THE NEXT RUN

A UC BERKELEY STUDENT'S RISE TO MAJOR 60S POT SMUGGLER

TOM JENKINS

THE NEXT RUN
A UC Berkeley Student's Rise to Major 60s Pot Smuggler
by Tom Jenkins

Published by Rider Avenue Press
South Pasadena, CA

Copyright © 2024 by Tom Jenkins
tomjenkins1187@gmail.com

This book was set in Adobe Caslon Pro.
Cover concept by Casey Rogers
Cover design by Illumination Graphics
and Casey Rogers

Identifiers:
ISBN: 979-8-9860263-7-4

Manufactured and printed in the United States of America

This is a true story—true down to the sentence level. The many coincidences, close calls, and ironies I describe all happened. At times I relate events told to me by others. While I have no reason to doubt their accounts, there could be inaccuracies. I have changed some names as well as a few minor details to protect people's privacy.

*This book is dedicated to the many people who
appear in it as characters, even the bad guys—
people who stole from me or betrayed me—
for they all in their own way helped
make this a fascinating story.*

PROLOGUE

THE FIRST TIME I EVER HEARD OF MARIJUANA was in Miss Russell's class in third grade. This was in 1955. Miss Russell showed us a black-and-white clip of two Black youths smoking reefer on the steps of a paintless wooden shack set in a weed-choked field in what could have only been the Deep South. Then she showed us a clip of a young couple getting arrested as they tried to bring drugs back from Mexico in their car. Either the actors were very good or the clip was footage of a real bust because the couple looked so genuinely miserable and repentant that my eight-year-old's heart went out to them. I didn't want them to go to jail. Maybe this story could have a different ending, I thought to myself. I raised my hand.

"How did the police know they had drugs in their car?" I asked Miss Russell.

She seemed unprepared for my question and didn't answer for a long moment.

"Because of their eyes," she said finally. "Drug addicts have red eyes."

CHAPTER 1

I COULD WRITE ABOUT THE BIG TIME when I drove an Aston Martin DB5 convertible, maintained a Swiss bank account in the Bahamas, carried a .45 semiautomatic pistol I didn't really know how to use, and was bringing in tons at a time remotely—that is, without having to go anywhere near the stuff. One of my biggest runs was six tons and all I ever saw of it was a brick a trusted distributor brought by to complain there was shake in the load. The brick was unopened.

"I just picked one at random."

I opened it and indeed there was a small amount of shake mixed in with what was otherwise good-quality pot.

"They're all like that. . . . Don't get me wrong now. I can sell this stuff. Only it's going to take time. Now if you could drop the price a nickel—or better yet a dime—I could probably off my share in a week."

I went out to a pay phone, called the Mexicans, and told them the load had shake in it and was going to take time to sell, but if they wanted it to go faster, they could drop the price by ten dollars a pound. The grass was partly fronted and they jumped at the chance to get their money back sooner rather than later. A week later the load was gone and my cut remained the same, netting me a six-digit figure in 1975 dollars.

During the Big Time I spent long hours going from bank to bank changing small bills into hundreds. By the late sixties, the American hundred-dollar bill had solidified its position as the smuggler's currency of choice. With hundreds the payment for a load took about a half hour to count and fit in a briefcase. With smaller bills it would have taken hours and required a suitcase.

Whenever a shipment came in, there was pressure to offload it as quickly as possible before something bad happened, and my distributors would spend

1

their days driving all over the Bay Area and points beyond with no time to change the many fifties, twenties, and tens given to them by the smaller distributors they were supplying. That job fell to me and I made a science of it. Small bills went into the left door panel of my pickup and after they were changed to hundreds, they went into the door panel on the right. I wore cowboy boots and could fit $3,500 in small bills into the left and right side of each boot for a total of $14,000 at a time. I especially liked dense financial districts where there were three or four banks within walking distance of one another. Upon entering a bank, I would remove small bills from my boot and upon leaving, I would tuck back in hundreds. Thirty-five hundred, I had learned, was close to the upper limit you could change before the teller would be required to call over a manager or make out a report to the IRS. Many of the tellers changed my money in a bored, mechanical fashion, but if they seemed at all curious, I would excitedly tell them how I was going to see a used Porsche for sale and wanted to flash hundred-dollar bills in front of the owner as I made my offer.

"New ones if you've got 'em."

Most of the mistakes I made in the business could be filed under the heading of forgetting what I was about. I had changed fourteen grand in small bills one day and was heading back to my truck when I happened to pass a store window with the exact model of Adidas basketball shoes I had been looking for. I swerved right in. The clerk found my size to try on and without thinking I yanked off my boot—only to see a shower of hundred-dollar bills flutter across the shoe store floor.

"Oh, I just went to the bank," I blurted truthfully as I scrambled to gather them up.

The clerk never said a word, just averted his eyes till I had picked them all up, as though my bills were somehow obscene.

Anyway, I could write about the Big Time and I will. And not just Mexico but Colombia too, with a twin-engine cargo plane picking up loads under cover of darkness and dropping bales into the lee of a deserted atoll off the coast of Florida to be recovered by waiting speedboats and brought into Miami harbor the following morning complete with water-skiers in tow to make everything look cool. I'll write about all that. And Morocco and Afghanistan too. But for me the best times, and what I'm going to write about most, were the early small-time days when everything seemed so lighthearted and romantic, and all of us in my crowd were still friends with no jealousies or betrayals, and I truly and wholeheartedly believed that flooding the country with pot was the most wonderful thing I could do.

*

On a rainy December night in 1965, I was playing cards with my two best friends, Bill Gretsch and Arf, as we wondered what we should do over the

Christmas break. Arf and I were studying engineering at UC Berkeley and Bill was going to Merritt Junior College. Neither Arf nor I had any interest in engineering, but we were both good at math and science, and engineering was the only science-related major that didn't have an English requirement. We had been traumatized by our English teachers at Berkeley High, who always seemed to want something more from us, though we could never figure out what, and asked questions like What does the river symbolize in *Heart of Darkness*? To us it was just a river. Anyway, this is what we were basing our future careers on: avoiding English class.

Arf came here from Puerto Rico in tenth grade, and our teacher introduced him to the class and then asked me to show him how to use a slide rule. I introduced him to our crowd and he told us people called him Raf, short for Rafael, but because we liked to mangle words, and especially because Raf wanted nothing more than to blend in here in this new country and not stand out in any way, we changed Raf to Arf. At first he hated the name. One day I called him by it and he drew himself up to his full six-foot Latin-macho height and said, "The name is Rafael Agustín Lopez Loera!" I figured I would never be calling him Arf anymore, but a few days later he called me up, saying, "Hey, what's new? This is the Arf."

Above us we could hear the rain with its random pounding on the roof of Bill's flat as we concentrated on our cards. We were playing hearts and I was always trying to "shoot the moon" while Bill and Arf kept trying to stop me. For a long time none of us said much, then while Arf shuffled, Bill said, "Say, we ought to go to Mexico over the break. We could take your truck, Tom, and Arf here could do the translating."

Now I had dreamed of going to Mexico ever since I was partly raised on my grandparents' farm in the Salinas Valley, where I saw Mexicans driving around in their long, low, rattly cars with the sarape over the rear deck and a pile of kids going wild in the back seat while their mother sat placidly in front. A Mexican family lived next door to my grandparents and I used to play with their kids and envied the secret language they had for talking among themselves. I vowed I would learn Spanish and even got a little, red Morocco-bound Spanish dictionary to carry with me wherever I went.

So by the end of the evening, it was decided: we would go to Mexico over the break. Then as a complete afterthought, Bill said we should bring some pot back in order to defray our trip expenses. Pot was still something of a mysterious unknown in 1965, at least in our circles, and none of us knew much about it. Bill had tried it several times, I had tried it twice, and Arf had never tried it at all. Coming from an aristocratic Latin family, he regarded pot as low class. The game broke up with our deciding vaguely to look into it.

Bill used to live in La Jolla, where he learned to surf, and a few nights later he called to tell me one of his old surfing buddies was in town. "He's been to Mexico," he told me, then whispering over the phone, "He knows where to score." We met with him the very next night at a Mexican restaurant in an industrial area of west Oakland. Arf was there, along with Bill and his friend, and we took a booth at the back, next to the kitchen. Bill's friend kept looking behind him as though the cook might be listening.

"Mazatlan's the place to score," he told us in low tones, leaning close. "Just hang out on the beach there. Watch out you don't get burned, though. A lot of cats will sell you weed and then turn around and have you busted. They get their weed back as part of the deal. Just ask some surfers where to score. They'll hip you to the right people."

A few days later I ran into Arf on campus and learned he had no intention of scoring grass. He had only been playing along with the idea for the excitement of plotting something dangerous and evil. He called our plan a pipe dream and said it would never happen. "Anyway, what am I going to do with a bag of pot?" He waved his hand in a deprecating way that was like a habit with him.

"Sell it for a small fortune."

"I don't know anyone who would buy pot."

"I'll sell it for you. Better yet, I'll *buy* your share."

He thought this over, the prospect of easy money seeming to interest him. "But we'll get caught."

"No, we won't. Remember, bad stuff only happens to other people."

We both laughed because this was a conclusion we had come to recently during one of our late-night, philosophical discussions. I eventually got him to go along with our plan, and the next day the three of us checked my truck out for hiding places and decided the door panels were the safest place.

CHAPTER 2

WE LEFT ON A CRISP WINTER DAY. I picked up Bill and Arf and they each laid their gear in the back of my pickup, arranging the heavier items on top so nothing would blow out in the wind.

"Don't ever grow old!" Arf said as he slid into the cab. In his left hand he was holding a paper bag gripped by the neck. He was upset about his grandmother.

"All she does all day is sit in a chair and dream about Puerto Rico. She has no friends here. How can she? She doesn't speak the language."

"Well, she needs to learn," said Bill. "She should take a class. She could make friends that way."

"Anh," Arf waved his hand. "She'll never learn English. You know what she told me last night? . . . She's just waiting to die!"

"What's in the bag, Goose?" Bill said then, quoting our favorite television commercial.

Arf reached in and pulled out a bottle of eggnog his grandmother had given us for the trip. He passed it around and to our surprise, it had rum in it—lots of rum. Evidently Arf's grandmother saw nothing wrong with giving alcohol to three teenagers on a road trip to Mexico. It was gone by the time we reached San Jose.

Now we were on the 101, the King's Highway, El Camino Real. Everywhere we looked, it seemed, there were signs of Mexico and we eagerly pointed them out, hyping our trip. We exulted over the littlest things: a prickly pear in someone's front yard or a black-on-white license plate that said only "B.C." In Gilroy we lusted over the brown-skinned Mexican girls selling fruit at rickety stands. And every time we passed a place name in Spanish that I didn't know, I would ask Arf what it meant. We passed a sign that said "Salsipuedes" and

Arf said it referred to a game kids play where they pretend to be birds and try to pour salt on each other's backs, the folk belief being that if you pour salt on a bird's tail, it can't fly. Arf explained this in a very authoritative tone, warming as he was to his job as chief interpreter for our trip. "If I don't know it, it's not Spanish!" he declared with a laugh. I later learned his explanation was nonsense and not at all what Salsipuedes meant, but at the time I believed Arf's every word.

Late that afternoon we were approaching King City when we came up behind a stake bed truck carrying Mexican women laborers home from the fields. By now the sun lay just above the horizon, a huge, red ball bathing everything in a thin, wintry light. The truck in front of us had no tailgate, affording us a clear view of the fifteen or twenty women in back. All were standing save for a lone teenage girl who sat at the tail end of the bed, facing us, her legs dangling over the edge. She wore a dirt-smudged peasant blouse and was big-boned with strong worker's arms, full breasts, and skin that shone like copper in the fading light. We guessed she wasn't wearing a bra, for every time the truck went over a bump, her breasts jiggled. She caught us staring at her breasts and to our surprise, she grinned. We pulled out to pass and she waved. Her boldness blew us away. Bill then declared she was a good omen and signified that we were all going to get laid when we got to Mexico. This led to a discussion of the Tijuana Donkey Act and sex in general, with Bill speaking from true experience while Arf and I could only pretend to know what we were talking about based on what we had learned from books and off john walls and the like. Bill was already living with a girl but rarely even referred to this fact and never questioned Arf or me when we intimated stuff he likely knew never happened.

We made it past L.A. and threw our sleeping bags out under a row of palm trees along a deserted farm road domed with stars. In the morning there was dew over everything and a chill in the air, so that we had to work up to getting out of our bags. We found a Flying A station and used the restroom to wash up, drying our faces with paper towels as we joked about all the *señoritas* we were going to ball when we got to Mexico. At a roadside café we ate huge breakfasts of eggs, pancakes, and hash browns, with plenty of bacon and sausage on the side and coffee to wash it all down with. The bill came to over eight dollars, but we figured it was as good as paid for by the grass we were going to bring back.

We cut inland and next thing we were crossing the border at Calexico. This involved navigating a maze of tall concrete corridors bearing intimidating signs that read, "All narcotics addicts must register with US Immigration before entering Mexico. Federal law." The corridors finally opened up and ahead of us lay Mexicali. "Wow!" we murmured to ourselves. Instantly, I fell in love with this place. It was crazy: brightly colored buildings, cars zooming about, people everywhere, little shops sandwiched between the big ones, wooden stands where there was no more room for shops, pushcarts for the vendors too poor to afford a stand, and signs everywhere, many of them hand-painted, often in red and blue, which are at opposite ends of the visible spectrum, so that the letters seemed to scintillate. And the cars! Many dated to the thirties: long four-door sedans with suicide doors and running boards, and the men driving them in white linen suits and white sombreros looked just like gangsters out of a tropical version of *The Untouchables*.

We got caught in traffic and a peddler rushed up to sell us a piñata. He had an immense bundle of them hunched over his back. We told him no, but he kept jogging alongside us, quoting lower and lower prices, his absurd burden of piñatas bouncing. To get away from him, we turned down a side street, but it was one-way the wrong way and a motorcycle cop pulled us over. We were so excited to be in this new, crazy country that we acted silly in front of the officer. Arf rolled down his window and pretended not to speak Spanish. The cop kept asking for "*dinero para los cafés.*"

"*Los cafés?*" Arf repeated with a thick gringo accent, scrunching his face up in puzzlement.

"*Sí, sí. Los cigarillos,*" the cop tried.

"Oh, you want a cigarette?" Arf whipped his pack out and deftly shook it so that a single cigarette popped up.

The cop gave up and strode back to his motorcycle, shaking his head in disgust. As he roared off, we roared laughing. We can get away with anything here! we told ourselves. We headed on, and at the very edge of town sat a squat cinder block store advertising "*Cerveza.*" We decided to take a chance. We pulled over and walked in making conversation in deep, manly tones as we pulled a six-pack of Bohemias from the cooler and brought it up to the counter. Sure enough, the clerk sold it to us without asking for I.D.

"He hardly looked twice at us," I said as we got back in the truck.

"This country's wide open!" exulted Bill.

We drank while we drove, figuring there was no law against it, and flipped our empty bottles out the window and up over the cab so they landed in the bed. Later I got the idea to ride in back and made a comfortable pallet out of our three sleeping bags as we headed on. We were in the great Sonoran Desert now. Beneath me the truck's drivetrain made a reassuring drone that varied in pitch with the dips and hills in the road, and above me arched the blue immensity of the Mexican sky. From time to time a raw, red-earth road cut flashed by. I sucked in the pure desert air rushing past and thought how all these years I had dreamed of going to Mexico and now I was finally doing it and had the wonderful feeling that this was going to be the beginning of a whole new life for me. I punched my fist into my palm and shouted, "Yeehaw!

. . . You're doing it! . . . You're gonna make it!" along with other crazy things only the rushing wind could hear.

I took the wheel later that evening as we passed through a barren stretch of desert with only the occasional, pale yellow lights of a lonely *ranchito* to break the monotony. There was no moon out and the surrounding land was inky black. Once in a while headlights would appear, grow brighter, and flash past. The three of us sat slouched in the cab, and for a long time none of us spoke, each lost in his own thoughts as we hurtled through the night. It was while we were in this pleasant, dreamy state that a great orange glow flared up from behind a dark hill just ahead of us, lighting up the sky. "A fire!" we all cried out at once, jerking up in our seats. I pressed the pedal to the floor.

It had to be some horrible accident, we figured. I pushed my poor truck for all it was worth, propelled by teenage visions of pulling a beautiful Mexican girl from the wreckage. We topped the hill doing ninety and there below lay the burning wreck. It was off the highway and cars had already stopped and there were people milling about. No one seemed to be approaching the wreck and as we drew closer, we saw why. It was an inferno. Flames were reaching twenty to thirty feet into the sky. "Whoever was in there didn't have a chance," Bill murmured. We pulled up, jumped out, then stood there dumbly watching like everyone else.

Looking around, I saw there were several Mexican families and four or five lone Mexican men. I didn't see anyone excitedly telling how they had just narrowly escaped death. Bill shook his head.

"Even if someone had managed to get out, the nearest ambulance is probably a hundred miles away."

I looked around and, aside from the fire, there were no lights anywhere, just miles and miles of desert with bleak buttes casting their purple bulk against the dark of the sky. We were in big, bad Mexico now, we told ourselves. Anything could happen here and no one to save us. It felt exhilarating. I wanted something to happen that would shake up my life and this seemed like the perfect place.

We watched until the fire began to die down. Two kids had already lost interest and were playing in the dust alongside the highway. A car took off and we decided to leave too. There was nothing we could do here to help anyone and anyway we had a mission ahead of us. But as I opened the door to my truck, I took a last glance at the burning vehicle and had a sense of *What's wrong with this picture?* By now we could make out the silhouette of the vehicle and it appeared to be an older pickup, probably from the forties. Then I saw it: the vehicle had no wheels! It was propped up on blocks! This was no fiery accident, but just an old stripped wreck someone had doused with gasoline and set on fire for God knew what reason. Realizing this, we looked around, wondering if the other people knew this too or had maybe even started the fire. It was hard to tell. Anything *could* happen here, we decided, but it might not always be what it seemed.

CHAPTER 3

AT THE LONELY BORDER TOWN OF SONOYTA we waited in line with other drowsy travelers as a clerk typed up tourist visas by the light of a naked bulb surrounded by moths. From here the highway turned south into the interior of Mexico and after a while we came to a brightly lit inspection station with pylons in the road diverting us in. We rolled to a stop and a bored officer approached, asked if we had any radios or appliances, and waved us on when we said no. In the lane next to us, a Buick was being searched by soldiers with rifles slung over their shoulders while the apparent occupants, two Mexican men, looked on. Leaving the station, Bill said, "Did you see which way that Buick was pointing?" Arf and I both had. It was pointing north. Sure enough, we pulled onto the highway and saw that pylons were set out to divert northbound traffic into the station as well. This was sobering. We hadn't counted on having to go through any inspections in Mexico. Obviously the grass would have to be well hidden before we got back here. It was going to be like running the border twice.

We drove on till we grew tired and then pulled off onto a lonely set of tire tracks and and threw our bags out on the open desert. With no lights around, we could see every star in the sky. I picked the dimmest, tiniest star I could find, a star no one else would ever think to pick, and got bearings on it from nearby larger stars so I could find it again and decided this would be my star forever, my star to wish upon.

In the morning we took off and a peasant couple flagged us down. We let them ride in the back of the truck and soon more *campesinos* flagged us down and before we knew it, we had eleven men, women, and children riding in the back of the truck. My poor truck! I worried that the springs would break. Thankfully they were all going to the same nearby village and we soon had our truck to ourselves again. And this is how we learned about the Mexican style of hitchhiking, which involves several quick waves of the index and middle fingers, which to us gringos looked as though they were flagging us down.

In the afternoon we grew hungry. All along the highway we had seen signs for restaurants, some of them little more than letters painted on a board. Anyone, it seemed, could call their place a restaurant and put out a sign. I got the idea that we should eat at the beatest, most tumbledown place we could find and Bill and Arf went along with this crazy plan. Soon we found a squat adobe hut with no panes in the windows, no door in the doorway, and a bald tire hung up on a post out front with the letters "*RESTAURANTE*" hand-painted across the top of the tire in white. We walked in and a young couple hurried to seat us at the only table, a rickety affair situated next to the stove. The back doorway had no door and looked out over a ragged vegetable patch carved from a field of weeds. The couple set the table and I told Arf to ask them for the menus.

"Are you kidding? There's no menus."

I looked around. "Well, ask them where the bathroom is."

Arf nodded toward the field out back. "There."

"Yeah, and that's where our food's coming from too," put in Bill, whose father was in public health.

The couple served us and Arf said, "You know we're eating their dinner, don't you?"

"What do you mean?"

"You didn't see them chase their kids out as we were walking up? This is their dinner."

Meanwhile, Bill had picked a piece of lettuce out of his taco and was holding it up to the light. "Hm. . . . Salmonella City."

While he and Arf carefully picked all the vegetables out of their meals, I made a show of eating everything on my plate. "Wimps!" That evening, though, I got sicker than I had ever been before in my life. For the first time on our trip we had to pay for a motel. I got in bed and felt so chilled, I had Bill and Arf pile all three of our sleeping bags on top of me and still shivered miserably and couldn't get my teeth to stop chattering. Every few minutes I had to jump up and run to the bathroom to throw up or have diarrhea or both. Finally I grew so exhausted that I couldn't even get out of bed when I needed to and fell into a deep, coma-like sleep.

Morning came and I woke up feeling strangely refreshed and full of energy. I took a long, thorough shower, left a fifty-peso note for the hapless maid, and we headed on. Our next stop was the Tropic of Cancer, which was marked by a truncated stone pyramid with an inset bronze plaque. Bill and I had never crossed the Tropic of Cancer before and we pulled over to check it out. No one was around as we crossed the highway and walked up to the monument. "I piss on the Tropic of Cancer!" Bill declared and proceeded to do just that. Arf and I quickly followed, laughing as we aimed so that our three trajectories intersected at the same spot on the stone.

Then came Mazatlan. I will never forget our first sight of it because there was a dense, white mist lying over the lowlands between us and the town, which made it look as though Mazatlan were floating on clouds, like a city out of a fairy tale. We came to a fork in the road with a sign offering *El Centro* or *La Playa*, which seemed an easy choice, and soon found ourselves looking out over the most beautiful stretch of beach I had ever seen. The sand was white, the water blue and clear, and there was practically no one around. To the north, the nearest hotel was over a mile away. To the south, two men were building the second story to a small cottage. One man stood on the ground next to a wheelbarrow full of bricks and lofted them up one at a time to the other man, who was kneeling on the second floor, trowel in hand, as he laid a wall. "Mexican efficiency," commented Bill. We parked right on the sand next to a patch of ice plant, threw our trunks on, and jumped in the water. Bill taught Arf and me how to shuffle our feet along the seafloor to kick up stingrays, but we soon stopped bothering. There were no stingrays here. "This is just like Puerto Rico!" Arf cried and went rolling over and over in the sand until he was covered with it and only his eyes gleamed out.

We pitched our tent right there on the sand and rolled some bleached logs over to serve as benches. As we were sitting there admiring our new digs, we spotted a man heading down the beach from the north, the first person we had seen since the two laborers. He was thin, older, and wore a white muslin shirt and pants but no hat, his bald scalp red from the sun. On spotting us, he headed in our direction. Then, to our astonishment, he stepped into a tall bush, squatted, and proceeded to hang a shit right there on the beach. We could see him grinning through the branches. After using some leaves to wipe himself, he strode up to us with his hand extended. Bill and I shook hands with him, but Arf just let the man's hand dangle there in midair. The man ignored the snub.

"Good morning!" he said in reasonable English. "I am pleased to offer to you my services as your guide to Mazatlan. I can get for you whatever you need. You like peyote? Mushrooms? Grass? Bennies? Reds? . . . Nice Mexican girls?"

He said he could get us Acapulco Gold for ten dollars a kilo. We asked to see a sample and he said for the trouble to get it, he would need five pesos, which amounted to forty cents. This we readily gave him and watched him head on down the beach, which was the last we ever saw of him. When I realized he had gotten our hopes up just to beat us out of forty cents, I got pissed and wanted to go find him, but Arf just laughed and said it was a typical Latin trick.

After that, no one approached us. The days went by and we spent our time body surfing or roaming the crooked Mazatlan streets all lit up with Christmas lights. For dinner we ate freshly caught seafood at thatched-roof restaurants that hung out over the water and in the evening we built bonfires out of driftwood and talked our hearts out late into the night. When we were too tired to talk anymore, we threw our bags out just above the high tide line and let the crash of the waves lull us to sleep. The sun on our faces woke us up in the mornings.

The days passed and I eagerly took note of little details of this new country that I somehow knew was going to become an important part of my life: pelicans flying parallel to the waves as they inspected them for fish, a cur lying in the shade of a beached skiff, the lanterns in the restaurants made out of dried blowfish, and at night the way the reflections of the green and red neon signs danced gently over the rolling waters. At a restaurant, I held up a salt shaker to show the cute waitress how someone had put grains of rice in it as a joke and she smiled and told me they were put there on purpose to keep the salt from caking in the humid air.

We were having the time of our lives, but our plan to score grass was going nowhere. We had seen a few American surfers in town, but they looked so sullen and cliquish, we were afraid to approach them. We told ourselves we should do something and decided to try scoring at the most popular stretch of beach, which was in town, across from the Hotel de Cima. We went there, purposely dressed in street clothes and street shoes and wearing shades. It was the middle of the day and the beach was crowded with people lying on towels while their kids played tag with the waves. The air smelled of salt and suntan lotion. Circulating among the tourists were the usual vendors, peddling everything from dried blowfish to opals to bracelets made of abalone shell set in silver.

We walked back and forth across the sand, doing our best to look sinister and heavy, stopping from time to time to raise our shades and peer mean-ingfully over the crowds. No one paid us any attention. Paralleling the beach was the Avenida del Mar, which was six to eight feet higher than the beach and separated from it by a stone wall, interrupted every so often by a set of concrete stairs. On the street side, the wall was only a couple of feet higher than the sidewalk and wide enough to make a convenient bench. The sidewalk and bench-like wall were called *el malecón* and served as an esplanade, where vendors sold mangos and *paletas*, lovers sat holding hands, and cab drivers stood about looking for fares. Arf suggested we hire a cab and ask the driver where to score, but after discussing this for a good half hour, we couldn't quite get up the nerve to do it. Bill then pointed out that we hadn't scored grass and hadn't even gotten laid, yet were having the best vacation of our lives.

"I would do it all over again and don't give a damn about the cost because it's money well spent!"

Arf and I agreed and in a way it was a relief giving up on the idea of scoring pot. We had discovered paradise and began talking about our next trip down and all the friends we couldn't wait to bring.

CHAPTER 4

ABOUT A WEEK HAD PASSED AND WE KNEW we had to leave our wonderful paradise soon in order to get back in time for classes. The problem was we had lost all track of the date. We tried to figure it out by counting backward, but the days all ran together in a blur. We were sitting at our favorite hangout, a *cocos helados* stand set on a concrete platform that projected out over the beach a few blocks north of the Hotel de Cima. The tables here were thick, round concrete disks with red and blue tiles set in them checkerboard fashion and were shaded by parasols. A faint breeze off the ocean kept us cool.

We watched as the proprietor selected three coconuts from a rusted ice chest and deftly cut the tops off with a machete before serving them to us with straws. After we had sucked out the sweet milk, he cut them open for us and gave us spoons to dig out the meat, which is soft if the coconut is truly fresh. We looked out over the beach, where the usual vendors paced back and forth plying their wares with the persistence of the tide. This was their lot in life, I thought to myself, and wondered what my lot was going to be. I had no idea. The prospect of earning a living daunted me and was something I didn't like to think about. There were a lot of things I didn't like to think about. I was still living with my parents and was dying to move out but didn't have any way to make money. I was nearing the end of my teens but didn't feel at all ready to go out in the world as a competent adult. I wasn't sure how well I would get along with people. In high school the kids who were socially awkward or didn't have friends were called gimps. I hated that word and went to absurd lengths not to be thought of as a gimp. A couple of times I even made up stories that made me sound like someone exciting. More often I didn't commit myself, only hinting that I was up to something secretive and important. In reality, I was up to nothing. Berkeley High had social clubs made up of jocks, cheerleaders, and other popular types, and there was even a consolation social club for the kids that couldn't get into the desirable ones. My friends and I weren't even invited to the consolation club.

While I was thinking all this, a vendor came up to us offering woven palm leaf hats. Arf had taught me how to say we weren't interested, but before I could get the words out, the vendor was speaking to Arf in rapid Spanish. Arf leaned across the table toward Bill and me.

"This guy says he can get us grass."

I stared at the vendor and he grinned, nodding up and down as if to affirm what Arf had just said. He was dark-skinned with smooth, broad, almost feminine features and a pencil-line mustache, like a Mexican version of Muddy Waters. Later I would come to appreciate this wasn't entirely coincidence. The vendor came from Guerrero, where many of the inhabitants have African blood that can be traced back to the days when slaves were imported to work the plantations there. He said his name was Meche and handed a hat each to Bill and me.

"He says to look at them as though you're thinking of buying them."

While Bill and I feigned interest in our hats, Arf and Meche spoke in rapid-fire Spanish. Meche said the beach there was *muy caliente* — very hot — meaning there might be agents or informers around. He asked where we were staying and said he would meet us there in an hour.

He arrived at our camp and straight off handed us a piece of folded newspaper with pot inside. Grinning in a way that was almost like a giggle, he explained how he sold hats on the beach as a way of meeting Americans who wanted to buy grass. While he and Arf discussed terms, I used a piece of the newspaper to roll a joint. I lit it and offered it to Meche, but he declined, saying he would be back the next morning to see what we thought of it.

He left and Bill and I passed the joint back and forth. Arf still looked down on pot and refused to try it. Before long a feeling like you get in a fast-dropping elevator spread out my arms and legs to my fingertips and toes. I became aware of the sun blazing down and felt the salt on my skin tingle. I lay down and let myself go limp on the sand. I thought how lucky we were to have found Meche and began to laugh. It was a soft kind of laugh that welled up in my throat like bubbles in a spring. Arf frowned, thinking I was hamming it up, and seeing him looking skeptical like that made me laugh all the harder. Bill just smiled and took drags off his cigarette. Bill never got the giggles. He was too mature in a way.

I laughed and laughed. I laughed until my sides began to ache and said I needed to calm down with a fresh orange juice at the Rocamar, which was a restaurant perched on a rocky bluff a half mile down the beach. The whole way there I couldn't stop laughing. We climbed the narrow steps to the entrance and I worried there might be a lot of people inside—I was still laughing—but the only other patrons were four surfers sitting at a far window overlooking the ocean. The surf must not have been up, for the surfers looked very sullen and morose, which caused me to laugh all the harder. The waiter came and Arf had to give him my order. My orange juice finally came and as I felt the golden liquid go down my throat, I thought of the Peruvian Indians who poured molten gold down the throat of the Spanish governor who tried to overtax them and fell into a pensive mood.

"So you think this stuff is pretty good?" I heard Arf asking me as though from the far end of a tunnel. I turned to stare at him.

"Arf," I said in the most serious tones I could muster—as though if he had had lapels, I would have grabbed them. "We have *got* to bring some of this stuff back."

Meche approached our camp the next morning, taking long, quick strides over the sand. He asked how we liked the grass, flashed a quick grin when we told him we liked it, then turned serious. The deal had to be done today, he said, his people couldn't wait. The price was ten dollars a kilo. We made some crude attempts to calculate the volume of the door panels and told him we wanted twelve kilos. He asked to see our money, then told us he would be back at noon to take us to the score. We broke camp, packed everything into the back of my truck, and waited.

Just like that, the character of our trip had changed. Before, we had been happy and carefree and now we were worried and nervous. This was our plan, though, and we were determined to go through with it. We tried to imagine what the score would be like and worried we might get cheated on the weight. Arf said we could drive into town and buy a scale, but we stayed where we were out of grim inertia.

Meche arrived nearly an hour late, appearing nervous and agitated. He asked to see our money again and the four of us piled into my truck. I drove, following Meche's directions interpreted by Arf. Soon we were in a poor *fraccionamiento*, far from the usual tourist spots. Deep potholes pocked the road and Meche kept jerking his hand up at every one as though I couldn't see them for myself. People were everywhere: in doorways, by the side of the road, hanging out on street corners. They must know, I thought: three gringos crammed in with a Mexican waving his hand like a maniac in an area where tourists never go. I cursed my truck for being painted a bright construction yellow. Bill hardly spoke, I noticed. He was chain-smoking and had his hand outstretched against the dash to steady himself against the jolts. Arf was the only one who seemed at all calm.

We crested a small hill and Meche directed me to pull over next to an adobe home painted phosphorescent pink. Arf stepped out to let him out and he disappeared inside. Instantly, we were surrounded by a gang of ragged kids staring up at us and giggling at our foreignness.

"This is the score?" Bill said. "This is crazy. There's a million people watching."

"He said not to worry about the people."

Bill gave a faint snort, looking around. "Someone'll turn us in for the reward, for sure."

I glanced behind us. "See if anyone gets our license number."

"Meche's probably already got it."

"I don't think so," said Arf. "If he had an arrangement with the police, I don't think he'd be so jumpy."

Several minutes went by. "We've still got the money," Bill said. "We ought to split."

His words lingered in the silence that followed. He had said them in a half-joking way, but I could tell he meant them. Showing fear was considered a sign of weakness in our crowd and his words felt embarrassing to me. Arf wasn't saying anything, but I suspected he felt the same. I was still contemplating this when we suddenly became aware of two men at the back of the truck. We turned in time to see them lay two large cardboard boxes in the bed. The contents of the boxes were concealed by sheets of newspaper neatly folded so that they just fit inside the boxes near their tops. Meche appeared at the passenger-side window, hissing, "¡El dinero! ¡El dinero! ¡El dinero!" Arf moved to step out and make sure the boxes really had grass in them.

"Just pay him and let's get the fuck out of here!" cried Bill.

Arf handed Meche six twenty-dollar bills and I gunned the truck down the road.

The kids scattered. My poor truck was bottoming out from taking the potholes too fast, but all I cared about was getting away. I imagined Mexican cops closing in on us any second. Out of the corner of my eye, I saw something white flash in the rearview mirror and felt my heart freeze. It was the folded newspapers flying away in the wind! Inside the boxes we could see loose, dark-green pot jiggling with the bumps in the road and spilling out over our gear. "Pull over and let's cover them," Arf offered reasonably, but I was too panicked. Instead I turned left, right, left, trying to find the way out.

Fraccionamientos are like American subdivisions in that they often have only one way in and out. Every road we tried came to a dead end and I kept jerking my truck around to try a different way. This seemed to go on forever. People in doorways stared as we careened past for the second and third time. Finally I found a way out, only it led directly to the center of town, where we had to stop for a red light at a major intersection. A crowd of pedestrians proceeded to cross the street directly in front of us and one of them, a young man, slanted behind us, right past the open grass. "Grim," we muttered to ourselves, "grim" being the latest word in our crowd for anything that wasn't cool. "Grim, grim, grim," we chanted over and over like Buddhist monks as we waited for a light that seemed never to change. "This is really grim!"

At last we were out of town and pulled over onto a deserted side road. Arf and I jumped out, grabbed the boxes, and ran them into the jungle, where we left them like live bombs while we debated what to do. Our problem now was that the grass took up far more space than we had imagined. Back home we were used to seeing grass in tiny amounts and had imagined twelve kilos might take up the space, say, of a briefcase. These boxes were big, though. There was no way all this grass was going to fit in the door panels. We searched my truck for other hiding places and discovered that the cab was double-walled. By removing the dome light, we were able to access this hidden space. I began poking grass through, using a pencil to move it along, but after twenty minutes of this I had managed to pack only a few ounces. It was going to take a day or more to pack the whole load, and I wasn't that happy about opening my truck up like a tuna can to get the grass out when we got back to the States. It was mind-boggling: we had an amount of pot worth a fortune back in the States, but with no way to cross it, it was worth nothing. About a pound had spilled in the back of the truck, and Bill used a branch to sweep it out onto the ground in a gesture of mock extravagance.

It was growing dark and we decided to bring the boxes back to the truck and head north, hoping an idea would come to us before we reached the Mexican inspection station south of Sonoyta. If not, we would simply have to abandon the grass on the desert. We placed the two boxes in the truck bed, covered them with our gear, and took off. Night fell, and everything seemed different now that we were holding. I felt very alert and took notice of little details along the road. We passed a bus with *Amor es perder* finger-painted in red on the back bumper. "To love is to lose." Many of the semis on the road had replaced the lights outlining their trailers with colored Christmas lights, adding cheer to the night. In the purple fold of a distant hill, I spotted a faint yellow light and wondered what sort of conspiracies were being hatched there. The Mexican night seemed filled with mystery and now we were a part of it.

We approached an agricultural checkpoint with a sign saying, "All trucks must stop," and in the dim light we could make out a police cruiser parked out front. After stopping at several of these on the way down and getting waved on, we had concluded they only applied to commercial trucks, not pickups. Just the same, my heart pounded as we barreled past. Later we rolled into Culiacan and I spotted the motel where we had stayed when I got sick, and got an idea.

*

The desert air felt cool against my face as I stared up into the night sky. With no lights around, I could see every star. Underneath me, my truck's drivetrain made the reassuring drone I found so soothing. I figured it was well after midnight. I had our three sleeping bags over me to keep warm and beneath me was our grass, packed into a large duffel bag. At the mouth of the bag, we had stuffed our dirty clothing, including at the very front, a pair of underpants we had purposely soiled with poop watered down to resemble diarrhea.

I felt the truck slow down and the whine of the drivetrain dropped in pitch. The whine changed again as Arf downshifted to second, and when the stars faded, giving way to a brighter light, I knew we were entering the Mexican inspection station. I felt us roll to a stop and closed my eyes. I heard an officer ask Arf for papers, heard some rustling, then felt a bright light in my face. I half opened my eyelids, letting my eyes roll upward, and gave a faint groan as I turned away.

"*Está muy enfermo,*" I heard Arf say. "He's very sick. We need to get him to a doctor in the States."

A moment later we were rolling again.

Adrenaline kept us driving through the night and the next morning we were in Mexicali. Everywhere we looked, it seemed, the streets were filled with kids wearing brand new holsters and brandishing shiny cap pistols. After several blocks of this, it finally dawned on us: today must be Christmas Day!

From Mexicali we headed west and shortly before Tijuana we pulled over on the desert and got the grass out. We knew the sick-in-the-back-of-the-truck routine wouldn't stand up to U.S. Customs and decided to stash the grass in the hopes of finding someone to cross it for us when we got back home. By stomping on it, we were able to get it all into a large aluminum cooler my parents had loaned us for the trip and then buried it five paces south of a lone mesquite tree opposite kilometer marker 2695. It was a relief to be rid of that grass, but I felt bad about my parents' cooler. Ever since I could remember, that cooler had been a part of family camping trips and picnics with my grandparents. It seemed kind of sordid to be packing it full of pot and burying it, and I had an uneasy feeling I might never see it again.

CHAPTER 5

IT RAINED THE DAY WE GOT BACK and the campus poolroom was filled with students who hadn't left town for the holidays, their umbrellas making little puddles of water where they were leaned against pillars and walls. I knew most of the regulars and made the rounds of the tables, telling people about the grass and asking if they knew anyone who might run it for us. Everyone wanted to hear about our adventures, but no one wanted to run the grass. I was hoping a sandy-haired guy named Thorpe would show up. He played pool a lot and I knew he sold grass whenever he could get any. I ran up three or four hours of table time, then went to The Blue Cue on Telegraph Avenue. Thorpe was there and brightened on seeing me.

"So, I hear you've got twenty kilos stashed on the other side of the border."

"More like twelve," I laughed. "The pool hall grapevine may be fast, but it's not too accurate."

"So when are you going to get this stuff back up? I'd like to cop some when you do."

"As soon as we find someone to run it for us. Why don't you run it? We'll give you a good cut."

"No, thanks," he grinned. "Taking risks is not my bag. I'd like to help you sell it when you get it up, though."

I asked all our old high school crowd if any of them wanted to run the grass. A friend I had grown up with nicknamed "the Bub" seemed tempted but couldn't quite bring himself to do it. Classes started and the break was over. My parents asked about the cooler and I told them I had left it at Bill's place and would get it when I saw him next.

A week went by and I told Bill and Arf we should get together to decide what we were going to do about the grass. We met at the campus poolroom.

21

I was taking the problem of getting our grass back very seriously, but Bill and Arf seemed to have written it off. I didn't blame Bill; he wasn't the enterprising type. He had his girlfriend and was working part-time sacrificing lab rats for the health department while he took classes at Merritt Junior College. Arf, though—Arf was sharp. It seemed to me he was being lazy and letting me do all the work of finding a runner. I gave him a hard time about it and he laughed and apologized, but I could tell he had pretty much lost interest in the deal.

Dead Week came, the week before final exams. I was crossing Sproul Plaza when a guy named McDermott approached me. I had seen him around the poolroom but never spoken to him. He was tall, thin, and pale and had long, stringy black hair that fell across his shoulders. Few guys had long hair in 1966. He told me he had heard about our grass and was interested in running it. He said he had a '62 Valiant and had discovered a good hiding place between the back seat and the trunk wall. I looked him over.

"You'd have to cut your hair, you know."

"For sure," he nodded earnestly. "I'd get it cut really short and wear straight clothes and everything. For sure."

"Would you do it alone?"

"No, I'd do it with my old lady. I think that would look better for customs."

"Well, there are twelve kilos in all. What if we give you a fourth for running it? Does that sound reasonable?"

He nodded. "That sounds reasonable."

"How soon can you do it?"

"This weekend if you want."

"This is a sure thing then?"

He nodded. "It's a sure thing."

I jumped in my truck and drove straight to Arf's place to tell him the good news. On the way, though, I got to thinking how little he had done to find a runner. He was just leaving his parents' house when I pulled up.

"Hey, I think I found someone to run the grass."

"Mellow! Anyone I know?"

"McDermott? He hangs around the poolroom?"

"That beatnik type?"

"Right."

"I don't really know him."

"Well, it's not a sure thing yet. I mean, he said it was a sure thing, but you never know."

"How much does he want for doing it?"

"Well, like I said, it's not a sure thing yet, which is why I wanted to talk to you. I was thinking I could just handle the whole thing and pay you something for your share."

"You mean in advance, whether the stuff makes it back or not?"

"Right."

He thought a moment and shrugged. "Well, I spent $105 on that trip. Give me $105 and you can have my share."

"It's a deal," I said, and we shook on it.

I went to the bank and got the $105. I was living off $3,000 my parents had given me for my college education. I was only halfway through my freshman year and had already spent nearly a third of that money on motorcycle repairs, table time at the campus poolroom, and hamburgers at the Bear's Lair. In another year the money would be gone. I hated thinking about it because I had no idea where I could get a part-time job or what I could even do that people would pay me for.

That night I found Bill and offered him the same deal I had offered Arf. He surprised me by telling me he no longer owned his share. He had traded it to a friend of ours named Ken in place of some money he owed Ken. The whole thing was becoming like some big stock deal!

The next evening I visited McDermott at his home in the Berkeley flat-lands, where he lived with his girlfriend and several other people. He opened the door and a smell just like the Berkeley dump wafted out. I followed him through the kitchen past stacks of unwashed dishes and bags of garbage no one had bothered to take out. On the door to his room was a Polaroid of him in midair as he was jumping up and down on an American flag. I felt a sudden wave of dislike for him. I'm just hiring him to do a job, I told myself, and drew a detailed map for him showing where the grass was buried and left.

That weekend I was on pins and needles. On Sunday afternoon McDermott called and said I should come over to his place. I didn't recognize him when he answered the door; he looked so different with his hair cut short. He led me back to his room and showed me a large plastic bag full of pot.

"This is a little over half the load. That's all we were able to fit into the hiding place. We're going back next weekend to get the rest."

I ran my hands through the grass and it was just like the sample Meche had given us on the beach. We smoked some and McDermott smiled tolerantly as I went through the giggles. I decided he was an OK guy after all.

"Did you bring back the cooler by any chance?"

"No. It's still buried with the rest of the grass in it."

He told me to take as much of the grass as I wanted and I took half and he gave me a Co-op shopping bag to carry it in. It was still light out as I walked back to my truck carrying enough pot to buy me a prison sentence. I passed a woman pushing a baby in a stroller and she barely noticed me. I'm just a young man carrying a bag of groceries to her, I mused.

I gave two pounds to Ken and sold the rest as lids. It was fun having lids for sale. Before, I had always been in awe of anyone who had the least access to grass and now I was a connection. A cute girl I knew saw my lids and seemed to notice me for the first time. "*Some*body's been to Mexico," she grinned, drawing out the "some" in "somebody" in a way that made my heart skip.

Finals came and I did poorly. My last-minute cramming hadn't made up for all the times I had cut class to shoot pool. The weekend passed and there was no phone call from McDermott. I phoned his place Sunday night and a roommate said he wasn't home; he didn't know where he was. I hoped he was on his way home from getting the rest of the grass. The following afternoon I walked into the campus poolroom and there he was, shooting nine-ball with a friend. He was in the middle of laughing when he saw me and turned serious. We stepped to the side.

"I've been meaning to call you."

"Did you get the rest?"

"No. That's why I've been meaning to call you. We went down there and it was gone."

I felt my stomach drop. "Gone? How could it be gone?"

He pursed his lips, looking very sincere, and shrugged. "That's what I've been asking myself."

"Did anyone see you dig it up? They shouldn't have. You can see cars coming for miles in either direction on that road."

"I don't think anyone saw us. No cars drove by while we were digging it up."

"This last time?"

"No, the first time. No one drove by this last time either, but like I told you, it was gone."

"I don't believe it. . . . I just don't believe it."

McDermott shrugged. "I don't know what to say. I know you lost a lot of money, but I lost out on a lot of hassle and expense myself. I had to buy a new water pump for my car."

"What about the cooler? Was it there?"

"No. Nothing. Just a hole in the sand."

"I just don't believe it."

McDermott didn't say anything, just stood there holding his cue propped on the floor.

"Well, there are other people involved in this," I said, trying to sound ominous. "We're going to have to decide what to do about it. I'll be at your place at nine tonight."

McDermott shrugged. "Suit yourself. I don't know what there is to do about it, though."

I strode around the corner to the Bear's Lair. Arf was there playing cards with some friends, and in a low voice I told him what had happened while he shuffled.

"I just don't see how anyone could have stumbled across that grass. On the other hand, how could McDermott have the nerve to keep it and claim it was gone?"

Arf rolled his eyes. "God, how can you be so naive, Tom? Of course, he kept it. Why shouldn't he? He hardly even knows you. Even if he did, what difference would it make? What are you going to do, threaten to kill him? I'm surprised you even got those few pounds out of him."

Arf and I were always having arguments in which he would accuse me of being naive and I would accuse him of being cynical.

"You just don't believe anyone has morals," I told him.

He rolled his eyes again. "You—you don't even know what people are like."

I drove home, went up to the attic, and found a switchblade knife I had had since I was a kid. It still worked. At nine o'clock I was at McDermott's house. As we went back to his room, I glanced in the other rooms half hoping to spy some sign of the missing grass. His room had no chairs and we sat at the opposite ends of a mattress lying on the floor. McDermott folded his legs in a lotus position and rested his hands lightly on his knees. The expression on his face was innocent and quizzical. I pulled out the switchblade and right when I was supposed to flick it open, the way I had been planning all along, I lost my nerve and just hefted it a couple of times, trying to act tough.

"OK, McDermott, I want the rest of that grass. Now where is it?"

McDermott didn't even flinch. I felt sure he had seen the knife but he seemed to be making a point of not looking at it. He was looking me straight in the eye. He cleared his throat and wet his lips. Speaking slowly and carefully as though parsing his words, he said, "I told you, we went down there and the grass was gone. I don't know what happened to it. I don't know where it is. I don't know what else I can say."

I was dumbstruck in the realization I had no plan what to do next. I hadn't even thought about what McDermott might say or what I should say in response. A wave of shame swept over me. The knife was now an embarrassment and I closed my hand around it, hoping maybe he hadn't seen it after all. I looked around. I could demand to search his house, I thought. Or I could demand to quiz his old lady to see if her story matched his. Instead, I got up and walked out.

Driving home, I tried to think of ways to get even with McDermott. I was furious with him. But on some level I knew I was really furious with myself and my stupid *West Side Story* notion that pulling a switchblade on someone would get me what I wanted. Arf was right: I didn't know people and didn't know how to act around them. I needed to learn. And as for McDermott, there was always the possibility he was telling the truth. I would never know.

CHAPTER 6

I SOLD OFF WHAT I HAD LEFT of our grass, making a small profit, and that seemed the end of that—nothing more than a story to tell my grandchildren as the saying goes. I tried to focus on getting better grades in school. It was hard, though. Arf and I had the bad habit of sitting at the back of the lecture halls, where we smoked cigarettes and made fun of the foreign students up front, tapping their feet with nervous energy as they frantically took notes on the professor's every word. Plus, we were spending too much time in the campus poolroom. "How is it ever going to affect your future life if you cut this one class?" we were always asking in order to get the other to play. As a result, we were cutting classes half the time and getting Bs and Cs when we should have been getting As. One day we were riding with friends and passed a building where we could see men on the second floor hunkered over draft boards. These were real engineers. "There's us in a few years," I told Arf and we both laughed in awful rue because we knew deep down in our hearts that the way things were going, it was never going to happen.

Summer came and I got a wonderful job driving cars and buses for UC. I got it through the Bub. Many of the drivers were moonlighting Berkeley policemen, the Bub's father among them, which is how the Bub got the job, and when they needed another driver, he thought of me. I had never driven a bus before and was nervous about it, so one night the Bub took me to the cavernous garage where the buses were kept and let me drive one around to get the feel of it. While I was making figure eights around the concrete pillars, I saw the Bub disappear behind one of the other buses carrying a five-gallon jerry can and a siphon hose. It was like a point of principle with the Bub never to pay for something he could get for free.

My first job was to chauffeur Dr. Edward Teller back and forth between

Berkeley and the Lawrence Radiation Laboratory in Livermore. Dr. Teller was commonly known as the father of the hydrogen bomb, a sobriquet he hated. "On the contrary, I am the father of a wonderful daughter named Wendy," he was known to say. I knew Wendy because she and I were in the same accelerated class at Berkeley High. "Just tell him you know her," one of the other drivers told me. "He loves talking about her. You'll have it made."

On my first day, I picked Dr. Teller up at his elegant, older home in the Berkeley hills. He was a stout man with dark Groucho Marx eyebrows and spoke with a thick Hungarian accent that made him seem stern. As soon as he was settled in the back seat, I mentioned being in the same high school class as his daughter and he seemed pleased. We talked about her a little and then he fell silent. A while later, I thought of something else to say about her, only this time he didn't seem as pleased. Later yet, I thought of something else to say and he interrupted me.

"To you it may not seem as though I am doing anything back here but I am always thing-king. And when you talk to me, it interrupts my thing-king. So from now on during these trips, I would like you please not to talk."

So that's how it went with Dr. Teller. After several weeks he began bringing a stenographer with him and would dictate letters during the ride. He especially liked to write to President Johnson, warning him of the "red threat," which is how he referred to Communist China.

At the UC Garage there was a big black book listing all the driving jobs and I would check it frequently and sign up for jobs that didn't conflict with my classes. I drove forestry students to the Sierra, architecture students to elegant homes in San Francisco and Marin counties, and engineering students to a factory that built ship engines with piston rings big as hula hoops. I also drove the Regents frequently, including Mrs. Randolph Hearst and Lieutenant Governor Anderson. Many of the driving jobs required a fleet of buses and I would end up hanging out with the other drivers, mostly moonlighting Berkeley cops. At first, I was a little nervous around them, but they seemed friendly enough. One of them slapped me on the back and told me, "Just cut your corners wide and don't park under any low-lying tree limbs. You'll do fine!" A burly, blond cop winkingly told about a phone conversation he had had with some fraternity brothers after they caught a Black man trying to burglarize their fraternity. The fraternity brothers felt bad because they had roughed up the suspect in the course of subduing him, but the blond cop told them not to worry about it, that they might even have to rough him up some more if he tried to get away and in fact, he and his partner were going to stop for coffee, so it would be a while before they got there. The other cops all got a good laugh out of this. I could see it made a big difference which side of these guys you were on.

I had been dying to get out of my parents' house and with the money I made driving I was able to rent a cottage on Neilson Street for sixty dollars a month. It was just a one-room cottage behind a house, but the room was big enough to accommodate my bed, which doubled as a sofa, and a table, where I could eat or do homework. The walls were made of knotty pine, which gave it the feel of a cabin. To dress it up, I hung a large poster of Einstein on one wall and got an old Chianti bottle to put in the middle of my table for burning drip candles. After a few weeks the bottle was covered with red, orange, yellow, green, blue, and purple wax. Behind the cottage was a huge tangle of blackberries and behind that, the railroad tracks. I worried that the trains might bother me, but I soon learned to love the mournful sound the whistle made and the way the trains made my whole cottage tremble as they passed.

Strange days followed. I began smoking pot a lot and hanging out with a friend named Fred Swaha, who had attended a prep school back east and was now going to Cal. I happened to be with him when he rented an apartment in a rundown Victorian above Moe's Bookstore on Telegraph Avenue. The landlord told us that the previous tenant had jumped out the window into an alleyway on LSD and killed himself. He had been a writer and the landlord showed us the hole in the wall where he threw his typewriter right before he jumped.

Fred and I began spending evenings getting high and playing honeymoon bridge on his bed, which was next to a window where we could see everything going on down on Telegraph Avenue two stories below. Telegraph Avenue, or "The Ave" as it was called, had become a scene where longhairs congregated on the sidewalk and talked revolution. These were the first hippies and every evening the street would clog up with carloads of straight folks coming all the way from places like Hayward and Castro Valley just to see the strange, new long-haired freaks.

The apartment next to Fred's was occupied by a luscious brunette named Kathleen, who worked as a go-go dancer in The City. She didn't have a car and on nights when Fred and I had nothing to do, we would drive over at two in the morning to pick her up. One time the bouncer let us in briefly to see her topless, but all other times we had to wait outside because of our age. At closing time, Kathleen would come out and give us big hugs, wearing only a fur coat thrown over her go-go outfit and trailed by straight, business types, who gave Fred and me dirty looks because they thought we were making it with her. Actually, she was waiting for some guy in jail. Coming home one night across the Bay Bridge, we heard a terrific roar and felt the whole bridge shudder as four Hells Angels shot past on their overpowered Harleys. They must have had their throttles pinned because they were leaning back on their sissy bars, hands clasped behind their heads, feet propped on their handlebars.

They came to the curve past Treasure Island and simply leaned smoothly into it, barely moving a muscle. It took our breath away, such a display of raw power. I felt my heart soar. This is it! I thought to myself. Young people are going to take over the world! There really is going to be a revolution!

I had been smoking grass for some time now but had never seen a brick, which was the way I knew most grass came packaged. One evening a friend of the Bub named LaDue mentioned that he knew of some bricks for sale. LaDue was a short, skinny kid who had dropped out of high school and had acquired the manner of a salesman. "These are full kilos too," he was saying. "Not just two-pounders like most of the bricks you see nowadays."

I decided to buy one and fronted him $125. I was supposed to get it the next day and called him, but he sounded defensive, saying there had been a "slight delay" though everything was "still cool" and I would get my brick by the weekend. I got the sinking feeling that comes with throwing away $125, but on Saturday morning he showed up at my door with a brick. "It's a little underweight," he apologized, "but that's about all you can expect with the weed market being so dry." I invited him to come in and smoke some of it, but he declined, saying he "previous engagements."

I locked the door, pulled the shades, and set about examining my brick. It was the size and shape of a Roget's Thesaurus and came wrapped in red cellophane. The cellophane looked shrink-wrapped, it was on so tight, and I imagined a large, clandestine factory somewhere in Mexico run by God knew what sort of sinister criminal types. Underneath the cellophane was beige construction paper, which had a syrup smell to it and was damp in places. This struck me as odd. I undid the paper and saw that the grass itself was damp and sticky. I tried to smoke some, but it wouldn't stay lit. This couldn't be right. I was about to go looking for LaDue when the Bub dropped by. He had heard I got my brick and hoped to hit me up for a smoking stash. He told me not to worry about the stickiness, saying it was the way most grass came these days.

"They pack it with sugar water. It's just a cheap Mexican trick to boost the weight."

He told me to break the brick up inside a pillowcase, run water through it to get all the sugar out, then wring it out and spread the grass out on a tray and place it in the oven under very low heat. I followed his instructions and eight hours later my pillowcase was stained an indelible brown, my cottage reeked of caramel, and my "kilo" had been reduced to all of twenty-two ounces. But the grass got me high and I was satisfied. I called all my friends to say I had lids for sale, and in two days the grass was gone and I was ahead seventy-five dollars—money it would have taken me thirty hours to earn driving buses. I got ahold of LaDue and bought two more of the same bricks.

These sugared bricks were on both coasts and were practically the only bricks around. Word was that they were brought up by the Mexican Mafia, whoever that was. While I was cleaning my new bricks, I had the radio tuned to a hip station and heard the D.J. ad-lib the following:

Hysterical female voice: "My God, John! What are you doing with your head in the oven?"

Bored male voice: "Relax, Martha. I'm just checking to see if the pot is dry yet."

I was part of a nationwide conspiracy!

The second bricks took longer to sell. Most of my friends had bought lids from the first brick and I began offering grass to wider and wider circles of friends. I sold to students in my classes, to the mechanics at the UC Garage— even to people I met driving buses. I carried lids hidden in my truck and sold one to a hitchhiker, assuming he was cool for the sole reason he was wearing burgundy cords, the latest sign you were hip. People often wanted to try the grass before buying it and I would get high with them. A few hours spent socializing netted me more than I made in a week driving buses.

I didn't wait to run out of grass before contacting LaDue again. He lived in a big communal home on College Avenue and I got there around dusk. As I strode up the walkway, I could hear "Sunshine Superman" playing at high volume. I knocked and someone opened the door for me and drifted off. I stepped into the living room, which smelled of pot smoke and was dark save for several candles burning on a low table. Eight or ten people lay around, listening to the music. I made out LaDue slumped in an overstuffed chair in a corner and went over to him. He became animated on seeing me and pulled out a piece of folded tin foil.

"Nepalese Black, man. It's the best you can get. Made by priests high up in the mountains in Nepal. They run through the fields barefoot wearing leather robes—"

I told him I wasn't interested in hash; I wanted more of the red cellophane bricks. He pulled out a pill bottle and handed it to me. In it was a single small flowering tip of grass, a *colita*.

"Pure Acapulco Gold. It'll blow your fucking mind apart. I can let you have it for ten dollars."

I stared at it. There couldn't have been enough grass there to roll two joints. LaDue snatched it back, pocketing it. "Actually, it's worth more like twenty."

I started to ask him about the bricks again when a sudden movement caught my eye. I turned to see a guy in Levi's and a blue windbreaker showing off a gun, pointing it in people's faces and trying to scare them, saying, "This is a police raid!" then grinning stupidly. One of the first things I had learned about smoking pot was that it could make you paranoid and it was considered really poor form to try to scare people when they were stoned. This guy was an ass and I felt like telling him so but turned back to LaDue. "What about those red cellophane—"

LaDue wasn't paying attention to me. He was staring past me, his eyes going wide. I turned again to see uniformed police officers bursting into the room. "Everyone in this room is under arrest for possession of marijuana!" shouted the guy in Levi's.

"Bullshit!" I didn't have any marijuana on me. I wasn't even high.

A blond cop was on me in an instant, grabbing my arms. I resisted briefly, thought better of it, and let him twist my arms behind me and handcuff me. He then shoved me down on a couch. I didn't like having my hands behind me and instinctively flopped back, drew my knees up to my chest, and quickly wriggled the handcuffs under my butt so that my hands were now in front of me. I held them up, expecting abuse, but the blond cop only grinned.

"That's pretty good. Not many people can do that."

"Anyone else got anything to say?" baited the guy in Levi's. No one spoke. He lowered his gun and looked around. "Geez, what a bunch of deadbeats. We burst in here and no one even moves. What's the matter with you guys? Are you really that fucked up on drugs?"

No one said a word. A girl in a corner began to cry.

"I can't go to jail!" she burst out between sobs. "My parents'll kill me and besides, I have diarrhea."

The guy in Levi's looked embarrassed.

"Why don't you quit taking drugs?" offered one of the cops. "Then maybe you wouldn't get diarrhea."

The guy in Levi's gave orders and cops fanned out through the house searching for drugs. Some stayed in the living room, grabbing pillows off the couch, knocking books off shelves, and pulling drawers out and turning them upside-down so that their contents fell all over the floor. In the middle of this, a young guy came to the door not realizing there was a bust going on, took one look, and ran. Two cops ran out after him. Moments later, they brought him back blubbering, his face bright red and smeared with tears. "They maced him," I heard a girl's voice whisper. We were lined up and searched in turn. Two people were caught holding, one of them LaDue. He had ditched the hash but somehow failed to get rid of the colita. They also found several grass plants growing in tin cans in a back room. For this they arrested the whole lot of us.

Outside, the police formed a cordon as we were marched single file to a waiting van. I recognized one of the policemen I had driven buses with and stepped up to him.

"Hey, you've got to get me out of this! I just came here to get a book from a guy. I'm a student."

31

He threw me an uncomfortable look. "You're going to have to tell it to the judge," he murmured. "Keep moving!" he shouted loud enough for the other cops to hear.

Fourteen of us were herded into a small van with hardly any ventilation. The benches on either side were quickly taken and the rest of us had to stand with nothing to hang on to. We could barely move our arms, we were packed in so tightly. The doors shut and it got hard to breathe. Two cops slid in front, separated from us by a window and a thick wire mesh. The driver revved the engine, popped the clutch, and the van took off with a purposeful lurch. People tumbled against each other and for a moment I thought there was going to be panic. LaDue's voice rang out.

"Everyone stay cool! Put out your smokes! Breathe slowly! . . . Everyone do yoga!"

Now that we were moving, fresh air began to filter in. I was near LaDue, who didn't seem that upset by the fact he was caught holding. In fact, he seemed to enjoy his new role as guru. He had his face pressed to a narrow, mesh-covered window and gave a running account of our progress through the streets. At Haste and Telegraph the van stopped for a red light and LaDue shouted to two longhairs standing on the corner. "Peace, brothers! Peace!"

He wheeled, exultant. "They flashed us the peace sign!"

He began singing "We Shall Overcome" and people joined in, the sound swelling with each chorus. It reminded me of the parties held in the backs of semi-trailers during Prohibition. The cops looked back and shook their heads, causing everyone to laugh and sing all the louder. Even the girl with diarrhea was singing. The only one who didn't laugh or sing was me. I was furious. Even though I had gone to LaDue's for the purpose of buying grass, the cops had no way of knowing this, and their failure to respect the letter of the law enraged me.

We were booked and bail was set at $1,100. A friend came and bailed me out, and because he didn't happen to have $1,100 in cash lying around that time of night, he had to pay a bondsman ten percent, which meant I was out $110. I was the only one who bailed out. I had to because I had a bus run scheduled for six-thirty the following morning. Everyone else spent the night in jail and in the morning the judge dropped charges against everyone except LaDue and the other guy caught holding.

For days afterward, just thinking about the bust would make my face go hot with anger and shame. Fuck the Establishment! I told myself. I bought an American flag and tacked it down over my doorstep so anyone coming to visit would have to step on it. Anyone who isn't willing to tread on the American flag is no friend of mine! I told myself. But after a few days, having that flag there felt weird, and I pulled it up, dusted it off, and folded it away in a drawer.

CHAPTER 7

FINALS WERE COMING UP AND FOR ONE of my engineering courses I had to submit a design for a barbecue grill that could be used indoors, which meant it had to have a way to ventilate out an open window. I gave the project some thought but had no real interest in it and didn't get started until two days before it was due. When I turned it in, I had to wait briefly while a guy ahead of me turned his in. I saw that he had produced incredibly elaborate drawings, including exploded views with every bolt and nut labeled according to gauge, length, and thread. This guy was going to be a real engineer, I thought to myself, and positioned my sad drawings so others couldn't see them. A week later I got my drawings back with "C-, Wouldn't work!" scrawled across the top.

Summer was passing and I signed up for as many bus runs as I could, drifting along with no real plan other than to keep studying engineering, which, aside from the math, held little interest for me. One afternoon Arf and I met to play pool and on a whim I said we should play at the Kue and Kushion on San Pablo Avenue in Albany. We had never played there before and I was longing for something new and different. We got there, and because there were no parking places in front, I turned the corner and parked on a side street. We played for a couple of hours, and if we had played a minute longer or a minute less, my life might have turned out differently. But we left when we did, and because I had parked on a side street, I found myself driving through an area of Albany where I normally never went. It was a quiet neighborhood of squat stucco houses with neatly kept lawns and concrete walkways painted red.

"I could never live in a place like this," I told Arf. "I would rather live in a tenement."

"I know what you mean," he said. "The conformity is depressing."

The street was narrow and when a car approached, I had to slow nearly to a stop to get past. The car was some nondescript car and made no impression on me until I happened to glance at the driver and recognized the Bub! And sitting next to him was his best friend, Ron! They were ignoring us, though, staring straight ahead as though they could have possibly failed to notice my yellow pickup. This was weird! And the car they were driving, I now saw, was a Rambler and looked like an old lady's car. This was weird too. The Bub normally drove cars that were raked and had chrome reverse rims and the like; I wouldn't have expected him to set foot in a Rambler. "Something's up!" I told Arf as I pulled over and laid on the horn. We turned to watch as the Bub and Ron drove on, saw them turn to each other as though to confer, then saw them slowly, as though reluctantly, pull over at the end of the block. "Come on!" I cried to Arf and jumped out.

The Bub, whose real name was Steve, was nearly six feet tall, big-boned, with big hands, pale freckled skin, and light red hair. He was the first in our crowd to grow his hair long. Throughout my childhood the only two people I knew of with long hair were Jesus Christ and Prince Valiant. If longhairs had curly hair, they looked like Jesus Christ to me, and if their hair was straight, they looked like Prince Valiant. The Bub had straight hair and looked like Prince Valiant.

Ron was Bill Gretsch's younger brother and was like the classic bright kid gone bad. He was tall, thin, and pale and wore wire-rimmed glasses that made him look like a character out of a Thomas Mann novel. He purposely carried himself in a loose, floppy manner that was like a calculated affront to macho types, used "ain't" and double negatives a lot, and was said to have a genius IQ. He had already been in trouble with the law twice, both for pot. Because the two were younger than our crowd and had dropped out of high school, we considered them to be immature and referred to them as "the Bubblegummers," which soon got shortened to "the Bubs." The name stuck more to Steve, though, than it did to Ron, so if you used it in the singular, everyone knew you were talking about Steve.

By the time we caught up to them, they were standing on the sidewalk with freshly lit cigarettes.

"Nice car," I laughed.

The Bub took a drag off his cigarette and blew smoke down toward his shoes. "It's alright."

"Where'd you get it?"

"The papers."

"You mean it's yours?" I had expected him to say it was his aunt's or something.

"It's a boss car, man. Gets good mileage."

I laughed. "When was the last time you paid for gas?"

"You know, just trying to save a little coin."

"Face it, you guys are up to something. What's going on?"

The Bub started to say something when Ron stepped forward and waved his hands like a director about to yell Cut!

"We ain't sayin' nothin'!"

It took a while and Arf and I had to wheedle and plead, but we finally got them to tell us their secret. They said they had bought the car for running grass and that it was the straightest, most innocent-looking car they could find. Having revealed this to us, they began stumbling over each other to show off all the car's straight-looking features.

"Dig the two-tone color job," grinned the Bub. "Green and white. What colors could be more straight?"

"Check out the College of Holy Names decal on the rear bumper!"

"The body hardly has a dent in it."

"Check out the whitewalls!"

The Bub grabbed a sack off the back seat and pulled out a hubcap. "Hardly even scuffed. We're going to keep them like that and put them on just before the border."

"It's the classic little-old-lady-from-Pasadena car!"

"It's even got overdrive and reclining seats. It's a boss little car!"

"But most of all," exulted Ron. "It's a *Rambler*. What car symbolizes middle America better than a Rambler?" He staggered off the curb, holding his cigarette and tittering. "Customs isn't even going to *see* this car!"

The Bub went on to describe their plan. He popped the trunk and showed us a Rambler gas tank they had bought at a wrecker's. They had already chiseled a square hole in the top of it for packing in bricks. Their plan was to fill this gas tank full of bricks and install it right before crossing the border. During the crossing, the car would run off an auxiliary tank they were going to devise.

"God, I can't believe you guys ran across us like this," the Bub said as he shut the trunk. "We haven't told a soul about this car. We've been keeping it hidden in a rented garage here in Albany. This is only the second time we've taken it out and the only reason we did was 'cause I just gave it a tune-up and wanted to see how it was running." What they needed now, he said, was a contact in Mexico. "Say, you guys know something about that, don't you? From that time you went down with Bill?"

I spent the next week helping the Bubs outfit their Rambler. Helping the Bub would be a better way to put it as Ron scarcely did a lick of work. He made up for it, though, by providing moral support. He referred to their plan as the "All-time Crime" and said they were going to become "multi-thousandaires." One day he brought some cocaine by, laughing to me on the sly that this was his way of making sure he got a full day's work out of the Bub. It was the first time I had ever seen cocaine. "You'll see," Ron grinned. "One hit off this shit and the Bub'll be humping butt all day!"

We all snorted and, sure enough, the Bub and I began working with twice our normal energy and loving it. Even Ron chipped in, using a rag to clean the windows, although ten minutes later he was back on the sidewalk, smoking, while the windows remained streaked with soap. Somewhere along the line it was decided that I would be a third partner in the run. I was a natural because in addition to a contact, the Bubs also lacked financing, and I had both.

With the rigged tank in place, we took the Rambler for a spin on the auxiliary fuel tank and it ran perfectly. The auxiliary fuel tank was just a five-gallon can we had wedged way up inside the right rear quarter panel. A neoprene hose led from a fitting at the base of the can, joined the taillight wiring in the darkness of the quarter panel, followed the wiring into the trunk space underneath the trunk mat, and ducked down a small drainage hole and through the chiseled hole in the top of the gas tank to join the regular fuel line from *inside the tank*, where customs would never be able to see it. Customs could follow the car's fuel line from the engine all the way back to the tank and not find a thing amiss. Where the neoprene hose joined the taillight wiring, it was wrapped along with the wiring in black electrical tape.

To get the can up inside the quarter panel, we had passed it through a rectangular hole at the bottom, flush with the undercarriage. On shining a flashlight up there, we saw that the can was plainly visible. We spray-painted it black, but it could still be seen. So to hide it, we fashioned a piece of plywood to block off the rectangular hole that was the quarter panel's access. Then we spray-painted the plywood black and while the paint was still wet, we threw dust and grit against it till it perfectly matched the rest of the undercarriage. For symmetry, we covered the hole on the other side in the same way. Only someone who had worked on the Rambler assembly line would know the difference. I lay underneath the car for a moment admiring our work. If only my engineering professor could see this!

The tank would hold about thirty kilos, we calculated, and in order to make the run profitable for the three of us, we decided to buy sixty kilos and do two crossings. I would finance the run with my college money and manage the score, and the Bubs would transport the grass up through Mexico and across the border. We would split the grass three ways. At the last moment I worried that my Spanish wasn't good enough for dealing with Meche and invited Arf to come along in return for a cut of the grass. He declined, saying he didn't think the plan had a chance. I then offered him a hundred dollars plus expenses up front. He saw this as an inexpensive way to see Mazatlan again and agreed to come.

The Bub got a crew cut, but when Ron came back from the barber, his hair was still down to his ears. We made him go back again, but when he returned, it was hardly any shorter. "Oh, ma-an, cut off my hair and you'll cut off my love life!" We made him go back yet again and it was worth it because in the end he and the Bub looked like a pair of kids off a fifties cover of the *Saturday Evening Post*. All they needed was a couple of fishing poles and a can of worms. As a final touch, Ron stuck a "Yes on 14" sticker on the front bumper of the Rambler, where it could be plainly noticed by customs. Proposition 14 was the famous anti-fair housing proposition of the time. "Customs ought to be able to relate to that," Ron laughed, stepping back to admire his work. "They're all a bunch of redneck bigots anyway! He-he-he!"

As the four of us headed south, Ron kept us entertained with stories of jail. "There was the greatest saying scratched into the wall above my bunk. It said, 'Society deserves every criminal it creates.' Ha! It's so true! He-he-he!"

I told him about the College Avenue bust and he sympathized. "The police are just a bunch of fucking cowboys. Fuck 'em!"

I wondered how Ron got along in jail, carrying himself in the unmacho, almost effeminate way he had. "The tough guys didn't give you any trouble?"

"No, they never messed with the hips. They thought we were crazy! He-he!"

"How could they tell who was hip? Don't you have to get your hair cut in jail?"

"No, not everyone. And even the ones that do, you can still tell they're hip by the white patches where their beards and mustaches used to be. He-he-he!"

We slept by the side of the road somewhere past Los Angeles and ate breakfast the following morning in San Ysidro. At our booth was a chromed fortune-telling machine with a picture of a seer in a turban. "Swami knows all! Ask Swami any question that can be answered yes or no." Ron put a penny in and asked, "Will this run pull through?" He pulled the lever and a small card came out with the word NO printed on it. He laughed and then the Bub put in a penny and got another NO. We all laughed and started quaking and making groans and grimaces of mock fear as we put penny after penny in the machine—only to get NOs. Not until our seventh try did we finally get a YES, and in a way that's how the run turned out.

CHAPTER 8

WE CROSSED AT TIJUANA, BOUGHT MANDATORY Mexican auto insurance, and drove out of town to the desert, where we followed a set of tire tracks till we came to some large creosote bushes that made a perfect place for stashing our rigged gas tank. I made sure the Bubs had the spot memorized and we headed on.

That evening we came to the Mexican inspection station south of Sonoyta. I had learned a little about this station since our first trip, when we drove the grass through here on balls and a whim. Its purpose was to enforce a tariff on manufactured goods entering the interior of Mexico. The only reason northbound travelers had to stop here was to turn in their car permits and tourist visas and show that they still had any radios or appliances they had taken into the interior for their personal use. Theoretically there was no reason for northbound travelers to be searched. I remembered seeing that Buick getting searched, though, and figured the authorities were catching on to the fact grass was passing through here. The Bub took care to memorize the kilometer marker here and said the grass would be well hidden before they passed back through. We continued driving, taking turns at the wheel, and around two in the morning, while Arf was driving along a dark, unlit stretch of roadway, we slammed into a calf that had wandered onto the road.

This was one of the hazards of driving in Mexico. Well-maintained fences were rare, and everywhere you drove, there were signs warning of cattle on the road. None of us was hurt and we jumped out and played a flashlight over the front of the Rambler. The grille was smashed, the hood was buckled, and the right front fender was caved in. A puddle of water was forming on the asphalt and the smell of sulfur hung in the air. We managed to pry the hood open and saw that the radiator was smashed back into the fan blade and the battery had broken loose and lay dashed against the block. It broke our hearts to see the

Rambler wrecked like this after all the work we had put in to make her perfect. The calf gave a dying groan by the side of the road and I figured that might as well be the death knell for our trip, but then Arf got out our insurance papers and discovered that collisions with cattle were covered.

As soon as it grew light, Arf hitchhiked to the nearest town and was back in a few hours with an insurance adjuster. The adjuster had the car towed to Nogales for repairs and took us there in his pickup. We found an inexpensive motel and settled in to wait out the delay.

Nogales was going through a hot spell at the time and our motel with its foot-thick adobe walls would stay cool till about noon, then heat up like a brick oven. We spent afternoons wandering the shady sides of the Nogales streets and hanging out in parks that had trees. In the evenings we lingered over dinners at a Chinese restaurant we found that had good air conditioning. Each day we visited the repair shop, only to find that no work had been started yet on the Rambler. The foreman kept telling us he was waiting for parts. The left front tire had been cut in the crash and we asked him if he could at least replace the tire while waiting for parts, and he promised he would, only it wasn't done the next day or the day after. "Things happen slow around here," Ron laughed and dubbed the country "Mexislow."

One night our wanderings took us to the Nogales red-light district. We came to a building with a concrete platform in front, like a loading platform, where available girls paraded about. From below we could see up their mini-skirts. One approached us and stooped down, offering us a view of her breasts. "You like fuckee fuckee? . . . Suckee suckee?" She ran her tongue over her lips.

"How much?" Ron asked her.

"Ten dohlars."

I had spent so much time trying to imagine what sex would be like, it seemed hard to believe I could find out right now for money I had right in my pocket. Ron was all for it, but we had already spent more than we planned on account of the delay, and if we spent much more, we wouldn't be able to buy as much grass.

"Aw, ma-an . . . "

More days went by with nothing getting done on the Rambler and Arf began talking about going home. I wasn't about to give up and felt I needed him for the score. The small smoking stash we had brought with us was long since gone and I figured we needed some more pot to boost our morale. Even Arf was smoking grass now and had taken to it like a kid to candy. I offered to try to score some and Ron volunteered to go with me. In part I viewed this as a rehearsal for the real score, which I worried I might have to do without Arf.

It was the hottest part of the day and we went to a nearby park. There, we studied the people to see who we thought might have grass. We didn't want to approach people who looked straight, of course, but the people who didn't look straight looked sleazy, and we were afraid to approach them. The whole time, too, Ron was acting like a goof, giggling and holding his cigarette in the effeminate way he had. He seemed to view life as some sort of play he had been thrust into against his will and in order to get even, he acted the opposite of the role he imagined he was supposed to play and screwed things up even more by laughing all the time. We spent a half hour at the park getting nowhere and decided to ask a cab driver.

At a major intersection we found a line of cabs, slid into the back seat of the first in line, and asked the driver if he could get us grass. He assured us he could and turned down a side street. Soon we were in an area I recognized as being near the red-light district. We came to a pool hall and the driver stopped, disappeared inside, and came back accompanied by a burly man with a long scar over his left cheek. The scar was jagged and I imagined it had been made by a knife. The two men got in the cab, the driver drove on, and the burly man turned around and handed me an envelope containing about twenty joints. "*Cien pesos,*" the cab driver said. By now we were in a hill land with only a few scattered homes, and the driver pulled over onto a patch of dirt overlooking a garbage-strewn slope. There was no one around and I wondered if the cabbie had driven here because it was a safe place to score or if he had other reasons. I pulled out a packet of *cerillos* and started to light one of the joints, but the cabbie stopped me, saying the smell would linger in his cab.

"*No te preocupes* — Don't worry. This grass is very strong." He held up his right fist and shook it to indicate strength.

"What's going on?" Ron demanded.

I interpreted for him and he frowned.

"Well, if we can't smoke it, tell 'em we ain't buying any!"

The burly guy craned his head around to see what was going on, affording me a full view of his scar.

"Wha'f they 'ave knives?" I murmured to Ron.

Ron did a sort of double take and jerked up his right index finger.

"Tell 'em we'll take it!"

I handed the cabbie a hundred-peso note and stuffed the envelope inside my underpants as the cabbie started the car.

He let us off at the intersection where he had picked us up, a giant inter-section where several wide boulevards met at odd angles. It was now rush hour, and a police officer stood in the middle of the intersection directing traffic from a wooden stool. We set out to cross, and as I was passing the policeman's back, I realized Ron was no longer beside me and simultaneously felt a tickling sensation along my left leg. I glanced down in time to see a joint slip out from my pant leg. Horrified, I grabbed my crotch to keep any more from falling out and looked back to see a trail of neat, white joints leading right behind the policeman's back to where Ron stood stooping over to pick them up! I hurried on without looking back. By the time Ron caught up to me, I was halfway down the next block.

"I got 'em all!" he panted, holding them up for me to see.

"Put those away, you fool!"

He glanced back as if to see what the trouble was about.

"Man, everything's cool."

Our motel was a mile farther on, and the whole way there I tried to look as though it were the most natural thing for me to be walking along with my left hand tightly gripping my crotch.

At the motel we burst into our room like heroes. Arf couldn't believe we had scored, having bet the Bub we would come back empty-handed. We lit up a joint and passed it around, and since they were small, we lit up another. "Funny-tasting grass," commented the Bub. We lit up a couple more. Arf was the first to complain he wasn't getting high.

"Let me see one of those joints," said the Bub. He unfolded it at the table where we were seated and used a pencil to tease apart the contents, picking up pinches and sniffing them.

"Pure parsley and tobacco. . . . I thought this stuff tasted kind of funny."

An argument ensued whether the eight dollars Ron and I had just blown could be considered a community expense.

"I mean it's a joke," Arf said. "You guys think you can pull off the All-time Crime and you can't even score a lid."

He said he wanted to go home. I didn't want to do the score without him, though, and got him to agree to the following plan: he and I would catch the next train to Mazatlan, where we would score the grass and then stash it in the jungle, after which he could go home while I waited for the Bubs to come down once the Rambler was repaired.

The following morning we visited the repair shop and Arf told the foreman in his sternest Spanish that the car had to be done by the end of the week without fail. "I will get it done if I have to drive to Tucson and get the parts myself," the foreman assured us. At the train station I gave the Bubs enough money to make it to the end of the week and for the drive to Mazatlan and told them to find me at the Hotel Olas Altas, a hotel I remembered from our first trip down.

CHAPTER 9

STEPPING OFF THE TRAIN AT MAZATLAN WAS like stepping into a steam bath. It was the rainy season here with thick, humid air and muddy water in all the potholes. The surrounding hills were carpeted in green. Arf and I checked into the Olas Altas, then went straight to the beach, where we spotted Meche showing hats to two middle-aged American women. They appeared to be bargaining with him, but when Meche saw us, he grabbed his hats back and hurried over, leaving the two women staring at us with indignant looks.

"*¡Qué milagro!* — What a miracle! I thought you were in jail!" Meche laughed heartily.

Arf frowned. "Jail? What made you think we were in jail?"

Meche shrugged. "So much time passed and you never returned, *pues*." He laughed again.

Everything was very hot now, he told us, glancing over his shoulder. The new harvest season had started and the government's annual campaign against grass was underway. Over a thousand *federales* were garrisoned right here in town. Each day they drove out on the highways in long convoys and fanned out into the *sierra* looking for grass. They searched ranches and stopped any cars or trucks they considered suspicious.

"If they catch you with grass, they beat you till you name your suppliers." Meche sucked in air to make a hissing sound like spit on a hot stove and laughed. "*¡Qué barbaridad!*"

He said he could still get us grass, but we would have to pick it up in the sierra north of town; that was as close as his people dared bring it. We said we preferred picking it up in the sierra. We told him we wanted bricks this time and he assured us it would come in neat, tightly packed bricks. The price was still ten dollars a kilo. After settling a few more details, we set the score for six o'clock the next day. Dusk was the best time to do a deal, Meche explained. "It will be hard to see, yet not so dark that you have to use lights. Furthermore, people are tired at that hour and thinking only of their stomachs." He patted his belly and laughed.

At a fledgling Hertz agency Arf and I rented a VW bug, then drove out the highway north to the general area where Meche had said the score would take place. After the score, we planned to take the grass quickly to a place where we could safely stash it. It had to be a place we could find again easily in the dark yet where no one would stumble across it—two potentially conflicting requirements. We pulled off on a dirt road, followed it a ways, and pulled over and got out. The lush vegetation here gave off a sweet fragrance like the fragrance of freshly cut alfalfa, which is similar to the fragrance of pot, so that we kept having to look around to make sure we weren't stumbling across someone's crop.

We checked out a number of places like this, working north, but none of them had any landmarks that would enable us to find them again easily in the dark. Eventually we came to the Tropic of Cancer monument, where we noticed a dirt road directly opposite that led up into the jungle. We followed it up a gentle slope and after about a quarter mile, it abruptly dead-ended. We got out and looked around. There was nothing here—no structures, no fences—nothing but jungle. We walked a ways into the jungle and aside from the road, there was no sign that people had ever been here. This was ideal. The Tropic of Cancer monument would be easy for us to find in the dark, and as long as we carried the grass well into the jungle, no one should run across it.

This was going to be the "deal of sixes." We were to meet Meche at six o'clock and would score sixty kilos for $600. The afternoon of the score, Arf and I ate seafood at the Playa Norte and drank Superiores. I felt a little nervous, though more excited than anything. I asked Arf if he felt at all nervous and he said, "A little," then added, "But if you want to enjoy life, I think you have to take risks." And in a way, that could have been the credo for our crowd.

At six o'clock we met Meche along the malecón. Meche hurriedly shooed me out of the passenger seat, telling me to get in the back, which left me feeling insulted until he explained why. It could be dangerous for a gringo to be seen with Mexicans during the harvest season, he said, and told me to lie down out of sight. Arf, of course, could pass easily for a Mexican, but with my fair skin I made a poor imposter. I did as told and looked up to watch the tops of trees and telephone poles flash by against the deepening blue of the sky. Every now and then a colorful open-air bus would pass by packed full of campesinos returning home from the fields.

Out on the highway, Arf told me there were no other cars around and I sat up. As we drove, I recognized dirt roads we had checked out the day before. After a few miles, Meche indicated a dirt road ahead on the right and told Arf to turn. Arf slowed and Meche looked around to make sure no other cars were coming as he didn't want anyone to see us turn off. "*¡Derecho! ¡Derecho!*" he cried suddenly. "Straight! Straight!" A stake bed truck carrying federales had just appeared around a bend ahead. Arf kept going straight and we passed the dirt side road. I was staring at the federales in fascination when Meche wheeled on me.

"*¡Escóndete!* — Hide yourself!"

I ducked down and moments later the stake bed flashed by, providing me a quick glimpse of the upper halves of the federales standing in back. They were dressed in olive drab, wore helmets, and had rifles slung over their shoulders, some hanging on to the railings for balance, others cupping their cigarettes against the wind. They looked young and were all dark-skinned. It stood to reason, I supposed, they would be drawn from the poorest segments of society. What struck me most, though, was the impassive look of their faces. "Indoctrinated morons," I thought to myself. If they caught us, we could forget mercy.

Several more army trucks and a jeep followed, after which the road was clear. Arf made a quick U-turn and headed back for the dirt side road. As we approached it, Meche looked behind us and cursed. "*¡Hijo de la chingada!*" Another army truck had appeared behind us. Again we had to pass the dirt side road and continue straight, now heading back toward town. Before long we caught up with the first Army vehicles we had seen and fell in sheepishly behind. Soon the army vehicle behind us caught up with us and behind it more army vehicles appeared. Here we had tried so hard to avoid any heat—only to end up in the middle of a federales convoy! It wasn't until we were nearly back to town that we came to a paved arterial sufficiently well-traveled that Meche felt we could turn off without attracting suspicion. After rounding a bend we pulled over and peered through the foliage to watch the convoy go by. After the last truck had passed, we let a good five minutes go by before getting back on the highway. This time we finally made the turn onto the side road, and as the bug bounced off the pavement onto the dirt, I noticed Meche flicking his fingers across his chest in the sign of the cross.

The road wound back and forth up into the sierra, and the sky now was a butterfly-wing blue I had only seen in the tropics. Behind us the foliage had lost all its color save for a lone *amapa* tree in bloom glowing a lambent pink. After twenty minutes or so, Meche told us to pull over at a small clearing, got out, and disappeared into the gathering darkness. We got out and saw that we were stopped next to a large pit about thirty feet across and fifteen feet deep. We looked down and could make out red Tecate cans at the bottom glowing like fluorescent blood. We lit smokes and made jokes about ending up in the pit. Some time passed and it grew completely dark. We flipped our butts into the pit and stood watching the coals slowly fade when we heard a rustling sound and turned to see what looked like two ghosts materializing from the darkness.

The ghosts were two campesinos dressed in white muslin with white sombreros, each carrying a squarely bulging white flour sack slung over his shoulder. They came up, dropped their burdens at our feet, and shook hands with us Mexican style—just a brief, light grasp of the other person's palm between thumb and fingers. So these were the growers, I thought, these two humble, older campesinos. We smiled at each other in conspiratorial kinship. I wished I could learn all about them—their lives, their wives and kids, and what they did during the day—but Arf said it would be improper to ask any of these questions and I supposed he was right. Meche appeared and Arf counted out thirty twenty-dollar bills to him while the campesinos helped me load bricks into the bug. Some fit in the shallow trunk in front, and I was hoping the rest would fit in the well behind the back seat, where I could cover them with a sarape we had brought, but there were a lot left over and I simply dumped them on the floor of the back seat and threw the two flour sacks over them. Arf and I shook hands with Meche and he and the campesinos disappeared into the darkness, leaving Arf and me alone in the sierra with a car full of pot.

I took the wheel and we headed down the hill, following Meche's advice to keep our lights off till we got to the highway. When I needed to slow down, I used the parking brake so as not to flash brake lights. We hadn't seen a soul on the way up, but halfway down we came across a cowboy smoking a cigarette as he leaned against the fence of a corral. With one boot propped behind him on a low railing and his elbows hooked over the railing at the top, he looked as though he were auditioning for a Mexican version of the Marlboro Man. He watched us pass without altering his pose and must have wondered what we were doing with our lights out, but I wasn't going to turn them on just for him. All the while, I was feeling very alert but not that nervous. We were committing a serious crime for which we could do hard time in a Mexican prison, but at the first sign of trouble, I figured I could jump out and quickly lose myself in the jungle.

We came to the highway and during a lull when there were no other cars on the road, I pulled on and turned on our lights. To our right was a steep canyon and now I began to feel nervous knowing I could no longer get away that easily if we were pulled over. I consoled myself with the thought that the Tropic of Cancer road was only a few miles farther on. I didn't realize how nervous I was until a car approached and began flashing its high beams at us. The car was the same make and model that the California Highway Patrol was using at the time, and for a panicked instant I imagined this was a sheriff signaling for us to pull over.

"It's your high beams. You're blinding this guy."

I stomped all over the floor with my left foot but couldn't find the dimmer switch. The car passed and another car appeared, the driver likewise flashing his high beams. I continued stomping.

"Where the hell's the dimmer switch on this car?"

Arf didn't know either. Neither of us had ever driven a VW before.

More cars appeared. Our whole goal was to be as inconspicuous as possible and here we were, attracting the attention of every car on the road. I began trying all the knobs and levers I could find. Two thin streams of water struck the windshield, trickled down over the dust and dead insects, and were smeared to an even blur by the windshield wipers. In desperation I even tried the radio knob. Mariachi music welled up inside the car at full volume and I twisted the knob off with such force that it broke off in my hand. I hurled the useless lump of plastic on the floor.

"Calm down, for Christ's sake." Arf had his arm braced against the dash.

"Fuck these imported cars! Why can't they put the switch on the floor like everyone else?"

A semi was coming. The driver began flashing his high beams like a strobe. Desperate not to blind him, I pushed our light switch in so that only our parking lights showed. Instantly, the roadway went black and I could no longer see the reflector posts by the side of the road. The truck was approaching and I instinctively edged to the right, then felt our right-side tires drop off the pavement. Knowing the shoulder was only a few feet wide with no guardrail and an abyss beyond, I jerked the wheel back to the left. The right-side tires jumped back onto the asphalt and we swerved left, straight into the path of the truck. Just in time I corrected right again and heard the blast of the truck's air horn right next to my ear, dropping in pitch as it passed. The right-side tires dropped off the road again and I hit the brakes, fishtailing to a stop. I turned on the headlights and saw there was a huge boulder just a few yards in front of us. Beyond Arf's door gaped the black void of the canyon.

"God, you almost killed us," Arf breathed, letting his arm down from where it was braced.

I felt bad, knowing he was right. I took a deep breath, managed to calm myself, and began searching again for the dimmer switch. In so doing, my left wrist accidentally knocked the turn signal lever backward and the headlights obediently dimmed.

I convinced Arf I was OK to drive and a short while later we reached the Tropic of Cancer road. We followed it to the end and stashed the bricks on top of the exposed roots of a large tree deep in the jungle. Heading back to

Mazatlan, I had a feeling of letdown and tried to analyze why. Was it because I had panicked and Arf hadn't? I felt bad about that, but no, that wasn't it. Was it because I knew Arf would be gone soon and I would miss him? No, no. All I could conclude was that I missed the feeling of holding—that exalted feeling of doing something clandestine, dangerous, and evil.

At the bus station, Arf and I drank Mexican Fantas in the thick air as occasional raindrops thudded on the corrugated tin roof overhead. We each had to pee and laughed as we held our noses against the imponderable stench of the station lavatory. Then Arf's bus came and I saw him off and realized, walking back to the car, that I was farther away from home than I had ever been before alone.

CHAPTER 10

THAT NIGHT RAIN POURED DOWN IN TORRENTS. I sat up in bed, and the streetlamp outside my window was just a vague, gray blur. I was on the top floor of the hotel and could see water cascading from the roof gutters in a long arc to where it dashed on the sidewalk three stories below. Every few seconds there was thunder. My heart sank as I thought of our grass getting soaked and ruined. I considered driving out to try to rescue it but doubted the VW would make it up the Tropic of Cancer road because of the mud. Somehow I managed to sleep, and in the morning the sky was clear and the sun was out. I looked out the window to see kids in their Catholic uniforms walking to school along steaming sidewalks. I drove out to the Tropic of Cancer and was surprised to find the dirt road not the least bit muddy. Not only that, but our grass was as dry as if it had never rained. The canopy of the tree above and the fact it was lying on exposed roots had apparently saved it. I moved it even deeper into the jungle and made sure to place it on the exposed roots of a similar, even larger tree. Hiking back to the car, I spotted a lime tree, picked a lime, and rubbed lime juice over the spaces in the car where the bricks had been in order to mask any lingering smell before returning the car to the Hertz agency.

I figured it would be several days before the Bubs arrived and passed the time trying to improve my Spanish. I had brought a copy of Fabian's *Essentials of Spanish* with me and would study it for several hours, then go out to practice with the locals. There was a park near the hotel where old men hung out, and they made ideal conversation partners. All I had to do was take a seat at one of the white-painted, ornate iron benches, and before long one of them would approach me. They didn't care if I made mistakes and seemed to have all the time in the world.

One morning I decided to tackle the familiar form of the second person preterit. This involved words like *caminaste* and *dijiste*, which struck me as odd-sounding, not like real language, and I wondered if they were the type of words you found only in textbooks, not in actual speech. Just the same, I memorized them, practiced using them with the common verbs I knew, then headed out to the park for a road test. No sooner had I sat down than an old man came up to me, pointed to my obviously new huaraches I had bought the day before, and asked, "*¿Cuánto pagaste?*" A morning of studying vindicated! It was exciting, too, to think that I could learn a new language with just a book and my own efforts.

The days passed and I began to worry that something had gone wrong at the Bubs' end. To burn off nervous energy, I took long walks all over town, trying to stay away from the hotel as long as possible in order to maximize the probability of finding the Bubs waiting for me when I got back. "Has anyone come looking for me?" I would ask the hotel clerk upon returning. He got so used to my question that he would shake his head no as soon as he saw me coming.

I let a total of eleven days go by before giving up on the Bubs. By the eleventh day my money was running low and it seemed clear something fatal had gone wrong with the run. Most likely the Rambler never got fixed and the Bubs got tired of waiting and went home, I imagined. I could just see our whole crowd laughing at the fact I was waiting down here for nothing and even imagined them making bets as to how long I would hold out. The $800 I had spent on this run was a good chunk of what was left of my college education money and I thought of all the driving I would have to do at $2.25 an hour in order to make it up. I packed my suitcase and took a last look out the window at the sea. It was sunny and the waves were up. Why not go body surfing one last time? I thought to myself and fished through my suitcase for my swimsuit.

I swam and body surfed for over an hour, continually checking the beach road to the north in hopes of spotting the Rambler. Finally, I got out and walked back to the hotel, thinking about the two days I would have to spend riding buses in order to get home. At the entrance to the hotel, I turned to take a last look for the Rambler. The Olas Altas was perched partway up a short hill, and I scanned the beach road as it led down the hill, passed some cafés and the ancient Hotel Freeman, rounded a *glorieta*, and was lost from view around a point. Just then a car appeared rounding the point, and even though it was too far away even to identify its color, my heart leapt because something about it made me think it could be the Rambler. I studied it intently as it followed the beach road and, sure enough, it was green and white! It was the Rambler! Soon I could make out the Bubs' faces heading toward me! But then other details caught my attention. There was a gaping black hole where the grille should have been and the hood was still buckled and being held down by a sheet wrapped underneath the car and tied in a knot above, making the Rambler look like a caricature of a car with a headache. The Bub was driving and upon reaching the hill, there was a sound as of a thousand marbles being dropped on metal. The Bub downshifted, the car coughed and sputtered, he downshifted again, and the car lurched forward and died yards from where I was standing. I ran up as the Bubs jumped out looking haggard and unshaven. Before I could say anything, the Bub gripped me by the shoulders and shook me—the first time he had ever even touched me in the many years we had known each other.

"Did you get the dope?" he demanded.

"Yes, it's in the jungle."

He released me and let his whole body go limp with relief. "Good! That's all I care about!"

The Bubs said they were starving and we stepped into the Olas Altas restaurant. Over heaping plates of tacos and enchiladas, they told me what had happened.

"That asshole foreman never did do any work on the car," said the Bub. "He kept putting us off and it was a bitch 'cause we couldn't speak Spanish. We finally realized he was never going to do anything and decided to fix the car ourselves. He wouldn't even let us work on it in the shop, though. He made us sign a release and push it out of his shop. We just pushed it onto a vacant lot next door. The workers saw what was happening and felt sorry for us. They were super cool. They loaned us tools behind the foreman's back and told us where to get the best deal on used parts and stuff. One of them even pounded out the front fender for us and put on touch-up paint."

"The lumpenproletariat pulls through!" exulted Ron.

The Bub grinned. "Anyway, by now we were running out of money, so we ditched the motel and started camping out in the Rambler and cooking up food on the Coleman stove. We got a used battery and a reconditioned radiator and got the car running. The right front tire was shot, but we didn't even have enough money for a recap, so we just threw on the spare. We hardly ate 'cause we were trying to save money for the car. The workers must have sensed what was going on, 'cause they gave us this huge tin can full of refried beans and a stack of tortillas. That's all we've eaten for the last five days!"

Ron waved air past his nostrils as he wrinkled his nose. "Man, I've never farted so much in my life! He-he-he!"

"Anyway, by now all we had left was five dollars and we spent it all on gas. We took off and to save gas we kept our speed down to fifty-five. It drove me nuts 'cause I was afraid if we took too long, we were going to miss you, but if we went any faster, we'd run out of gas. That gas got us as far as Los Mochis and then we searched the glovebox and the cracks in the seats and came up with another dollar and sixty-seven cents to put in the tank. With that I thought we had it made, but then right before Culiacan we came to a bridge with this big sign over it saying there was a toll of forty cents. We pulled up and I told them our story, hoping they'd let us through for free, but the cop running the tollbooth got all pissed and threatened to arrest us if we didn't back up and get out of other people's way.

"So we backed up and pulled over to the side of the road and decided as soon as a car with American plates came along, we'd run up and beg forty cents. By now it was just starting to get light—we'd been driving all night. We flipped coins to see who had to run up and beg and Ron lost, but then this car with California plates pulled up and he chickened out."

"Man, I was going to do it, but by the time I got my nerve up, they were already moving."

"After that no Americans came by for about an hour. I was in a real sweat. I knew you weren't going to wait forever. Finally, this late-model Cadillac with Texas plates pulled up. Ron was supposed to go up to it—he swore he was going to do it this time—but I didn't even give him a chance. All of a sudden my legs just started running."

I thought how hard this must have been for the Bub as he was basically a shy guy.

"I don't know what got into me. I just knew I had to do it. I didn't want to take a chance on Ron chickening out again. Something told me you were just about to give up on us."

"You shoulda seen it!" tittered Ron. "The guy in the Cadillac was some kinda redneck businessman in a ten-gallon hat riding with his fat redneck wife and they looked at the Bub like he was a piece o' shit! He-he-he!"

"They gave it to me, though," grinned the Bub.

"If they only knew what it was going for!" Ron clutched his sides in laughter.

"Anyway, we drove on, but the needle on the gas gauge went down to 'E.' I did everything I could to keep that car going. I was feathering the accelerator and cutting the ignition every time we came to a downhill. Then about twenty miles out of Mazatlan we finally ran out of gas. I thought we were going to have to beg for gas, but then I remembered the white gas for the Coleman stove. I threw it in the tank and that's what got us here. The engine's pinging like a mother, though."

The Bubs' food came and they proceeded to wolf down huge mouthfuls. The waiter passing by paused to comment on their hearty appetites. *"Muchas días, nada comer,"* Ron grinned, trying out some Spanish he had learned.

"Man, I'm so glad you waited all this time for us," Ron said after the waiter had left. "Otherwise we'd be stuck here without a fucking dime." They ate, and I started thinking how bad the Rambler looked, all patched together the way it was. It seemed bound to stand out at customs. Even if it got searched, though, the pot would be so well hidden, customs would be unlikely to find it—as long as the Bubs kept their cool and didn't act nervous. I wondered how they felt about it.

"You know, with the Rambler looking the way it is, if you guys don't want to go through with this, I would understand. I don't want you to feel obligated."

The Bub had just taken a huge bite of food and waved his fork back and forth till he could get it swallowed.

"Nothing could stop us from running the border now!"

CHAPTER 11

THE BUBS COULDN'T WAIT TO SEE THE GRASS, so we got gas and drove out to the Tropic of Cancer road. The grass was right where I had left it and we brought it back to the Rambler, which we had parked at the end of our dirt road. The Bub got down on his back under the left quarter panel, I got down under the right, and we removed the pieces of plywood we had fashioned and began packing as many bricks as we could up into the quarter panels. The quarter panels were more than safe enough for passing through the Mexican inspection station, we reasoned, and this is where the grass would stay until the Bubs reached the desert outside Tijuana where the rigged tank was stashed.

As we worked, we could hear the shouts of a road crew down on the highway. I had noticed these road crews when I was checking out hiding places with Arf. They were ragged groups of young campesinos with machetes, hired to hack back the vegetation that threatens to take over the highway every rainy season. After a while the shouts grew unusually loud. I couldn't imagine they would bother clearing vegetation on our lonely road but told Ron to go down and take a look just the same. He came back running.

"They're coming!"

The Bub and I leapt to our feet. Bricks wrapped in bright blue construction paper were scattered everywhere. I said we should set up a bucket brigade. Ron positioned himself partway in the jungle and the Bub took up a position farther in. I tossed bricks to Ron, who tossed them to the Bub, who tossed them farther yet into the jungle, where they wouldn't be seen. This should have worked smoothly, but Ron kept dropping easy passes, giving lousy passes to the Bub, and laughing about it the whole time. He seemed committed to playing the goof no matter the stakes. We barely got the job done in time, and the campesinos arrived to find us standing around the Rambler trying to appear casual. They were young guys from the *campo* and seemed more shy of us than we were of them. They probably wondered what we were doing here but were too polite to ask. They stood around with bashful smiles and offered us water from a pink plastic jug they were carrying. We politely declined and they headed back down the road, taking occasional swipes at the bushes with their machetes.

We recovered the bricks and were able to pack thirty-six into the quarter panels, where they were held in place by our pieces of plywood. The rest we simply threw in the trunk for the time being. Before passing through the Mexican inspection station, these would have to be hidden better, and the Bub said he was pretty sure he could pack them all under the hood in two sacks on either side of the Rambler's six-cylinder engine.

Now it was my turn to be seen off at the Mazatlan bus station. I gave the Bubs all the money I had left save for a few dollars and wished them luck. Fifty-two hours later, I staggered into my cottage, feeling almost surprised to see it exactly the way I had left it. Einstein still stared wild-haired from the wall and one of my engineering texts lay on the table right where I had left it. So much had happened since I was last here that I half expected things to be different.

I slept till noon the following day, then got a paper and pencil and tried to calculate when the Bubs should arrive. If they made really good time, they might arrive in a day, but more likely it would be two or three. I could barely stand the suspense and tried to think of ways I could kill time. I went to the UC Garage, but there were no runs to sign up for.

"Yo, Baby!"

I turned to see one of the mechanics hailing me. Al was from Chicago, where he and a partner used to own a couple of "bebop houses" as he called them. This was back in the fifties, and they used to get pot hidden in shipments of frozen shrimp from Louisiana. They were busted, though, lost their bebop houses, and now Al only bought grass in small amounts for his personal use. He strode up to me, wiping his hands with a rag, and we shook hands in the three-part hip style. He lowered his voice.

"Hey, you got any mo' o' that reefer you was sellin'?"

I told him not right now but probably in a few days. Just then a cute young driver named Linda walked up.

"An' so yo' truck's runnin' fine now and the carburetor ain't givin' you no mo' trouble, you say?" Al made a show of changing the conversation, but I knew Linda was cool.

Al drifted off and Linda smiled, studying my face. "Wow, where'd you get so tan?"

"Mazatlan."

"Mazaltan? Where's that?"

"Mazatlan. It's in Mexico."

Linda had just moved here from Texas and somehow got to be one of the UC drivers. She was blonde, thin, cute, and perky, but awfully naive at times. On an impulse I asked her if she wanted to drop by my place later and get high. We could listen to Jimi Hendrix records, I told her. I wasn't thinking of it as a date so much as just a way to kill time. I was still feeling racked with suspense. She smiled, seemed to study me in a new light, and said, "Sure."

I went home, cleaned my cottage, and dusted off my Chianti bottle, which by now was heavy with colored wax from late-night, stoned discussions with Arf, Bill Gretsch, Fred Swaha, and the rest. Linda came by around twilight. I opened the door and stood stunned for a moment. I was used to seeing her in her Texas cowgirl clothes, but tonight she was wearing tight slacks and a halter top that showed off her midriff. She had on lip gloss and was wearing perfume.

We sat at my table and I lit the candle in the Chianti bottle and turned off the light.

"Oh, they have candles like that at Revol's," she said, naming a bar on Solano Avenue.

"Revol's? How did you get into Revol's? You're not twenty-one."

"I borrowed someone's I.D."

That surprised me. Maybe she wasn't as naive as I thought.

We got high and I told her all about the run. She knew the Bub from bus driving and had met Ron, so the story came alive for her. Her eyes went wide.

"Gol, I can't believe you guys did all that."

We talked till nearly midnight. She was throwing me smiling looks across the candlelight and I started thinking how she would be the perfect girl to make it with for the first time, she was so sweet. I wondered if she had ever done it before. I doubted it, but then she was so naive, some fast-talking guy might have talked her into it.

I tried to think how to do it. I had to kiss her first, but if I leaned across the table, it would be awkward, and if I got up and went around, it would seem too premeditated. I was getting all hung up on logistics.

"Well . . . ," Linda said, trailing off.

"Yeah, it's getting late," I said, immediately cursing myself for being so timid and lame.

We both got up. I knew this was my chance but couldn't bring myself to do anything and walked her to the door. Just then a loud knocking from the other side startled us both.

"Open up! It's me and Ron!"

There was no way they could be here this soon. It was some kind of trap.

"Are you sure it's you?"

"Of course, I'm sure," came the Bub's voice. "Come on. Open up!"

I opened the door and the Bub strode in, followed by Ron, both grinning. The Bub had a bulging sleeping bag slung over his shoulder, Santa Claus style. Seeing Linda, he balked.

"She's cool," I told him. "I told her all about it."

Then in a move he'd obviously rehearsed in his mind, he grabbed the sleeping bag by its bottom with a flourish and shook twenty blue-wrapped bricks out onto the floor.

"There's your share!"

With a guilty grin he added, "We were going to go up to Tilden and pick out the twenty lightest to give you, but we figured you earned your share!"

Linda and I were stunned.

"But how did you get here so fast?"

Over a joint rolled from the newly smuggled grass, the Bub and Ron explained.

After seeing me off at the Mazatlan bus station, the Bubs decided they were too excited to sleep, so they checked out of the Olas Altas and headed north. With money for gas now, they pushed the Rambler in overdrive, averaging eighty most of the way. Every time they passed a Tres Estrellas bus, they honked, just in case I was in it.

"Did you see us?" Ron asked. "I thought I saw you waving at us once, but couldn't tell for sure 'cause of the tinted glass."

They drove in shifts, intent on making time so they could get the run over with. They were so intent, though, they forgot all about the Mexican inspection station. With the twenty-four bricks still lying in the trunk, they flew over the top of a rise and saw the station dead ahead.

"You shoulda seen it!" tittered Ron. "The Bub slammed on the brakes and went flying back over the hill in reverse like in an old-fashioned movie!"

Hidden from view by the hill, the Bub packed the twenty-four bricks into two gunny sacks and laid them underneath the hood on either side of the engine before going through the station.

"It's a good thing, too. They didn't search that hard, but they would have found them in the trunk."

By the following morning they reached the desert just outside Tijuana, beat from having driven so hard. They found the rigged gas tank, but when they thought of all the work involved in packing it and setting up the reserve tank, they decided not to bother with the beautiful plan we had worked so hard on. Instead, they simply left the thirty-six bricks packed in the rear quarter panels and stashed the remaining bricks in the desert. They scraped the Turista decals off the car's windows—telltale signs they had been to the interior of Mexico—then drove to Tijuana and had the car washed to remove the mud and dust of their long journey. If customs asked, they were going to say they had only driven to Tijuana for the day. After getting the car washed, they drove down a dirt road until the Rambler acquired just the right patina of dust consistent with having spent a few hours in Tijuana. They flipped coins and Ron had to drive crossing the border. They pulled up to customs and after stating their citizenship, they were waved through.

Now they were home free with thirty-six bricks and felt sorely tempted to head north, but for the three of us to make a decent profit, they knew they needed the other twenty-four. They stashed the thirty-six bricks in some bushes, went back, and packed the rest into the rear quarter panels. This time it was the Bub's turn to drive and as he pulled up to customs, he took one look at the inspector and knew there was trouble.

"I could just see it in his eyes. He had these cold, blue eyes that seemed like they could see straight through me. He asked us a bunch of questions, then made me go back and open the trunk."

Ron clutched his sides, laughing. "You shoulda seen it! The Bub whipped on back to the trunk like he was on speed!"

"You know why? I was scared shitless and wanted to get the key in the trunk lock before the customs dude could see how bad my hands were shaking!" The Bub shook his head. "Next time I'll be sure to leave the trunk unlocked." He thought for a moment. "There won't be a next time, though. Two times is enough!"

The Bubs were exhausted. In fifty-two hours they had driven the 1,500 miles from Mazatlan to Berkeley and had run the border twice. They left and Linda and I were alone again. The success of this run made me feel I could do anything. Next thing I knew, Linda and I were in a clutch on my bed. The following morning I woke up, felt Linda's warm body next to mine, looked down at all the bricks still lying on the floor, and thought, Fuckin' A, my life is starting to take off!

CHAPTER 12

BILL GRETSCH DROPPED BY MY COTTAGE LATER in the morning, saw my bricks still lying about, and stated, "God, Tom, this is the best thing you've ever done." That struck me as an odd thing to say, but the more I thought about it, the more I thought, Yeah, maybe this *is* the best thing I've ever done. The Bubs dropped by and Ron strode in, tittering.

"Check out the Bub's new shoes!"

The Bub grinned and stuck out his foot, lifting his pant leg for us to see better. "Florsheims," he stated proudly. Bill and I stared. He was wearing wingtips. He must have just polished them too, for you could see specks of brown left in the holes.

"But those are businessman's shoes," I told him.

The Bub shrugged. "I think they look boss."

Ron roared laughing. "Check this! He's got another pair just like 'em. Admit it, Bub!"

"So what? They're boss shoes." He withdrew his foot.

Ron collapsed on my bed laughing. "The Bub's true bourgeois nature comes out!"

I asked the Bubs if they had sold much of their grass yet and the Bub said he had sold eight kilos already.

"Eight? What are you getting for them?"

"Hundred and a quarter."

"Man, you're blowing it. I'm selling all mine as lids and quarter pounds. I'm going to make the most out of this deal."

"Check this," Ron grinned. "I just sold a half pound for seventy-five dollars!"

His brother, Bill, frowned. "What kind of guy would pay seventy-five dollars for a half pound?"

"Just some chump who doesn't have any contacts!" Ron fell back on my bed to laugh some more.

Over the weekend I paid a visit to my parents. My dad was a dentist and had several medical texts in the house, which I used to pore over when I was a kid. The books used to fascinate me though I never imagined growing up to become a doctor because I had a strong aversion to needles and blood and had even fainted several times when I got shots. When my parents were in a different room, I grabbed one of the books to look up some information I needed, then drove to the UC Garage, where Linda was due back from a run.

She arrived and I drew her aside and asked her when her last period was. She looked taken aback.

"Gol, I don't know. About three weeks ago. Why?"

"Well, you know, I'm trying to figure out if there's any chance you might get pregnant."

"I'm on the pill."

"Oh."

I quickly changed the subject to cover how stupid and naive I felt.

Fall was near and the air got that dry leaf smell that makes you feel exhilarated. My cottage had become a hangout and nearly every evening friends dropped by to get high and talk. We would clean the seeds out of a lid, roll joints, and then psychoanalyze ourselves based on what we had learned reading Freud. Grass was opening my mind to so many things that I considered it a miracle drug and thought the whole country should be smoking it. Ron was usually there for these late evening talks and he and I were becoming fast friends. We poured out our life stories to each other, analyzed them, and drew conclusions that changed from night to night.

Talking with Ron, I made the amazing discovery that I had been unhappy much of my life. I had never fully realized this before—that was how closed off I was to certain parts of myself. Once when I was six, I was walking along the side of our house minding my own business when a blackness struck me with the force of a hammer blow. I ducked into our basement, where no one could see me, and tried to deal with what was happening to me. There was no reason I could see for this awful feeling but it was truly awful and I think if someone had told me I was to spend the rest of my life in a dungeon being tortured, I couldn't have felt worse. I decided that this awful feeling was coming from inside me, that there was something terribly wrong with me, and that I must hide this feeling and not let anyone even suspect it, for if they did, the whole world would shun me as some vile aberration of a human being.

There was a spading fork in our basement and I grabbed it and took it to an unused portion of our backyard, where I began spading the earth by planting the fork upright and jumping repeatedly on the back of the tines with all of my forty pounds in order to sink it into the ground. When I had tilled a five-foot square patch, I went inside, found a potato, cut it into pieces each with an eye, and planted them. By the time I was done, the black feeling was gone. The black feeling hit me other times during the following years and each time planting potatoes or some other intense physical activity made it go away. Once when my father was giving me a lift to school on his way to work, the radio announcer came on to say that a recent study discovered that one out of every ten children was "emotionally disturbed." He's talking about me, I thought to myself silently. I'm emotionally disturbed.

At first, when Ron talked about being unhappy, I was repelled. Being unhappy seemed like the ultimate in uncool. In high school no one wanted to hang out with the kids who were shy or seemed sad, and I had gone to great lengths to hide the least trace of being unhappy. But the more Ron talked about it, the more I realized he could have been speaking for me.

"I always felt left out as a kid," I told him. "I'd go somewhere with my family and look at other families and get this feeling that they had something we didn't. I'd see them laughing and play fighting or goofing off and wish we were like that. It was like we were only pretending to be a family."

"Right! I used to look up at other people's houses at night, at the windows with all the shades pulled down, and get this really sad feeling wondering what was going on inside."

"Me too!"

Pretty soon we were rushing to top each other's moanings. Ron described a feeling he used to get that was like throwing up. "You get so sad you feel like throwing up, only you never do. It's like a queasy feeling in your stomach and you feel all blah. It's psychological." This was so familiar to me that I nearly jumped out of my chair. I used to get that same nauseous feeling too as a kid but had never told anyone.

The Bub was always quiet when Ron and I talked this way. He seemed to like it better when we talked about grass or the latest Jimi Hendrix album. One night Ron confronted him. "How come you never say anything, Bub?" Arf was there and we all turned to see what the Bub would say. The Bub was leaning back in his chair, his hand draped lightly on the edge of my table to balance himself. By the candlelight his features seemed larger and more pale than usual.

"Man, I'm listening. I'm digging it."

"Well, don't you ever get depressed?" Ron asked him.

The Bub started to shrug, accidentally leaned back too far, and had to grab the table quickly to keep his balance.

"Sure, I get bummed out sometimes. You know, if something happens to bum me out."

"Dig the Bub!" Ron exulted. "All his life he's been trained to think it's uncool to be unhappy, so he's afraid to admit it!" He broke out laughing.

"Ma-a-an." The Bub shook his head and gave a slight snort. Ron turned serious.

"Shit, Bub, I've hung out with you. I know you get depressed. Why don't you just admit it?"

The Bub looked at him evenly. "I don't know what you're talking about, Ron."

Ron burst into gleeful laughter.

"Not too wasted, are you, Ron?"

Throughout all this, Arf had tried to keep from laughing but could no longer contain himself and burst out with a high-pitched, explosive squeal. I was laughing too. We were all high.

Our discussions became more and more intense. Over the following weeks we came to all sorts of conclusions. Life was absurd, there was no purpose to it, everything was arbitrary, nothing mattered, and even if it did, there was nothing we could do about it anyway because we were products of our environment—our upbringing as well as our genes—so that all our actions were determined by forces beyond our control. We came up with these theories on our own, so when we discovered authors like Sartre, Camus, Kafka, Hesse, and Dostoevsky, we interpreted them as supporting our theories and flipped out.

One theory followed another. Bill said we felt the way we did because we could never live up to our parents. "They went through the Great Depression and World War II. We'll never be able to match that." Ron said he always looked back on himself as the fool. I knew exactly what he meant. I would have interactions with people, say things spontaneously, and then look back a week later and think what I said was embarrassing and stupid. I spent a lot of time worrying what others thought of me—even in simple situations like walking into a café. If people looked up to see who was walking in, I would feel self-conscious, almost as if I didn't have a right to be there.

I tried to explain to Ron how I had often looked at myself as if from outside, the way we were doing now on grass, even when I was a little kid, only I hadn't realized I was doing it then. I just did it without thinking so I could guess what other people thought of me and modify myself to please them.

Ron said people spent all their lives in fantasy and reminiscence, fantasy of the future and reminiscence of the past. The present almost never existed. Memory had a way of twisting things around so that the past always looked better than it really was. One day we would probably look back on these days of moaning over our unhappiness and feel horrible nostalgias. Yet the strange fact was, we were having truly wonderful times.

I was dying to talk to Ron more about this, but the next night he didn't show. The following morning, the Bub showed up at my door, acting stagey. "What's up?" I asked him, to which he replied, "Not much."

We walked out onto the grass because it was a nice day outside. There he dropped it on me.

"Ron's busted."

"You're bullshitting."

"I'm not bullshitting. They got him last night."

"How?"

"He sold to a narc."

"No-o shit. How could he be so stupid?"

"Some guy he knew from DVC turned him on to the narc. He thinks the guy was probably an informer working off a bust."

I gave a low whistle. "Where is he?"

"In the Berkeley jail. Bill and I just saw him. They're going to send him to Santa Rita."

"Can't he bail out?"

The Bub shook his head. "Bail's ten grand."

"How about his parents? Can't they help him out?"

The Bub gave a short laugh. "They're not even going to visit him. They said they're sick and tired of him getting in trouble all the time and maybe jail would do him some good."

"No-o shit. He's liable to be there for a while. This is his third bust."

"I know."

We stood around.

"Is he really bummed out?"

"Not too, I don't think. He was laughing about it and stuff."

"How much did they get him for?"

"Two and a half bricks."

"No-o shit . . ."

CHAPTER 13

THEY TRANSFERRED RON TO GREYSTONE, which Bill told me was the worst section of the Santa Rita County Jail. He said it was a grim concrete building with no windows and no provisions for exercise, where prisoners spent twenty-four hours a day in small, gloomy cells. This was the section for prisoners awaiting trial, prisoners not even found guilty yet of any crime. Bill and the Bub visited Ron and came back with reports that he was looking pale and might be in poor health.

Usually defendants want to postpone trial for as long as possible. With time, the arresting agents' memories become vague and they grow less emotionally involved with the case; evidence might even get lost. After a month, though, Ron couldn't take it any longer in Greystone and claimed his right to a "fair and speedy" trial. At least if he was found guilty, he would be placed with the general jail population, where he would have a better cell and use of the day rooms and exercise yard.

His trial took place at the Berkeley courthouse on a sunny afternoon. Our whole crowd went after first meeting at my cottage to get in the proper spirit with a couple of joints. With me were Ron's brother, Bill; the Bub; Arf; Fred Swaha; and Dan Miller. It was Fred, with his prep school sensibilities, who suggested we all wear coats and ties to the trial. "To show our respect for the court!" This got instant approval and we all piled into the Rambler and drove to the St. Vincent De Paul Thrift Store in West Oakland, where we picked out the loudest, most outrageous coats and ties we could find. I got a tie that was at least four inches wide and had bright orange flowers like calla lilies against a maroon background. Arf found a purple and white checkered coat with squares big enough to play chess on. Fred found a baggy old bum's jacket that actually looked good on him.

Dressed like this, we arrived at the courtroom just as Ron's trial was about to start. We walked in shuffling our feet, coughing, and making various ambiguous noises calculated to fall just short of contempt. Ron's parents were there and turned to look, then turned quickly away with pained expressions. Naturally they blamed us, Ron's friends, for all Ron's problems. I thought Bill might feel weird goofing in front of his parents like that, but he was making more noise than any of us. We took seats in the very first row.

"Oyez! Oyez!" shouted the bailiff. "Court is now in session! All rise!" We all shuffled to our feet save for Bill, who made a show of having to tie his shoe in that moment. The judge strode in and we sat down again. When they brought in Ron, my stomach dropped.

He was pale and seemed to be in a daze. He glanced at the judge, squinting as though unused to light. He stumbled and the deputies on either side of him had to hold him up. For the first time it hit me what a serious game we were playing. This is what I'm risking, I told myself, and felt almost nauseous with fear. But then Ron spotted us in our St. Vincent De Paul rags and became suddenly animated, breaking out in a grin and flashing us the peace sign. I should have known the dazed thing was all an act! It was just like Ron to make a goof of his own misery!

The prosecution began by bringing out Ron's two and a half bricks, which they introduced as People's Exhibits A, B, and C. It felt strange knowing I had seen those bricks before, looking peaceful and benign where they lay on the roots of a tree in the Mazatlan jungle. Now they were being presented as something unspeakably vile. A roach clip and several hash pipes were introduced, followed by a laboratory report describing the bricks as "leafy green vegetable material, to wit, marijuana." The agent who busted Ron then took the stand and described meeting Ron through a third party, buying a half pound from him, and raiding his apartment six weeks later. "And the person who made that sale to you," asked the prosecuting attorney, "do you recognize him here in the courtroom?"

The agent pointed to Ron. "That's him there, the defendant."

Ron's lawyer followed. She was a fiery, young public defender by the name of Penny Cooper. "Mr. —," she began, addressing the narc. "When you allegedly purchased the half pound of marijuana from the defendant, isn't it true you were under the influence of marijuana at the time?" This was an interesting tack. If the narc was high at the time, his testimony might be discredited.

"No, that is not true."

"Isn't it true that before purchasing the half pound, you asked to try some of it?"

The agent hesitated. "That may be true. I don't remember."

"Isn't it true that the defendant then rolled a marijuana cigarette, lit it, and handed it to you?"

"I—don't remember."

"I see. Is smoking marijuana such a common experience with you that you wouldn't remember?"

"Objection!"

"Objection sustained."

Penny Cooper nodded.

"Mr. —, I'm going to ask you again and please try to remember. Did you or did you not accept a lit marijuana cigarette from the defendant on the date in question? Take your time to recall."

The agent shifted in his seat. "It's possible. I frankly don't remember. Sometimes I pretend to smoke a marijuana cigarette as part of my cover and I may have done that."

"I see. And just how do you 'pretend to smoke' a marijuana cigarette?"

"I don't inhale."

"You just suck the smoke into your mouth, hold it there a while, and blow it out?"

"No, I don't suck any of it into my mouth."

Penny Cooper frowned. "You don't? Wouldn't it be rather obvious you were faking?"

"Objection! Calls for a conclusion on the part of the witness."

"Objection sustained."

"Mr. —, have you ever smoked marijuana?"

"Objection!"

"Sustained."

In the end there was nothing Penny Cooper could do. Ron had been caught red-handed and everyone knew it. I never imagined the agent had really gotten high; I thought Penny Cooper was simply trying the only angle she could think of to get Ron off. But months later and with no reason to lie, Ron told me the agent had gotten wasted out of his mind, pupils dilated and everything.

During closing arguments the prosecuting attorney picked up People's Exhibit B and waved it menacingly while shouting phrases like "moral subversion" and "threat to the general welfare of the community." Whenever he referred to the grass, he called it "leafy green vegetable material, to wit, marijuana," never once shortening this phrase despite having cause to repeat it many times. Ron was found guilty and given a year in the county jail.

Ron flashed us the peace sign and was led away. We filed out of the courtroom behind the grim backs of Ron's parents several paces ahead. It was still sunny outside. The Rambler was parked across the street next to Provo Park and we stood around on the grass fingering our St. Vincent de Paul ties. The

Bub shrugged.

"You guys want to go for a ride up to Tilden? I've got some leafy green vegetable material in the car."

"You mean, to wit?" quipped Bill.

"Ma-ri-juana-a-ah!" intoned the Bub in a deep, evil voice as we all laughed.

We jumped in the car and the whole ride to Tilden all you heard was "Pass the leafy green" and "Don't bogart the to wit." I could see these were going to be the big expressions for weeks to come.

CHAPTER 14

I WAS GETTING NOWHERE IN ENGINEERING and even flunked a course I had kissed off out of lack of interest. Both Arf and Fred had flunked courses too, but by going to their advisor and claiming stress, they had been able to get their Fs changed to incompletes. I didn't even have the heart to go bullshit my advisor and let the F stand.

The engineering department let me take a course in complex analysis that wasn't part of the standard curriculum and I did extremely well in it. Ever since grade school, I had been interested in math and even developed some of the rudiments of calculus before I was exposed to it. I had no one to guide me in my math pursuits and simply made up problems for myself and tried to solve them. My parents knew I was bright in math and saw me spending hours on it, but for whatever reason they never encouraged it, only rarely even commenting on it. They had a very hands-off approach to parenting and liked to talk about the weather and how the hydrangeas were doing. Both came from difficult pasts. My dad's father was a well-to-do Chicago stomach doctor who drove a Chalmers but died of the flu while attending patients during the 1918 pandemic. My dad was only four at the time and his eccentric mother soon squandered the family fortune on bad investments and outright cons. During particularly difficult times, my father would be farmed out to a cruel aunt who liked to beat his knuckles with a ruler.

My mother grew up with a difficult Old World father, whose relationship to her can be summed up by what he said when she graduated at the top of her class at UC Berkeley, earning the Founders Award. He told her, "The other students must have been pretty stupid."

The complex analysis professor was a visiting mathematician from Columbia and had a sardonic sense of wit. At the end of the course he drew me aside to compliment me on how well I had done. He had assumed I was a math major and appeared shocked when I told him I was majoring in mechanical engineering.

"So what do you want to do with your life?" he asked me. "Design the perfect waffle iron?"

That was all it took for me to switch majors to mathematics. I was instantly happier and went to the campus bookstore and bought wonderful texts, including Suppes on set theory, Bartles on real analysis, Niven on number theory, and Kelly on general topology. I loved math because it was rational and pure and required only a pencil and paper and your mind. A lot of the mathematics majors hung out in the Bear's Lair and talked about the latest developments in math while they played cards. Paul Cohen at Stanford had just proved the consistency of the Axiom of Choice with the Continuum Hypothesis and I couldn't wait to understand concepts like this.

Of course, I now had to take the English courses that I had so dreaded and were the sole reason I had started in engineering. To my surprise, they turned out to be some of my favorite courses. They were nothing like my high school classes, where the teachers were hung up on what everything was supposed to symbolize. Here we talked about life. We studied many of the existentialists I had already read and also Freud's *Civilization and Its Discontents* and Hare's *The Language of Morals*, two books that had a lasting effect on the way I thought about things.

*

Fred Swaha had now taken to dropping acid nearly once a week and sometimes more. He would drop in the most casual way, often alone and without telling anyone. He had an amazing constitution and could tolerate immense quantities of drugs while appearing to remain perfectly sober. Once, after beating me in a long, complex game of chess involving beautiful combination plays and during which he knocked off a bottle of Cribari Zinfandel, he casually remarked that he was also on acid. He never tried to get me to drop, though, and in fact, never even suggested it.

I had another friend, named Ray, who was encouraging me to drop every time we met. He described acid as the most wonderful experience in existence. If it was that wonderful, I asked him, how could you keep from getting addicted?

"It's not like that," he said. "You don't want to drop again right after you've dropped. It's like sex—well, maybe that's not the best example," he laughed. "Anyway, it's too intense. You wouldn't want to be high on acid day after day." Without knowing exactly why, I was afraid of taking acid. Just the same, I let him give me five capsules and stashed them at my cottage at the bottom of a half-full Quaker Oats box.

With the money I made off the last run I bought a BSA Hornet. This was the café racer of its time, and to this day I think it was one of the most esthetically beautiful, badass motorcycles ever built. It was designed for flat tracking and didn't even come street-legal; you had to add mufflers and lights. Mine had a black frame and a red fiberglass tank with no markings or indentations on it, giving it a sleek, customized look. The torque was amazing; you could be doing eighty and still feel your neck snap when you cracked the throttle.

I loved math, but so much was happening that it was hard for me to concentrate. Nearly every day there were people on campus speaking out against the Vietnam War, and often there were demonstrations and even riots. Arf had already gotten a Notice to Report for Physical from the Selective Service System and was looking around for a friendly psychiatrist to write him an excuse. Bill saw a psychiatrist who promised to write a letter to the Selective Service, but when Bill reported for his physical, he learned that the letter said he was "a fine young man who would make an excellent soldier." Bill never went and I forget how he got out of it. I still had my 2S (student) deferment and hadn't yet been hassled.

Crossing Sproul Plaza one morning, I saw a crowd gathered around Ludwig's Fountain and cut over to take a look. In the middle of the fountain, soaking wet, was a young guy with a beard, wearing a bright orange kimono covered with political buttons and with a sign hanging from his neck saying, "TV makes you sterile." He wore a Russian fur cap and in his right hand he held a candle that had been snuffed out by the spray. This is a trip, I thought to myself, and worked my way toward the front.

"Now you're probably all wondering why I've gathered you here today," he announced to the rapidly growing crowd. "Well, it's on account of this!" And he pulled out an official-looking paper, which immediately became drenched.

"For those of you who aren't close enough to read, it's titled 'Notice to Report for Physical.'" A sympathetic murmur arose from the crowd. "And a little lower down it says, 'May twelfth, nineteen sixty-six,' which is today!" There was a collective gasp. "And after that there's a time: 'one p.m.' In other words, in three hours I've got to report to the Oakland Induction Center, where the U.S. Army is going to decide whether or not I would make a good soldier. Now I propose to convince them that I am mentally unfit"—he paused to brush water out of his face—"that I am, in fact, crazy. And here's where I need your help. I need you to tell me whether or not you think I'm crazy."

"You're crazy!"

"Nuts!"

"Flipped!"

The guy held his hand up. "No, that's way too easy. You've got to be hard on me! Put yourself in the place of an Army recruiter! But first, the facts."

He began ticking them off, using the fingers of his free hand.

"At age four I distinctly recall shitting in a small box, wrapping it up with a ribbon, and giving it to my mother.

"At age six I talked my younger sister into sticking a birthday candle up her vagina.

"Throughout my entire childhood I was never allowed to play with war toys.

"At age twelve I owned, not one, but an entire collection of dolls.

"I have smoked marijuana.

"I have dropped LSD.

"Now the question I want to ask you is this: If you were crouched in a foxhole in some rice paddy with the Viet Cong firing all around you, am I the sort of person you would want to have by your side?"

"No-o-o!" shouted the crowd.

This was too good to enjoy alone, I thought, and ducked down to the pool-room, where I found Arf shooting by himself.

"You've got to see this guy!" I told him.

"I can't. I waited half an hour for this table."

"Forget the table. This is history in the making."

He shrugged. "What do I care if some guy's making a fool of himself? Grab a cue, why don't you? Let's shoot." He tapped in a shot.

"Man, where's your sense of the times? These are special times we're living in. Everything's changing. People are burning their draft cards in public. Professors are dropping LSD. The whole world's changing and we're right in the middle of it. Doesn't it make you feel like taking part?"

"What do you mean? I'm here. I'm alive, aren't I? I'm going to school. Grab a cue!"

"I've got a class in twenty minutes."

"Cut it."

"I just cut yesterday."

"Cut it again."

"I'm already behind."

He stopped shooting for a moment. "How's it ever going to affect your future life if you cut this one class on May whatever-day-it-is in nineteen sixty-six?"

Instead I went back up to watch the guy in the fountain some more.

"How come we have so many right angles anyway?" he was asking the crowd. He waved toward Sproul Hall. "Why not left angles?"

The crowd finally dwindled and the guy in the kimono stepped out of the fountain and headed in the direction of the Oakland Induction Center trailing water. Several days later, the Daily Cal reported that he got the 1-Y (psychiatric) deferment he was looking for.

Instead of going to class, I went back downstairs and ended up shooting pool with Arf. Shooting pool was how I usually spent my time whenever I cut class. The first five or ten minutes were always excruciating because I knew if I wanted to, I could still rush out and catch most of the class. My whole body would break out in pinpricks of guilt. After a while, though, it would be too late to make the class and I could relax—until it was time for the next class to be cut.

We shot for several hours. Then in a fit of remorse I sped home to get some studying done. I made coffee, cleared my table, sharpened a bunch of pencils, and got out my math texts. Leafing through them, it was hard to know where to begin. It all looked so wonderful. I began by working out some proofs in real analysis. The sun shining through my window kept distracting me, though. I got up and pulled the shade, sat down again, and worked out some more proofs. Now the sun was sneaking in past the side of the shade, casting a bright strip across the pine-paneled wall. I was suddenly overwhelmed with boredom.

So often when I felt like this, I would end up smoking a joint. Once I got high, I would leaf through my math texts and wonder how I could have possibly felt bored. The material in these texts was so fascinating! You start with the simplest possible notion, that of counting, or better yet, the notion of membership in a collection of objects, a set, and from there you construct the integers and eventually build up theorems of startling power and elegance. Imagine you have a piece of paper lying on your table. You pick it up and crumple it without tearing or stretching it and set it back down. Brouwer's Fixed Point Theorem states that at least one point in the crumpled paper will lie directly above where it lay before. I would immediately want to get to work trying to understand these amazing concepts, but of course, being high, I wouldn't be able to make any sense of them. If only I hadn't gotten high!

I got up and paced around. I didn't want to go through the routine of smoking grass again and then wishing I hadn't. I felt like doing something drastic, something that would change my life. On an impulse I went over to my Quaker Oats box, fished out a capsule, and swallowed it. What the fuck am I doing? I thought a minute later and began to panic. But the panicky feeling soon faded and I poured myself some milk and sat down to wait for the trip.

About twenty minutes later I began coming on, and it was everything Ray had promised and more. My stomach went light, but not in a scary way, and I felt in love with life and the world and everything in it. Why can't we all love each other? I thought to myself and wanted to hug everyone I ever knew. I

71

looked around my room. Colors were vibrating and a Grateful Dead album seemed to burst into flames. I felt so happy I was almost nauseous—like a surfeit of euphoria.

I spent an hour or so in my cottage, staring at things with my new acid eyes and feeling things with a new sense of stonedness. Then I went out. Just stepping out the door seemed an amazing adventure—the smell of the lawn, a warm breeze, a strange car driving by on the late afternoon street. I decided to go for a ride on my bike; I felt in complete control. I fired it up and the engine sounded like thunder in a narrow canyon. The throttle was like lightning in the palm of my hand. The next thing I knew, I was several blocks away, cruising in third. I didn't even remember shifting. Several more isolated points of consciousness like that and I found myself at Bill's place. Bill wasn't home, but his girlfriend, Susan, invited me in.

"Wow, your eyes look really red," she said.

"I've been riding my bike."

She stepped into the kitchen to tend to something and I wandered about the living room. She came back wiping her hands on a towel. "So, what's up?"

"Not too much. . . . I'm on acid."

"You are? Oh, wow!" she said eagerly. "What's it like?"

I dropped my casual act and grinned. "It is absolutely and totally out-of-sight! You have got to try it!"

"Oh, I want to. I've been thinking about it. Bill's kind of chicken, though. . . . Here, sit down. So when did you take it? Are you hallucinating yet?"

"Not actually hallucinating, but colors are jumping around and everything."

"Oh, wow. Well, can I get you anything? How about a cup of coffee—oh, no, that might bring you down. How about some hot chocolate?"

"No, thanks. I'm not the least bit thirsty. In fact, I don't even think I could swallow."

Susan shook her head. "God, I can't believe you just went and dropped acid like that all by yourself."

I grinned and didn't say anything. We were quiet for a moment.

"Gee, I don't know what to say. I feel like I should guide your trip or something."

I laughed. "Don't worry about it. It's not like that. I just feel extremely mellow. . . . I know what," I said then. "Let's go wander around The Ave. You want to?"

She said sure and offered to drive.

It was still sunny out. The Avenue had its usual crowds: longhairs, freaks, serious-faced foreign students, TAs wearing tweed coats and jeans. I thought how there was no other place I would rather be. We walked in the direction of campus. "Hash? Acid? Grass?" dealers whispered to us from doorways. At the entrance to campus, Holy Hubert, the evangelist, was preaching to an amused crowd.

"My friends, there is no place in heaven for marijuana smokers! . . . There is no place in heaven for LSD droppers! . . . There is no place in heaven for ho-mo-sek-shoowuhls! . . . And if you sleep with a woman, that woman better be your wife because if she isn't, you're a fornicator, and it says in the Bible that fornicators shall not go to heaven!"

A street person stood up and shouted, "The way I heard it, the Lord said, 'Go forth and multiply,' and that means fuck!"

We watched them argue for a while. The poor street person was having trouble making himself heard. Through years of preaching, Hubert had developed super-human lungs that enabled him to drown out anything anyone else said.

The street person finally gave up and drifted off. Hubert grinned, revealing several dark gaps where his teeth had been knocked out by people he had irritated to the point of violence. "God bless your dirty little heart!" he hollered after the street person.

We moved on. I told Susan, "They say Harvard Square is the crossroads of the earth but for me it's Bancroft and Telegraph."

Susan eventually had to go cook dinner and I ended up at Fred Swaha's place, above Moe's. "Welcome to the club," he said when I told him I had dropped. We spent the evening playing honeymoon bridge on his bed and had the window open that overlooked Telegraph. Snippets of conversation floated up to us.

"The revolution's gonna happen, man, for sure."

"Have you tried strychnine yet? It's the ultimate high."

"Trees are our brothers."

The acid had peaked and was beginning to fade. I felt like one of those aboriginal teenagers who has just succeeded in jumping headfirst off a tower with vines tied to his ankles.

CHAPTER 15

ANOTHER QUARTER STARTED. I SHARPENED all my pencils, bought brand-new notebooks with colored dividers, and eagerly signed up for classes. Two weeks later I was already bored. One night I was forcing myself to study when the Bub dropped by to tell me about a "pot party" he had been to. He said there were two secretaries there getting off on the fact they looked so straight that no one would think they smoked pot. They were apologizing for their straight appearance, saying they had to look that way for their jobs. One of them remarked that they would probably make perfect smugglers as customs would never think to search them. The Bub drew them aside and asked if they wanted to do a run and they said yes.

"You gotta see them," the Bub told me. "They're super straight-looking. They've got fingernail polish and everything. They're not super good-looking, but I figure it's better that way." He paused to grin at his own logic. "That way they won't get hung up by some horny customs dude hoping to catch looks."

The Bub wanted me to go partners with him on a run, but I told him I couldn't. "At least not till the next break."

"When's that?"

"About eight weeks. The quarter just started."

"Oh, man. They might not even want to do it by then. Can't you take a week off?"

"I'd flunk. Anyway, you know it would take longer than that."

He left disappointed and I tried to get back to my studying. All I could think about, though, was the run. I got out my Schedule and Directory and looked up the last possible date for withdrawing from the quarter. It was six days away.

I attended class in a daze. I tried to pay attention to my lectures, but my mind kept wandering to the thought of the secretaries and the possibility of a run. To drop out seemed unthinkable, though. I recalled my father once speaking of a neighbor girl who had dropped out of college, using the same grave and pitying tones he might have used had she gotten knocked up. I just couldn't do it. But on the afternoon of the sixth day I found myself walking up the Sproul Hall steps as though in someone else's body. I stopped at the Registrar's Office, filled out a withdrawal form, and handed it to the pretty coed behind the window, half expecting her to ask me for a reason or even talk me out of it, but of course, she didn't. She just smiled. I walked back down the steps, thinking I was now a "non-student." You saw that term all the time now in the Daily Cal. Non-students were getting blamed for all the demonstrations and riots taking place and there was even talk of banning them from campus.

I cut down to the poolroom and found Arf there, practicing on a snooker table by himself. We hated snooker and I gave him a hard time about it. He jerked his hand up.

"What can I do? All the good tables are taken. I'm next in line, though. What's up?"

"I just dropped out of school."

"Oh sure." He didn't even bother looking up from his shot.

I showed him the receipt.

"You've flipped," he stated, resting his cue on the floor. "I mean, you'll be bored out of your mind in a week."

"No, I won't. I'm taking up smuggling with the Bub." I told him about the secretaries and he shook his head.

"You really have flipped. Face it, that one time with the Bubs was just a luck-out. I mean, you might get lucky one or two more times, but if you keep on breaking the law, sooner or later you're going to get caught. You don't see that? The government has agents specially trained to catch guys like you."

"We'll outsmart them."

He rolled his eyes. "Anyway, you can't speak Spanish well enough."

"I'll learn."

This seemed to irritate him.

"You don't realize the amount of hassle I went through with Meche. He's completely uneducated, you know. You have to go over everything with him twenty times, and when he says yes, you have to know if he really means it or if he's just saying it. It's not just the language. You have to know Latin culture. You can't just go and learn that."

"Well, why don't you join us then?" I suddenly realized what a great idea this was. All his talk had begun to scare me a little. I glanced at the clock.

"There's still time to make it to the Registrar's Office. You could be a third partner. The Bub would go for it. He likes you. You keep saying how much you hate school. Well, here's your chance. Drop out!"

He chuckled in a paternal way. He was trying to act very above-it-all, but my offer had touched him, I could tell. He didn't say anything for a long moment.

"Come on, do it."

"No, thanks," he murmured finally. "I've got better things to do."

I glanced at the snooker table. "Yeah, right."

We both laughed.

"It's true I hate school," he said then. "I'm just trying to graduate so I can get a job. Having a job has got to be better than this. I just want to put in my four years and get out of here. That's my plan."

Just then Stony, the one-armed poolroom manager, called his number.

"Hey, I got a table. Want to play?"

"No, thanks. I really do have better things to do."

We laughed again and I moved to leave.

"Hey. . . . Be careful. I mean, you're a prick and everything, but I'd hate to see you end up in jail."

I hadn't even talked to the Bub—that's how impulsive this move was on my part. For all I knew, the secretaries had changed their minds. I called the Bub and he took me to see them that evening. They looked every bit as straight as he had described. One was brunette and had schoolteacherish glasses that swept up at the sides, and the other had long, straight blonde hair and looked like she belonged on a horse. They seemed extremely nice and even apologized for how particularly straight they looked, saying they hadn't had a chance to change since getting off work. They told us to have a seat on their couch and opened a bottle of wine for us to drink while they put on comfortable clothes. After pouring glasses for us, they left the bottle on the coffee table in front of us and told us to be sure and help ourselves to more. I glanced around the apartment they shared. There were shelves with a lot of hand-thrown pottery, and tacked to a wall was a large poster of Bob Dylan tipping his hat and grinning over the top of a blues harp.

They came back dressed in peasant blouses and bell bottoms and poured themselves wine. I told them what the Bub and I had in mind. Since our last run the Bub had had the Rambler body cherried out and I told them how clean and straight it looked. I envisioned a run just like the last one, using the quarter panels and making two crossings. I said for this we could offer them $300 apiece. Their eyes went wide.

"Wow, that's almost as much as we make in a month," said the blonde.

"You know where it's going to go, too," laughed the brunette. "Dinners at Norman's!"

"Oh, and that dress I saw at Little Daisy!"

"And the purple scarf!"

In a minute they had it all spent.

Things were pretty much settled and they opened a second bottle of wine. We talked about things having nothing to do with the run and before we knew it, it was almost midnight. The thought struck me that this was like a perfect first date, only if it had been a real date without the run as an excuse, I would have been all nervous and bumbling.

We got up to leave, but it seemed to me the secretaries were agreeing to this almost a little too blithely. "Before we shake on this," I told them, "I want to make sure you know what you're getting into. I mean, smuggling's a federal offense. If you got caught, you'd probably go to jail. I don't know. Maybe not since you obviously don't have records. Anyway, we think it's a safe run, but it's up to you to make up your own minds."

I could feel the Bub giving me Shut up! vibes as I was saying this and the secretaries stared at each other and shrugged.

"I don't see where there would be any problem," said the blonde.

"Neither do I," said the brunette. "I just don't see how they would ever suspect us."

We shook hands on the deal and I gave them sixteen dollars each for airfare to San Diego.

Back in my truck the Bub said, "Man, what did you have to bring up all that jail shit for?" I knew he was going to say this.

"I just don't want to feel like I'm conning anyone into anything."

He shook his head. "You could have killed the whole deal."

It remained only to tell my parents I had dropped out. I was surprised how well they took it. They seemed to realize I was going crazy in school and needed time off. Of course, I framed everything in the right light, telling them I wanted to go to Mexico to improve my Spanish and learn more about Latin culture. My mother asked where in Mexico I was going, and I told her Mazatlan. "And maybe Guadalajara too," I added just to muddle things. I wouldn't have told them I was going to Mexico at all save that I needed a notarized letter of permission from them. Mexican law required it for minors.

CHAPTER 16

THE BUB GAVE THE RAMBLER A FINAL TUNE-UP and we headed south. Passing the Seminary exit, I got a sudden, intense feeling of, What the fuck am I doing? According to testing, I was the brightest kid to pass through my grammar school since 1947, leading everyone to assume I would grow up to become a great scientist. Now here I was, dropping out of college in order to take up smuggling with a high school dropout. Yet it somehow felt right. It felt really right. We lit up a joint and I stared out the window at the green hills and spotted a lone house, like a Mediterranean villa, with curved orange roof tiles and wrought iron railings at the balconies, and I tried to memorize every detail about it because I wanted to remember this feeling forever, this strange feeling of kissing off everything I was supposed to do and be and feeling wonderful about it.

"You gonna sit there holding that joint all day?"

We took turns driving and made it to Mazatlan in two days, arriving on a Sunday morning. We went straight to the beach, but this time Meche wasn't there. We cruised up and down the full length of the beach but couldn't find him. We then drove to the top of a hill and the Bub broke out a joint of Acapulco Gold he had been saving for a special occasion. We smoked it, staring out over the water. From our perch we could see the Rocamar, which now stood vacant, having been shut down after a ton of grass was found on the premises, so I had heard. Below us, a bulldozer was clearing a stretch of beachfront land where developers were just starting to take hold. Lazy shouts of the laborers floated up to us. I had no idea what we were going to do if we couldn't find Meche, but somehow I didn't even care.

Now we had the munchies and headed to the Olas Altas to eat. On the way, we scanned the beach again for Meche but with no luck. At the Olas Altas we ate *combinaciones mexicanas* and this was possibly the best meal of my life. Every bite was like a sensuous reverie thanks to the Bub's pot. Afterward we went back to the beach, and this time Meche was there.

Communicating with him wasn't as difficult as Arf had predicted. Arf hadn't considered how badly Meche and I would want to understand each other. We took our time, repeating things however many times it took for the other to understand. Over the next two days we met four or five times just to get everything straight. North of the Hotel de Cima there was a stretch of beach where few people went because of rip tides, and we could talk there without worrying about being overheard. Meche had a rapid way of talking that took me a while to get used to. Except for nouns, he seemed to have no concept of language as individual words; he just blurted everything out in spurts. To him a phrase like "so nobody will suspect" was a single entity, *paraquenadiesospeche*, incapable of being divided into smaller parts. Sometimes words failed us, and we would kneel down and draw pictures in the sand. I wanted the bricks to be more compact than the ones we had gotten the last time and sketched a large, lumpy brick and then next to it, a smaller, more squared-off brick. Pointing to the first one, I said, *"Este, no. Malo,"* and drew an X through it. I pointed to the second one. *"Este, sí. Muy bueno."* And I made a circle with my thumb and forefinger.

"Sí, sí, sí. All of them will be like this one," Meche said, pointing to the more squared-off brick. *"Bien macizos."* Glancing around, he quickly obliterated my sketch with his palm.

Meche was more friendly to us than on previous visits, possibly because we told him we were committed now and expected to return on a regular basis. He invited us to a ranchito in the sierra, which I suspected might have some connection to his suppliers. The owner of the ranchito was an amazing old widow who smoked black cheroots, which she rolled herself. She had five sons, all strapping youths with light skin and green eyes. They stood around grinning while the four of us sat talking at a rickety wooden table. The kitchen was open to the air on two sides and chickens ran in and out at will while pigs grunted in the shade of a nearby tree. A picture of Christ hung above a simple altar with a lit votive candle, and on the far wall hung a photograph of a man I assumed was the widow's deceased husband. He appeared very light-skinned and aristocratic in the dressed in a formal suit with silk tie and seemed to be frowning as though disapproving of everything that was going on at his ranch now that he was gone.

The widow wanted to know where I lived and if there were any ranchitos there like hers. I told her I lived in the city and there were no ranchitos, just a lot of houses all close together. She shook her head in wonder. "I have always dreamed of going to the States," she told Meche. "That is my one wish before I die."

I tried to tell her she had a better life here where she was. "You have clean air. The people here are friendly. No one tells you what to do."

She shrugged, unconvinced. I supposed I wasn't going to talk her out of her dream. Still, I hoped she never made it. I could just imagine the welcome she would get in the States: a leathery old woman who couldn't speak English and smoked black cheroots.

One of the sons stepped timidly forward, holding a hide. He showed it to me, wanting to know the name of the animal it had come from in English.

"Deer."

"Djur."

The other sons laughed.

"Deer."

"Djeer."

The other sons hooted and slapped their knees. The son holding the hide gave an embarrassed smile and retreated, mumbling "djeer" to himself. We talked some more, and then a small, barefoot boy brought in a full pail of milk, straining with both hands to carry it. "*¡Ah! ¡Leche natural!*" Meche exclaimed, rising to help him. And this was the main point of the trip. The whole way here Meche had talked about drinking *leche bronca* straight from the cow. He took the pail from the boy and set it on the table, cupping his palms around it.

"Feel it. Still warm!"

The widow got plastic tumblers and served the Bub and me first. I had never seen raw milk before. It was thinner than I had imagined, almost bluish-looking, with the cream floating on top in worm-like threads. The Bub stared at his glass as though it were poison.

"I ain't drinking that shit," he murmured.

"You got to."

"No way. Tell 'em I'm allergic or something."

I thought of all the diseases you could get from unpasteurized milk, but that almost made it more exciting and I drank it down. It was good, kind of sweet-tasting. The widow noticed the Bub hadn't drunk his and asked why.

"He's afraid of getting sick," I apologized. "We Americans have weak stomachs."

"This milk won't make him sick. It's pure. Tell him it's pure."

I had to interpret while she and Meche did everything they could to get the Bub to drink his milk, even getting a little offended toward the end, but it was no use. There was no way he was going to touch that milk.

Back in Mazatlan, the Bub and I made final arrangements with Meche for the run. We were walking along the beach road past an adobe wall plastered with old political posters when I thought to ask Meche for his address. "So we can write to you," I told him. He said he would give it to me later. I was afraid we would forget, though.

"Why not now?"

"We do not have a pen and paper."

"I have a pen and paper," I offered brightly and produced them. He held my pen poised over my pocket notebook, not writing anything, then glanced around. Some schoolboys in Catholic uniforms were playing in a nearby lot.

"*Espérate* — Wait here."

He hurried over to the schoolboys and handed them the pen and paper. One of them wrote, then handed the pen and paper back to Meche, and Meche came back and handed them to me. He asked me to read it, which I did.

"*Sí, sí.* That is right," he nodded, satisfied the schoolboy hadn't played a trick on him.

So Meche couldn't even write his own name. . . .

That night two campesinos handed the Bub and me four sacks of bricks across a barbed wire fence along a dirt road not far from the old widow's ranchito. The bricks were square and compact as Meche had promised and we deposited them at the end of the Tropic of Cancer road, then returned to Mazatlan clean, just like the run before. I liked this approach because it gave things a chance to cool off after the score. The following morning we drove back to the Tropic of Cancer road and packed the bricks into the rear quarter panels at our leisure. I loved the jungle here because it was quiet and green and fresh-smelling and felt safe. The Bub packed one quarter panel while I packed the other, lying on our backs on the cool ground and listening to the birds singing. I recalled the road crew stumbling across us here on the run before, but that was such a freak occurrence, I couldn't imagine that it would happen again. So when the sound of voices floated up to us, we were caught entirely by surprise.

Women's voices! Speaking in English! We scrambled to our feet. Loose bricks were lying about and we frantically kicked them under the car. Two middle-aged women dressed like Americans soon appeared, walking quickly and carrying binoculars. "Birdwatchers!" the Bub murmured in disgust. By now all the bricks were under the car and we had positioned ourselves on either side of the Rambler, effectively blocking the path. The women stopped just short of us and one of them eyed the Rambler's stateside plates.

"You speak English, I take it?"

We said, "Yeah," and she said they were following some rare type of parrot and described it, asking if we had seen it. I immediately said no, but the Bub was thinking faster than I was.

"Yeah, I saw that bird. It just flew right over there." And he pointed to some trees back down the road behind them. The women didn't seem to believe this but felt obligated to train their binoculars where he had pointed. Gradually, they panned around to the trees ahead of them, where they thought the bird really was. One of them put her field glasses down and I could tell she was trying to figure out how they could get past us. We had parked in a level area just short of the end of the road, and to get past us, they would have to step through the jungle, which wasn't that difficult but would be socially awkward considering we weren't getting out of their way. While they considered, the Bub and I stood there, giving off Go away! vibes. After a long moment, the two women gave up with a sigh and left.

"I really did see that bird," the Bub laughed after they were gone. "The whole time they were here, it was sitting right there in that bush." He pointed. "I had a hard time to keep from staring at it!"

We finished packing the quarter panels and about half the bricks were left over in accordance with our plan of doing two runs. The Bub then got the idea to pack the remaining bricks into the back and bottom sections of the back seat. "We're figuring the car won't get searched anyway. The secretaries would probably rather do one run and get it over with as long as we're paying them for two."

I didn't like this idea but he talked me into it. As I watched him rip the springs out of the two parts to the seat, my heart sank, knowing they could never be put back properly. But when he had finished, the seat looked perfect. It didn't have so much as a wrinkle in it. It was incredible what the Bub could do with his hands. The only problem now was that the seat was as hard as a stone park bench and hurt your butt if you sat down on it too quickly. We decided the seat should have souvenirs all over it in order to distract from the hardness. Twelve bricks were left over and we stashed them in the jungle for the next run.

We headed north, making good time till the following night when we rolled into Santa Ana to find the entire highway blocked with parked cars and people milling about. We got out and learned that the bridge on the other side of town had been washed out by recent floods. With the car locked, we walked about a mile past solid parked cars till we came to the Río Magdalena, where, sure enough, we could see the ragged ends of the broken highway jutting partway out over the inky waters. People were everywhere, wandering about or huddled in groups, the strange scene illuminated by bonfires and oil pots. Some people even had tents. Army vehicles were parked in a line and federales patrolled in pairs. One pair noticed our long hair and stopped short. I thought sure they were going to come over and question us and murmured to the Bub, "We got here hitchhiking."

We pretended to be unaware of the federales and after a while they moved on.

"If we ever get stopped, don't let them know about the car."

"I know. I had the keys in my hand the whole time and was ready to ditch them if they hassled us."

We talked to some of the men milling around. Everyone had a different opinion as to when the bridge would be repaired. One man said three days. Another said two weeks. One man, who seemed to know what he was talking about, said it would never be repaired, that they would have to build a new one, and it was going to take months. Heading back to the car, I spotted a teenage girl squatting furtively in the darkness. Already the place was beginning to smell of urine. We consulted our map and decided to head back to Hermosillo, a large agricultural town where we could wait out the delay without having to worry about federales.

CHAPTER 17

WE GOT A ROOM AT THE HOTEL KINO, a quiet, older hotel that was first built in the 1860s and hadn't changed much in decades. Our room had lace curtains and looked out over a courtyard with two diagonal footpaths making an X. Two large laurel trees grew in the courtyard and from our second-floor interior balcony we could reach out and touch their leaves. I thought about the washed-out bridge and how we were now delayed for God knew how long and was surprised to find that I didn't care. Time no longer meant much now that I had dropped out of school. I could just be.

Someone told us the people at the telegraph office would be the first to know of any news regarding the bridge and we drove there in the morning. The potholes in the streets were filled with muddy water from recent rains and just to tease me, the Bub headed straight for a particularly big one. I knew the Rambler could make it through and didn't say anything, but there happened to be a rock at the bottom and the Rambler bottomed out on it with a horrible crunching sound. The Bub turned to me with an abashed look and apologized. At the telegraph station the clerk told us there was no news on the bridge but that we should check with him every day.

Our days fell into a routine. We would wake up and light a joint, blowing the smoke out our second-story window that overlooked the street. Then it was down to the hotel restaurant for our free continental breakfast, which consisted of a freshly baked *bolillo*, real butter, and delicious, freshly brewed coffee. The restaurant was a fancy affair with cloth-covered tables and waiters dressed in livery, and we couldn't help but laugh because it was all so formal and we were stoned. The waiters seemed to enjoy our hilarity and even laughed with us as though we were all in on some common joke. Afterward we would drive to the telegraph office, where the news was always the same: no progress yet on the bridge. In the evenings we would get high again and wander the yellow-lit streets. The Bub loved the roasted corn sold at corner stands and we always made sure to pass a certain shop where the purple Berkel sign in the window looked psychedelic.

One morning we had nothing to do and sat on a park bench staring at a fountain like two old men. Across the way were the Gothic buildings of a university and something about the well-dressed students there, carrying books and looking so full of purpose, appealed to me. Maybe I'll go back someday, I thought to myself. The Bub was staring at the rainbow colors in the fountain's spray and commented, "Psychedelic."

"Yeah. Too bad we don't have any acid."

The Bub then inverted his belt buckle to show me a wad of foil hidden in the hollow of it.

"We do."

He unfolded the foil to show me three purple Owsleys. "We could split one. I've gotten off on a quarter before."

We dropped and headed out to the desert, the Bub driving. Every now and then we stopped to wander out among the cactuses. I especially liked the accordion cactuses because their wavy lines are the exact sort of thing you flash on. Everywhere I looked, I was seeing shifting splotches of purple, like the afterimages you see after staring for a long time at something yellow.

"Ever notice how you tend to flash on the color of the tab?" commented the Bub.

I went up to a tall saguaro and touched my fingertip carefully to one of the spines. The only sound we heard was the faint crunch of our footsteps in the sand. The desert seemed somber and mysterious and I had the crazy notion that somewhere hidden here we might find the secret to life.

We continued driving. We came to lonely crossroads and turned or went straight at random. The Bub began eyeing the rearview mirror. "I'm hallucinating smoke coming out of the back of the car," he told me. I looked back and it looked like smoke to me too. We got off on the fact we were having a shared hallucination. We kept on driving and each time we looked back, the smoke looked more and more real to us. We finally stopped to check, got out, and saw and smelled real smoke pouring from the right rear quarter panel. The Bub dove underneath the car.

"It's the piece of plywood!"

I got him a screwdriver and he undid the plywood and tossed it out and I threw sand on it to get it to stop smoking. Then he tossed out the brick that was directly above it. A large part of it was burnt and I used the screwdriver to scrape out the char.

"What happened?"

The Bub got up and brushed himself off. "The tailpipe got too close to the piece of plywood and it caught fire." He fished the plywood out of the sand. "This thing's shot."

"We can have another one made up at a *maderería* in town. We can buy black paint and match it to the undercarriage just like we did before. But how are we going to hold the bricks up in the meantime?"

"I think they'll stay up there. They're wedged in pretty tight."

"You're sure?"

"Yeah, I'm pretty sure."

"What about the tailpipe?"

"I moved it back. The bracket was bent, but I straightened it. It'll hold."

We tossed the partly burnt brick into the trunk and took off, heading back toward town. The adrenaline rush we had just experienced wore off and the acid seemed to come back with pent-up force. I watched the bushes by the side of the road burst into purple flames. I looked over at the Bub and it seemed as though the skin on his face was translucent and I could see splotches of blood underneath. He was studying the rearview mirror again. "Don't look back," he said, "but there's a fifty-eight Pontiac I think is following us. It's got Arizona plates."

"Who's in it?"

"Two beaners. Both wearing black leather jackets."

We were coming to a deserted crossroads.

"I'm gonna turn left and see what happens."

He turned left and continued checking the rearview mirror.

"Are they still behind us?"

"Yeah."

A moment later there was a siren sound. "Pigs!" muttered the Bub. I looked back and saw that the Pontiac had a red police light mounted next to the side view mirror.

We pulled over and I opened my door. "I'll go back and handle it. How do my eyes look?"

The Bub looked at my eyes and glanced down. "They're all right."

I went up to the driver. "*Buenos días. ¿Hay algún problema?*" He was burly and had an obvious bulge behind his leather jacket.

"*¿Ud. habla español?*" He seemed slightly surprised.

"*Sí. Algo.*"

He flashed a badge, got out, and motioned brusquely for me to go back to the Rambler. "*Vámonos.*"

The Bub had stepped out and was standing there trying to look casual. I knew he was thinking the same things I was: Did one of the bricks fall out on the roadway? And why the fuck did we toss that partly burnt brick in the trunk for anyone to see?

The cops asked to see our papers and studied them carefully, then went to the front of the Rambler to make sure our license plate matched what it said in our papers. My hopes rose with the thought these cops might be part of a stolen car detail. Maybe they weren't that tuned in to dope. I thought I saw a way to handle them.

"This car is ours," I began. "Our registration is in order and we have a car permit."

"That may be," said the burly cop. "Just the same, many Americans come to Mexico to sell their cars illegally." My hopes shot higher.

"Well, we have no desire to sell this car." And I began talking about what a wonderful car it was, struggling with my Spanish to describe the reclining seats and the great mileage it got. They nodded noncommittally and I sensed the moment had come to up the game a notch.

"So if you are really police, how come you drive an old, beat-up car?"

The burly cop smirked. "In order to catch criminals by surprise." I pretended not to notice the pointed way he regarded me on the word "criminals."

"And the Arizona plates?"

He smirked again. "The same reason."

Here I went all out. "And that bulge under your jacket? I suppose that's your gun?"

This felt good. It felt close to the opposite of the way I imagined a guilty, scared shitless kid on acid would act. We were two innocent and naive kids being stopped by real live Mexican undercover cops and couldn't wait to tell all our friends about it when we got back home.

The burly cop took a long moment to respond, studying me as though trying to decide whether I was for real. Wordlessly he drew his jacket aside to reveal a .45 semiautomatic in a shoulder holster. Not to be outdone, his companion then lifted his pants leg to reveal a small pistol in an ankle holster. I made a point of acting impressed. The Bub acted impressed too, having picked up on my approach. Sure enough, the two men now seemed slightly embarrassed for having shown off to two nerdy kids and reconcealed their guns. The burly one handed our papers back and turned to leave. My heart soared with the expectation we were home free, but then the smaller cop went up to the Rambler and pressed his nose to the right rear window, cupping his hands on either side of his eyes to see better. It seemed too much to hope for that they wouldn't ask to look in the trunk, but they didn't. They got in the Pontiac and peeled out, burning rubber.

The Bub and I took off, and as soon as the cops were out of sight, we turned down the first side road, jumped out, and popped the trunk.

"What do you want to do with this thing?" the Bub asked, grabbing the loose brick.

"Throw it away. It's half gone anyway."

"I agree," and he heaved it out on the desert for the rats to get high on.

"Man, when those guys first stopped us, I thought sure a brick had fallen out on the road."

"I can't believe they didn't ask us to open the trunk."

Heading back to town, I connected some dots to realize it was the Bub's fault we had nearly gotten busted. The reason the tailpipe got shoved up against the piece of plywood had to be the rock the Bub hit when he drove through that puddle trying to scare me. I wondered if he had reached the same conclusion but decided not to bring it up.

Back at our hotel, we talked about how stupid it was for us to be dropping acid and driving around with a car packed full of dope—especially with our long hair and hip clothes. Two days later, though, we dropped again, and we dropped a third time after that. This last time was my first less than pleasant trip. Recently, there had been a small element of fear in my trips, but I was always able to keep it under control. This time I wasn't sure. We were parked at a Pemex station and the Bub went in to get a Coke. I had told him I was bumming and wanted to get out of here, and it ticked me off that he was taking so long. He finally came back, walking at a saunter.

"Hey, man, I'm on a bummer. Let's get the fuck out of here!"

"Oh, sorry. Here, want some Fanta? They didn't have any Coke."

He drove out to the desert, stopping wherever I said it felt right to stop. We got out and wandered in the absolute stillness, our boots crunching over the sandy, crusted soil. We didn't speak much but when we did, the desert seemed to suck up our words instantly into the silence. What did I want from dropping acid? I wondered to myself. It seemed to me it was like a test. Ever since I was a kid, I had worried from time to time about losing my mind. It was never clear to me what losing my mind meant, though. I guessed it meant becoming detached from reality, screaming, yelling, revealing awful secrets I didn't want anybody to know—secrets I might not even know myself. But if I could hang onto my sanity on acid, then I was probably OK. It was like taking a risk just to make sure you can manage things, a stress test of your mental stamina. Dropping acid was like race car driving, I thought to myself. Race car driving of the mind.

After we had driven around for a couple of hours, I felt better. The Bub was talking about all the different names for marijuana: grass, pot, weed, reefer, Mary Jane, and so on. But the one he liked best, he said, was dope. "It's like what it really is without having to make it sound like something else. Just dope. . . . Dope." He said it in a really evil voice. "Got some dope?" He began yelling it out the window and laughing. "Do-ope!" I did too. The Hands up!

saguaros would have seen a green and white Rambler zooming past with two maniacs leaning out the windows hollering "Do-o-o-o-o-o-ope!"

CHAPTER 18

TWO WEEKS PASSED AND THE CLERK at the telegraph office couldn't understand why we didn't go home through Nogales. "That is what everyone else is doing. For you it would be easy—you are Americans." Back at the hotel we considered it.

"Our plates are going to stand out there," I told the Bub.

"We could 'borrow' some Arizona plates. We could probably pay a beaner to borrow some for us."

I didn't like the idea, though. The secretaries would have to pretend they were from Arizona and could easily get caught in a lie.

We drove to a *papelería* and bought a detailed map of northern Mexico to see if there was some other route we could take. Sure enough, the map showed a tiny jeep trail that led from Kino Bay to Desemboque, effectively bypassing the washed-out bridge. We checked out of our hotel and headed straight for Kino Bay.

On arriving, we were surprised to find a huge trailer park filled with older Americans. There were hardly any trees around and the trailers looked like giant aluminum sow bugs glaring blindingly in the sun. We asked around and learned that most of these people were snowbirds: American retirees who spent winters here, traveling from the States in large caravans.

"Think what a nightmare it must be for customs when they go back," I told the Bub. "They couldn't begin to do a thorough search of all these huge rigs. They probably just wave most of them through, figuring old people wouldn't be involved with drugs."

We stopped at a store to get refreshments and heard one of the older Americans talking to another. "Yessir, we're completely self-contained. Got enough food, water, and gasoline to last us three months. We don't have to depend on the Mexicans for a thing." Outside we saw the rig he was talking about.

"Think of the bricks you could pack in that thing," I told the Bub. "Only problem is, how would you find an old person to run it?"

"You'd have to find a crooked straight," observed the Bub.

The jeep trail turned out to be impassable for our poor Rambler. At the point where we gave up, an Indian family sat passively in the searing sun, surrounded by their meager belongings. These were the Yaquis that Carlos Castaneda had immortalized in *The Teachings of Don Juan: A Yaqui Way of Knowledge*. They were a ragged lot. The man of the family came over and begged from us. I gave him a ten-peso note and he stared at it, expressionless, before walking back to his family without so much as a *gracias*. Back in Hermosillo we learned that the Río Magdalena was much lower now and cars were being towed through by tractors. We immediately headed north.

It was dark by the time we arrived, but cars were still being towed through, the whole operation lit by floodlights. They had three tractors going and federales were everywhere, supervising. We pulled into a long line of cars and waited. While we were waiting, a van carrying an American band was towed through heading south. They pulled over near us and began hauling out all their instruments and gear, cursing because water had gotten into their van. We watched them pull out soggy sleeping bags and swear. They told us they were headed for Mazatlan, hoping to find a gig there. Mazatlan was already filled with wandering mariachi bands, and I wondered what sort of reception these guys would get. Later, one of them came over and asked if we had any weed on us. "You're just gonna have to throw it away when you get to the border anyway." We said no, but after he left, the Bub asked if he could give them a little bit of our grass, saying it would be good karma. I said sure and the Bub discreetly lifted up the back seat, pulled a brick out, broke a chunk off it, and went over and gave it to the guy. That chunk would have brought forty or fifty bucks in the States, but giving it away seemed worth it for the spirit of things.

Dawn broke and our turn finally came. Our tractor driver was lean and had black hair and a Zapata-style mustache. He kept eyeing our long hair and grinning in a way I didn't like, but the Bub said I was just being paranoid. Federales were everywhere. We stood around, stamping our feet against the cold, when I noticed the tractor driver kneeling by the right rear quarter panel, right next to the bricks. I rushed back in a fright.

"*¿Qué estás haciendo?*"

He stared up with a surprised look and held up a grimy rag. "I am only stuffing your tailpipe so that water will not get in your engine."

We made it through the river without incident, checked the bricks, and found they had hardly gotten wet. Next, we had to deal with the Mexican inspection station several hours ahead. We got out a bunch of cheap trinkets we had bought and scattered them over the back seat to distract from its hardness. In the early afternoon we topped a hill and saw the station ahead in the valley below. A lot had happened since I rolled through here lying on top of a load of grass in the back of my truck. Marijuana wasn't so much in the public's consciousness back then, but now, at least in the States, it was in the news nearly every day. The papers had documented the fact it was grown in the interior of Mexico and had to be transported to the border, and it stood to reason the authorities at the station knew this too and were on the lookout for smugglers.

I told myself we had the grass well hidden and there shouldn't be a problem. Still, I couldn't help feeling this might be a mistake. The Bub headed down the hill and I figured there was no going back and tried to lose myself in details of the scene. It had grown warm and the sky was clear blue save for a few wisps of clouds in the far distance. The station was whitewashed and there were no trees around to shade it from the full glare of the sun. We rolled in and a corpulent middle-aged officer in a blue uniform came up to us, followed by two young federales in olive drab, rifles slung over their shoulders. The officer grinned jovially and pointed to a man in civilian clothes standing back at the station wall. "That man says you have marijuana in your car." My heart jumped and I stared at the man he was talking about. He was lean and had black hair and a Zapata-style mustache. The tractor driver!

The Bub and I got out and the two federales proceeded to search the car. One began picking up each of the items on the back seat to examine it, just as we had intended, but the other ordered us to open the trunk and seemed to know exactly what he was doing. After a brief search of our belongings, he began tapping carefully against the side wall of the trunk, his fingers literally a sixteenth of an inch away from the grass. The metal yielded a dull sound and he leaned closer to hear. In a feeble attempt to project innocence, I told the officer, "If we wanted marijuana, there is already plenty of it where we come from."

"Is that so?" the officer replied, seeming to evince great interest as he rocked back and forth on the balls of his feet, hands clasped behind his back.

The federal at the back seat was still hung up examining trinkets, but the federal at the trunk had his ear cocked very close to where he was tapping and looked as though he was on to something. I couldn't imagine how we were going to get out of this when the officer gave an order I didn't quite catch and the two federales quit searching and stepped back. It seemed as though we could go. I couldn't believe I was reading things right but got in the car just the same. The Bub shut the trunk and followed suit. I started the engine and when no one stopped us, I took off.

"I can't believe this," murmured the Bub.

"I can't either."

"Are they playing cat and mouse with us or what?"

"Don't look back."

"Don't worry!"

I drove like an old lady until we had finally topped the hill leading out of the valley and were out of sight. I then floored it for a mile or so till we came to a dirt side road, where I turned sharply right. The side road soon dead-ended and we jumped out and ran up a short bluff that afforded a view of the station in the valley below. Nothing was happening. No police cars were giving chase. The only vehicle on the road was an old pickup laboring up the grade. We were safe.

Later I was able to make sense of what had happened. We weren't tipped off and the man standing against the wall wasn't the tractor driver. Many Mexican men are lean with black hair and Zapata-style mustaches, and it was only my paranoia that made me think he was the tractor driver. It was unrealistic to think that the tractor driver would have abandoned his job in order to jump in a car and race past us to the station. Most likely the man against the wall was just some guy hanging out, and when he saw us pull up with our long hair and California plates, he voiced the logical conjecture that we had grass in our car, a conjecture the officer then passed on to us. If the officer had had a solid tip, he never would have called off his federales so quickly.

Most people following such a close call would probably have quit taking risks or at the very least cut their hair. I did neither. In fact, the experience had the opposite effect on me. I began to believe I was special in the eyes of a benevolent greater power and could get away with anything.

CHAPTER 19

IN TIJUANA WE FOUND A QUIET MOTEL with an enclosed yard where the Rambler would be safe and left it there, using cabs to get around. It was Wednesday and the secretaries wouldn't be able to do the run till Saturday, giving us three days to kill. After eating dinner downtown, we bought a six-pack of Corona de Barril, caught a cab, and gave the driver the name of a motel several blocks from the one where we were really staying. The driver was about forty, had a friendly manner about him, and spoke good English. While we were stopped at a light, he caught our eyes in the rearview mirror and said, "You boys want to buy grass? I'm not talking about small shit. I'm talking kilos. I can tell you boys are interested in quantity." The Bub and I exchanged looks in the back seat.

"How much are kilos going for here in Tijuana?" I asked him.

"Twenty-five."

Any professional smuggler would have kept his mouth shut at this point, but I couldn't resist showing off.

"No, thanks. We've got a car packed full of bricks on the other side of town. We paid ten in Mazatlan."

The light turned green and the driver shrugged as he shifted through the gears.

"Well, be careful, boys. The border is pretty hot these days."

He seemed like a nice guy and we offered him one of our beers. He took a deep slug off it and positioned it between his legs.

"Say, do you mind if I take side streets? If anyone from the company saw me drinking this, they'd can me in a minute."

We told him to go ahead and soon found ourselves in a poorly lit neighborhood with pocked streets. It turned out the cab driver used to be a smuggler himself from way back. He got excited just talking about it. "Say, you boys have some time, don't you?" We said sure and he drove to the top of a hill overlooking all of Tijuana and the States beyond. He cut the engine and turned sideways, leaning against the car door in order to face us better. Below us lay the warm, twinkling, yellow lights of Tijuana, and beyond were the harsh white lights protecting warehouses and irrigation pumps in the States. In between was a thin dark line punctuated by the bright lights of the border station.

"We used to run it in Hudsons," the cabbie was saying. "You know those old cars that look like upside-down bathtubs? We used to pack it under the fenders. You could pack a hundred kilos that way. Customs caught on, though, and got these sticks with mirrors on the end for looking up underneath your car. Everyone switched to Falcon Rancheros. You can pack a hundred and fifty kilos in the quarter panels of a Ranchero. We used to put spacers in the rear springs so the rear end wouldn't sag. Customs caught on to Rancheros too, though, and they got hot—really hot. You couldn't run the border in a Ranchero now if you was a nun." He gave a laugh. "Now everyone uses something different. Keep 'em guessing, that's the best way. Mercuries are good, around sixty-one or sixty-two. So's a fifty-nine Plymouth."

We told him we were just starting and this was practically our first run. He asked if we were going to run it ourselves and we told him no, we had runners. He looked relieved.

"I was going to say, you guys wouldn't stand a chance with your hair like that."

"The last run me and another guy ran it," said the Bub. "We had really short hair, though."

"You gotta look straight."

We all took slugs off our beers.

"You know those rooms above the lanes with one-way glass that you can't see into? Customs has spotters up there watching the cars to see if anyone looks nervous. Make sure your runners act relaxed while they're waiting in line. Tell 'em they shouldn't even smoke a cigarette. Sometimes if the inspector on the line is suspicious, he will reach in and put his hand over your heart. I don't care how much balls you got, if you got a load in your car, your heart's going to be beating like crazy. We used to take some kind of pill for that. I forget what it was called."

"Our runners are women," I told him. It took him a second and he laughed.

"Oh, well, I guess you don't have to worry about that!"

He seemed impressed by the fact we were using women. I got the impression not many smugglers were using women runners at the time.

He stepped out to pee and the Bub turned to me with his eyes wide. "This guy's like the living encyclopedia of smuggling!" We could hardly believe our luck. The cab driver stepped in again and we drank a second round of beers.

"We used to learn the inspectors' shifts. When they first come on, they're all eager to catch smugglers." He made a grabbing motion with his hand and laughed. "At the end, though, they're tired and just want to go home. That's when we used to cross. Now they stagger the shifts. There's other tricks, though.

"Study the border. You know the Friendship Bridge that crosses the high-way just before customs? You can stand there all day and watch how they operate. They can't hassle you. Watch to see which cars get through and which get searched. Learn everything you can. When you're through, though, go away for a month before you cross, so you won't be hot. Or better yet, cross at a different town. You'd be amazed how many finks there are in the border towns. They get the slightest suspicion of you and they turn your license number in to customs just for the chance of getting a reward. Never spend time in a town where you're going to cross. Don't spend the night there. Don't even stop for coffee. Just roll into town and do it—bam! That's the only way."

The six-pack was finished and we stared at the view for a while. Across the street from us, a television set cast flickering shades of gray against the wall of the home next door. I thought how amazing it was we had met this cab driver. What were the odds? Could there be such a thing as destiny? I couldn't help thinking, too, how no other adult had ever spent even five minutes with me talking with love and passion about his line of work. The cab driver glanced at his watch.

"Well, I better get home or my wife will start worrying about me." He told us he had two daughters and showed us their pictures.

"When my first daughter was born, that's when I decided to give up smug-gling. Now all I do is help people score sometimes. It's no good to be in jail when you have a family."

"Were you ever busted?"

He held up two fingers. "Twice. The second time there was an ounce of shit in with the load and I got ten years. I've been in Terminal Island, Lompoc, and Victorville." He ticked them off with a laugh. "That's how I learned to speak English so good!"

He fired up the cab and drove us to the motel we had named and we got out.

"If you ever need any help, just look me up. My wife will always know where I am." He jotted down his name and address on a scrap of paper and handed it to me. The Bub and I each shook hands with him through the car window, and I pulled out a ten-dollar bill and handed it to him, immediately wishing I had made it a twenty. He wouldn't take our money, though, not even for the fare.

"It has been *my* pleasure!" And he drove off. We walked into the office of the motel that wasn't ours and killed a minute buying a couple of Cokes at a machine. On the way to our real motel, I pulled out the scrap of paper with the driver's name and number on it and studied it for a moment, then tossed it into a cactus bed. I felt kind of sad doing that, but we had gotten all we could from him, and having his name in our possession could only lead to trouble.

The next morning we walked to the top of the Friendship Bridge as the cab driver had advised. We weren't the only ones there! Ranged along the railing were a number of Mexican men of varying ages and a couple of men who looked vaguely Asian, possibly Filipino. One was dressed in a gaudy green suit and wearing gold jewelry. We wondered whether they were studying the border like us or possibly following the progress of a certain car in the lines below. Maybe they were simply staring wistfully at the States.

Many of our previous suppositions regarding customs were confirmed. Women were searched far less often than men, and pairs and groups were searched less often than single individuals. Out-of-state cars were frequently searched and so were cars that looked dusty or had *turista* decals indicating they had been to the interior of Mexico. Anyone hip-looking was immediately sent to the inspection area.

"Notice how they sometimes pop the hood right in the lane," commented the Bub. "They only do it to sixes, though, never to a V-eight." This made sense as you could hide a fair amount of grass on either side of a six but not a V8. It impressed me that the Bub would notice such a subtle detail as it required knowing which cars had sixes and which had V8s.

Saturday came and with the Rambler safely parked in the fenced lot of our motel, the Bub and I took a cab to the border, walked across, and caught a cab to the San Diego airport. We waited out on the tarmac and got something of a shock when the secretaries stepped off the plane. In our memory they had looked happy and wholesome, but now their faces were pale and they looked frightened and glum. They spotted us and didn't even smile. Compared to all the suntanned San Diegans happily greeting their families, they made a conspicuous contrast. "Are you sure you want to go through with this?" I asked them after we had entered the terminal and stepped to one side.

"Yes. We said we would and we will."

Heeding the cab driver's advice, we decided they should cross at Mexicali instead of Tijuana, where we had been hanging out for the last three days. This involved driving them from Tijuana to Mexicali, then bringing them back from Calexico to San Diego, a two- to three-hour drive each way. The secretaries went to the women's room and I told the Bub, "There's no sense in both of us going." He threw me a baleful look.

"I suppose that means you want me to do it?"

"The Rambler's registered in your name. If anything happens, you're already involved. No sense both of us getting in trouble. At least I'd be in a position to help you."

He gave a snort and sighed. "Man, those broads are so fucking nervous I don't know if I can stand being with them that long."

The secretaries came back and we waited outside for a cab. I coached them on how to act in front of customs, mentioned the trinkets on the back seat, and said they should feel free to buy more. They seemed terribly down and I tried to cheer them up by talking about things we would do after the run. To celebrate, I said we would take them to a great Italian restaurant we had discovered in North San Diego. I told them it had checkered tablecloths and candles on every table and even had *Spoonful* on the jukebox. The secretaries didn't say anything and bit their lips.

We got a cab and the driver let me off at the Best Rest Motel in North San Diego. I wished the secretaries luck and watched the cab disappear down the hill. It was about ten in the morning and I calculated it would be a good six hours before they got back from the run. I got a room, ate lunch at a nearby café, then came back to my room and wished I had thought to bring a book to pass the time. I found a Gideon's Bible in the nightstand and began reading it, getting off on the fact I was reading the Bible for the first time while waiting for a run to pull through. So much stuff I had heard about all happened in the first few pages: Adam and Eve, Cain and Abel, Noah and his Ark.

Around the time the Lord was advising Moses how to deal with lepers, I grew bored and got up. Nearly eight hours had passed and the light outside was starting to fade. I began to worry something had gone wrong. If there was a bust, I knew the Bub would never fink on me, but I wasn't so sure about the secretaries. I imagined agents bursting in to find me sitting here like a fool. I began gathering my things when there was a crunch of gravel outside and knocking at the door. I opened it to find the Bub standing there grinning and giving me the thumbs-up sign. I stepped out and saw the secretaries in the back seat of the Rambler looking worlds different from the way they had looked just a few hours ago. Their faces were flushed, their hair mussed, and they wore huge grins, reminding me of caricatures I had seen in Playboy of women who had just had sex. As I slid into the front passenger seat, they began stumbling over each other to tell what had happened.

By the time they got to Mexicali, they said, they were so nervous that they secretly planned to back out of the run. The Bub left them and they decided to go to the marketplace as planned, just to put off disappointing the Bub. There they could hardly believe the deals they saw. They rushed from stall to stall, buying embroidered blouses, scarves, sandals, jewelry, and leather handbags. Before they knew it, three hours had passed. Suddenly, they remembered the run and realized they were no longer that nervous about it. "Anyway, by that time we'd spent so much money that we had to do it!" they laughed. They drove up to customs, were waved through, and met the Bub at a preassigned corner where he had been waiting for them after crossing the border on foot.

They held up different items they had bought.

"Can you believe it? Only five dollars!"

"This is all hand-embroidered."

"This would cost you forty if you tried to buy it in the States."

"God, it's so easy to run the border!"

We went to the Italian restaurant I had promised them and ate spaghetti while we listened to *Spoonful* played over and over. I ordered a pitcher of beer and the waitress didn't even card me. By the candlelight the secretaries' faces still had a flushed glow. Afterward, the Bub and I took them to the San Diego airport, and after seeing them off with hugs, we headed home with the satisfied feeling of having enough pot in our car to further our reputations as folk heroes and leave us each several thousand dollars richer.

CHAPTER 20

WE DROVE THROUGH THE NIGHT, arriving in Berkeley on a cold, foggy morning, then headed up to Tilden Park, where we unpacked the bricks in a mist-shrouded clearing surrounded by eucalyptus trees dripping dew. I emptied one quarter panel, the Bub got the other, and we packed the bricks into two gunny sacks, which we laid in the trunk. I stepped over to the quarter panel the Bub had unpacked, gave it a loud thump with my fist, and grinned. "You didn't leave any bricks wedged up in there, did you?" We hadn't yet gotten a count on the bricks and it would be just like the Bub to leave a couple up there for himself and blame the bad count on Meche. The Bub gave me a baleful look and faintly snorted.

We drove to a garage I had rented in Albany and dumped the bricks into a large, battered trunk I had acquired. We talked about counting them but were both dead tired from driving all night and decided to do it later. I had bought a combination lock for the garage door and twisted the knob several times to make sure it was locked. The pointer of the lock ended up on the number sixteen.

I drove home and got barely two hours of sleep before a friend phoned, wanting to buy four bricks. I didn't want to wake the Bub and drove to the garage, figuring I would tell him about the four bricks later. The number on the lock was still set to sixteen, but when I entered the garage, I got the feeling that someone had just been there. I couldn't put my finger on it; it was just a feeling. I stared at the only window, which was at the back and had a cracked pane covered with dust through which you could barely make out the blackberry brambles pressed up against the other side. No clues there. I opened the trunk lid and the bricks seemed just the way we had left them. But when I went to count them, there were two less than there should have been. Not only that, but several of the bricks at the bottom were lying on their long edges, which didn't seem natural considering the way we had dumped them in. Could the Bub have taken two bricks and compulsively "fluffed" the pile so it wouldn't look low? I considered this for a while, took out the four bricks my friend wanted, set the combination lock to sixteen again, and left.

Back at my cottage I called the Bub several times, but no one answered. After several hours, I grew anxious and drove back to the garage. The lock was still set to sixteen. I went in and started counting the bricks and saw that even more at the bottom were set on edge. Sure enough, another three were missing. Was he planning to tell me he had taken them? The way he had fluffed the pile made me think not. Only three, I thought to myself and laughed. No guts! I took five, didn't bother fluffing the pile and left. Down the street I found a pay phone that allowed me to keep an eye on the garage while I called the Bub. This time he answered and I said we should split up the bricks and waited for him to come by. I decided that if he came clean about the missing bricks, I would tell him about the ones I had taken, but if he didn't say anything, then I wouldn't either.

He arrived and we entered the garage, closing the door behind us. I opened the trunk, and when he saw how low the pile was, his face fell a little, but he didn't say anything. I began divvying up the bricks. "One for you, one for me . . ." They came out even and he left with his sack of bricks while I lingered a while, laughing to myself. I didn't laugh quite as hard, though, when I thought how he had been sly enough to set the lock back to sixteen each time.

*

This was the beginning of the car runs. The Bub and I fell into an easy groove that worked perfectly for us. I was the brains of our outfit and he was the mechanic. I handled all the Spanish speaking and he made sure the Rambler was running perfectly and did things like packing bricks into the back seat. He liked mothering the car: checking the oil, listening to the motor for unwanted sounds, and making sure the radiator was full. We respected each other and hardly ever argued.

In Mazatlan we discovered María Luisa's *casa de huéspedes* on a narrow side street in the south end of town. This was a guest house frequented by Mexicans as well as a few hips that had stumbled across it or heard of it through the grapevine. It was a large building that dated to the 1800s, and the rooms were on the second floor and had ceilings fifteen feet high. Three ancient deaf women lived there and wandered mutely through the large common room like apparitions out of a T. S. Eliot poem. The rooms all had railed balconies that overlooked the street and in the early morning vendors would pass by below, shouting, "*¡Pla-a-a-a-a-atanos!*"

I was getting to know Mazatlan well. Each trip we would check out the marketplace, where we often spotted the Mazatlan Monkey Man, a poor, deformed youth who loped through the stalls on all fours, his butt up in the air like a chimp. We always spent time, too, at the *cocos helados* stand north of the Hotel de Cima. Sitting there staring out over the water as we reviewed the plans for our latest run, I felt just like a Marseille gangster.

After scoring, we would head north, passing through towns with romantic names like Guamúchil, Guasave, Los Mochis, Navojoa, Ciudad Obregón, Guaymas, Hermosillo, Santa Ana, and Caborca. Between Mexicali and Tijuana there was a bridge where we had to slow down for a toll, and young girls in Catholic uniforms would rush up to us holding out white cans with a red cross on them. We always donated a generous amount, figuring it was good karma for the run. The money went to a local orphanage and I knew what a rough lot orphans had in Mexico, having seen them sleeping under buses on cold nights for the warmth the engines gave. After the border, there was always the decision whether to take the 101 or the 99. The 99 was quicker unless there was tule fog, in which case it took forever. The 101 had the ocean, windbreaks of eucalyptus, and green velvet hills, while the 99 had railroad cars, wisteria-covered barns, windmills, and horse trailers. Whichever way we took, we always stayed tuned to Wolfman Jack.

Heading north from the border one time, the Bub was driving and noticed a green and white Border Patrol car tailing us. In it were two Border Patrol agents. We were in the middle of three lanes and the agents pulled up alongside us on our left. Once when I was twelve, I heard a friend's father say, "Never catch a cop's eye. That's a sure way to get a ticket. Pretend you don't even know they're around." The Bub and I had discussed this more than once during long hours on the road and decided we agreed with my friend's father. So we stared vacantly ahead and pretended not to notice these agents. They then dropped back, switched lanes to the right, and pulled up alongside us on our right. My heart began pounding, thinking we had somehow been identified as holding and were about to be busted. Turning to the Bub, I began a contrived conversation to make it seem realistic that I wasn't noticing these two agents staring at us from just a few feet to my right. I could feel the adrenaline coursing through my veins, but then the agents abruptly sped ahead and were gone. A wave of relief swept over me, but mixed in with the relief I was surprised to find an element of disappointment. Did a part of me want to get busted? I then wondered to myself. In trying to analyze this, I decided that it wasn't that I wanted to get busted, but that a part of me longed for some kind of interaction with authority figures. Maybe I just wanted to mess with them, I thought. That didn't seem quite right, though. Then I fantasized having some kind of showdown with them in which I would be exonerated from vague, unnamed Kafkaesque accusations of me and everything would be all right between us. I didn't really know why I felt that twinge of disappointment.

During these car runs we spent a lot of time walking back and forth at the Tijuana border and the customs agents there got to know us. "Here come the hippies," they would say. Our attire consisted of long-sleeved shirts rolled up at the sleeves, jeans, cowboy boots with the jeans not tucked in, and Mexican sombreros, which only partly covered our long hair. The reason we crossed so often was to eat American food and take advantage of the American telephone system while waiting for runners to come down. We both loved Mexican food, but there was a monotony to it that got to us after several weeks on the road, and what Mexican food lacked can be perfectly summed up by a hamburger and milkshake, which were the first things we ordered every time we crossed into the States.

We got used to being frisked and interrogated when we crossed. Often the customs agents would interrogate us separately to see if our stories matched. Our number one rule was to never mention the Rambler, so we prepared stories how we had been traveling by bus or hitchhiking. Inevitably our stories would break down. The agents would ask questions like, "Who bought the tickets? How much did they cost? Did you both go up to the ticket window or did one of you wait behind?" It was impossible to predict all the questions they might ask and after a while, I would go quiet on them or say I didn't remember. Once, I went quiet on an agent at the very start and he got so angry, I was afraid he was going to hit me. It seemed they didn't like being deprived of the opportunity to make liars out of us.

One of the Tijuana agents had a style that was entirely different from the rest. He never worked the line but had his own office with a desk, and the agents on the line often brought us in to see him. We had no idea what his rank was, but because he seemed to be in charge, we took to referring to him as "the lieutenant." He had a pipe he was always smoking and liked to lean back in his swivel chair. He would say things like, "So you're back again. Where did you go this time? . . . Kino Bay? . . . Lovely place! My wife and I were there just last month. Did you get a chance to do any fishing while you were there? . . . That's too bad, the fishing there is fantastic. My wife and I each caught marlins. How about Pepe's Bar, did you spend any time there? . . . No? . . . Never even heard of it? . . . That's strange. I thought everyone who went to Kino Bay spent time at Pepe's. Hmm."

We assumed he was just biding time until he had something on us at which point he would move in for the kill.

One time we were crossing the border every day while waiting for runners to come down and the customs agents got so used to us that they actually warmed up a little. I decided to play a joke on them and wrote out a note, which I folded up and tucked inside the sweatband of my sombrero. We crossed and as luck would have it, they didn't search us and missed the note.

Next to the customs building was a Greyhound station and we went in and took seats at the counter. Our hamburgers had just come when we heard the door open, followed by the sound of heavy boot steps and the creak of leather. By a subtle intuition that had developed between us, the Bub and I both knew that we each knew there were cops in the diner, and we bent to our food without looking around. I then glanced up, not realizing there was a strip mirror directly opposite us, and my eyes accidentally locked there with the eyes of a grim-faced highway patrolman. Moments later we were being told to get up from our seats.

There were two of them. One was tall, dark-haired, and appeared to be in his thirties, and the other was young, blond, and looked like a high school football player—a rookie, I presumed. They checked our IDs, then had us stand spread-eagled against the restaurant wall as they proceeded to search us right in front of the other patrons. This seemed like a gross violation of our rights but we knew better than to object. The first thing the rookie did was to pull off my sombrero and fish inside the sweatband, where he found my note. He unfolded it to read, "Won't you cops ever wise up?"

His response was hilarious. He grabbed me, jerked me around so I was facing him, slammed me back against the wall, and red-face shouted, "You could go to jail for this!" Those were his exact words, too. He really said exactly that.

He then showed the note to his partner, who seemed less impressed. Nevertheless, they decided to take us into the station and grabbed our arms. I said, "Wouldn't you like us to pay for our meals first?" The rookie looked slightly embarrassed and let go of me, and I stepped over to the Chinese counterman and handed him a ten-dollar bill, telling him to keep the change.

At the station we were taken in to see our friend, the pipe-smoking lieutenant. "We found this on them!" the rookie exclaimed as he slapped my note down on the lieutenant's desk. The lieutenant read it and chuckled.

"What should we do with them?" asked the rookie.

"Well, you can take them to separate rooms and search them if you like."

They did this and brought us back, the rookie now beside himself with excitement. "This one says they've been riding buses the whole way and this one here says they hitchhiked part of the way. Not only that, look what this guy was carrying!" He indicated me and laid $300 in cash down on the desk. It was a mistake on my part not to have hidden most of it back at our motel.

"What should we do next?"

The lieutenant was trying to light his pipe and had to flick his lighter several times before it would stay lit. He clicked the lighter shut and blew smoke to the side.

"Let them go."

The rookie stared at him, aghast.

"But we know why they're here. We can't just let them go like that!"

"We've got nothing on them."

We took this as our cue to leave and scraped our possessions off the lieutenant's desk. The rookie stood there, speechless, his face red with emotion. We could feel his impotent animosity boring into our backs as we beat it on out of there.

CHAPTER 21

A BIG PROBLEM FOR US WAS GETTING PAST the Mexican inspection station. If I had any thoughts about trying to run it again, they vanished the day I opened the Daily Cal to find an article there about three Berkeley students who had gotten caught at that station with two kilos hidden in their truck. One of the students, a coed, had tried to run, and federales shot her in the leg. I gave a low whistle reading this. There was no need to shoot that poor coed. It was broad daylight when the bust took place and the inspection station is surrounded by open desert. There was no place she could have run.

I figured there had to be a way around the station. "The Mafia's probably got a superhighway out there," I joked to the Bub. I went to the UC Berkeley Map Room and found the most detailed map they had of that area, but there were no roads marked that led around the station. Still, I felt there had to be one. Mexico was crisscrossed with dirt roads, some of them little more than tracks in the sand; there was no way a cartographer could chart them all.

For lunch I headed over to the Terrace, where I ran into Dan Miller. He came from a wealthy family and was an intellectual type with horn-rimmed glasses and pale, tapered fingers. I loved talking about our runs with him because he appreciated all their moral and philosophical aspects—unlike the Bub, who just looked at them as an easy way to make money.

"This whole pot thing's going to explode," I told him. "Even professors are smoking it. The Bub and I are getting in on the ground floor. Not only that, it's a chance to commit a serious crime without doing anything immoral!"

Dan began complaining about his schoolwork and on an impulse I said, "Hey, why don't you drop out and join us? The Bub's great at handling the mechanical details and you and I can be the brains. We'll form a syndicate. We'll be bigger than the Mafia!"

The very next day he dropped out.

I found the Bub at his parents' garage cleaning motorcycle parts and told him I had invited Dan along. He turned to me, his hands dripping black solvent. "I suppose that means we've gotta split everything three ways?"

The three of us headed south and right away I began to see it was a mistake bringing Dan along. He took over the wheel around Fresno and cruised along doing all of sixty. "Geez, Dan, we'd like to get there before Christmas," the Bub told him. Dan dutifully accelerated to seventy but lacked control at that speed and kept drifting back and forth in his lane. The Bub and I had grown up in a culture where mastering all things automotive was like a requisite of manhood, and it pained us to see a guy who couldn't drive well. Whenever Dan had to pass a car, he would stay in the left lane long after he had passed—even when there were no other cars around. "What are you trying to do, Dan, attract cops?" asked the Bub. I had to explain to Dan that it was safer to speed in the slow lane.

The Bub and Dan weren't getting along at all. Whenever the Bub got on Dan's case, Dan would say, "Take it easy, Beeyelzuh," which the Bub knew was some kind of intellectual putdown that only Dan and I understood. Later that afternoon it began to drizzle and our right rear tire went flat. The Bub got out and began replacing it with the spare. Dan was sitting in the back seat and rolled his window down. "Can't you hurry up?" he asked the Bub, sounding for all the world like some rich asshole speaking to his chauffeur. The Bub rose to his feet holding the jack in one hand, the lug wrench in the other, lifted them both up, and then thrust them down on the ground, where they crashed with a steel clatter.

"Fix it your fucking self, Dan."

To keep the peace, I ended up fixing the flat.

On previous runs, the Bub and I had never argued about who should do work. It was an unspoken point of pride between us that we each work as hard as the other. Now with Dan along, no one wanted to do chores. We ended up having to flip coins every time something had to be done—even chores as trivial as getting out to pump gas or cleaning the windshield. On our first night in Mexico we got a flop motel for all of four dollars and when Dan discovered the hot water wasn't working, he was livid. "Get the manager over here right now!" He had no understanding of the way things worked in Mexico. He didn't even like the cute Mexican girls, saying they had skinny legs as well as bad complexions from eating too many tacos. In Mazatlan he thought the water was too cold and while the Bub and I body surfed, he stood around the beach in his street clothes.

I thought sure we could find a road around the Mexican inspection station, but on the way down we spent the better part of a day searching and couldn't find any. Many dirt roads led out onto the desert and we followed every one, but they all eventually faded into soft sand. It seemed we had no alternative but to hike the grass around.

The score went smoothly and the following morning we drove out to the Tropic of Cancer road, packed the bricks into the quarter panels and the back seat without incident, then headed north, planning to arrive at the Mexican inspection station the following evening. We had learned to recognize the hill that lay just before the long valley where the station was located and arrived there while it was still light. We pulled over before the top of the hill and spent a pleasant hour watching the sun go down behind the flat-topped mesas to the west. The sky first turned a deep orange-red over the horizon with apple green above, slowly faded to purple, and finally it was dark. The Bub and I unpacked the bricks and repacked them squarely into two gunny sacks, each weighing about eighty pounds. After tying their ends closed with twine, we placed them in the trunk. Without the bricks, the back seat was now limp, like a Dali version of a back seat. The inspectors at the station might wonder what that was about, but they wouldn't find any grass in the car.

The Bub got behind the wheel and during a space when there were no other cars on the road, he pulled onto the highway with our lights out. From the top of the hill we could see the brightly lit inspection station ahead as well as the headlights of several southbound vehicles heading our way. The Bub pulled over and waited till there were no cars coming in either direction, then pulled out again and headed down the hill with our lights still out. We were about a kilometer away from the station. "A little further," I told the Bub. "A little further . . . OK, good." He and I jumped out and grabbed the two gunny sacks out of the trunk while Dan slid behind the wheel. I told Dan to pull over and wait a while to give us a chance to get well into the desert before he drove on to the inspection station. The Bub and I crossed the highway, and I could feel the asphalt press up hard against my boot soles because of the weight I was carrying. The inspection station was on the left side of the highway, and we had decided to hike around behind it rather than across from it, though it shouldn't make a difference either way; with the bright lights at the station, the officials would see only darkness in every direction.

The night was just cool enough to keep us from sweating much. The air was pure and exhilarating and the stars offered just the right amount of light. Our plan was to hike in a semicircle around the back of the station and meet Dan an equal distance away on the other side. I did the math and figured we had a little over two kilometers to go. That seemed easy though the terrain was rougher than we had expected. We kept having to angle back and forth to dodge cactuses and every few yards there would be a dry arroyo where we had to slide down the sandy bank and scramble up the opposite side. A few of the arroyos were so steep that we simply let the sacks roll to the bottom and then one of us would push them up to be grabbed by the other, kneeling on the opposite bank. My arm and shoulder grew tired and I switched my sack to the other side. Then my other arm got tired and before long I was switching the sack back and forth every fifty yards or so. We took a break. The sound of a car passing on the highway caught our attention and the Bub cocked his ear. He had an uncanny ability to identify cars by their engine sounds and stepped up on a rock to look. "Yep, it's Dan, all right." So Dan was headed for whatever fate awaited him at the station.

I commented that the hike was turning out to be a lot harder than I had expected.

"It's these sacks," said the Bub. "They're a bitch to carry."

He picked his up and began experimenting with it.

"Here, try this." He was stooped over and had his sack lying across his upper back. I tried it and sure enough, the sack was much easier to carry, balanced like that.

Still, it was rough going and we began to angle inward from our planned semicircle, edging ever closer to the station. "As long as they don't have dogs, we're probably OK," I said. The desert floor was littered with spiny pods that kept sticking to our boots and accumulating and we kept having to stop and kick them off. Soon we grew adept at kicking them off as we hiked, saving time. I felt a sharp sting over my right shoulder and thought I had been stung by a wasp, but it turned out to be one of these spiny pods. Thankfully, I hadn't swatted at it. The Bub used a stick to pry it off me, and a short while later the same thing happened to him.

"Man, it was like that thing jumped on me!"

We stopped to investigate and guessed the pods were coming from the drooping articulated limbs of a tree-like cactus that was all around. To test this theory, the Bub picked up a large rock and heaved it at the base of one of these cactuses: a whole rain of pods came down. This was the diabolical method of seed dispersal this plant had acquired: the mere tremor of an animal passing underneath caused a pod to fall on the animal, which then carried the pod to new territory. I later learned this cactus is called cholla or "jumping cactus."

By now, we had given up on our semicircle plan and were set to pass right behind the station, perhaps only fifty yards from it. We waited till we felt refreshed, then hurried quickly and quietly past. If I could relive moments of my past, this would be one of them. There was something so beautiful about the crisp night air, the starlight, the physical exertion, the camaraderie between the Bub and me, and the fact we were hauling grass right behind the federales' backs. Once past the station, we cut over to the barbed wire fence that par-alleled the highway and followed it until we found Dan waiting on the other side.

"They hassled the shit out of me!" he whispered. "When they saw the back seat was fucked up, they took me inside and made me strip. They held me for two hours! I didn't think—"

"Save it for later, Dan," interrupted the Bub. "Where's the car?"

Dan pointed to a vague shape in the darkness. Somehow the Bub got over the fence with his sack and I handed mine to Dan. Now, I had carried that sack for half the night and it didn't occur to me that Dan wouldn't even be able to hold it up, but he couldn't. He dropped it right on the fence and the taut barbed wire let out a *Tzing-tzing-tzing!* that telegraphed straight to the station.

"Damn, Dan!" hissed the Bub.

The three of us froze, our eyes on the station. I felt guiltily glad I was on the desert side of the fence as I would have a head start if we had to run for it. Several minutes passed with nothing happening and we rushed the sacks to the car and took off. A while later, we turned off on a faint road that took us deep into the desert, where we stopped, hid the sacks a good distance away, and threw our sleeping bags out on the sand and crashed.

In the morning, Dan was off somewhere doing his business while the Bub brought the bricks back to pack in the Rambler. I heard my name whispered and turned to see him beckoning me over to where he was resting on his knees beside the right rear quarter panel. He glanced around, then held out a brick.

"Look what I just found stuck up in the quarter panel. I can't believe I missed it when I unpacked them." He glanced around again and sniggered. "Dan doesn't know it, but he ran a brick last night!"

CHAPTER 22

WE MADE IT TO THE BORDER—ONLY TO LEARN that the secretaries no longer wanted to run grass for us. It was all because of a CBS special they happened to watch the night before. The special showed an operation similar to ours in which the runners ended up getting busted. "If we hadn't seen that special, we would have done it, and I'm sure it would have turned out all right, but now we'd be so nervous, we'd probably blow it." They felt bad and apologized, but I told them not to worry about it, we could easily find other runners. I had no idea where we were going to find other runners but didn't want them to feel bad.

We drove to the same place where we had stashed the rigged gas tank from the run with Ron and Arf and found the tank still there, looking exactly the same save for a thin line of bright orange rust along the edge of the square hole cut in the top. Seeing it made me think of Ron still in jail. I missed his flip attitude and goofy jokes, and seeing the tank there with its strange hole that begged explanation gave me a twinge of sadness. We buried the grass, then walked away from it backward, wiping our footprints out with a branch the way I had seen it done so often in Westerns on TV. In Tijuana we found a tuck and roll shop and bought some foam rubber scraps, which we stuffed into the back seat so it wouldn't look so bad.

We drove to the border and it may have been just as well the secretaries backed out, for as we pulled up to customs, agents came running out with their hands on their guns. "Hassle time," murmured the Bub. It seems the Rambler had somehow gotten hot. The agents escorted us into a large room filled with agents sitting at desks and left us there. Two New York-style punks dressed in dark clothing and pork-pie hats were also being detained and stood several yards from us. In a lame attempt to impress these punks, I said, loud enough for everyone to hear, "It sure is great to be back in the States!" A dog-faced sergeant looked up from his typewriter.

"Hey, you don't like it here, how about if we take you back to Mexico when we're through with you?"

"You can't do that. I'm an American citizen."

The sergeant lumbered to his feet, walked over, and thrust his mug in my face. "One more word out of you and we'll take you out in the black-and-white and beat the shit out of you."

I said nothing and looked down and the sergeant lumbered back to his desk. I couldn't help stealing a glance at the punks and saw they were staring blankly ahead, appearing to have registered nothing. They had refined their cool to glacial levels.

The agents eventually let us go and we drove back to Berkeley, where I made the rounds of the campus poolroom and the Bear's Lair, putting the word out that we needed a runner. "Back to burying stuff in the desert again?" chuckled Arf. A couple of weeks passed and it felt weird inviting Arf and Fred to do things, only to be told that they couldn't, that they had to study. I began to get a panicky feeling that I had made a mistake by dropping out, that I was wasting time.

The Bear's Lair by now had become a major gambling center. I don't think many people realized this. Patrons probably thought the young men playing cards at the first several tables as they walked in were simply students taking a well-deserved break from their studies. In fact, many of them were physics and math majors who had dropped out and were applying their genius IQs to playing cards. The main game was bridge and it wasn't uncommon during the course of an evening for hundreds or even thousands of dollars to change hands. No money was ever flashed at the table, of course; rather, all bets were carefully recorded on paper and settled in the men's room. Servicemen and gamblers from as far away as Denver and New York City kept the games alive. One of the strongest gamblers was a seventeen-year-old kid named Kyle Larson. I once saw him drop acid in the middle of a game and continue to win nearly every hand. Kyle would go on to win two world bridge titles as well as nearly a dozen national titles.

Eventually we got one of the Bear's Lair gamblers to do a run for us, a guy named Barrere. As a single guy, I knew he wouldn't make nearly as good a runner as the two secretaries, but we decided to have him do a dry run first, and if the dry run went smoothly, we figured the real one should too. As it turned out, the dry run was a failure, but it ended up being a memorable experience just the same.

The Bub and I headed south and got a room just a block away from the border at a motel with a large sign out front depicting a somnambulist bear.

The following morning we had several hours to kill before Barrere was to arrive and bought newspapers, drove out of town, and read them at a lonely turnout shaded by sycamores. If the dry run failed, it would be useful to know how carefully customs searched, I thought, and came up with a plan, which I explained to the Bub. We drove back to town, bought a dozen paper bags, drove back to the turnout, and hid a bag stuffed with crumpled newsprint in each of the quarter panels and the bottom and back of the back seat.

"Want to hide one under the hood?" the Bub asked and I told him to go ahead while I hid one up underneath the dash. Hiding these bags was fun and we began hiding them all over the car until there were none left.

We picked Barrere up at the San Diego airport and I told him about the bags. "That's OK," he said. "Just so long as there's no dope on the car." I checked the car's ashtray to make sure it didn't have any seeds in it.

At our motel the Bub and I got out and Barrere took over the wheel. I gave him ten bucks and told him to buy a sombrero in Tijuana and lay it on the back seat to support his image as an innocent tourist. He took off and I bought a six-pack of beer with some phony ID I happened to have at the time. Our motel room had a balcony that afforded a view of the border station, and we pulled up chairs there and drank beers as we watched for Barrere. When an hour passed with no sign of him, we figured he was getting hassled.

Yet another hour passed before we saw the Rambler dart out of customs and jerk to a stop in front of our motel. We could hear Barrere taking the metal steps outside two at a time. The Bub opened the door for him and held out a beer.

"Thanks! I could use one about now!

"I think your car is hot," Barrere said after shutting the door behind him and taking a long pull. "I didn't do anything to make it hot either. All I did was buy something to put on the back seat like you said. I didn't buy a sombrero; I bought a poncho. Anyway, I went to the border after that and when I pulled up, a bunch of agents came running out and made me get out of the car. It was a trip! They had their hands on their guns and everything. They grabbed me by the arms and as they're taking me into the station, this woman comes up and says, 'I'm so glad to see you men are doing your job. I think criminals like him ought to be put away for good!' I told her, 'But lady, I didn't do anything!' She just ignored me and told the agents, 'I hope they throw the book at him!' It was weird!

"Anyway, they shoved me inside and took me to this third-degree-type room. They were really interested in the car. They wanted to know who owned it. I didn't tell them a thing. I just told them I borrowed it from my girlfriend and she borrowed it from someone else, so I didn't really know who owned it. I don't think they believed me, but they finally left me alone.

"So they split and left me locked up for over an hour. At first I wasn't scared. I just figured, big deal. Then I started thinking, What if there really is dope in the car? What if this is the real run and you guys only told me it was the dry run so I wouldn't act nervous? I wasn't in the marketplace that long, but what if you somehow got the dope in the car while I was in there? I mean, I know you're an honest guy, Tom, but sitting in a tiny room like that, you start thinking all sorts of things!

"Anyway, get this: all of a sudden the door bursts open and four agents come rushing in and one of them's holding up one of those bags you guys hid and he shoves it in my face and says, 'All right, we found the drugs and we've got your partner in the next room! He told us everything, so you might as well, too! It'll go easier on you if you do!'

"Well, when they said that, I knew I was safe. I mean, it was such a joke of an act. They were pricks, though. They kept hassling me. They actually took turns trying to get me to talk. I told them, 'If you've got something on me, arrest me so I can call a lawyer. Otherwise, let me go.' One guy acted real pissed and kept socking his fist into his palm, coming really close to my face. Fucking asshole! They finally let me go, though. Ma-an . . . "

Barrere took another long slug and grinned. "I'll tell you one thing, though: they sure were interested in those bags!"

The Bub and I couldn't stop grinning, hearing this story. We tried to imagine the elation the agents must have felt when they first found the bags, only to be followed by intense disappointment on discovering they contained only newsprint.

Barrere couldn't get over the incident with the lady. "I mean, like, she's never even seen me before."

The Bub told him not to worry about it. "It was probably all an act anyway. She probably had a bag of heroin up her cunt."

We finished our beers and headed out to the car. Another good laugh awaited us when we saw our crumpled bags and newspapers scattered all over the back seat. We guessed by law customs wasn't allowed to throw them away. We drove around a while to make sure we weren't being followed, then pulled over into a vacant parking lot behind a market. The Bub got a screwdriver and went to check the quarter panels while I got the back seat and other places.

"Find any?" he asked me after some time had gone by.

"No. How about you?"

He shook his head.

"You mean they got the quarter panels?"

He nodded. "Yep."

"They took off our pieces of plywood and put them back on again?"

"Yep."

"They searched for a long time," put in Barrere.

On the way to the airport, Barrere said, "This job seems a lot harder than I thought. I don't think I'm going to be able to help you guys."

I was touched that he even felt the need to tell us.

*

"It's the Rambler's new identity!" grinned the Bub as he showed me a set of plates he had acquired at a wrecker's. It was the plates, we had decided, that were making the Rambler hot. Customs couldn't keep descriptions of every suspicious car reported to them and descriptions wouldn't be unique anyway. They had to go by the plates. Now, all we needed was a runner. I told Barrere about the new plates, but he had had enough with his one experience. I again put the word out in the Bear's Lair and the poolroom, but nothing came of it. A couple of weeks went by and I began to get that nervous, desperate feeling again that I was wasting time, wasting my life.

U Save was the hip place to shop for groceries and was located in the center of town at Grove and University. It never closed and in the late evening it would fill up with potheads looking to satisfy the munchies. Many Berkeley celebrities shopped there and you might see Mario Savio, Super Spade, or General Wastemoreland. Around midnight a different sort of clientele took over. These were guys you never even saw during daylight hours: freaks with pale skin and immense beards, often mumbling to themselves—a nocturnal variant of hip.

Leaving U Save one afternoon, I heard my name shouted and turned to see Ray, the guy who turned me on to acid. We knew each other from Berkeley High though we had never spoken then, coming from different crowds. Ray was part of a small surfing crowd, drove a woody, and had a heart-meltingly beautiful girlfriend named Marie Brandt. During lunch hour he and Marie would sit in his woody parked across from the school and stare out the windshield as though expecting the surf to come up over downtown Berkeley. Now, Ray was a dealer and he and I had become friends through the universal medium of drugs. He was thin and wiry and wore a fringed leather jacket with the fringes always bouncing about because of his nervous energy. He was subject to fits of paranoia and I was never able to decide whether this was a deep-rooted affectation—the way he thought a dealer should act—or whether he might perhaps be developing schizophrenia.

Ray and I did the three-part hip handshake, to which Ray had added several embellishments, and he glanced around, lowering his voice.

"Say, you don't have any more of those blue-wrapped bricks, do you? I could move loads. I've got connections *back east*."

"I don't—"

"Shhhh!" Ray put his finger to his lips. He looked around, narrowing his gaze on a Plymouth going by, driven by a housewife. A shopping cart rattled and he startled. "I don't like it here," he declared. "Let's go somewhere where we can talk."

His apartment was down the street and we walked. I had never been to his place before and wondered if he still knew Marie Brandt. He pointed to the street signs on his block indicating there was no parking between four and six p.m. "Know how I know the narcs are on to me? . . . Yesterday I left my car out here all during rush hour and didn't get a ticket. They don't want to take a chance on scaring me off."

I told him I didn't think the narcs had anything to do with the meter maids and he exploded.

"Oh yeah? Well, how come every other car on the block got a ticket and mine didn't? Answer that!"

Ray's apartment was in an older building fronting directly on the sidewalk. We walked up a dim flight of stairs and Ray undid a couple of locks. Inside, all the shades were pulled and it took me a few moments to adjust to the dim light. I looked around and saw an old sectional with a TV opposite. In front of the sectional was a coffee table made from a resined hatch cover and on it were a couple of sand candles and a packet of Zig-Zags. A bureau stood in the corner and poking up behind it, I noticed the tip of a rifle. Underneath a chair I spotted a pair of women's shoes.

Ray came back from the kitchen with a couple of Cokes and I asked him if he was living with anyone.

"Yeah, Marie Brandt. She was in our class, remember?" He grabbed a framed photograph off a shelf and handed it to me. It showed her wearing a low-cut dress and faintly smiling. I felt my heart race.

"You've been going with her for a long time."

"Used to go with her," Ray corrected. "Now we just live together. We haven't made love in a year and eight months. She sleeps in her bedroom and I sleep in mine. We're free to do our own trips. I watch out for her, though. I wouldn't let anyone take advantage of her. She watches out for me, too. It's really beautiful." He pursed his lips as though seeking words to explain.

"You see, Marie and I don't need to make love. We've already been through that. I couldn't make love to Marie—not anymore. She's like my sister. She's my family." A strangely intense look passed over his features. "We've been having the most beautiful talks lately . . . "

He asked again if I had any bricks and I told him I hoped to have some soon. I told him about the grass stashed just across the border and that we were looking for someone to cross it. As I was talking, Ray's eyes went wide as though I was missing the incredibly obvious, his look of disbelief morphing to a huge grin.

"Marie and I'll run that grass for you!" he exclaimed. "It's perfect, don't you see? We'll pose as man and wife! . . . Don't worry," he added, seeming to read my mind. "I won't blow it. I can act really straight when I want to. I can act just like a stockbroker! I've done it before!"

He began planning it all out. Marie could wear her grandmother's wedding ring. He thought maybe he should wear a ring too, maybe just a plain gold band. He needed a short haircut, something conservative. He knew the perfect haircutting salon. He might even get a manicure while he was there. Oh, and a suit—he needed a suit.

"Yeah, maybe you guys can front me a suit since it's your run."

"A suit? For Tijuana?"

"OK, OK. I've got some slacks and a sweater I could wear."

I wasn't at all sure I wanted Ray as a runner. Just the same, I asked him, "How do you even know Marie would do it?" He slumped his shoulders in exasperation.

"Because I *know* her. That's what I've been trying to tell you all along!"

I told him I would think about the idea and we agreed to meet at his place later that evening. If nothing else, it was a chance to see Marie again. I was about to leave when Ray beckoned to me with a strangely coy look as he pulled out his wallet.

"You know, you really only know one side of me. You probably think of me as a mellow guy who likes to get high and everything. But look at this!" He handed me a plastic card with a rabbit's head in the upper right-hand corner. It was a membership card to the San Francisco Playboy Club.

"Where did you get this?"

"Sent away for it."

"How much did it cost?"

"Fifty bucks."

"Have you ever used it?"

He gave a chagrined look. "No, man. I don't have a suit. That's one of the reasons I need to do this run!"

I was back at Ray's apartment around dusk. Marie answered the door, looking as beautiful as I had remembered her from high school. She was wearing a wine-colored turtleneck that showed off her breasts and gave her a sultry, beatnik look. Her long, dark hair clung to the frizzy material in strands.

"Hi, I believe we went to high school together," I said, trying to be witty about the fact we had never even spoken to each other before. She studied me.

"I think I remember your face. Come on in."

Ray was in the living room, hunched over the hatch cover table as he rolled some joints. He was talking excitedly about some new ideas he had for the run.

So Marie had agreed to it, I thought to myself. She took a seat on the sectional and lit a cigarette, her lighter flaring prettily against her face for a moment before she snapped it shut. Ray had the run all worked out.

"Check this! We're going to have this bottle of Kahlúa on the front seat, and when the customs guy asks us what we're bringing back from Mexico, I'll hold up the bottle real innocent-like and say, 'Just this bottle of Kahlúa, sir. It's OK to bring back one bottle, isn't it?' Of course, he'll have to confiscate it and then Marie and I will act like, 'Aw, shucks, we didn't know the law,' and everything. It's perfect, don't you see? They'll never imagine we have weed in the car!"

He paused in the middle of rolling a joint. "No, maybe I should have Marie say that line. Or wait—how about this: I say the part about the Kahlúa and then Marie gives me this dirty look like she didn't want me to mention it in the first place. Then when the guy confiscates it, she starts acting pissed off, like we've been having an argument, get it? Then I tell her to be quiet or something and we have a few words. It's perfect! They'll think we're just a typical young couple getting on each other's nerves! What do you think? Pretty cool, huh?" He licked the joint and twisted the ends tight with a flourish.

Ray's ideas were terrible and I tried to explain to him that the less said at customs, the better.

"But if we act like we're in a hurry, it'll seem suspicious."

"Everyone's in a hurry to get through customs. You want to sit there and chat. *That's* suspicious."

Marie, meanwhile, had given no clue how she felt about the idea. She hardly spoke, yet I could tell she was taking in every word. I wondered whether Ray was somehow pressuring her.

It grew late and Ray abruptly got up and said he was going to U Save to get some beers. I was suddenly alone in a dimly lit room with Marie, a situation I could never have imagined back in high school. We were both sitting on the sectional, facing each other across a ninety-degree angle. The apartment seemed unnaturally quiet with Ray gone. Marie lit another cigarette. I was afraid she might somehow resent me because of this run.

"Ray isn't pushing you into this, is he?" I asked her. "I wouldn't want you to do it unless you really want to."

She took a deep drag off her cigarette and exhaled, staring thoughtfully past the smoke. Her legs were crossed and she flicked at an ashtray in her lap.

"No. He isn't pushing me into it. He told me about it when I got home and I thought it over and decided I want to do it." She turned to look me in the eye. "But thanks for asking." And for the first time all evening, she smiled.

CHAPTER 23

THE FOUR OF US HEADED SOUTH on a Friday morning, planning to do the run the next day. The Bub drove, Ray was in the passenger seat, and I was in the back with Marie. I was surprised how much she and I had to say to each other. Because she was quiet most of the time, I had assumed she was conceited, but in reality she was just shy. She told me she was "on the make" for a good girlfriend. For some reason she rarely made friends with girls, she said—only guys. I happened to tell her about my idea of running grass in an Airstream trailer and she said her grandmother would make a perfect runner.

"She'd probably do it for the hell of it; that's the way she is. She looks like a little old lady, but she's anything but. She smokes grass. I turned her on to it."

"Is her husband still around?"

"No. My granddad died a long time ago."

"I don't think it would look too good, a single old lady driving a big Airstream by herself."

Marie shrugged. "She could probably get some old man to go with her. She's got lots of admirers."

The city was behind us now and to our left were dry hills with subdivisions creeping up their bases. Marie stared out her window to the right. "What I need is a good session with a shrink," she said, apropos of nothing.

Later, after passing around a joint, we got the munchies and stopped in Ventura to eat delicious hamburgers and milkshakes. Ray then took the wheel and for a long time no one spoke. We were in that pleasant state that follows getting stoned and eating. The sun was dipping toward the ocean, bathing everything in a shimmering gold light. Ray broke the silence, enunciating his words in a tense, controlled voice.

"Nobody look, but there's a beige Ford following us. . . . Three men in suits." He had his eye on the rearview mirror. "I'm going to lose them."

The Bub turned to look.

"Don't look, I said!"

Abruptly he cut across three lanes of traffic, barely making an exit.

"What the fuck?" cried the Bub.

"Got to lose the tail."

Ray came to a red light, ran it, and began racing wildly through the city streets.

"That Ford didn't even get off!" said the Bub, looking back.

"Yeah, but the Camaro did."

"But the Camaro wasn't following us!"

Ray narrowed his eyes on the rearview mirror. "I wouldn't be too sure of that."

I glanced at Marie and she shot me a helpless look. Ray suddenly grabbed the emergency brake and cramped the wheel, executing a perfect 180 in the middle of the street.

"Hey, this is no sports car!" cried the Bub.

"It's OK," Ray said in a reassuring tone as he straightened the wheel. "I'm pretty sure I lost them."

We were now lost in some endless, flat suburb of L.A. The Bub and I told Ray to pull over so one of us could drive, but he refused. His pride was at stake. "OK, OK," he insisted sullenly, promising not to take any more detours. The Bub turned to shoot me a What the fuck? look.

Ray managed to restrain himself though I could see him checking the rearview mirror every few seconds. We finally made San Diego, but when we tried to get a motel room, we learned there were three large conventions all taking place here at the same time and no rooms were available. We kept looking and found ourselves on a long boulevard with arc lights that lit up the Rambler's interior periodically like a strobe. I was beat and lay back in the seat and closed my eyes. Marie tapped my shoulder. "Why don't you lie down?" She scooted over next to her door to make room. I lay down with the top of my head just grazing her thigh. "No, here," she said, indicating her lap. I could hardly believe this was happening! I lay my head in her lap and felt her warm thighs against my cheek. Her body had a sweet smell to it that wasn't perfume but just the natural fragrance of her skin. My heart was pounding. Every time the car went over a bump, I could feel my cheek nuzzling her thighs.

We ended up on an unlit side street and the Bub spotted a green neon sign half hidden behind the branches of a drooping pepper tree. I sat up and saw what looked like a secret sign out of a Hesse novel. It read, "The Family Village, Cottages," and by the starlight we could make out a half dozen small bungalows scattered like dice across a dark hillside. Between the bungalows were huge maguey cactuses twice as tall as a man. This was like the ultimate gangster hideaway! We found the office and rented the only bungalow left available.

Ray pulled the Rambler into a rickety garage that adjoined our room and went in, followed by the Bub. Marie and I were now alone in the back seat and began kissing. As we kissed, she held my face between her two palms. No girl had ever kissed me like that and it made me think of movie stars. She took off her blouse and undid her bra and I took off my shirt. "Let me lower the seats," I told her. No one had bothered to close the garage door and the stars outside looked like pixie dust.

In the morning Marie and I went inside to find Ray in a state of agitation. "The manager knows," he told us grimly. The Bub shot me an eye-rolling look. Ray explained that as part of our "cover" he had gone to the manager and asked him if he had any brochures showing points of interest we might like to visit during our stay here in San Diego. The manager, a short, balding man who smoked cigars behind a butt-stained counter, had looked at him funny or so Ray thought. Ray threw his hands up. "He knows, I'm telling you. He knows!"

Marie was able to calm him down some and the Bub and I left to have breakfast at a café down the street. We walked. This was our first chance to talk alone since the trip began.

"The guy's flipped."

"Usually he's not this bad."

"He's flipped."

We fell quiet for a few paces as we passed a man watering his front yard.

"Are you saying we should call it off?"

The Bub shrugged. "Who else have we got?"

At the café we took a booth and ordered. Our coffees came and the Bub smirked over the top of his cup. "So, did you get a piece of ass off that broad last night?" I debated whether to bullshit him.

"Not quite," I said truthfully. "She says she wants to get to know me better. I think it'll happen really soon, though."

Our breakfasts came and we put away link sausages and stacks of hotcakes. Whenever I felt nervous, food always made me feel better. We had just finished when Ray and Marie walked in. We heard the screen door creak and turned to look. Ray was holding it open for Marie in an elaborately polite pose, dressed in his border-running clothes: white shirt, gray slacks, and a blue vest. With his short haircut he looked quite straight. I raised my hand to beckon them over but quickly lowered it when Ray shot me a fierce look. Evidently, we weren't supposed to know each other. Marie managed to throw me a helpless look as Ray steered her to the far side of the café. The Bub shook his head.

"Like the place was filled with narcs!"

The waitress approached them and Ray addressed her in overly polite tones. "Excuse me, miss, could you tell me if your pancakes are made with real buttermilk? And could you bring two waters, please? My *wife* and I are very thirsty." The Bub shook his head in disgust.

"Let's split."

"Where to?"

"Our room."

"We don't have the key."

"Who has it?"

I nodded toward Ray.

The Bub groaned. "Are you sure?"

"I saw him carrying it when they walked in."

"Well, fuck it. Let's just go over and ask him for it."

This was just talk, though, as neither of us dared setting Ray off.

As we nursed refills on our coffees, Ray got up and headed toward the men's room, which took him on a path directly past our booth. He was staring rigidly ahead and just as he passed, I saw his wrist flick and felt the room key land in my lap.

Back at the cottage, the Bub removed the Rambler's plates and put on the cool ones he had gotten at a wrecker's. "What do you want to do with these?" He held up the real ones.

"Stash them at a Greyhound locker."

Ray and Marie came back and Ray strode up grinning. "Hey, how'd you like the way I got the key to you? Pretty cool, huh?" He glanced down with affected modesty. "Oh, I know you guys think I'm paranoid and everything. I just figure you can't be too safe in this business."

He, Marie, and I went inside while the Bub tended to the Rambler. Ray asked if he could borrow my razor. "It's the one thing I forgot!" I gave him my razor and shaving cream and saw him hold the razor up to stare at it before stepping into the bathroom. Marie and I were alone and I went to hug her, but she edged away. "Careful, you'll wrinkle my dress." It was her border-running dress. She stepped over to the tarnished mirror and began touching up her lipstick.

"It's going to be a while yet," I told her. "We still have to dig up the dope."

"I know." She snapped her compact shut.

"Are you feeling nervous?"

She sighed and managed a brief smile. "A little. More than I thought I would."

"We could drop by a drugstore and try to get something."

"I'll be all right."

She paced for a while, then sat down on one of the beds. I couldn't think of a thing to say. I caught myself looking at myself as if from afar, as though

I were some other person. Outside, a truck groaned. Marie was seated on the bed with her back to me, and I went to kiss the back of her neck, but this involved kneeling with one knee on the bed, which was an ancient Army surplus affair, and my knee caused the bed to sag so badly that Marie was thrown backward and our heads collided.

"Ow!"

"Sorry!"

She wheeled to face me, but in that same moment Ray stepped out of the bathroom, his face covered with blood. All across his lower face were horizontal cuts the exact width of my razor. The cuts were bleeding and where the blood mixed with leftover shaving cream, it had turned a phosphorescent orange. Ray was holding my razor up and grinning. "This is the first time I ever used one of these. I couldn't seem to get the hang of it. I'm used to an electric."

Marie rushed to him. "God, are you all right?"

"Aw, it's nothing." He dabbed at himself, holding the towel in such a way that Marie could see all the blood on it. "I just couldn't seem to get the hang of it," he repeated, dabbing at himself.

"Well, why didn't you stop when you saw you were butchering yourself?"

Ray threw me a hurt look. "I kept thinking I would get the hang of it."

"Well, there's no way you can go through customs looking like this!"

I stepped out to the garage. The Bub had just finished checking the oil and shut the hood. I nodded in the direction of our room. "Check out Ray's latest trip." The Bub wiped his hands off on a mechanic's rag and went in just as Marie was coming out. She and I stood there and stared at each other and sighed. "You want to go for a walk?" I said.

"That sounds like a great idea."

She took my hand and we walked along a street that led up a steep hill to a park. We walked to the edge and could see the town below and the ocean beyond. At the other end of the park, a sailor was talking to a young woman who was pushing a small child in a swing. The sailor got down on his knees as though to plead.

"It's going to take a while for those cuts to heal," I said.

Marie nodded and stared out over the water. We stood there for a while.

"You don't really want to do this run anymore, do you?"

Marie turned to face me. "It's not that I don't want to do it. It's Ray. He's been acting so crazy lately. I'm afraid of what he might do."

"Well, let's not do it then."

"It might be better that way."

She smiled and next thing we were all over each other. Neither of us cared anymore about her dress getting wrinkled.

Back at the cottage no one was sorry to hear the run was off. We threw the Rambler's real plates back on and headed home. We all got high and Marie and I began necking in the back seat. Ray suddenly remembered something he had to do and we dropped him off at Los Angeles International. The poor Bub got stuck driving home while Marie and I tried every conceivable position in the back seat, the goal being to touch as much skin as possible. Somewhere near Morgan Hill, we stopped for burgers and Marie did something I will always love and remember her for. We were in line when two jocks behind us began making comments about my long hair and beat clothes. "Why don't you get yourself a real man?" one of them murmured. Marie wheeled to face them, stared them down, then took my face between her two palms and soul-kissed me right there in the A&W line.

CHAPTER 24

I MOVED IN WITH MARIE AT THE FLAT she was sharing with Ray and we were like a little family. Marie made simple home-cooked meals and Ray would come home in the evening and gripe about his work. "I don't care if it is purple Owsley, no way I'm going to pay two dollars a hit!" After dinner we often drank wine, and if we ever needed anything, U Save was just down the street.

Ray picked up a case of the clap somewhere and seemed quite proud of this development, which he managed to work into conversations with total strangers. He was taking antibiotics and left his pill bottle on the coffee table as a conversation piece. He seemed in good spirits and only got moody when he talked of the narcs. More than ever, he seemed convinced they were poised to close in on him. He owned a number of guns and kept repositioning them around the apartment, his goal being to have one in hand on three seconds' notice no matter where in the apartment he happened to be.

One day two guys from my high school class came by to score some grass from Ray. These were two jocks who had belonged to one of the most desirable social clubs back in Berkeley High. I guess they must have heard of my reputation, for they kept stealing glances at me. One of them spoke to me and his tone was downright deferential. Considering they barely knew I existed back in high school, this was heady!

Each night Marie would take a bath, put on a negligee, and come to me. The weird thing was I was rapidly losing interest in her that way. In high school this would have been the fulfillment of my wildest dream, yet now that I had her, I didn't really feel that attracted to her anymore. I felt bad for Marie and told her there must be something wrong with me. She considered.

"I don't think there's anything wrong with you. I think you've just psyched yourself out."

We slept together anyway. This went on for a week.

Ray knew I liked motorcycles and took me to a rented garage one day to see an old Harley he was rebuilding. On the way, he mentioned that he had a friend who had a car with a good hiding place. "He'd really like to run your keys. He needs the bread for his car payments." I asked what kind of car he had and Ray said it was a Mustang. I didn't think a Mustang would hold much and didn't give it further thought.

At the rented garage, Ray undid several locks and flipped a hidden switch to get in. "Anyone tries to break in here, they're in for a surprise. I've got a double alarm system." He locked the door behind us. "I'm planning to wire my bike so if anyone touches it, they get electrocuted."

The bike wasn't much. The heads were off and starting to rust and the seat was torn. The tank, which was purple with pink flames along the sides, lay on the floor covered with dust. Ray grabbed a tool chest and a heavy duffel bag and we drove back to the apartment.

He parked, grabbed his tool kit and some other items, and said, "Say, grab that duffel bag for me, would you?" We went inside and I went to the kitchen to get a drink of water. When I came back to the living room, Ray was weighing bricks on a scale. The bricks had come out of the duffel bag.

"Hey, next time carry your own dope!"

"OK, OK."

Marie came home, and a short while later I could hear her arguing with Ray in another room. "I suppose you think we fuck like pigs every night! Well, if you want to know, he's hardly touched me that way!"

My time here, I could feel, was running out.

That same afternoon Marie left to visit her mother in Sacramento and said she wouldn't be back till the following day. Ray was around for dinner, then disappeared. It grew late and I went to bed. Several hours later I was awakened by loud knocking at the door. I supposed it was one of Ray's customers eager to buy acid or grass and tried to ignore it. The knocking kept up, though, and I couldn't sleep. Finally, I leapt up, threw on my robe, strode to the door, and jerked it open—only to see four large men huddled there, poised to burst in. "Is Ray in?" asked the closest one, whom I recognized as the guy in Levi's who had led the College Avenue bust. His name was Brian Corliss, I had since learned, and he was widely regarded as a malevolent asshole among dope circles.

"No," I said, simultaneously slamming the door in his face. He had his boot toe in the jamb, though, and I couldn't get the door to close. For about two seconds I was able to resist the force of these four narcs and then the door burst open and I was flung back against a wall. In an instant a narc pinned me and held a pistol to my face, actually touching the tip of it to my nose. Corliss flapped a badge. "Police agents!" he shouted and began reciting something about "In the name of the law—"

"Yeah, I know who you are."

Corliss stopped to take a closer look. "Have I busted you before?"

"On College Avenue."

"Oh, the College Avenue bust!" He slipped his badge back. "That was a big one. Fourteen people. Strange bust, though. We burst in and everyone just sat around."

His tone was oddly conversational, as though I might enjoy reminiscing with him.

Meanwhile, the other agents had fanned out through the apartment and were dumbfounded when they couldn't find Ray. It turned out they had been watching the place since we returned from Ray's garage and hadn't seen him leave. One of them reported back to Corliss. "There's a back way that leads down to an alley. He must have cut through the alley to the next block."

So Ray's paranoia finally paid off!

The narcs didn't handcuff me or tell me to stand in any one place and I moved about and watched as they searched the apartment and gathered Ray's guns, which seemed to alarm them. "Christ, this one's got a bullet in the chamber and the safety's off!"

An agent picked up Ray's duffel bag and held it toward me. "What was in this?"

"I don't know."

"Bullshit. We saw you bring it up here."

He took it over to the light, turned it inside out, and found a seed in the seam.

"We could arrest you for this, you know."

Another agent produced a pocket knife and dug an old roach out of a candle that was lying on the resined hatch cover. After that they didn't find much. They seemed to be wrapping up when Ray abruptly walked in on his own bust. It was hard to tell who was more surprised, Ray or the narcs. Ray was the first to recover.

"Hey, you guys need a warrant for this!"

Corliss showed him the warrant. Ray spotted all his guns gathered on the floor.

"You can't take those! I've got a permit for every one of them except the shotgun and the thirty-aught-six, and I don't need a permit for those!"

The agents seemed to know Ray and called him by his first name in an overly familiar way.

"Say, Ray, how come you have so many guns lying around?"

"Self-protection."

"Yeah, sure. I bet you'd love to blow our heads off, wouldn't you, Ray?"

"Maybe you should quit doing things that make people feel that way."

Corliss in particular seemed attuned to Ray's excitable personality. "Say, Ray, how come you didn't see us following you down University this afternoon? We were right on your bumper the whole way. When you stopped for that orange light at Grove Street, we practically slammed into you. We thought you were going to run it. I can't believe you didn't notice us."

Ray hung his head. Corliss was fueling Ray's paranoia for months to come.

An older agent picked up Ray's clap pills. "What are these?"

"Ampicillin. It says so right on the label."

"What's it for?"

"Gonorrhea."

The agent set the pills back down in disgust. "Figures!"

"Aw, come on. I suppose you guys didn't mess around when you were our age."

The agent hesitated, seeming to search for the right macho response that wouldn't put him on the same level as Ray.

"Well, maybe we did, but at least we had the sense to stay clean."

In the end, all the narcs found was the roach and three caps of mescaline stashed in the refrigerator. The bricks from the duffel bag had apparently all gone out the back way. They had Ray, though, for selling to an agent a month earlier, which was the basis for their warrant. Corliss had him placed under arrest. One of the agents jerked his thumb in my direction.

"What about this guy?"

"Let him go."

"But we saw him bring that bag up."

"That's not enough."

The agent stepped over to me. "What were you trying to hide when you saw us at the door?"

"Nothing."

"How come you tried to slam the door on us then?"

"I didn't know who you were. You could have been robbers."

"I thought you said you recognized Corliss from that other bust."

"I didn't recognize him right away."

The agent turned to Corliss. "Come on, he's not playing ball with us. Why should we play ball with him?"

"Leave him for next time."

CHAPTER 25

MARIE SHOWED UP THE NEXT MORNING JUST as Ray was returning from jail, having posted bail. I was on my way out and the three of us ran into each other on the sidewalk next to Ray's woody. No one had much to say. I put my arm around Marie, but she didn't respond. Ray drifted off and Marie told me she was actually in love with someone else, someone she had been going with on and off for over a year. I knew him. He was in our class at Berkeley High and was part of the metal shop crowd. I gathered my things, feeling a little hurt, but by the time I got back to my familiar cottage, I felt more relieved than anything. The Bub came by and consoled me. "There's got to be something wrong with that broad anyway for her to be hanging out with Ray."

Ray convinced me to see his friend with the Mustang and we met at a vacant parking lot. Martin was an amiable, heavyset construction worker and his car was a bright red '66 fastback with two broad black racing stripes down the middle and chrome reverse rims. Martin had a toolkit with him and proceeded to remove the back seatbelts and the back seat. He undid all the screws to the plastic molding on one side, and when he pulled it away, what I saw made my eyes bug out. Behind the molding was nothing but sweet empty space and lots of it! God knows why the Mustang engineers chose to waste all this space, but I was grateful for it. And it was hard to get to, having taken Martin a good half hour to undo everything. I immediately agreed to do a run. Martin's car was a hot rod, but it was a factory rod, the kind of car a father might buy for his son, while the hot rods that tended to get searched were mostly custom jobs.

We estimated the Mustang would hold about forty bricks. This was little more than half what the Rambler held, but the Mustang seemed many times as safe. Martin wanted five bricks for doing the run, which seemed fair, and

Ray put in that he expected a brick for introducing us.

I said the run should be done on a weekend and Martin said he could only do it Saturday, which meant we should drive down Friday. Ray threw his hands up. "Oh man, I've got a court appearance Friday!" I didn't know he was expecting to come along and gave a secret sigh of relief that he couldn't. I called the Bub and we agreed he didn't need to come either.

On the way down, Martin let me take the wheel along a deserted stretch of the 101 south of Salinas. I couldn't wait to see what it felt like to drive a 390 cc engine capable of cranking out 320 horsepower. He had a Hurst shifter and I went through the gears, then floored the accelerator till we were doing 140. The frame leaned down with perfect stability through the curves while the dashed white lines of the roadway zipped by like bullets. I was keeping a close eye on the rearview mirror and felt my heart sink when I noticed a tiny pinpoint of red light miles behind us. I let off on the gas and we quickly slowed to sixty-five. A highway patrolman eventually caught up to us and pulled us over.

"Geez, what's this thing got in it anyway?" the patrolman asked as he approached. Martin popped the hood and showed him.

The patrolman shook his head. "You know, if you guys hadn't've slowed down, I couldn't have caught up to you. Look at my radiator."

We looked and saw it was boiling over. It turned out the patrolman was a hot rod enthusiast himself and a really nice guy at that.

"Tell you what. I know you were doing at least a hundred and thirty, but I'll write you up for eighty."

The cop left and a short while later, through some kind of automotive commiseration, the Mustang began overheating too. We discovered a leak in one of the hoses, but it was a small leak and all we had to do was remember to add water to the radiator every hundred miles or so.

Night fell as we crossed the border at Tecate and headed to where the grass was buried. It was a dark night with no moon out and hardly anyone on the road. A car with the dome light on appeared heading toward us and we could see two Mexican girls inside. The one on the passenger side was bending down as though searching for something, and right as we passed, she sat up, leaned forward to be seen, and held a liquor bottle toward us, grinning.

"Holy shit! Did you see that?" Martin exclaimed, hitting the brakes. He was all for turning around and catching up to them, but I told him we had a run to do. I felt bad, though, knowing I would never know what those girls were up to and secretly wished I was the kind of guy who could drop what he was doing in order to chase after a couple of chicks.

We dug up the grass and Martin was able to pack forty-two bricks into his car—a little over half our stash. It was now three in the morning. We took a motel room in Tecate, intending to get eight hours' sleep, but Martin was up at dawn, ready to do the run. I coached him on what to say at customs. Somewhere he had learned to pronounce "Tijuana" correctly and I told him to pronounce it "Tee-uh-wanna" like any other gringo.

We drove to Tijuana and Martin dropped me off near the border. I walked across and was escorted into the station, where I had a pleasant, if fictional, conversation with the pipe-smoking lieutenant before being allowed to go on. I walked about a mile up the road, checking to make sure I wasn't being followed, and entered Nelson's Restaurant. No sooner had I sat down than Martin strode in wearing a huge grin. Back in the car, he began shouting football cheers, socking his fist into his palm, laughing, and generally being a complete goof. It was the same hysterical relief I had seen in the secretaries!

"Get this! I pulled up to customs and the guy there was older and looked just like my father. He asked me where I was born and when I said the U.S., he waved me on! It was that easy! Just to make it perfect, I said, 'Do you know where I could get some water? My radiator's been overheating a little.' He pointed to a gas station down the street and I said, 'Thanks,' real friendly-like and smiled and he smiled back!"

I didn't bother telling Martin just how stupid this extra conversation was. I didn't want to ruin his good spirits and anyway, I wasn't even sure I wanted to use him again. I already had other ideas. But if that customs inspector had been a little sharper, he might have wondered why a guy would ask about water when there were no less than three service stations within plain sight of where Martin was idling.

Martin was in a hurry to get home and very apologetically asked if I would mind driving his car back while he caught a plane. Would I mind? Was he really even asking me this? This was like a high school dream come true! I saw myself cruising up the 99 with *Heat Wave* playing at top volume while I stopped at every drive-in between here and Berkeley. I couldn't wait!

We arrived at the San Diego airport and Martin was still so happy and excited that I felt I should go in with him and see him off, a courtesy that proved fatal. As we headed to his gate, who should be heading a mile a minute in the opposite direction but Ray! On seeing us, he skidded to a stop, leaning backward. "Man, I was just about to rent a car and come looking for you guys!" So much for my dream of having Martin's car to myself!

Because Martin was Ray's friend, Ray felt he had more of a right to Martin's car than I did and insisted on doing most of the driving. He first became paranoid around Modesto. We were seated at a diner when he suddenly yanked me up by the arm, saying, "I don't like the vibes here!" Back on the freeway, he hunched over the wheel with his head low, peering down side roads and under overpasses. "Know how I know that isn't a narc car?" he said, pointing to a late-model Buick driven by a man with his wife and kids in the car. "Because of all the chrome and the deluxe hubcaps. Narc cars are always real plain." That night he pulled one of his lose-the-tail routines and we ended up lost in some godforsaken area of Concord. After casting about, we found ourselves on a broad boulevard with block after block of car lots. We needed directions, but it was the middle of the night with no one around. I spotted a police cruiser parked up ahead, and more just to rile Ray than anything, I said, "Pull alongside and let's ask this guy."

"Don't even look at him!"

"What? Just because we ask him for directions, he's going to demand to search the quarter panels?"

"Don't look, I'm telling you!"

Ray stared rigidly ahead as we passed the cop, and about a mile later he swerved into the parking lot of a motel. Before I could stop him, he had jumped out and was headed for the office. There was a night bell and he stabbed it twice. I watched him smooth his hair back with his hands and knew he was preparing his overly polite act that he put on for straights. The door finally opened and a big bear of an older man stood there in his night robe. I watched Ray make little bowing and scraping motions. He was too far away for me to hear him, but the older man's voice rang out loud and clear.

"You mean you woke me up in the middle of the night to ask directions? What, are you some kind of numbskull?"

Ray hurried back to the car with a sheepish look.

"What, are you retarded or something?" the man shouted after him.

Ray got in and fired up the car with the man still yelling at him. I was doubled over in my seat with laughter. It was everything I had wanted to say to Ray all day!

CHAPTER 26

THE BUB AND I NOW HAD THIRTY-SIX BRICKS of stony grass. Everyone kept saying how much higher prices were back east, so Why not go? we asked ourselves. Neither of us had ever been back east, but many of the Cal students I had gotten to know were easterners, and when I sounded them out about the idea, they said, "Do it! You'll make a fortune!" They gave me names and numbers of friends and relatives who would want to buy grass, and before long I had an envelope full of paper scraps with addresses stretching from Des Moines to Boston, about half of them in New York City. Scribbled along with the names and addresses were messages like, "Tell Patty I still love her," and, "Ask Sam whatever happened with that girl he picked up at Bailey's." Our trip was going to be like a giant liaison between the two ends of the continent! I couldn't wait!

We packed our bricks into the quarter panels of the Rambler and on a chilly January day we took off. I looked back at a freeway sign that said, "Berkeley, Next Three Exits," and told the Bub, "When we get there, it'll probably say, 'New York City, Next Forty-seven Exits'!"

We crossed the Sierra and encountered our first setback in Nevada, where we were stunned to find the state covered in snow. Coming from California, we thought of snow as something that only happened in the mountains, never on the desert. Our plan was to avoid motels, and we pulled over onto a snowy field and tried to sleep on the Rambler's reclining seats using the light sleeping bags we had brought but spent half the night shivering. In the morning our lack of sleep lent an ethereal quality to the day that was almost pleasant. The Bub drove while I composed poetry. Upon learning that the entire country was going to be covered in snow, we stopped at an Army Surplus store and bought heavy clothing.

On entering Utah, we were greeted by a thicket of billboards advertising guns. "No waiting period! Anyone over eighteen can buy! Choose from our selection of over 5,000 new and used firearms!" A gun seemed like the perfect thing for New York and we stopped at a gun shop in the first small town, which happened to be filled with gun shops. We told the proprietor we didn't want to pay too much and he pulled out a battered .22 revolver and laid it on the counter for us to inspect. The metal was partly green with corrosion and someone had scratched the initials "D.H." on the frame. Four notches had been carved into the plastic handle, signifying God knew what.

"Are you sure this gun works?"

"Everything we sell has been thoroughly inspected and tested before it's ever put on display."

We told him we'd take it.

"You'll be needing some ammunition for that now, will you, boys?"

We bought fifty rounds.

I asked for a bag to put it in, but the proprietor shook his head.

"You're going to have to take that pistol out of here in plain sight, boys. It's the law."

The Bub drove while I put bullets in the gun, eager to try it out. Soon we were out of town and I rolled down my window, intending to shoot at the first sign we encountered. One came up and I couldn't help but laugh when I saw it was already shot full of holes. I might as well add one more, I thought, and pulled the trigger. There was a report and simultaneously a blast of powder struck me in the temple, nearly hitting my eye. I stared at the gun.

"This thing's a piece of shit."

"That guy saw us coming."

We rolled through Denver, where The Family Dog had recently been busted, and the Bub said it was with our dope. He had sold to someone who sold to them. Then we were in Des Moines, the first stop on our list. We went to the address and found ourselves in front of one of several squat bungalows next to a river. No one seemed to be around. It was eerily quiet save for a skeletal clacking sound coming from the river. I looked and saw that there were willows overhanging the river, and where their branches dipped into the water, they had become gloved in ice and were knocking against each other in the current, thus accounting for the spooky sound.

The bungalow seemed deserted. We peered through a window and saw graffiti on the walls saying things like "Fuck the Establishment" and "The landlady is a fascist pig." A woman bundled in winter clothing approached and asked what we wanted. We told her and she said the people we were looking for didn't live here anymore. She asked us if we wanted to rent the bungalow and we told her no. She eyed our long hair pointedly. "Because for you the rent would be $800 a month." She seemed to want to argue and we left.

Next on our list was Buffalo, New York, and to get there, we found ourselves on a lonely Pennsylvania farm road at night during a fierce blizzard. The snow fell so thick that one of us had to jump out every few miles and wipe snow off our headlights. The side of the road was blotted out by falling snow and we couldn't even see if there were any farmhouses around where we could get help if we got in trouble. No one else was on the road. We had the heater turned to high and the air coming out of it was barely warm. We shivered with cold and worried if the Rambler broke down, we would probably freeze to death. The Bub got the idea to stuff newspapers in front of the radiator and that had the effect of heating up the engine so that the heater now worked. Eventually, we made it to a crossroads service station, where we went in and warmed ourselves by the large potbelly stove there. The proprietor ran a towing service and his radio crackled with emergencies. Abruptly, he jumped in his tow truck and took off without even bothering to close his shop. This back east is dangerous! we told each other.

At dawn we rolled into Buffalo to the sight of Black workers in dark clothing trudging to a soot-black factory surrounded by white snow. Our contact here was a friend of Fred Swaha named Jenner and, unlike most of our contacts who might buy enough for themselves and a few friends, Jenner was an actual dealer, so Fred had said. We called him and he invited us to his place, which turned out to be a second-story flat in an older wooden building along a street lined with leafless elms. We entered his flat and it was like walking into an acid trip. Every square foot of the flat was meticulously and colorfully decorated. Colored parachute cloth billowed from the ceilings and the walls were lined with hundreds of framed photographs, many of Native Americans and the Old West. There were two fringed hammocks in the main room, and tatami mats and brightly colored cushions lay everywhere on the floor. Even the loops at the ends of the pull cords to the shades had been hand-painted with minutely detailed floral designs. "It's because of the weather," Jenner told us with a chagrined look. "We spend so much time indoors compared to you guys out in California. We've got nothing better to do."

He had a friend who wanted a kilo right away and we drove to his home. The friend came to the door dressed in a baggy sweatshirt and carrying a cup of coffee, and by his relaxed and thoughtful manner, I got the impression he might be a professor, but I was way off as I would find out much later. He bought a brick for $200—$75 more than we would have gotten in California. Jenner then told us, "I can see why you wanted to come here with no advance warning. That makes sense. But it takes people a while to get money together."

He said he didn't even have anyone else we could sell to right away. We decided to head up to Rochester and Syracuse, where we had more addresses. The Bub and I both had good feelings about Jenner and fronted him five bricks to sell while we were gone.

In Rochester we sold a brick to three university students who had been busted recently and had strange graffiti written along the stairway to their apartment. One of the scribbled notes had an arrow pointing to their doorway that said, "Dear Narcs, the grass is in there." The Bub and I were leery of these guys and tried to set up a bust-proof drop-off, a subject we had discussed often during long hours on the road. We found a desolate farm road outside town and buried a brick in the snow next to a speed limit sign. The Bub then dropped me off at the guys' apartment, and I rode with them in their car to a place near where the brick was buried and gave them directions how to find it. At this point they were supposed to pay me but discovered they were forty dollars short. I said they could mail it to me and rather reluctantly gave them my address. They let me off and went to get their brick while I waited for the Bub to pick me up as planned. Time went by, though, and he failed to show. I was getting chilled waiting for him and ended up hiking the five miles back to town. I had no idea how the Bub and I were ever going to find each other again, but as I headed to a coffee shop to warm up, the Bub happened to drive by and spotted me. He apologized, saying he had gotten confused and couldn't find our farm road. The three guys never did pay me the forty dollars they owed.

In Syracuse we sold a brick to a fraternity guy who kept getting calls about a party he was throwing later that evening. He didn't think to invite us and didn't even want our number in order to do future business. We went to the campus to grab a snack at the cafeteria there, and a cute coed with curly hair sat down next to us. We told her we had driven here all the way from California, and when she asked why, I ended up telling her—bragging, really. She saw some friends walk in and abruptly got up to go join them at a nearby table. "Watch," I told the Bub. "She'll tell them about us and they'll all turn to look." We watched out of the corners of our eyes, but they never looked.

We drove back to Buffalo, where Jenner surprised us by paying for the five bricks and telling us in his understated way, "I think I can sell the rest of your grass for you." And he did. All in one night, too. This is how we did it: buyers came by at staggered intervals and paid Jenner cash, which he used to pay us where we waited in a separate room, not to be seen. We then gave Jenner however many bricks people were buying. At any given time we kept only six or seven bricks at his place, and when we needed more bricks, we headed out to the Rambler, which we kept parked several blocks away on a side street. When getting bricks out of the quarter panels, we would jack up the car so that anyone seeing us would assume we were changing a flat. By midnight our entire load was sold.

Jenner told us we were welcome to stay at his place as long as we wanted. Two girls were living at his flat as friends and it was fun hanging out with them. I think the Bub could have spent the rest of the winter there, lying in Jenner's hammocks and listening to Grateful Dead albums all day, but after just a few days I grew bored and wanted to head home. Here, the Bub did an amazing thing: he gave his beloved Rambler to Jenner. Jenner was the perfect recipient too, because he viewed the Rambler as a work of art and had commented often on its fine touches, such as the Yes on 14 sticker and the College of Holy Names decal. In return, Jenner insisted on treating us to lunch before we caught a plane home, and for some reason he took us to a Howard Johnson's. This was a straight establishment and upon seeing us with our long hair and the girls wearing beads and all, the maître d' went back to confer with the manager. The result was that they took us upstairs to an empty banquet room where our presence wouldn't offend other patrons. The banquet room was on the second floor and offered a floor-to-ceiling view of Lake Erie with its icy shoreline framed by beautiful snow-draped conifers. Furthermore, the service was excellent—probably because they were eager to get us fed and out of there. And that is how we ended our trip back east: by getting treated like VIPs at a bourgeois Howard Johnson's restaurant!

CHAPTER 27

I SEARCHED THE WANT ADS AND SOON found a fastback Mustang the same make and model as Martin's but that wasn't hot-rodded. I figured this car was going to revolutionize smuggling. Coincidentally, the guy selling it confided that he needed the money to complete his flying lessons so he could fly grass in from Mexico. He even showed me his aeronautical charts with the route he intended to take. A billion-dollar industry was springing up and everyone wanted to get in on it! I was finally learning to keep my mouth shut and didn't let on that I knew anything about grass. Anyway, flying grass back in a plane seemed too grandiose to me at the time. I didn't think his plan had a chance and didn't even bother keeping his number.

For a runner I approached Linda. She seemed eager to do it after I showed her the Mustang and told her how safe I thought it was. The Mustang was metallic green, didn't have a scratch on it, and looked like the kind of car a secretary might buy wanting to look sporty. Currently, the car had Texas plates and I knew I had to register it in California but didn't have any false I.D. at the time. I wrestled with this problem for several days without finding a solution, then went to the DMV one day on impulse and registered it under my own name. I knew this was bad form, but that's how safe I thought the Mustang was.

The Bub and I drove south, picked Linda up at the San Diego airport, and continued on to the desert outside Tijuana, where our grass was buried. We dug it up—only to find that ants had gotten into it, attracted apparently by the slight amount of sugar water used to pack it. They had eaten divots in many of the bricks and loose grass was spilling out. I proceeded to shatter the desert silence with just about every swear word I could think of when Linda came up to me and gently touched my shoulder. "I'm really sorry ants got into your grass, Tom." That made me feel kind of weird, considering she was about to risk a prison sentence for us when all I had lost was a few pounds of grass and some time.

There was no *papelería* in Tecate and we had to drive all the way back to Tijuana to buy construction paper and tape. We came back and set up an assembly line, shaking ants off the bricks, wrapping them in new paper, taping them, and packing them in the Mustang. By the time we were done, it was late afternoon. I wanted Linda to do the run before dark, figuring a single woman after dark might not look as good, but when we went to leave, the Mustang wouldn't start. The Bub and I popped the hood but couldn't find anything wrong. We finally got it started, but it wasn't running right. At the top of a rise, where we could roll-start it if we had to, we stopped and the Bub and I got out and popped the hood again. Again, we couldn't find anything wrong. We conferred, shielded from Linda by the upturned hood. The Bub thought we should go ahead with the run.

"What if they ask her to pop the trunk? She's going to have to turn the engine off and what if it doesn't start again?"

"She could keep the trunk key separate."

"Nobody keeps the trunk key separate."

The Bub shrugged. I said I wanted Linda to spend as little time as possible at customs and the Bub considered.

"You're probably right. That broad's so dingy, no telling what she might tell them."

We needed to get the Mustang repaired and rolled into Tijuana just as storekeepers were pulling down the metal curtains to their shops. Eventually, we found a backyard mechanic willing to work on the car, and I told the Bub to take Linda to a motel down the street and get a room so she could watch TV and get her mind off the run. Meanwhile, I stayed and watched the mechanic work on the Mustang by the light of a grease-printed bulb hung by an extension cord from the upturned hood. Two of the mechanic's friends came by and watched him work and drank beers. Eventually, the mechanic determined that a relay had gone bad and said he might be able to get the part tomorrow, a Sunday, but that he would likely have to wait till Monday. By now it was around eleven p.m.

At the motel, I found the Bub and Linda watching TV. Shortly after I walked in, the Bub discreetly undressed and got into one of the two beds. We hadn't discussed sleeping arrangements and I undressed and got in the other bed. Linda then turned off the TV and turned out the lights, and by little rustling and unzipping sounds, I could tell she was undressing. Moments later she slipped into my bed. I felt her leg press against mine in a way that didn't seem accidental and next thing we were embracing. It was exquisite too, moving ever so slowly and trying not to pant so as not to disturb the Bub.

The mechanic couldn't get the part Sunday and it wasn't until Monday around the middle of the day that the Mustang finally got fixed. I recalled the words of the friendly Tijuana cabbie: "Never spend time in a town where you're going to cross. . . . Just roll into town and do it—bam!" I knew we should drive to Mexicali and do the run there but was eager to get it over with and convinced myself we had done a good job of lying low, so there shouldn't be any trouble.

Linda took the wheel and dropped the Bub and me off just short of the border. We crossed on foot without getting hassled and caught a cab to the Greyhound station in San Diego, where Linda was to meet us after crossing with the Mustang. The cab driver had a transistor radio tuned to a rock and roll station and between songs the DJ happened to announce that today, May fifteenth, was National Law Enforcement Day. The Bub and I exchanged looks in the back seat. What better day to do a run than National Law Enforcement Day!

At the Greyhound station the Bub bought a comic book and I bought a Newsweek and we settled in to wait for Linda. We expected her any time, so when a half hour passed with no sign of her, I began to worry that something had gone wrong.

"Maybe there's a long line at customs."

"On a Monday afternoon?"

The Tijuana cabbie's words began haunting me and I wished we had driven to Mexicali to do the run. The only reason we hadn't was that we didn't feel like driving all the way to Mexicali and back. Sheer laziness! I tried to imagine what might happen if Linda got busted. She would never purposely fink on us, but she was so naive, customs could probably trick her into giving them information. I imagined agents bursting into the station any moment and kept looking around.

It was a typical bus station crowded with weary travelers and sailors toting duffel bags. Two skinny kids were playing pinball at one end, the *Whinkadinkadink!* of the machines adding to the general din. We were the only longhairs in the place. I hadn't shaved and felt disreputable-looking. I began to feel conspicuous and imagined people nudging each other: Hey, check out the two dope smugglers waiting for a run to pull through! I didn't realize how nervous I was until a man in a trench coat strode quickly in and I felt my heart freeze. The man paid no attention to us, though, bought a ticket, and took a seat at the lunch counter. I got up.

"I'm going to the men's room to shave," I told the Bub and grabbed my travel kit.

The men's room was on the basement floor, a large room with white hexagonal tile flooring, a row of urinals, and stalls beyond. Opposite the urinals was a shoeshine stand, where a middle-aged Black man in a blue smock stood, patiently waiting. I shaved, and as I was putting my razor away, the loudspeaker blared the following: "Will all those people not actually in the process of boarding a bus please remain inside the station!" My heart jumped. They've cordoned the place off!

I wheeled around. The shoeshine stand was on an elevated wooden platform about three feet above the floor. Underneath there had to be empty space. I pulled two twenties out of my pocket and thrust them in the shoeshine man's face.

"Man, you gotta hide me! This is all I've got." His answer was bizarre.

"Guys come in all the time axin' me that. I's sorry. I cain't help you."

He was standing with his hands clasped behind his back, regarding me warily. I looked around again. The stalls! They wouldn't bust a guy while he was hanging a shit, I thought desperately and headed for a stall.

"Hey, you in some kind o' trouble, go somewheys else an' hide. I don' wan' no trouble in this heah lavatory!"

I wheeled around again. A man who had just finished urinating stared, keeping a distance from me as he passed. I caught sight of myself in the mirror. My long hair! They'll be looking for a guy with long hair! I rushed back to the shoeshine man.

"Well, at least loan me a pair of scissors!"

"Scissors? What you need a pair o' scissors fo'?"

"To cut my hair!"

"You wan' a haircut, they's a barbershop across the street."

"Yeah, but no one can leave the station!"

"What you talkin' about? You free to go wheyever you want."

Could I have misunderstood? I rushed out and hurried up the steps until I could just peer across the concrete floor and see what was going on. Everything seemed normal. Then it hit me: huge crowds were pressing up against the glass doors leading out to the buses and the management didn't want people spilling into the area where buses were pulling up. That's all the announcement was about. Still, Linda was now over an hour late.

I ran over and found the Bub calmly reading his comic book. I was still in a hyperexcited state. "This run's a bust! Let's get the fuck out of here!"

Alarmed by my tone, the Bub jerked to his feet. "Where are we going to go?"

"Let's catch the first bus out of here. Not here, though—Continental Trailways is just down the street!"

As we headed for the door, I had visions of myself as a fugitive working on a ranch to get by. For some reason I pictured the ranch in Iowa. I had only been there that one time on our trip back east, but it seemed an unlikely place to find a dope smuggler. I envisioned myself tanned and muscular from loading hay all day. I would meet Iowa cowgirls and if they asked about my past, I would just nod vaguely and stare off into the distance to let them know it was something mysterious and heavy, not to be talked about. Oddly, I wasn't that bummed by the prospect of this new life.

We left the station to find the sidewalks mobbed with people getting off work. We tried to hurry, but it was like wading through water. Suddenly there was a girl's voice shouting my name. We wheeled and saw Linda waving to us across the top of the crowds. The Bub and I took one look at each other and hurried on.

"No, wait! Everything's cool!" Linda shouted over people's heads. "They searched the car and didn't find it!"

We slowed just enough to let her catch up to us, each edging away to make it look like she was with the other. Poor thing! She led us to the car, and after walking past it several times to make sure it was cool, we jumped in and took off. Linda leaned forward in the back seat to tell us what had happened.

As soon as she pulled up to customs, she said, agents came running out and took her inside. They wanted to know whose car it was and she told them it was her cousin's. They put her in a holding room, and when she saw them walking out with tools, she thought she was done for.

With her in the holding room were three hips, two guys and a girl. Linda noticed that the girl was crying softly to herself and patted the girl's knee, asking what was wrong. Between sobs, the girl said they had scored a kilo in Tijuana and hid it under the seat of their van and now customs was sure to find it. Linda told her not to feel so bad. "I've got forty kilos hidden in my car. I'm probably going to go to prison."

Upon hearing this, the Bub and I mimed having heart attacks in the front seat. But there was more. Linda thought there might not be telephones in prison and worried what we would think when she didn't show up. So she told the hips if they somehow got out, could they please call me, and proceeded to give them my name and phone number! Thank God customs didn't have a listening device planted in that room! And thank God the hips were either too righteous or didn't think fast enough to give customs my name in the hopes of getting a break. Linda said she spent over an hour in the holding cell. When agents returned and handed her back her keys, she said she nearly blew it by simply standing there in disbelief.

"God, I've never been so scared. I thought sure I was going to prison."

Poor Linda! The Bub and I paid no attention to her. All we could talk about was what a great car we had that it could get tipped off and still make it through customs. We were callous clods. And when Linda asked to be let off at Los Angeles International rather than ride home with us, I actually felt slighted.

*

Back in Berkeley we unpacked the Mustang in the Bub's parents' garage, knowing they were out of town. I heard a cracking sound and said, "What was that?"

"Nothing."

I looked over and saw that the Bub had put a small crack in the plastic molding trying to fit it back in.

"BFD."

"It is a BFD! Customs is trained to notice little details like that. Why would there be a crack there unless someone was messing with it?"

That same afternoon I went to Golden Bear Ford and ordered a new piece of plastic molding. They said they would have to special order it and it was going to take six weeks. Out on the sidewalk, I remembered that Alan Jacques lived nearby. He was a fellow smuggler I had known since junior high and I decided to pay him a visit.

I had never asked him, but I suspected Jacques was born into a criminal environment. In junior high I once saw him riding in a pink Cadillac with two men who looked like gangsters and a woman who looked like a prostitute. In ninth grade he was already shooting heroin. Now he was smuggling grass and had gotten into it well before I did. I sometimes went to him for advice and he enjoyed giving it, treating me like a protégé. He lived with his girlfriend, Cindy, and she was as wholesome-looking and beautiful as a Midwestern cheerleader. How Jacques latched on to her, I often wondered. She looked like the last person to shoot heroin, but I knew Jacques was strung out and wondered if she might be too.

He and Cindy lived on the second floor of an older apartment building overlooking University Avenue. The foyer had that cloying smell that pot leaves when smoked in older wooden buildings. The woodwork was dark and the carpeting on the stairs was worn through to the wood in places. I knocked on Jacques' door and Cindy answered. Alan wasn't in but would be back soon, she told me, and invited me to come in. "He won't be that long and he'd be sorry to miss you." She served me tea and said, "Actually, I'm kind of glad you came by. I was just about to do up. You can tie me off."

Well, that answered that.

I hated needles and was loath to tie her off but didn't want to seem a wimp. I waited while she produced an envelope and shook a horse-sized dose of white powder into a blackened spoon. "This stuff's been stepped on a million times," she said, seeming to read my mind. She cooked up over the stove, then sat down quickly in an overstuffed chair by the window. She handed me a wrinkled tie and said, "Here, quick, tie me off." She had her sleeve rolled up and I tightened the tie around her upper arm and tried to focus on the traffic passing below on University, not to feel faint.

"Tighter!"

I cinched the tie down tighter. Some time passed and I heard her say, "Damn!" I looked down and saw a little pool of wine-colored blood lying in the crook of her elbow, like a rose petal lying on the smooth white of her skin. She had missed.

"Quick! Tie off my other arm."

I moved the tie to her other arm.

"Tighter! Haven't you ever tied someone off before?"

This time she hit and I loosened the tie and she slumped back in the chair and gave a sigh. She was up in moments, though, putting her kit away and cleaning blood off the floor with brisk efficiency. She stepped over to me and put her hand on my shoulder, letting her body rest against mine.

"Do me a favor and don't mention this to Alan, OK, Tom? I know he's been taking hits on the side and I'm just trying to catch up."

After cleaning up, she took me out on their balcony overlooking University and showed me some champagne she and Alan were making. I didn't know you could make champagne in your own home like that.

"Sure, it's easy!" She picked up a bottle. "This one here is going to be grape-fruit-flavored." She hoped they would be done by the time her father came out to visit.

We stepped back inside and she shut the door. "I keep them out there in case the corks pop off. So far none of them have, though."

"Where's your dad coming from?"

"Indianapolis."

"Is that where you're from?"

"Yeah." Her tone was vaguely apologetic.

"We're trying to think of places to take him. We'll take him to Fisherman's Wharf and across the Golden Gate, of course." And as she said this, I had a sudden vision of Alan ducking beneath the girders to cop a fix.

"Does he know you're, like, into drugs?"

She turned to face me. "He knows I've done heroin before if that's what you mean."

I gave a bland look to show I hadn't meant anything and she went on.

"My dad's not your ordinary father. He's really cool. I can tell him anything. When I first told him I was doing heroin, he got all worried and asked if I wouldn't get addicted, but I explained to him I was just chipping every now and then to relax and there was no way I'd get strung out. He has complete confidence in me." In a strangely defiant tone she added, "He's never once tried to interfere with my life."

"Does he have long hair?"

She laughed. "My dad? No, he's really straight-looking. Actually, he's starting to go bald."

"What does he do?"

"Sells plumbing supplies. Most of the time he's at the track, though." She sighed. "As soon as he gets here, I know he's going to want to go straight to Golden Gate Fields."

She had work to do in the kitchen and I took a seat in the living room to wait for Alan. The fact Cindy and Alan were doing heroin seemed exotic and exciting to me, but I knew it wasn't going to end well for them. Suddenly, the door burst open and Alan rushed in, making it halfway across the room before spotting me. He managed a smile. "Tom! Hey, great to see you." He was excusing himself even as he pumped my hand, "Gotta use the can." He was in the bathroom a good five minutes and I never heard the toilet flush. When he came out, he was the picture of relaxation itself, his movements languid, pupils pinned. "So, Tom, what have you been up to? I can't wait to hear."

We talked and as always the conversation turned to smuggling. I told him all about the Mustang, from buying it off a would-be smuggler to Linda's near bust to the crack in the molding. I told him about ordering a new piece of molding at Golden Bear Ford, expecting him to be impressed with my attention to detail.

"Why bother?"

"What do you mean?"

"You ruined that car for running the day you registered it in your own name."

And the moment he said it, I knew it was true.

"Say your runners get busted. You don't think they're going to trace that car back to you? You need to sell it and get another one."

Just then Cindy stepped in. "Alan, can I talk to you for a minute?"

Alan got up and they stepped into the kitchen. I could hear them arguing. Cindy was accusing Alan of holding out on her. Alan was speaking to her in low, placating tones. I got up and quietly let myself out.

CHAPTER 28

I NEEDED A NEW CAR AND A NEW RUNNER as I couldn't ask Linda to do another run, but then everything changed as a result of a chance meeting at the No Name Bar in Sausalito. The Bub had been hanging out with a racing crowd of late and became friends with a race car driver named Rust. I knew Rust because, like so many people in this story, he was in my high school class. The Bub and Rust were having drinks at the No Name one evening when an acquaintance of Rust named Bruce Sutherland happened by. The three of them got to talking and it came out that Bruce was an experienced pilot interested in flying grass into the country from Mexico. The Bub was at my cottage first thing the following morning.

"I told him about our runs and he really wants to meet you."

"What's he like?"

"He's a couple years older than us and has a British accent. He acts really straight, but Rust swears he's cool."

"Sure, bring him by." I still thought plane runs didn't have a chance but felt flattered that an older guy was eager to meet me. At age twenty I already had a field of expertise!

The Bub brought Bruce by, and when I saw him walking up the pathway to my cottage, my heart jumped because he looked so straight. My first thought was Narc! But then no narc would ever dress this straight—or with so much class. He looked like he belonged on a yacht. Or in Playboy. He looked like a Kennedy.

The Bub introduced us and we took seats at my table. Bruce took in my poster of Einstein, my drip candle, and my Grateful Dead albums and broke out in a grin as if to say we came from different worlds but that was no reason we couldn't do business together. I in turn studied him. He was about six feet tall with curly blonde hair and rugged features and was wearing a white shirt

146

with cufflinks, gray wool slacks, and a blue blazer. I offered him coffee and he asked if I had tea. I made him some and he asked if I had cream, which I did. I had never seen anyone drink tea with cream before. He began talking about race cars.

"The Brits used to build some bloody fine racing machines. They've gone downhill, though. It's the fault of the factory workers. They no longer take pride in their work." I was checking out Bruce's accent. It seemed clipped yet casual at the same time—very suave.

The Bub lit a joint and offered it to Bruce, but Bruce declined, slightly wrinkling his nose.

"You don't like grass?" I asked him, taking a hit.

"I wouldn't know. I've never tried it." He was grinning as though he had been through this before.

"Aren't you curious?"

He shook his head. "Not in the slightest."

I hesitated. "You don't think grass is bad for you, do you?"

"Well, isn't it?"

"Whoa, let me get this straight," I laughed. "You think grass is bad for you, and if I've got things right, you're here to talk about flying large quantities of it into the country from Mexico?"

"That's right." And he grinned so wide his gums showed.

The Bub soon left and Bruce and I began talking details. Bruce said he had learned to fly as a teenager in Australia, which is where he was from, though he had modified his accent toward that of a sophisticated Londoner, I later learned. At age twenty he got a job as a bush pilot for a Malaysian construction firm and flew French contractors and engineers into remote jungle strips in Vietnam. "I mean to say, flying's no problem. I've flown all sorts of light planes under just about every conceivable circumstance." He said he had even ditched once, in the Gulf of Siam.

He asked me about my contact and I told him we had done a number of runs with him without getting burned or ripped off. He had never heard of Mazatlan, which surprised me. I got out a map and sat down next to him so we could both see it. I showed him Mazatlan and he in turn traced out the route he would take across the border. He took a pencil and began calculating various costs. "What makes you so sure you can get away with this?" I asked him and he looked up from his figures to shrug.

"What's to stop me?"

"I don't know, but I'm sure the U.S. government has thought of something."

"Well, there's your national defense radar, but with a light plane and flying low to the ground, they'll never pick me up on that—especially with all these mountains around." He used the pencil's eraser to tap the area around Tecate.

"Radar's line-of-sight, you know. And as soon as I cross, I intend to lose myself in the San Diego traffic pattern. Even if they did pick me up, there's so much bloody air traffic around here, they'd never be able to keep track of me."

"You don't really know, though, what sort of methods the government is using to stop people."

"Well, I know how radar works and while it's true I've never smuggled anything from Mexico before, I've done similar sorts of things elsewhere with no problem."

"Really? Where?"

"Well, Europe, for instance."

"Where in Europe?"

"From Holland to Britain."

"What did you smuggle?"

He hesitated. "Jewels."

"Why, is there some sort of duty on jewels coming into England?"

He held his palm up. "Some people hired me to take some jewels across and that's all I'm in a position to tell you. Take my word for it, though, I've done this sort of thing before."

I found myself fascinated by Bruce. He talked of places I had only dreamed of. He mentioned living in Uppsala and Paris, marrying an Asian woman briefly, and said he once owned his own insurance company covering air freight out of Borneo. He talked as though the world was his backyard. Every time there was a break in the conversation, he would go back to his figures. I wondered where all this was going and soon found out.

"There!" He circled a figure with a broad flourish. "Say we bring back a hundred kilos for starters. An investment of eighteen hundred dollars would net ten grand." He expected me to finance the run!

"You don't have money?" I blurted. By the way he was dressed, I had assumed he was rich.

"Well, I do, but it's all tied up right now. I won't be seeing a penny of it for another six months and I don't want to wait that long."

"What's it tied up in?"

"Some real estate in London."

"Can't you borrow against it?"

He shook his head. "It's not that sort of an investment. It's more of a private arrangement, actually. No bank would honor it."

"How come you tied up all your money like that?"

"I didn't intentionally. I simply made some investments that are taking longer to realize than I originally anticipated."

"How about friends? Don't you have friends who could help you out?"

"Shore, I have friends, but they're all flung out over various parts of the world and anyway, I'm not about to tell them what I'm up to."

We went on and on like this. The more Bruce tried to get me to put up the money, the more convinced I became this was all a con.

"We could start out with a smaller amount if you like," he was saying. "Say fifty kilos. I could carry that much in a Piper Cub. That would diminish the cost of the plane rental as well as fuel." He penciled it out. "We could do it for twelve hundred. Shorely you've invested that much in a run before."

"Yes, but I don't even know you."

"Well, I'm not going to run off with the stuff if that's what you're worried about. For one thing, I wouldn't have the slightest clue where to sell it."

"Anyone can sell dope."

He sighed. "If you want, you can come with me when I pick up the plane. I've got to bring the plane back."

"You could return it at a different airport."

He sighed again. "Gawd, you're a bloody suspicious fellow."

"Well, you're a con artist, right? Why don't you just come out and admit it? You're a con artist."

"I'm not." He shook his head and sighed. "I'm not."

CHAPTER 29

BRUCE DROPPED BY MY COTTAGE SEVERAL MORE times to try to convince me to finance a plane run. "Because if you don't, I'm going to have to do a car run to raise capital." It amused me the way he had come here knowing nothing about smuggling and was now throwing out terms like "car run." I figured this was just a ploy to convince me how earnest he was, so when he asked me to tell him all I knew about car runs, I played along with him. "You really ought to get a partner," I told him. "Single guys are pretty likely to get searched." He glanced down and sighed.

"You know, if you would just finance a small plane run, I wouldn't have to go through all this."

A week later Bruce shocked me by saying the car run was all set up and he hoped I would manage the score. His partner and financier was going to be Rust. That surprised me as I remembered Rust as a shy, quiet type. I was even more shocked when I learned what car he was going to use. He was going to use the secretaries' car! The very same secretaries we had used as runners!

"How did you meet them?"

"Through Clint and Harold," he said, naming two guys from my high school class who were now dealers. In a matter of weeks Bruce had met half my crowd and was talking them into things!

For a modest amount plus expenses, I agreed to arrange the score and took the bus all the way to Mazatlan in order to save Bruce money. I had no trouble finding Meche, and he invited me to stay at his home, which I considered an honor. The Bub would be impressed, I thought, and realized I missed him. Meche lived in a small home on an alley near the beach. His wife cooked a meal for us, and that night he led me up a lashed-branch ladder through a square hole up onto the flat roof of his home, where I was to sleep. By the

150

moonlight, I could make out a cot in the middle of the roof and at the far end, stacks of cinder blocks, a pile of rebar, and several sacks of cement.

"With the money I earn from *los negocios*, I am going to build a second story here and rent it out to tourists. It will be like a *casa de huéspedes*. I will find quiet guests and the *señora* will cook meals for them. Rooms go for a lot now: thirty, thirty-five pesos—maybe even more because we are near the beach. I might get forty. Every year the prices go higher. It is because so many of you gringos are coming here." On the word "gringo," he pointed to me and grinned.

"With the money I earn in rent, I will no longer have to do *los negocios*." He was still grinning and suddenly caught himself. "Except with you, Tom. I will always do *los negocios* with you. Whatever you need, I will always get for you. *¿Entiendes?*" He laid two fingers on my chest for emphasis.

"*Sí, entiendo.*" I was grinning too. I didn't care about his slip. He didn't want to be in the grass trade forever and neither did I. By the time he finished his second story, I would be doing something else too, I figured, though I had no idea what. Meanwhile, I was having the time of my life.

The roof was bordered with a row of decorative concrete blocks and we walked over and watched for a long while. The waves shone in the moonlight and we could hear the surf pounding. All around us were the city lights. Nearby, a mariachi band was playing and we could feel the *thump-thump* of the bass through our feet. It all seemed divine.

I looked to the north, where the bourgeois hotels were with their phony bands and menus in English. Straights don't know anything about this country, I thought to myself. They're going to go back home and say things like, "Pedro was the funniest waiter. You wouldn't believe the cute things he said." And of course, Pedro only says them in order to get a good tip and couldn't care less about these straights. They don't know the real Mexico, I thought to myself. I looked around, taking in the low-roofed houses of the *colonia*, the colored lights, and the several street vendors still out in the alleys shouting their wares. This was the real Mexico.

Meche went back down and I went over to the cot—only to find a dog in it. I went to the hole and shouted down. "*Hay un perro en la cama.*"

"*¡Échalo!,*" came the logical response.

I went over and went "Shoo!" a couple of times with no result. I then brought my boot up underneath the cot with a sharp kick and the dog leapt off with a yelp, followed by three fat ticks who scurried to the edge and jumped off after him. I lay down, pulled the thin blanket over me, and fell asleep, rocked by the thumping mariachi beat and listening to the surf.

A short while later, I woke up from getting bitten by *jejenes*, which are like our North American no-see-ums. I jumped up and waved my blanket to scare them off, but of course, they came right back. I tried covering myself completely with the blanket, but then I couldn't breathe. I lifted the blanket just a little to let in air and the *jejenes* got in. Every so often I got a really bad bite and knew it was a *sancudo*, which is a mosquito. Sancudo bites leave welts and tend to last for days and fester. The night dragged on like this, and finally dawn broke and every rooster in the colonia went off and I had gotten almost no sleep. I clambered down the ladder and on seeing me, Meche's wife looked concerned. "*Tiene granos* — He has pimples." I wanted to tell her they weren't pimples, they were bites, but was afraid she might take this as a criticism of their hospitality. After breakfast, I went swimming, and the soothing effect of the warm salt water against my bites felt so good, it almost made the whole experience worthwhile. To the north I could see the bourgeois hotels with their screened windows and beds with clean sheets and thought to myself, maybe the bougies didn't have it so bad after all.

Bruce and Rust arrived, and the score this time took place at a small hotel located at an intersection where five streets met at odd angles. We entered the lobby and two men brought the grass out from behind two potted palms. I determined that the grass was good and Bruce and Rust loaded the sacks into the secretaries' Plymouth. Bruce then slipped behind the wheel, but Rust remained on the sidewalk doing what looked to me at first like an Irish jig. I looked again and realized he was having some sort of paroxysm of nerves. Bruce had to yell at him to get in the car.

The run pulled through—sort of. The secretaries' car's hiding place wasn't very big and the bricks weren't that compact, so that Bruce was only able to pack half the load in the car. In order to get it all across, they would have to run the border twice and decided to take turns driving alone. Bruce went first and pulled up to customs, only to discover that his Australian visa had expired. As a result, he spent the next two hours filling out immigration forms and waiting for them to be processed while the car full of grass baked in ninety-degree heat in the customs parking lot. On hearing this, I thought how my hands probably would have shaken too badly for me to write.

"Weren't you scared?" I asked him.

"Well, I wasn't all that happy about it."

I began to see Bruce was the ultimate "rock," a guy who doesn't rattle no matter the stakes. In fact, he made light of this part of the story. The story for him was that when it came time for Rust to drive the rest of the grass across, Rust chickened out. Bruce figured he had become too well known at customs from his first trip and didn't want to chance a second one, so they came home with only half the grass.

"Gawd, that Rust is a bloody coward! I mean to say, if he had told me in the beginning that he didn't want to do it—or even in the middle of the trip. But to wait till after I had done my share!"

So Bruce was back nearly to square one. The half load he had brought back barely covered expenses. He didn't even pay the secretaries the $300 he had promised them. In his view, Rust owed them the money. He asked me again to finance a plane run, but despite his recent effort, I was still afraid to trust him.

A week passed and I ran into a high school friend named Harold. Harold dealt grass and had a cautious, diplomatic way of speaking. In straight life I'm sure he would have become an administrator. We talked for a while and he said, "By the way, I—uh, might be financing a little venture in the near future."

"The usual?"

"No. Actually, this is more in your line."

"Down south?" I was surprised.

"Yes. In fact, I believe you know the party involved. Bruce Sutherland."

"Bruce Sutherland? He's a con artist!"

"I don't think so."

"Well, maybe not a con artist, but I wouldn't trust him."

"I do. This isn't something I'm doing off the top of my head. I've given it a lot of thought. I've had some long talks with Bruce and I think he's a pretty sincere guy."

I told him about Bruce stiffing the secretaries.

"Bruce told me that story and I can see both sides to it."

"Well, have you fronted him any money yet?"

"As a matter of fact, I have."

So it was a done deal.

Harold wanted me to set up the score. He would pay my expenses in advance as well as a cut of the grass when it got back. At last I was going to see whether Bruce was for real and whether his idea would actually work—and without having to pay for it!

Harold and I flew to Mazatlan, where we learned that the government's annual campaign against marijuana was underway and the entire area around Mazatlan was crawling with federales. This time, Meche said we would have to do the score in the sierra twenty kilometers south of Mazatlan, near a small town called Villa Unión.

Bruce arrived with the rented plane, Harold rented a hatchback car, and the three of us drove to the area around Villa Unión, where we found a dried-up mud flat that would make a perfect landing strip. The score was then set for the following day. In the early morning, we dropped Bruce off at the Mazatlan airport, and Meche, Harold, and I headed toward Villa Unión. On approaching the town, we were dismayed to see a convoy of dark green Army vehicles parked in the plaza and dozens of federales standing around in their dark green uniforms, rifles slung over their shoulders. Harold was driving and seemed shocked and alarmed. To avoid them, we turned off on a dirt side road, and Meche managed to find a way to connect to the dirt road that would lead us to the score.

The road led uphill into the sierra and after a half hour or so, Meche indicated for us to pull over. We got out and a horseman rode up, followed by two campesinos on foot carrying two sacks filled with bricks. The horseman carried a revolver at his belt and had an unfriendly manner. He was having trouble keeping his horse still, which seemed to embarrass him, and he jerked the bit mercilessly. "Is this the way it usually is?" Harold murmured. I wanted to open one of the bricks to check the grass, but the scene seemed so tense that we just stashed them in the back of the hatchback, paid Meche, and took off with Harold driving. Why Harold had rented a hatchback I never asked him, but the sacks now lay behind us for anyone to see, looking in. In an attempt to conceal them, we took our shirts off and laid them on top. Harold and I were now two shirtless gringos with something bulky in the back of our car in an area of the sierra where no tourists go and at any point we could run across federales, who would almost certainly stop us. Harold's body was tensed and he looked as though he wished he had never gotten into this mess. It was one of those experiences you can only endure by looking at yourself from afar, as though this were really happening to someone else.

We made it to the mud flat and minutes later Bruce appeared in the sky and came in and landed. We rushed up and pushed on the wings to turn the plane around, and while Bruce taxied to the far side of the flat, we followed him in the car, jumped out, and turned the plane around again, for a plane should always land and take off into the wind. We loaded the two sacks into the plane and Bruce took off. As we watched him turn into a tiny white speck and disappear, Harold turned to me.

"So this is what you do down here. Well, you can have it!"

CHAPTER 30

BRUCE MADE IT BACK, PROVING HE WAS RIGHT all along about his method, but the grass was no good. We opened brick after brick, only to find immature plants, stems and all, some even with roots and a few with clods or rocks. I felt terrible and apologized profusely to Harold and Bruce. Oddly, Bruce didn't seem that discouraged. He seemed to take adversity in stride. By a laborious manicuring process, Harold found a way to extract a few ounces of reg weed out of these bricks and Bruce rolled up his sleeves and pitched right in. This time when Bruce asked me to finance a plane run, I didn't hesitate. We penciled out a run that would involve a slightly larger plane, a Piper four-seater, which could carry 200 bricks, with the total cost coming to $3,000. This figure was significant for me because it was all the cash I had and also because it was the amount of money my parents had originally given me for my college education. I was thinking of giving it back, which seemed the right thing to do if I didn't go back and get my degree.

After the last score, I wasn't eager to continue dealing with Meche and put the word out that I was looking for a new contact. One of the gamblers in the Bear's Lair put me in touch with a Black smuggler named Darnell Boucher. Darnell met Bruce and me at a café, decided we were cool, and invited us to his home later that evening. He had an apartment in the Berkeley hills with a deck that commanded a view of the bay and all three bridges. Inside, the rooms were carpeted in a thick, white shag. A real zebra hide covered his king-size bed, and on the wall was a poster of Huey Newton seated in a rattan chair. Darnell put on Coltrane and served us San Miguels. He was extremely excited about the possibility of working with us. "I can't tell you how long I've dreamed of doing a plane run. I've been fucking around hiking ten and twenty kilos across the border, and each time I make it, I feel great that I beat the

Man one more time, but you can't get ahead that way. I just know we're going to be doing business together because I've got the contacts and you guys have the method."

He told us about his career as a smuggler. "You guys can't imagine what it's been like getting as far as I've gotten. You guys can move around fairly easily, but me—talk about a sore thumb! I step off a bus and there's a hundred eyes on me. It's not prejudice either. It's just curiosity. You don't see many Blacks in Mexico—at least not in Culiacan. That's where my contacts are. That's the major dealing center in Mexico. You knew that, right?

"It's so weird. I've had little kids come up and touch me to see if I'm real. I'll tell you, though, I've hung around Mexico a lot and I've never encountered prejudice there. The Mexicans are some of my favorite people. They're the gentlest people I know."

I liked Darnell immediately, but Bruce was openly suspicious of him. "These contacts of yours. What sort of ashorances can you give us that they actually exist?" He was flashing his gummy horse trader's grin at him and I winced. Darnell didn't take it badly, though.

"Ask around. I've got a reputation in this town. You're not going to find a single person with a bad thing to say about me."

After some more talk, Bruce seemed reasonably convinced. A tentative run was penciled out and we agreed to meet again in two days. We were about to leave when Darnell said, "Hey, let me show you guys something." He opened a drawer and pulled out a .38 wrapped in an oiled rag. He was just showing it to us in a friendly way, thinking it might impress us I suppose, but Bruce took one look at the gun and appeared horrified. Darnell saw his mistake and quickly put it away, saying, "I just figure it's better to have one and not need it than to need one and not have it." Outside, Bruce told me the deal was off; he didn't want a thing to do with Darnell.

"Why are you Americans so bloody obsessed with guns? In Britain the police don't even carry guns. Your London Bobbies? They don't carry guns—just nightsticks is all. Have you ever read about any of our great train robberies? Fifteen guys subdued an entire train with nothing more than saps. You know what a sap is—just a sock filled with sand. I mean to say, if I thought I needed a gun in this business, I'd get the hell out."

Nothing more came of my attempts to line up a contact stateside and we decided to give Meche one more chance. Maybe he could introduce us to someone higher up. Bruce rented a plane and we took off on a windy day. As I looked down and watched the ground jerk away from us with the gusts, I thought, This is crazy! But at the same time I was eager and excited. Bruce let me take the "stick" as he called the yoke and by the time we reached Mazatlan, I could hold a steady course and make smooth turns.

We landed and as we were chocking the plane, a ruddy-faced American in a ten-gallon hat strode up to Bruce. "Howdy, partner! Just saw you pull in. I've got that twin Cessna over there." He pointed. "Bartlett's my name. Oklahoma's my state. What part of the country do you hail from?"

Bruce stared at him for so long that I was cringing inside. With an overly thick British accent, Bruce then pronounced, "San Diego." The Oklahoman left and we headed into the terminal.

"Bloody Americans! Why are they always coming up to you like that? I mean to say, in Europe you would never see that. A Brit or a Frenchman coming up to you with his hand stuck out? Never in a million years!"

We met with Meche, and when we told him we had a plane, he told us he had always dreamed of flying, so Bruce took him for a ride in the plane. Nothing came of our attempts to deal with him, though. He kept promising he could introduce us to big suppliers, but after four days we had met no one and our plane rental fees were piling up. Our last meeting with him was sad, too. We were at the restaurant La Faena, right across the street from the beach, and it was nighttime and Meche was drunk. I had never even seen him drink before. As Bruce and I walked up, he hollered loudly to the waiter for three more beers. Bruce wanted a soda instead, but Meche refused to order it for him. The beers came and Bruce let his go flat in front of him. "*¡Tómate!*" Meche insisted and told me to interpret. It was a battle between two strong wills. Poor Meche wanted so badly to impress Bruce, but instead he was accomplishing just the opposite. Even though we didn't need them, he ordered three more beers. Then he pulled his pants leg up to show Bruce a dime-sized scar. "*La policía*," he grinned and took another swig off his beer. What followed was a story I could never have imagined.

Meche was originally from Acapulco, he said, and had a wife and two daughters there. One day he found his wife in bed with another man and killed the man. The police came, and as he was fleeing, they shot at him, hitting him in the leg. He managed to get away and came to Mazatlan to start a new life, married again, and raised children who were now grown—all under a name that was not the one he was born with. So Meche had killed a man . . .

We left despite Meche's entreaties that we stay. I left a bill on the table for the beers I knew he could ill afford, and we crossed over to the malecón overlooking the water. I glanced back and Meche was still sitting there with his knees spread, his one pant leg rolled up. The colored lights of La Faena never looked sadder. This was the end of an era, I thought to myself, the era of Meche and the car runs. Well, there was nothing to do but look ahead. We walked on. Behind us I could hear Meche bellowing for the waiter.

CHAPTER 31

WE HAD TO FIND A NEW CONTACT, But how? Early the following morning we stepped out of the Hotel Olas Altas, and before I could stop him, Bruce had hailed a motorcycle-powered contraption with a bench in back for two, a fringed canopy on top, and a sign on the back that read, "El Shrimp Bucket." These were all over Mazatlan and I had avoided them, considering them bourgeois.

"Come on, chap. Don't be so stodgy. These are fun! They have these in Singapore."

Reluctantly, I got in and actually it was kind of fun with the salty breeze whipping our faces. The driver followed the beach road and we passed fishermen tending their boats on the beach, auto mechanics, waiters in restaurants, cab drivers, lone men lounging by the seawall. It was strange having to strike up a contact cold. You saw all these people going about their daily lives and you knew some of them were suppliers or at least had connections. But which ones?

We ate at a health food restaurant, hoping we might find someone interesting there, but no luck. Afterward, we walked around at random, noticing everyone we passed as though sooner or later we might run across someone with *CONTACTO* emblazoned across their shirt. "I reckon it's a little like chasing birds," Bruce commented. "When you purposely go looking for them, you can never get any, yet when you don't want one, you have to beat them off with a stick." "Birds," I had learned, was Bruce's word for girls and ranked right up there with airplanes and money as a favorite topic of conversation. As it turned out, Bruce's comment couldn't have been more prescient, for later that day we took a break to go to the beach and no sooner had we spread our towels out on the sand than a young Mexican approached us offering grass.

He was about my age, stocky, had acne-scarred features, and said his name was Esteban. I asked what kind of quantities he could get us and he shrugged. "Hundreds of kilos if you want." I told him we would need to see the grass first and he said for that we would have to travel to Culiacan. My hopes shot up, recalling that Culiacan was the city Darnell had said was the center for grass dealing. "Are you the owner of the grass?" I asked and Esteban said he was.

We agreed to go to Culiacan and Esteban said we could take the bus together, but I told him we would get there on our own and meet him. I wasn't yet ready to tell him we had a plane. He shrugged and said in that case he would need advance bus fare, round trip. I gave this to him and that same afternoon Bruce and I flew to Culiacan and got a room at the small downtown hotel where Esteban had said we should stay.

I opened the shutters to our hotel room window and leaned out to stare at the busy *avenida* below. Already, I was excited because this town seemed to have the feel of a major dealing center. For one thing, everything was in Spanish. There was none of the sappy advertising for El Shrimp Bucket and Señor Frog's and the like. Tourists didn't come here. People only came here for business and probably half that business was dope. As I was surveying the crowds, a motion caught my eye, and I could have sworn that a man at a far street corner was waving to me, but by the time Bruce came over, the man was gone. "Probably just some chap hailing a cab," was Bruce's guess.

We rented a VW bug, met Esteban that evening as planned, and drove to an outlying colonia to see the grass. Esteban directed us to pull over along a dark, unpaved street next to some small homes and we got out. Four men appeared, two of them carrying boxes, and the boxes were laid down for us to inspect. Inside were bricks and I broke the corner off one to check the quality. *"Mira como chingan los bloques,"* I heard one of the men mutter. "Look how they're fucking up the bricks." Headlights appeared and the men grabbed the boxes and vanished. We jumped in our car and took off. This little scene had accomplished nothing.

I assumed one of those men was the true owner of the grass and offered Esteban a cut for introducing us. He bridled.

"I am the owner of the grass."

"Who were all those men then?"

"My associates."

We spent the next couple of hours haggling. I wanted to see all the grass and have a better chance to check it out before proceeding, but he said we would simply have to trust him. He seemed to be losing interest in the deal and I decided to play what I considered to be our trump card.

"You have probably wondered how we plan to get this grass back to the

States. Well, we have a plane and my companion here is a pilot."

Esteban nodded. "Yes, I more or less imagined that." He seemed bored.

I decided to postpone the question of trust while we searched for a landing strip. The next morning we drove out to the countryside and cast about for a straight, cleared area that would be suitable. Esteban took no interest in the search and complained that we should be paying him for his time. I gave him three hundred-peso notes and he pocketed them, muttering that he could have made twice that much had he stayed in Mazatlan.

We found a dirt road we could use as a strip and it was back to the question of trust again. Esteban wanted us to front him the cost of the grass, but I wanted to pay for it C.O.D. at the strip. He shook his head.

"No one is going to deal with you on those terms."

We were at an impasse. With no clear plan in mind, we agreed to meet again in the morning.

That night Bruce was asleep while I lay awake, worrying about the score. Suddenly there was tapping on our door and the door partly opened. Incredibly, neither of us had thought to lock it. Two heads appeared in the partly opened doorway, one above the other. "*Shhhh*," whispered the higher head, a finger to its lips. "*Somos amigos.*"

I woke Bruce and we threw on our clothes and invited the two men in. They introduced themselves as Jesus and Miguel. They said they were the true owners of the grass we had seen the evening before and by following Esteban, they had been able to find our hotel. They said we should leave the hotel immediately and find another one where Esteban wouldn't be able to find us. I didn't have to be asked twice.

At Jesus's recommendation we checked into the Motel Tres Ríos at the north end of town. On waking the next morning, we found ourselves in a sunlit cottage covered in bougainvillea and surrounded by thick-bladed lawns shaded by palms. There was even a swimming pool. Jesus and Miguel arrived and I got to see them in better light. Jesus had an asymmetrical face with one eye slightly higher than the other, a goofy grin, and big, pointed ears that made you think of the devil, and yet despite all this, he was handsome. He had jet-black hair, a mustache, and looked like the kind of guy who probably had to shave twice a day. Miguel was shorter, broadly built, and had broad lips that curled outward and were the inspiration for his nickname: *El Pato* — The Duck. Both appeared to be in their early twenties. Jesus did most of the talking.

He said we should find a new landing strip, that Esteban might cause trouble with the old one out of revenge for getting cut. The four of us drove out to the countryside and, unlike Esteban, Jesus took a keen interest in finding just the right strip. In a short time we found one much better than the first, a deserted levee road that was near a large reservoir that Bruce could find easily from the air.

The issue of trust came up again that evening. Jesus wanted $1,000 in advance and said we could pay the rest on delivery at the strip. This seemed a reasonable compromise. I had a good feeling about Jesus and Miguel. Both seemed very eager and sincere and impressed me with the way they slowed their speech down and used sign language as needed to make sure I understood everything. I handed Jesus $1,000 in cash and he stared at it as though I had just handed him a turd.

"You don't have pesos?"

"No."

Jesus proceeded to explain that a few months earlier two Americans had bought a half ton of grass here, paying for it with dollars that turned out to be counterfeit. Not wanting to get stuck with them, the suppliers had passed them on to others, who in turn passed them on in a cascade that left so many people burnt that suppliers no longer accepted dollars.

"Let me see those bills," Jesus said. He studied them and a long odyssey followed in which we drove all over the neighborhood so Jesus could show the bills to different friends of his and get their opinions. None of Jesus's friends could find anything wrong with the bills, but none would commit to saying they were good. We ended up next to a trash-filled ravine, where a half dozen men sat on logs drinking beers. Again, Jesus passed my bills around. I got a sudden inspiration, which I struggled to explain in my newly learned Spanish. The bills consisted of hundreds, fifties, and twenties. If they were false, I told Jesus, they would all be of the same denomination because it was hard enough to make up one set of counterfeit plates, let alone three. A light bulb seemed to go on in Jesus's mind and he eagerly explained my reasoning to the men, who all nodded in assent. *"Eres muy inteligente,"* he told me. Back in the car, though, he got second thoughts.

"You are sure these bills are not false?"

"I got them at the bank."

"Because if they are false, I will have to kill you. I will find out where you live and come to your home and kill you."

I laughed. "Don't worry. You won't have to kill me."

Everything was set for the following day. The pickup was to take place at two o'clock in the afternoon. Toward noon Bruce was taking a last look at his aeronautical charts when there was knocking at the door. I opened it and was surprised to see Jesus—he and I were supposed to meet at a café downtown. He looked haggard and hadn't shaved. "What's wrong?" I asked, and he indicated for me to keep calm and have a seat on the bed. He drew up a chair and leaned close. "Tom," he said, calling me by my name for the first time. "I need the other two thousand dollars." My stomach dropped.

"Why?"

"In order to get the rest of the merchandise to the strip."

"But I thought you owned it!"

"I do."

"What do you need more money for, then?"

"Mis socios."

I groaned. It was back to the "associates" again!

I got up and paced around. I felt sick. It seemed like such an obvious burn: now that he had gotten the first $1,000 out of me, I would be that much more likely to throw in the other two.

"Trust me," Jesus was saying, looking me in the eye the whole while. "I know I said I owned the grass, but it's the same as if I owned it. It belongs to a close friend of mine, my *compadre*."

"Why won't he front you the grass then?"

"He just won't."

"Are you sure? Can't you change his mind?"

"Tom, I spent the entire night trying. I got down on my knees and begged him." Jesus proceeded to get down on his knees, demonstrating.

"What about the original $1,000?"

"Gone to pay expenses."

I paced back and forth, trying to analyze my options. I should be tough, I told myself. Either Jesus stuck to our original terms or we would go back to Mazatlan with the remaining $2,000 and try to strike up another contact. I didn't feel up to it, though. The thought of spending hours dropping hints to strangers with a third of our money already gone was depressing. Really there were only two options: pay Jesus the remaining $2,000 or give up and go home. And what then? Give up on the whole idea of smuggling? Go back to school?

I asked Bruce what he thought I should do.

"It's your money, chap. I honestly don't know what to advise you."

I would always remember him for that. He was dying to do this run and stood nothing to lose by encouraging me to risk all, yet he didn't. I stared at Jesus. Something about him made me want to trust him. I pulled the rest of the money out of my boot and handed it to him.

Jesus stuffed the money in his jeans pocket without counting it. "Do not worry. You will not regret this. We now have to hurry. You come with me. Tell the *piloto* to hurry up and get a cab!"

Jesus had a red Ford and I got in and he sped to a café downtown. There he introduced me to an older Colombian and said the Colombian was going to drive me to the strip as it would be dangerous for me to go in the same car as the grass. A moment later, Jesus was gone. The Colombian ordered a soda and I ordered a fresh-squeezed *jugo de naranja.* "There is still plenty of time," the Colombian said, glancing at his watch, and asked me all the usual questions. Where had I learned Spanish? How did I like Mexico? Had I been to Mazatlan? I got sick of answering these questions and told him, "Why don't you just admit this is a burn? There's nothing I can do now anyway. The money's gone. I'll just go home. I won't cause problems." The Colombian looked surprised and said it wasn't a burn.

"Have faith in Jesus," he told me.

I jerked my head up to see if he wasn't trying to make some kind of joke.

For the next hour I was miserable. I wanted so badly for this run to pull through but was afraid to let myself hope. The Colombian looked at his watch again and said it was time to go. We got in his car and he proceeded to drive in the direction of the strip. Once more I tried to get him to admit it was a burn.

"You worry too much," he told me.

He pulled over on a slope to one side of the levee road where Bruce was due to land and we got out and waited in the shade of a tree. The air was hot and still. We heard a faint drone and spotted a white speck in the sky. "*¡Ahí viene!*" cried the Colombian, pointing. Moments later we spotted a cloud of dust headed by Jesus's red Ford speeding toward us! Jesus pulled to a stop right as Bruce was landing. He opened the trunk and there was the grass. A quick check showed it was good. We loaded it onto the plane and Bruce took off. We watched him disappear into the hot, cloudless Mexican sky.

"Everything was difficult this time because it was the first," Jesus said as we walked to his car. "The next run will be easier. I would like to make this a regular thing." He turned to see how I would respond and I laughed out of crazy relief.

"Yes, I would like to make this a regular thing too."

It seemed like such an understatement.

CHAPTER 32

BRUCE MADE IT BACK WITHOUT INCIDENT, the grass sold, and I flew to Culiacan to set up the next run. Jesus and Miguel met me at the airport in a cherry red pickup with red fringe at the tops of the windows and a pair of furred dice hanging from the rearview mirror. They had a collection of tapes they thought I might like: Bob Dylan, The Doors, Creedence Clearwater. Jesus put me up at his home, which was a small adobe affair along a street full of immense potholes in a part of town called Tierra Blanca. I remembered Darnell saying Tierra Blanca was the section of town where most of the suppliers lived. Jesus had a beautiful wife named Alicia, who was thin and lithe and had smooth, walnut-colored skin. She took me out back and showed me where the bathroom was, a small structure next to an adobe wall topped with shards. There was no light switch and she demonstrated turning the bulb in its socket to get light.

Alicia prepared dinner for us and afterward we headed to a small warehouse the grass was stored. The grass was good and we headed toward town. Jesus said his compadre was very interested in meeting me. At last I was going to meet the true owner of the grass! Jesus cut down a side street, pulled over, and sounded the horn, and moments later a man stepped up to the car and introduced himself to me through the car window. He was lean, about five foot eight, boyishly handsome, and had a very gentle and friendly manner about him. "I've been very much looking forward to meeting you," he told me. He said his name was Abelardo. He and Jesus began talking across me, so I moved to get out and let Abelardo take the front seat, but he insisted I stay put and got in the back himself.

Jesus drove around and we checked out the Friday evening crowds downtown. From time to time Jesus would roll down his window in order to have a brief, shouted conversation with a friend. Abelardo handed me a packet of folded jeweler's paper and I opened it to find a large mound of white powder inside. I set it down and pulled out a bill with the intention of rolling it into a straw, but Abelardo asked for the packet back so he could demonstrate. He simply dipped his thumb and forefinger into the powder to get a pinch, snorted it, then rubbed his thumb and finger briskly beneath his nostrils, sniffing, to get the last bit. What a sensuous way to snort! I had never seen anyone snort like this and couldn't wait to show everyone when I got back home.

After snorting, I held the packet for Jesus so he could snort as he drove, and the cocaine came on. It must have been close to pure, for I was flying. "What do you think, *compadre*?" I heard Jesus say. "Should we take him to see *las viejas*?" I scrunched my face in puzzlement. To me, *"las viejas"* meant "the old women." They both laughed.

"O sea, las putas," Jesus offered.

This I understood. I gulped, never having been to a whorehouse before. I remembered Ron once telling about a whorehouse he had visited in Turkey where everyone did it in the same room. He said he ended up next to an Australian who compared notes with him as they were screwing. I didn't know if I was up for this. The only girls I had made love to were girls I had gotten to know and liked and seemed nice. Not wanting to seem unmacho, though, I said, "Sure."

Jesus swung the car around with newfound purpose. Soon we were in an area of closed parts stores and auto repair shops. Jesus pulled over onto a large vacant lot with a row of pine trees at the back, and by turning the steering wheel back and forth as he backed up, he was able to sweep the pine trees with his headlights until he found a break where he could drive through. Now we were on an unlit dirt road. I could see lights ahead, but before we got to them, an officer with a flashlight stopped us and asked to look in the trunk. While Jesus got out and opened it for him, Abelardo said that the officer was only checking to make sure we didn't have a woman in the trunk. Women, he explained, were required to pay a tax to enter this area.

The officer waved us on and we soon came to what looked like a set for a Hollywood Western. It was a broad dirt street a block long and flanked on either side by cantinas with wooden sidewalks and swinging doors. Men caroused in the streets and the whole scene was bathed in colored neon while *ranchero* music blared from every door. We parked and went into a cantina, where Jesus and Abelardo were warmly greeted by the manager, who evidently knew them. Black lights offered the only lighting, suffusing the place with a purple glow. The manager seated us at a table in front of the stage and in a short while trumpets and a drumroll announced the start of the *variedad*. A girl who looked like the young Brigitte Bardot came out and began doing a slow striptease to a bawdy tune that sounded like a Mexican version of "The

Stripper." "¡*Mucha ropa!*" the men shouted. "Too many clothes!" One by one the girl would take off a piece of clothing and toss it into the darkness behind her. Finally she was down to red pasties on her nipples and a red-sequined G-string. The men quit shouting and she lay down on the floor propped on her elbows facing upward, and began thrusting her hips up in time to the music. A hush fell as the men craned their necks to see, their white shirts glowing in the purple light. Gradually the band picked up the pace and the girl thrust her hips faster and faster till they were nearly a blur. Abruptly the music stopped, the girl let out a sensuous moan, the lights went out, and when they came back on again, she was gone.

Other girls appeared and men got up and danced with them or bought them drinks. The manager came over and after conferring briefly with Abelardo, he led us out a back door that opened onto an interior courtyard with rooms on three sides. Cactuses grew in the middle of the courtyard, looking silvery in the moonlight. The manager opened a door to a room and stepped aside so Abelardo could look in, but instead of going in, we went on to the next room and here, even though it looked the same, we went in. The manager left and Jesus and I lounged on the king-size bed while Abelardo took a seat in a chair. A young boy came in with a pitcher of ice water, followed by a waiter who brought a bottle of Old Parr and six tumblers. A three-piece band appeared at the door and took requests. The manager came back, asked if there was anything more we needed, then left after adjusting the door so as to screen us from the musicians' view while still letting in the sound of their music. Moments later, three of the best-looking girls in the house appeared.

We all stood up and Jesus and I made room for them on the bed. They were two brunettes and a blonde. Abelardo poured out shots of Old Parr and when one of the girls said she preferred amaretto, he gave a whistle and had a waiter bring it to her. We all raised our glasses and Abelardo toasted the girls' great beauty. Then he got out the coke. Here he used yet a different procedure for snorting, this time flattening the end of a *cerillo* with his thumbnail in order to fashion a little coke spoon. Another method I couldn't wait to show my friends back home! The girls snorted huge mounds.

Hoping to impress Jesus and Abelardo with my manliness, I began making a play for the blonde, who had beautiful round breasts and full lips. She would coo and bat her eyelashes at me, but every time I tried to touch her, she would remove my hand in a coy way or slip aside. Jesus and Abelardo watched with amused grins. They were acting very formal, I noticed, hurrying to light the girls' cigarettes and not touching them in any way. The coke got passed around again and I took the opportunity to slip my hand inside the blonde's lace bra, but she waved her finger at me.

"*No, chico.* For that, one must go to the other room."

So that's what the first room was about.

"Well, let's go then," I said boldly.

"*Vámonos,*" she said and grabbed her purse.

"What a Casanova!" Jesus laughed. Abelardo grabbed the bottle of Old Parr and said I needed another shot. Under this guise he drew me over and murmured, "Don't pay her. I will take care of it. She would cheat you."

We walked out and three girls across the courtyard turned to look. "*¡O, la la!*" they teased the blonde. "*¡Le tocó el güero!* — She got the white guy! . . . You'll have to tell us what he's like!" That added a little pressure I didn't feel I needed. The blonde paid them no mind.

We went in the other room and the blonde quickly stripped to her bra and panties and went into the bathroom. I undressed and slipped into the bed. I felt ready for action and checked myself a couple of times to make sure I wasn't losing it. The blonde stepped out and paused next to the light switch.

"Light or no light?"

I considered. "Well, not too bright."

She thought a moment, turned off the light, and left the bathroom light on with the door ajar. Then she took off her bra by jerking the clasp around to the front, where she could easily undo it. This was such a rough gesture, it made me think her nipples had no more feeling.

She got in bed, and I had read somewhere that prostitutes didn't like to kiss, so I began playing with her breasts while kissing her neck. She made cooing sounds and pulled away as though the pleasure were too much to bear. Meanwhile, she was trying to crowbar her leg under mine. We wrestled like this for a bit until it struck me that she just wanted me to hurry up and get on top of her and get the whole thing over with. I suddenly lost all heart. I checked and, sure enough, I was having an enthusiasm problem.

I struggled to think of an excuse. I ran the back of my hand across my forehead as though I were about to pass out and told her, "Too much Old Parr. . . . I don't want you to think we North Americans are not strong and powerful."

"Just lie there and relax," she said. "I will make it right." She sat up and kneeled next to me, brushing her hair back. "Promise not to tell the others, though. I'm not supposed to do this. I could get in a lot of trouble if anyone found out."

I grimly promised. This wasn't going to help, I knew. By now I felt totally psyched out. I was wrong, though. The blonde knew what she was doing. She was so good, in fact, that in no time it was all over. She jumped off the bed and began dressing, putting her bra on in reverse order of the same rough way she had taken it off. Now I had a whole new problem: how to avoid going back to the other room too soon. I didn't want Jesus and Abelardo to think I was a lightweight.

I took my time getting dressed and stopped midway to launch into a long story how I was here in Sinaloa to manage a silver mine I owned in the sierra. This was an actual story told to me by a middle-aged American sitting next to me on the flight down, and I was thinking of using it as a cover after doing some research on the subject. Once I got the mine into full production, I told her, I planned to buy a couple more.

Then I thought how creating the impression I had a lot of money wasn't such a good idea and started complaining how silver prices were down now and how hard it was to make a living mining these days. The blonde paid no attention. She was at the vanity, freshening her makeup and yawning.

I stopped bullshitting when I felt enough time had gone by that we could reasonably return to the other room. I finished dressing and moved to the door. The blonde stepped in my way with a coquettish smile.

"You can pay me now."

I told her Abelardo would pay her.

"Oh no. You have to pay me. That is the rule. You were supposed to pay me before, but I let you wait because you were a foreigner and did not know."

I hesitated. "Well, how much do I owe?"

She glanced down, batting her eyelashes. "Whatever you like."

I reached for a hundred-peso note, remembered Abelardo's words, and offered her a fifty. She exploded.

"Fifty pesos? For me? After what I did for you?" She was wagging her finger at me and fire seemed to spit from her eyes. "Listen, *chico*, this is a Catholic country. You don't get a blowjob in a Catholic country for any fifty pesos!"

I was afraid the others would hear and began peeling off bills. She snatched them with a hurt look and we walked out. In the next room she was all smiles again.

To my surprise, the girls soon left and Jesus and Abelardo never did anything with them. Once they were gone, things seemed more relaxed. We talked about the run and whatever else came to mind. We even talked about life and our dreams. Abelardo wanted to buy a ranch and I thought what a wonderful thing it would be to own a ranch in Mexico. Maybe I would buy a ranch too and imagined marrying a beautiful Mexican girl and raising cowboys and cowgirls. I was surprised how much I had in common with these two men whose background and culture were so different from mine. We lay around and talked like that till early morning. Abelardo then sat forward with his palms on his knees, gave a sigh, and turned to Jesus. "Well, *compadre*, what do you think? Are we going to avail ourselves of the pleasures here?" Jesus was red in the face from drink. He lurched to his feet, tossed off one last shot of Old Parr, and went off to have one of the girls. Abelardo never did take part.

While Jesus was gone, Abelardo drew his chair up to where I was sitting on the bed and laid his fingers gently on my knee. "So what are you thinking, Tom? Are you enjoying yourself with us? Do you feel at home with us?"

I told him yes and he held my eye.

"You are sure?"

"Sure."

He nodded, still holding my eye.

"Good. Because that is the most important thing, that you feel at home with us."

My mind was reeling. Here I was with a big Mexican grass supplier and instead of acting hard-assed and macho, all he cared about was that I feel at home with him!

Driving back, I thought to ask him how much the viejas usually charged.

"Thirty or forty pesos. Maybe fifty if you get a blowjob."

CHAPTER 33

JESUS SAID WE HAD TO FIND A NEW landing strip because a large
bust involving gunfire had taken place a half kilometer from our old one and
he was afraid the general area had become hot. Bruce arrived, and the four
of us—Jesus, Abelardo, Bruce, and I—drove out to the countryside to find
another strip. Much of the land here was devoted to sugarcane fields and if I
were ever brought here blindfolded, I would know as soon as we had arrived
from the *flubadubadub* the tires made running over the sugarcane stalks that
had fallen off overladen trucks. Abelardo said the farmers burned their fields
prior to harvesting, and when they did, snakes, rats, toads, and all manner of
wildlife fled across the road, conjuring up a Hieronymus Bosch-like scene in
my mind. When Bruce heard we had visited a whorehouse the night before,
he was instantly jealous.

"Why didn't you tell me, chap? I could have arrived sooner!"

"I didn't know they were going to take me to a whorehouse."

"Well, maybe they'll want to go again. Go ahead, ask them."

"You mean and postpone the run?"

"Shore. Why not?" He broke out in a lecherous grin. I couldn't believe
he wanted to delay the run just to chase after a few whores. He was married, too, having just wed a Pan Am stewardess he had been dating. I told
him they probably wouldn't want to go twice in a row and he screwed his
eyes up at me.

"You wouldn't be holding out on me now, would you, Mr. Jenkins?"

We found a strip a lot like the first one, another levee road with no one
around. We spent an hour or so pulling up tall weeds that could interfere with
the plane's wings and during that time not a soul showed up. Having satisfied
ourselves the place was cool, we left, planning to do the pickup the following

morning.

Dawn broke and Jesus and I drove out to the strip with Miguel following in a car with the grass. On approaching the strip, Jesus hit the brake as he slapped the heel of his palm to his forehead. *"¡Hijo de la chingada madre!"* There next to our secluded strip, an entire village had sprung up overnight!

They were migrant workers, drawn to the area, I supposed, for some sort of harvest. They had tents, wash lines, cook fires—all the workings of an itinerant village. We pulled over and stepped out to get a better look as Miguel came running up to join us. There's no way we can do the run in front of all these people, I thought to myself.

"Can you contact *el piloto*" Jesus asked me.

"He is already in the air!"

"You can't contact him by radio?"

I held my arms out to show I wasn't carrying a concealed radio.

Jesus sucked in air. "Well, we will just have to do it anyway. Do not worry about the people," he then told me. "They are only *campesinos*. They do not know anything. They will be afraid of us. They will think we are the ranch bosses. Anyway, they cannot do anything because they do not have telephones." And he mimed making a call and grinned.

There was a low rise on the side of the strip opposite the camp and we parked the Ford there in an open area, laid a white sheet over the car's roof, and weighted it with rocks—our signal to Bruce that it was OK to land. With my stateside mentality it seemed crazy to conduct a dope deal in front of several hundred witnesses, but here was a whole class of people who didn't seem to count.

Bruce appeared and we watched him circle overhead before entering a landing pattern. The wind was carrying the sound of his plane away from the area and none of the migrant workers seemed to notice him. Then with Bruce only a few kilometers away, an older campesino wheeled his bicycle up onto the levee road, jumped on, and took off with Bruce coming in right at his back! *"¡Híjole!"* cried Jesus.

We began yelling at the campesino to get off and waved our sombreros, but he only stared at us with a puzzled look and kept on pedaling. It was Jesus's idea to throw rocks at him. You would be amazed how much fun it is to throw rocks at someone when you know it's for their own good! We threw with all our might. The rocks made little puffs of dust all around the campesino, but this only made him pedal all the faster, right into Bruce's path. By now the entire village had dropped what they were doing in order to stare at the strange spectacle of three men throwing rocks at a poor campesino. A moment later Bruce dropped down right in front of him, clearing the campesino's head by about a foot. The campesino's sombrero flew off and in a belated effort he swerved his bicycle off the levee road and crashed. We ran up to the plane and hurried to turn it around. Bruce stepped out and when I told him he had cleared the campesino's head by barely a foot, he simply grinned.

"Did I? Quite frankly, chap, I couldn't have given fuck-all if I hit him. I wasn't in the mood to execute a missed approach."

*

And so began the plane runs. Bruce's most important principle, which he repeated many times over, was to stay as aboveboard as possible. Accordingly, he always filed flight plans—even for crossing the border. Here is how we did the first runs: Bruce would rent a Piper Cub in northern California and remove the passenger seats before flying to Culiacan. Sometimes I would go with him and other times I would take a commercial flight in advance in order to evaluate a new load of grass. The score would usually take place the day after Bruce arrived in Culiacan. Bruce would file a flight plan from Culiacan to Hermosillo, but on the way he would make an unscheduled landing at whatever deserted strip we were using to pick up the grass. At Hermosillo, where he had to clear outbound customs, he would park the plane at the far end of the airport, counting on the usual ninety-degree heat coupled with the laziness of the officials there not to get searched. As further insurance, he always made sure to give the head official a generous tip. "You should see him," Bruce told me. "He's my pal. He sees me coming and his whole face lights up."

At Hermosillo he would file a flight plan for San Diego and would underestimate his cruising speed, which would give him a later ETA. On crossing the border, he would fly low to the ground in order to get lost on radar and make an unscheduled landing at a deserted crop duster strip between Ramona and Escondido, where he would unload the grass and hide it in bushes. After clearing customs at San Diego and refueling, he would return to the strip, recover the grass, and fly it to the Bay Area.

This was the initial plan, which we refined with each run. As with the car runs, it seemed we were often just one step ahead of the authorities. On the second run, the pickup got delayed till one in the afternoon and Bruce was only able to make it as far as Ciudad Obregón before stopping to spend the night. As he was tying down the plane, a gun-toting Mexican official came up, pointed to the half dozen suitcases plainly visible inside, and demanded to search the plane. Bruce calmly explained that he was not required to clear outbound customs until Hermosillo. When the official persisted, Bruce grew furious, threatened to report him for abusing his position, and walked off in the direction of the terminal, leaving the official red-faced and sputtering.

When Bruce first told me this story, I thought he had somehow come up with the one act that could get him out of a desperate situation. But as I got to know him, I came to realize it was no act. Bruce actually saw himself as a member of a privileged class and had little tolerance for "petty officials" as he called them. Following this incident, we made sure the scores took place early in the morning so that Bruce would have plenty of time to make it to Hermosillo without stopping.

Hermosillo was an obvious weak point in our operation. To assume the officials there would never go out to look at the plane entailed considerable risk. The only solution here seemed for Bruce to make an unscheduled landing on the desert outside Hermosillo, unload the grass, go in with a clean plane to clear outbound customs, then fly back to the desert to reload the grass. By now we were using a Cherokee Six and carrying 500 pounds at a time. Bruce wasn't at all keen on having to unload and reload all that grass in sweltering heat, but we couldn't think of a way around it. "Oh well," he grinned. "I guess I'll just have to take a course at Vic Tanny's." On the very next run, Bruce found that his "pal" had been replaced by a hard-nosed inspector who declined Bruce's offer of a tip and insisted on going out to examine the plane.

Bruce's job of unloading and reloading the grass, which he now had to do both in Mexico and in the U.S., was complicated by the cheap suitcases Jesus was providing to hold the bricks. These were flimsy plastic affairs with a picture of the Mazatlan-La Paz ferry on the front, and the handles would often break off, so that Bruce would then have to lift them up by their bottoms. Sometimes when the handles broke off, they would take a big section of plastic with them and bricks would fall out. On my next trip to Culiacan I told Jesus about this problem and he invited me to come with him to the luggage shop. On the way we stopped at a *papelería*, where Jesus bought several hundred sheets of blue construction paper for wrapping bricks. The proprietor had this paper on hand, already cut to size, and sold it without so much as a wink or a grin. At the luggage shop the proprietor said he could get better suitcases but they would cost nearly five times as much and he would have to special order them. I decided we should stick to the suitcases we were using and Jesus bought twenty of them. To get them, the proprietor opened the door to a back room where I noticed literally hundreds of the same suitcases stacked floor to ceiling against the far wall. So we weren't the only ones using them! It amused me the way these small shops had adapted themselves to the dope trade. If the narcs had any smarts, they would stake out these two shops and soon know every supplier in town!

Another weak point in the run involved the crop duster strip, where Bruce was leaving the grass unattended in bushes. Harold had a van and for $3,000 a run he agreed to meet Bruce at the strip to pick up the load and transport it to Berkeley, where he would turn the van over to me and I would take the load to a rented garage. At any given time I usually had one or two garages rented and was always on the lookout for new ones as I didn't want to use the same garage for more than a couple of runs. I tried to pick garages in good neighborhoods where there was little crime, and I especially liked garages that were behind houses or at least set back from the street. In each garage I kept a can of Lysol spray, which I used liberally to keep down the smell of the bricks. For one of these runs I was using a garage on a property Bill Gretsch owned and he called to tell me he thought someone had tried to break in. I drove straight there and, sure enough, there were marks on my lock where it looked as though someone had tried to use a hacksaw on it. I immediately moved the load to a different garage.

Yet another issue involved flying to Culiacan. There, our rental plane stood out with its U.S. registration number that started with "N" while all the other planes' registrations started with "X" for Mexico. Mazatlan was a tourist destination where there was no end of planes whose registrations began with "N" and we decided Bruce should land there and avoid the Culiacan airport altogether.

Changing our dollars into pesos was another problem we had to resolve. For the second run we went from bank to bank in Mazatlan buying pesos, but this was time-consuming and risked attracting attention. Upon investigating, I learned there was a currency exchange house in San Francisco called Deak & Company where for a modest discount we could get all the pesos we needed.

CHAPTER 34

BRUCE AND I SPENT A LOT OF TIME together in the course of these runs. I was in awe of him because he was the most self-assured person I had ever met. He no sooner cared what others thought of him than I cared what kind of impression I might make on a dog. In fact, he seemed to treat people almost as if he were a different, superior species. People sensed this quality about him and were attracted to him, often approaching him, especially at airports. One of his techniques for getting rid of them was to pronounce the word "yes" to a question where it made no sense. Someone might come up and ask where he was from and after studying the person for a long moment, he would say, "Ye-es," drawing it out in such a way as to suggest they may have made some terrible faux pas. Other times he would simply walk away from them. I felt bad for these just snubbed people and would try to make conversation with them, but it was Bruce they wanted and they often walked away from me in turn.

Bruce believed we should treat ourselves well during these runs and taught me how to feel at home in fine restaurants. He taught me the order in which to use the array of silverware set before us and turned me on to drinking Rémy Martin at the end of a meal. The first time he suggested this was at an elegant restaurant in Hermosillo. The cognac came and he showed me how to warm it by holding the snifter in my palms as I inhaled the aroma. We took sips and I commented on how good it was, but he set his down and said, "Well, chap, I don't know what this is, but it's not Rémy Martin, I can tell you that."

He told me to call the waiter over but I refused, paling at the thought of creating a scene in an establishment where I already felt out of place. He then called the waiter over himself and used the little Spanish he knew along with sign language to get his point across. I felt sure the waiter would take offense, but he was courteous and soon returned with an unopened bottle of Rémy Martin, which he showed to Bruce before opening it. He then poured it into fresh snifters and waited for our approval. Sure enough, it was worlds better.

"You see, chap? There is a difference. This here is the real thing."

I learned about Bruce's childhood one run as we were flying south over Baja. I was in the back of the plane, dozing on the floor where the seats had been removed, and suddenly felt a strong jolt. I rubbed my eyes and sat up. Bruce glanced back with an abashed look. "Sorry about that, chap. We must have hit a pocket of turbulence." I looked out at a clear, blue sky and felt the plane running as smoothly as if it were standing still. There was no turbulence. Bruce must have pushed the yoke in on purpose, I realized, just to roust me. Figuring he might want company, I clambered into the copilot's seat.

He told me his father was extremely wealthy, a millionaire many times over—in pounds, he made a point of stressing. He was an attorney and also owned an advertising firm but had made most of his money in land speculation, taking advantage of powerful political connections he had cultivated. As a child, Bruce rode horses, played polo, raced sailboats, and learned to fly planes. He and his father didn't get along, though, and when Bruce was seventeen, they had a violent argument and Bruce left home. Since then he had roamed about, spending time in London, Paris, Singapore, Hong Kong, Brunei, Bombay, Uppsala, Madrid, New York, Sausalito, and Mill Valley. He occasionally exchanged letters with his mother and also his brother, who was the Australian ambassador to Yugoslavia, but never with his father.

"Do you think you'll ever go back and see him?" I asked and he considered.

"Not unless it was in a chauffeur-driven limousine and wearing an eight-hundred-dollar bloody suit with money dripping out of every pocket. That's about the only thing that would impress the old bugger."

In Mazatlan, Bruce and I generally stayed at the Hotel Olas Altas and took meals in the restaurant there, which was on the first floor and looked out over the sea. On one particular run we were enjoying lunch and overheard an American businessman at a nearby table trying to get his buddy to go visit a whorehouse. His buddy begged off, saying he was going to be home the next day and that his wife liked him to have a good, stiff hard-on when he got back. Bruce got the biggest kick out of this conversation.

"Say, chap, that's what we ought to do. Come on, now, you've got no excuse this time."

So we hailed a cab and the driver took us to a building he said was a brothel and dropped us off. The building was made of adobe and had two stories with an arched entryway that opened onto an interior courtyard. We wandered in past a wrought-iron gate and looked up at the interior balconies that ran the full length of each side. No one seemed to be around. We wandered up a set of stairs onto the balcony, which offered a view of a poor part of town and the ocean beyond. Presently, a woman appeared. She looked about thirty and wore casual clothing. She asked if she could help us and I explained why we were here, feeling rather embarrassed because I was beginning to think the cab driver had misled us and this wasn't a brothel at all. The woman explained that it was indeed a brothel, but that it was closed today because of elections. I interpreted for Bruce and he cursed our rotten luck. The woman sympathized, saying she knew how it felt when you had your heart set on something. She remained standing very close to us despite the fact we were total strangers, and anyone observing the scene would probably have imagined we were friends. She didn't tell us we had to leave and made no move to leave herself. Instead, she rested her arm on the balcony railing and stared out over the town as though this was precisely what she had come out to do.

I took a second look at her. She wasn't the type who immediately struck you as beautiful, yet the more I looked, the more I liked what I saw. She had long black hair and smooth brown skin and wasn't wearing any rings. I turned to Bruce, gave a faint nod in her direction, and held my palms up questioningly. He nodded yes and broke into a lecherous grin. So I asked her if she wanted to help us out herself, but she laughed and said no, that she wasn't one of the girls. And then she stayed right there and didn't even edge away from us. Bruce and I stayed too, enjoying the view and chatting with her from time to time. We were three people, each with our own needs, finding solace in the afternoon.

*

Another run was coming up and I went to change money at Deak & Company in San Francisco. I parked, and as I was walking to their office, I happened to run into a dealer named Postman Joe. He used to be a mail carrier and had started out selling lids, which he carried in his large leather mail pouch. "I'd like to see them try to touch the federal mail!" he was fond of saying. Now he had quit the post office and was selling kilos. He turned me on to some high-quality grass he had just acquired, and I got so stoned, I had trouble gathering the courage to walk into the staid offices of Deak & Co. There, the teller counted out my pesos so rapidly that I lost all track of the sum but was too self-conscious and paranoid to ask her to recount it. I just grabbed the stack of pesos and left. It wasn't until Bruce and I reached Mazatlan that I finally got around to counting them and discovered there were 4,000 pesos too many!

"Deak & Co. is fronting money in our run!" I told Bruce.

Deak & Co.'s mistake allowed us to buy that much more grass, and when I got back home there was a letter waiting for me, noting the mistake and asking me to please return the money. I did so and got a second letter telling me what an "upright and honest citizen" I was! On the next run, Jesus told us we could pay him in dollars and in fact, he now preferred it that way.

With each run the loads grew larger and I had to concentrate on customers who would buy large quantities. One by one I began dropping people who wanted only one or two bricks. I hung on to the mechanics at the UC Garage for a long time out of loyalty but finally gave up on them because of the grief they caused me. One of them, named Lonnie, would express amazement on finding himself ten or fifteen dollars short every time I sold him a brick. "I'll pay you tomorrow," he would tell me but never did. Another told me to meet him at his apartment and he would pay me for two bricks. I went to the address he gave and a total stranger answered the door and said, "Oh, you must be the connection. Here's the bread."

My biggest customer was Thorpe. He would buy several suitcases at a time and paid cash. He was also fronting money in our runs in return for double his money back. Bruce and I accepted a lot of front money for these runs as a form of insurance. If a run went bad, at least our losses wouldn't be that great. Our overall return on the grass wasn't that much, so paying back double on front money ate up a fair portion of our profits. None of those early runs ever did go bad, and if we had had the guts to invest more of our own money, we would have made much more than we did.

Another good customer was Postman Joe. As with Thorpe, he was now buying suitcases at a time. I enjoyed dealing with him because he was extremely enthusiastic and upbeat, making friends wherever he went. People who met him for the first time assumed he was on speed. He later tried to get into smuggling himself and spent three months waiting for a deal to pull through in the tiny coastal village of Manzanillo. Nothing came of it, but he returned with a priceless photo of himself and the Manzanillo chief of police, both grinning and holding beers while Postman Joe held the chief's own .45 to the chief's head.

My newest customer was Wade Maddox, introduced to me by Fred Swaha. Wade was over six feet tall with broad shoulders and muscles thick as hawsers that he came by honestly, for he used to work as a choke setter in the Northwest. More recently he had studied to be a civil engineer. He was very excited about the plane runs but declined to front money in them at first. "The way I look at it, any dope deal has a fifty-fifty chance at best," he told me. He saw Thorpe turn $5,000 into $10,000 on one of our runs and fronted money in every run that followed.

Jenner was another good customer who paid high prices, both because he could sell grass for so much more back east and because I was shipping the grass to him at my risk. The first time I shipped to him, I went to a thrift shop near my cottage and bought an old suitcase for twenty-five cents. The key to the suitcase had long since been lost, but the shop owner said I could get a replacement key for it at any locksmith and he was right. I wrapped nine bricks several times in plastic, placed them in the suitcase, sprayed them with Lysol, locked the suitcase with my newly acquired key, took it down to the Oakland Greyhound station, and sent it via Package Express. The bricks arrived without incident and a week later I got a letter from Jenner with an $1,800 money order inside.

I began sending Jenner larger and larger amounts. The local thrift store soon ran out of suitcases and I went to the mammoth St. Vincent de Paul store on San Pablo Avenue in Oakland, where they had a mountain of used suitcases. By now I had acquired seven keys that fit the majority of these old suitcases and would pick only those for which one of my keys worked. Most of the suitcases cost fifty cents, sometimes seventy-five. Occasionally I would see one priced at a dollar and would reject it as a gross rip-off.

At the other end, Jenner was breaking the suitcases open with a pry bar. This disturbed my sense of thrift and I told him he should get a set of keys like mine and even offered to send him a set. However, he said the breaking open of the suitcases had become a ritual he and his friends performed with candles and incense and they didn't want to give it up.

At the Greyhound station you had to declare what you were sending and I would put down clothes and textbooks. Clothes weighed less than grass per volume and books weighed more, so that some combination of the two would be consistent with the suitcase's weight. In order that no one remember me, I rotated among various Greyhound stations in the Bay Area. At the Richmond station one time, the clerk placed my suitcase up on a rack without weighing it and handed me the form to sign. I looked at the form and saw he had put "32" for the number of pounds the suitcase weighed. I was sending Jenner twenty-two pounds of grass and thought to myself, How could a small suitcase weigh ten pounds? I had a policy of saying as little as possible during these encounters but couldn't resist. "How do you know how much it weighs if you didn't weigh it?"

The clerk took the suitcase back down off the rack and hefted it a couple of times. "Yeah, I think thirty-two is right. Tell you what, I'll bet you five bucks it weighs within a pound of thirty-two pounds." I chortled to myself. How often does a person know the exact weight of the contents of their suitcase?

"You're on!"

The clerk placed the suitcase on the scale, stepping aside so I could see, and it weighed just short of thirty-two pounds.

"When you've been doing this as long as I have, you get pretty good at it," he grinned as he accepted my five bucks. Later I recalled buying a suitcase with steel reinforcement in the top and bottom and figured that must have

179

been the one.

Jesus and Abelardo had come to trust me deeply. The only limit to the size of these early runs was money to buy the grass, and Jesus helped us by fronting grass in addition to the quantity we were able to pay for. In return, we paid him back double for the portion that was fronted. On a typical run I would meet Jesus in Culiacan and pay him for the grass he had fronted on the last run along with a partial payment toward the run coming up. Bruce would then bring the rest of the money with him on the plane to be paid C.O.D. at the pickup. Money became such a relaxed issue between us that one time we forgot all about it. We had finished loading the plane and Abelardo, Jesus, Miguel, and I were all watching Bruce disappear into the sky when Jesus slapped his palm to his forehead. *"¡El dinero!"* It was still in Bruce's pocket!

We laughed and I told Jesus, "Whatever happens to this run—even if it gets busted—I owe you nine thousand dollars. I have that much at home and will go get it now and bring it back to you." Jesus offered to have Miguel drive me to the border and wait there while I got the money and provided us with a late-model Ford.

This was my first trip up Highway 15 since the car-running days and all along the route I recognized old familiar landmarks. I thought about the many times the Bub and I had traveled this highway and realized I kind of missed those days. I hardly saw the Bub anymore. By turning me on to Bruce, he had unwittingly brought an end to our partnership. After each run I always offered him bricks at a special price, but he never bought more than a few. Another person might have made a fortune buying at the prices I offered him, but he didn't have the mentality for dealing quantity.

Miguel tossed his beer bottle out the window and we heard it land with a crash. Both sides of the highway, I noticed, were littered with cans and shards glittering in the sunlight. Miguel turned to me, abashed. "We Mexicans are real pigs," he grinned.

Before this trip I had thought of Miguel as just a hired hand, but he turned out to be a really sweet guy. Every time he spoke of Jesus and Abelardo, it was with an affection that bordered on reverence. He was always striving to please the people around him and helped me with my Spanish. He taught me *caló*, which is the form of slang used by the Mexican underworld. Grass was *mota*, which I already knew, but could also be *mostaza* or *mostacita*, and the people who dealt it were *paquetones*. He even helped me perfect my accent, repeating words over and over for me until I got them just right.

In Los Mochis we stopped for lunch, and as we walked to the restaurant, a little kid ran up and offered to watch our car for five pesos. Miguel waved him away but the kid persisted, saying there were bad kids in the neighborhood who would scratch our car. Miguel wheeled on the kid. *"¡Pobre el que lo raye!* — Pity the person who scratches it!" We walked on and Miguel was in mid-sentence when he suddenly snapped his fingers, shook his head ruefully, and went back and paid the kid his five pesos. It amused me the way this six-year-old kid was able to extort money from a *paquetón!*

Miguel's sweetness was especially endearing considering the impression most people probably have of Mexican suppliers as hard-assed and macho. At the restaurant he confided that another American he and Jesus were supplying had stiffed them for $20,000. After putting them off for several months, the American had finally admitted he didn't have the money and said he had spent it on chemotherapy for his mother. While I was thinking, chemotherapy for his mother—that's a good one, a pained look crossed Miguel's face.

"Everyone knows one's mother comes first, but why didn't he simply tell us in the first place?"

He pulled out a worn black-and-white photograph and showed it to me. It was of a little African girl. He was sending her money every month so she could eat and in return she sent him letters. He had found her by responding to an ad at the back of a magazine.

We reached Tijuana, and I walked across the border without incident, flew home, got $9,000 in cash out of a hiding place in my cottage, flew back, walked back across the border to meet Miguel in Tijuana, and gave him the $9,000. With a warm *abrazo* we parted and when I walked back across the border, this time I got hassled. A heavyset inspector was watching the line and stepped forward to block my path. "Say, didn't you cross here just a few hours ago?" He pat-searched me and found my airline tickets, which I had foolishly forgotten to leave stateside. After studying them, he told me, "You're coming inside!"

He led me to the desk of our old friend, the pipe-smoking lieutenant, whom I hadn't seen since the car-running days. The lieutenant recognized me, smiled, leaned back, and lit his pipe. Reading from my airline tickets, the inspector told him, "This guy was just through here earlier this morning. At ten oh five he flew from San Diego to San Francisco, at two fifteen he flew from San Francisco back to San Diego, and now he's here again and he's got another flight back to San Francisco in an hour!" He handed my tickets to the lieutenant.

The lieutenant studied them and began questioning me. Possibly because I had been picking up traits from Bruce, I snapped at him after only a few questions. He held his palms up.

"We're not accusing you of anything, you understand. We're just trying to establish a reasonable explanation for your actions. . . . Now, why did you fly back to San Diego after you had just been there?"

"I lost something in Tijuana."

"What did you lose?"

"My wallet."

Here the heavyset inspector snorted, pointedly taking in my long hair and beat clothes. "Looks to me like he lost his identity!"

It was a good joke.

CHAPTER 35

I WAS SPENDING A LOT OF TIME with Jesus in Culiacan. I wanted to make sure he got us the best grass possible and would go with him to see different lots that were available. With the profits from these runs, he had bought a new home along one of the few paved streets in Tierra Blanca and it had an extra bedroom where I could stay. He would come and go, feeling no obligation to entertain me, which was great because I didn't want him to feel burdened in any way. He had bought five or six used cars, which he rented as taxis, and for drivers, he hired his friends. At the end of the day, they would drop by to settle accounts. The cars were always breaking down and Jesus spent much of his time working on them, which is what he liked to do anyway, having been an auto mechanic before getting into the grass trade. I often went with him when he had to go into town to buy parts, and every couple of blocks he would pull over to chat with friends he spotted on the street. I thought he must be the most popular guy in town. There were other stops too. He might spot a *camarones* vendor and stop to get fresh shrimp, and because of the heat, we often stopped to get cool *horchatas*, so that a simple chore like getting a distributor cap often turned into a half-day odyssey.

While Jesus worked on his taxis, visitors streamed through all day, giving his home the feel of a continuous party. Some were neighbors, some were drivers, and some had obscure purposes I never learned. Jesus treated them all the same, which meant if they wanted to talk to him while he was underneath a car, they could, or if they wanted to hang out in his air-conditioned home, that was fine too. While Jesus struggled with some obstinate part of a car, we stood around and ate the chili-covered pineapple rounds Alicia brought out to us. From time to time Jesus would take a break and sink into one of the plastic lawn chairs on his concrete porch at which point his young daughters would rush up and pester him by jumping on his lap and pulling his mustache, which he tolerated with an amused look.

Real parties took place at his home too, usually to celebrate the birthday of one of his four kids. Jesus had me stand on his roof and pull a piñata up and down through a pulley while blindfolded kids tried to swat it. I got a kick out of watching them try to beat the heck out of their favorite animals. Often the kids would end up directly beneath the piñata and I loved dropping it on their heads.

At times Jesus would disappear for the entire day and I would pass the time taking long walks through Tierra Blanca. During the middle of the day, the temperature often reached 110 degrees. My jeans would feel as though I had been sitting next to a hot campfire and I learned to walk with an economy of movement that minimized their contact with the skin of my legs. It was a trip, too, walking through Tierra Blanca with my fair skin and blue eyes, knowing that everyone who saw me knew exactly what I was doing there. In all the time I spent there, I never saw another gringo.

Alicia was eager to talk and I spent a lot of time with her. She was a fine woman, beautiful and very intelligent, but spent a lot of time complaining about Jesus. She knew he frequented the brothels and kept a mistress on the other side of town. In seventh grade, Jesus once told me, he fell in love with two girls and ended up marrying one and keeping the other as a mistress. One night while I was there, Jesus never came home. "Maybe he got drunk and fell asleep in his car," I offered, but Alicia shook her head, staring off.

"He is like Marcello Mastroianni. He never sleeps alone."

Alicia and I grew quite close and eventually sparks began to fly. This amused Jesus. "Whenever we have an argument," he told me, "she goes to my address book and copies down your number." He felt comfortable telling me this knowing I would never do anything to compromise him.

One day Alicia came to me holding a bottle of shampoo I had left in the shower. "Is this yours?" she asked in disbelief. "You? A man? Using shampoo?" Guys only used soap in her world. As she stood there confronting me with the bottle, I realized she was having trouble looking me in the eye, as though she had just discovered I was queer. What if she knew I had once tried crème rinse? I thought to myself. I figured I had lost big macho points in her eyes, but the next trip down I saw that exact same brand of shampoo sitting on Jesus's dresser. Alicia had bought it for him.

A chronic argument between Jesus and me involved the sugar water he was using to pack the grass into bricks. I had gotten him to use less and less, but he refused to eliminate it entirely, saying the bricks would fall apart if he didn't use a little sugar water to get the grass to hold together. I told him customers were getting very leery of sugared bricks. Often before buying, they would pull out a magnifying glass, and if they saw so much as a single sugar crystal, the price would drop ten dollars a pound. Jesus grew exasperated.

"Do you want to pack it yourself then?"

"Sure."

"Bueno!" he grinned. "I can play cards all night."

Jesus moved the grass to his mother's house, which he said was safe. His mother was a thin, ancient-appearing widow who wore black and wandered through her empty home like a sorrowful ghost. I worried a little what she thought of us packing grass in her house, but the only clue she gave me was a brief smile halfway through the night. We used a tack room at the back and to help me, Jesus commandeered his younger brother, Pablo, and Miguel. I think Pablo must have had a date planned for that night, for he was in an irritable mood and responded, *"Sí, mi capitán,"* sardonically to everything I asked of him.

The press consisted of a frame with a car jack welded to a plate that just fit inside a welded metal box the size of a brick. We tossed several sacks of grass into a shower stall and turned it over with a pitchfork with the shower running in order to get it damp. We then tried packing it, but when we went to remove bricks from the press, they fell apart.

"You are going to have to use sugar," Pablo warned.

Miguel and I persisted, though, and eventually developed a technique for wrapping the brick the instant it came out of the press, essentially not giving it time to fall apart. Even after we had perfected this technique, half the bricks crumbled at the corners, but we simply tossed the grass back onto the pile to be run through the press again. The job took all night but I considered it a success because it was an interesting experience and also gave me one more point of control over the whole smuggling process.

CHAPTER 36

A CLOSE CALL OCCURRED ON THE FIFTH RUN. By now we were carrying a half ton at a time, which was the maximum load for a Cherokee Six. A half ton took up thirty-three suitcases, which meant that the entire cabin of the plane, including the copilot's seat, was stacked floor to ceiling with suitcases. Bruce wasn't even visible from the starboard side of the plane. On this particular run he flew across the border with no problem, but as he homed in on the crop duster strip out of Escondido, he saw there was a tractor parked right in the middle of it. Looking around, he saw no sign of Harold's van.

I think most smugglers would have turned around and headed back to the safety of the Mexican desert at this point, but that wasn't Bruce's style. He flew on and landed at Palomar, which was a controlled strip with a tower and people around. After parking the plane at the far end of the strip, he hurried into the terminal, found a small car rental agency, rented a car, sped into town, and arrived at the local U-Haul center just as they were closing. All their trucks were rented and he had to settle for an open trailer. After hitching it to the car, he sped back to Palomar, drove out to the plane, and unloaded the thirty-three suitcases in broad daylight. Speeding back to town again, he accidentally clipped a Cadillac. Before the driver could get out of his car, Bruce was at the man's window thrusting hundred-dollar bills at him.

In town he got a motel room and transferred the thirty-three suitcases to his room. Meanwhile, I had just flown back from Culiacan. I walked into my cottage as the phone was ringing. It was Bruce, and it was the first time I heard him sound less than composed.

"Where the bloody hell is Harold? I've got to find some way to get rid of this shit! Do you realize I'm three hours late on my flight plan already? They've probably got the air-sea rescue service out looking for me! I don't know what

186

the fuck I'm going to tell them. Listen, I'm at a pay phone. I've got to get back to the room. The old bat who runs the motel saw me unload all those suitcases and she's suspicious as hell. Locate Harold and have him contact me ASAP!"

I was in a sweat as to how to find Harold. I figured he saw the tractor parked in the middle of the strip and panicked. My only chance was that he was holed up in a nearby motel. I got a friendly operator, told her this was an emergency, and she spent the next half hour phoning every motel, hotel, and inn in the Escondido-Ramona area asking person-to-person for Harold. Clerk after clerk said there was no one there by that name. Why would he register under his own name? I thought to myself. I should hang up and leave my phone line open, I was thinking, when a clerk said, "Harold Westover? Just a moment." I could hardly believe my luck! He had registered under his own name!

He came on and I told him what Bruce had told me and gave him the name of Bruce's motel. He drove there but balked at loading all those suitcases into his van, what with the bright lights of the motel and the landlady peeking out from behind her curtains every few minutes. Bruce told me later he had to load most of them himself. Harold then took off but was back in minutes looking white. Just north of town he had nearly run into an impromptu Border Patrol checkpoint. These checkpoints were set up to catch undocumented aliens, but the officers were hardly likely to ignore thirty-three Mexican-made suitcases stacked in the back of a van. In order to avoid the checkpoint, Harold had had to make a sudden U-turn across two double yellow lines.

Bruce then set out in the rental car with Harold following as they tried to find another route out of town. Three quick taps on the brake light was Bruce's signal to Harold there was danger ahead. They found Border Patrol checkpoints on every highway. Evidently the Border Patrol had set up a net around the area. At last, they found a small farm road that led to Route 15 and Harold took off, melting into the safety of the well-trafficked freeway. By now it was two in the morning. Bruce headed back to his motel, wondering what he was going to do about his flight plan, now ten hours late. An air-sea rescue search was undoubtedly underway. He was exhausted. An idea occurred to him.

He caught a couple of hours' sleep and was at Palomar at dawn. Using a piece of wire, he shorted out each of the plane's fuses across the battery, then put them back in place. He then flew to San Diego, where he made a low pass in front of the tower and rocked his wings—the aviation signal that he intended to land but did not have radio capability. Once on the ground, he closed out his flight plan, telling the authorities that he had been forced down by a freak thunderstorm over the Sonoran Desert and had to spend the night there. The reason he hadn't contacted them was that lightning had knocked out all his fuses.

The lower-level officials seemed satisfied with this story, but before he could get away, two senior customs officers showed up accompanied by two officials from the FAA. They didn't like Bruce's story one bit. They went out to inspect his plane and were appalled to see that the seats had been removed when all Bruce had in the way of luggage was a small travel bag. When they checked his pilot logbook and saw this was his fifth trip to Mexico in as many months, they were aghast. They proceeded to go over every square inch of the plane, even vacuuming it and emptying the vacuum bag in order to examine the debris, but found nothing. The plane was clean and in the end they had to let him go. The FAA officials were especially angry for having mobilized a search and rescue mission for an evident smuggler.

This near catastrophe caused us to make several changes to our protocol. Harold was too shaken to continue driving the van and I offered this job to the Bub. This seemed like an ideal opportunity to repay him for introducing me to Bruce. He had a van and for a minimal amount of risk, he could make a quick three grand. He surprised me by hesitating to accept.

"Why?"

"That guy Bruce is such an asshole."

"Are you kidding? I think he's ultra-cool."

"He's always ordering everyone around and stuff. He thinks he's Mr. Big Shot."

I convinced him Bruce would treat him well and he accepted.

Another change was to buy walkie-talkies so Bruce could communicate with the Bub. We checked our favorite strip and the tractor was now gone, but in case it returned, we found two other deserted strips in the area that we could use as backups. And in case the walkie-talkies failed, we worked out some visual signals to be used between the plane and the ground. Also, the Bub would bring the plane's seats with him in his van and he and Bruce would install them in the plane after unloading the grass, for the benefit of customs. I forget why we didn't worry that Bruce had become hot from his recent harrowing experience, but for whatever reason that didn't happen—surely a gross failure on the part of law enforcement.

Fall came and my landlord dropped by one day to say he was going to renovate my place and I had to move. So it was So long! to the pine-paneled walls and the blackberry bushes and the railroad tracks in back. So many good times had been packed into that tiny cottage. I didn't worry about it, though, figuring good times would follow wherever I went.

Arf was going through a reform phase and had sworn off pool and gambling and was back in school after having dropped out for two quarters. He had bought a blue cardigan sweater to celebrate his return to school and told me, "You're looking at the New Arf!" He was living with his parents and I knew he wanted to move out, so I asked him if he wanted to find a place where we could live together.

"I've often wondered why we never lived together before," he told me. "You know, for the companionship." He paused, glancing down. "I just don't know if my ego can take it!"

I promised not to lord my successes over him and we set about looking for a place. I could have paid the entire rent on a nice place in the Berkeley hills, but Arf insisted on paying his share, so we looked for places in the flatlands. We finally found a place at 10th and Addison and the neighborhood here was so bad, it was almost laughable. The flat sat above a garage and had a stucco and stone exterior that gave it the look of a fortress. Anything left outside was either stolen or vandalized according to its value. We didn't try to plant anything and the place had a bare look. Inside, the walls were painted landlord white. "Wow, this is like a Mafia safe house!" Wade Maddox exclaimed on visiting. But there was one thing the local vandals had missed, at least for the first couple of weeks, until one day I came home to find the dusty, never-used garden hose sliced by a sharp knife into foot-long sections.

Ever since I dropped out of school, I had flirted with the idea of going back. Each quarter I would register, but within a week or two I would drop out. This time I decided to stay in. A new phase of my life was beginning with the plane runs worked out and with my new living situation with Arf. I was happy.

Classes started and it was fun studying with Arf again. We took breaks together and made coffee in the spacious, older kitchen of our flat. It was early fall, the season was changing, and outside we could see dry leaves being whipped about in the wind. The runs were going so smoothly now, I scarcely had to miss classes. It was a heady feeling, too, crossing campus like any other student knowing I had this secret life on the side. I even wrote a paper comparing Hegel and Freud while holed up for the weekend at the Motel Tres Ríos in Culiacan.

Arf said we should take up guitar, that we could play duets together. He said it was a simple instrument and we could learn it in a week. I foolishly believed him, got an old guitar, and began struggling to get my fingers to land on the right strings. "It's supposed to be fun!" Fred Swaha laughed, watching me struggle to contort my fingers into a C chord. By a week I couldn't play much, but I was hooked. After I developed some proficiency, I began studying the old Black masters: Mississippi John Hurt, Blind Lemon Jefferson, Big Bill Broonzy, and Blind Blake. Arf never did learn to play.

A run pulled through and I took a sample to show Postman Joe, who lived with some other dealers in a commune on Shattuck Avenue. He was due to come home soon and I waited for him in his living room. A cute girl with strawberry blonde hair and dark eyebrows walked in, saw me, and said, "Oh, wow! Are you Joe's connection? I've heard so much about you." Her name was Mary and she asked if I wanted to smoke some PCP with her. I had never tried PCP before and said, "Sure."

The PCP came in the form of dried parsley that had been impregnated with the chemical so that in a bust, unless they were tipped off, the narcs would never imagine the parsley was anything more than what it appeared to be. Mary rolled a joint that was half grass and half impregnated parsley, lit it, and we passed it back and forth. The next thing I knew, I was kissing her full on the lips. "Isn't this a convivial drug?" she smiled, gently disengaging me. Wow, where did she come up with a word like "convivial"? I wondered to myself. I went to kiss her again but she stopped me. "Careful. My old man's in the next room."

Her boyfriend, I learned, was the source of the PCP, having learned how to manufacture it. His name was Gary and he was a close friend of Postman Joe. He and Mary were thinking of breaking up, and a few weeks later I managed to make it with her at my place. Afterward, we lay in bed and she said, "Well, what do you want to do now?"

"What do you mean?"

"Well, don't you want to do something?"

"Oh, sure. What do you want to do? You want to go shoot some pool?"

She threw her hands up. "Guys are all alike! All you want to do is have sex and then when it's over with, you can't think of anything to do!"

A school break came and I flew to Culiacan to set up another run. Jesus and Abelardo were in the habit of carrying pistols wherever they went, and they carried them tucked inside their belts aimed at their balls, which freaked me out thinking that if the guns accidentally fired, my friends would lose their personality as the saying goes. When I asked them why they carried their guns this way, they just laughed. I later learned this was a fashion statement observed by suppliers all across Sinaloa.

Jesus needed to get a radiator hose and I accompanied him for the fun of an odyssey. On the way, we stopped at a bank, and on the way out, I happened to catch sight of his pistol tucked at his waist.

"Do you realize you just went into a bank carrying a gun?"

Jesus slapped his palm to his forehead. "*¡Híjole!*" he laughed, then shrugged. "It doesn't matter. They all know me in there."

That night Jesus rushed into my room, saying he needed me to do some interpreting. By now my Spanish was quite fluent. It was dark out and we drove to a deserted area along a river and pulled up near two other cars. Two gringos from Florida were there and wanted to score a half ton of grass they planned to bring back to the States by sailboat. They had three machine guns in the trunk of their car that they were offering as a down payment. I got in the back seat of the third car and began explaining all this to the owner of the grass, who was a friend of Jesus. By the starlight I could tell I was talking to a lean kid who looked very young, probably even younger than I was. He talked rapidly, using a lot of *caló*, and after several minutes I asked him if he could slow down. He abruptly stopped speaking in order to stare at me.

"*¿Eres gavacho?*"

It was the highest compliment my Spanish had ever received!

The poor Floridians were extremely nervous and I did my best to put them at ease. "You've lucked out on a really good contact," I told them. "I know these people and deal with them. They're solid as gold." The machine guns were transferred to the third car, the gringos took down the telephone number and address of the young kid, and that was the last anyone ever heard from them.

Later I tried to analyze why I had been so friendly to those two gringos. Smugglers generally guard their contacts jealously and wouldn't reveal them to their best friends, let alone two strangers. If someone finds your contacts through you and starts dealing with them, that is called "contact jumping" and can arouse passions as strong as if they had slept with your woman. People have been shot for it. I decided I had been friendly to them because they found Jesus and his friend on their own, not through me, and also because they would be selling their grass in Florida, where it wouldn't have any effect on my sales. But upon analyzing it further, it wasn't prices really. The market for grass was so strong, you could throw tons at it and hardly drop the price. Really, it was the glory. I was enjoying the reputation of a folk hero in my community and wouldn't want anyone cutting in on my glory.

CHAPTER 37

THE FOLLOWING EVENING JESUS AND I DROVE to see his latest shipment of grass, which was kept at a ranchito near Bebelama, south of Culiacan.
I had come to know this drive well, and when we passed the brightly lit chicken
ranch on the right side of the highway, I knew we were getting close. Those
poor chickens were kept in such small cages, they could hardly turn around,
and I tried to imagine how they felt being enclosed like that, staring out all day
at a field they would never get to roam. Jesus interrupted my thoughts, saying
this time there would be a surprise waiting for me.

Jesus pulled off onto a dirt road and we soon came to a gate made of barbed
wire tacked to sticks. Jesus flashed his high beams three times and a campesino materialized from the darkness and pulled the gate aside to let us in.
"Don't ever come here alone," Jesus warned me. "They could shoot at you with
machine guns."

There was a charcoal fire burning and the smell of corn roasting. The
campesino lived here with his wife and two daughters in an adobe home
with no front wall, so that when you walked up, you saw everything that
was going on: the señora cooking and the two daughters staring to see
who was coming to visit. The older daughter was about fifteen, still developing, and had beautiful, smooth skin and soulful brown eyes. She and I
would sneak stares at each other to the point where I worried her father
might be wondering what was going on. I liked the way she returned my
stare and held it with no shyness at all, just a look of ragged wonder. This
humble family then was the "they" who might shoot at me with machine
guns. It amused me the way Jesus liked to exaggerate the gangster aspects
of our business together.

Abelardo soon arrived, jerking to a stop in a brand-new LTD. LTDs were the luxury car of choice among Tierra Blanca suppliers at the time. More prestigious cars like Cadillacs or Lincolns probably wouldn't have handled the Tierra Blanca potholes as well. Abelardo jumped out with his boyish grin and there were abrazos all around. Normally the grass would be stacked in sacks in a back room, but this time Abelardo led me to the field behind the ranch house and began stomping around in the dust with his boot. I wondered what he was doing when his stomp yielded a hollow metallic sound and he knelt down, felt around with his fingers, and lifted a sheet of corrugated metal that had been hidden under the dust. Beneath was a square concrete shaft about three feet wide. This, Abelardo explained, dropped down to a tunnel that led to a cavern where the grass was stored. He had had it built specially for our runs.

The floor of the shaft was about six feet deep and I started to let myself down, but Abelardo stopped me, saying we had to wait for the bad air to clear. I stepped back and saw fumes rising from the hole, making the distant hills and the starry sky beyond look wavy. Abelardo began fanning at the hole with the corrugated metal, but this raised too much dust and he laid it aside and used his sombrero. While he was fanning, the campesino brought out a shoebox full of figurines to show us. There were small people, birds, plugs for bottles, and beveled disks with yin-yang designs on the sides, all made of clay. "Those aren't real," Abelardo told me from where he was kneeling next to the hole, fanning. "They make those up at the marketplace to sell to tourists."

"No, they are real, *compadre*," said Jesus. "They found them right here in the ground."

The campesino nodded. "Every time we plow, we find many of these."

Abelardo got up and stepped over to see.

"You know, we are not the true Mexicans," Jesus said then and waited for effect. The campesino nodded, willing to agree to anything.

"We are not the true Mexicans, just as you, Tom, are not a true American. The true Mexicans are *los indios* and the true Americans are *los pieles rojas*. Am I not right?"

Everyone agreed and Abelardo said we could go down the hole now. He handed me a large, square flashlight and I dropped down to the bottom of the shaft, got down on my knees, and shone the flashlight down a horizontal tunnel. It looked long and was only a couple of feet tall and wide. I had broad shoulders and could barely fit. I got on my belly and began crawling like a Marine while pushing the flashlight awkwardly in front of me. I was feeling claustrophobic but kept it under control by thinking that at any moment I could scuttle backward like a crawdad and get out. My heart froze, though, when I heard a noise, craned my neck back, and saw Jesus crawling right behind me. So much for backing out! For a moment I thought I was going to panic but forced myself to go on and finally entered a concrete cavern where I could stand up, stooped, and move about, and the panic passed.

The cavern was about four feet tall and eight by ten feet wide and long. The *mercancía* as we called it lay stacked against the far wall and I picked up several bricks, opened corners of them to check the contents, and determined the grass was good. It may seem strange, but I no longer smoked the grass to see what I thought of it. I preferred simply to rub some between my fingers and inhale the fragrance. Before, when I used to smoke it, I would get all hung up thinking, Yes, this is good. . . . But am I as high as I was last time? . . . I think so. . . . Maybe not, though. . . . I'm not sure . . .

Actually, I didn't smoke grass much at all these days. Grass had opened my mind to so much in earlier days as well as providing a lot of good times but now seemed to have less to offer.

Jesus and I sat down to face each other cross-legged with the flashlight lying between us aimed up at the low ceiling. In that strange light and with his pointy ears, Jesus looked more than ever like the devil. "Prices have gone way up," he began in a ritual that had by now become quite familiar. I laughed.

"Again?"

He suppressed a grin. "No, this time they really have. Beans, flour, sugar—everything has gone up. I have the papers at home. You can read them."

"So how much do you want for it?"

"Fourteen."

"Fourteen? We would never make a profit."

"Can't you raise your prices too?"

I shook my head. "We would lose customers. We're not the only ones bringing this stuff up, you know. We have to compete with others."

Jesus considered this. "Can't you kill the competition?" He imitated a machine gun sweep. "*Ta-ta-ta-ta-ta-ta-ta!*"

I shook my head sadly no. "There are too many of them."

We put on grave looks.

"*Está bien,* Tom. Thirteen."

"How about eleven? That's what we paid last time."

Here the ritual took an unexpected turn.

"What about *la chiva*? It takes up much less space, so it would be easier for *el piloto* to cross. Furthermore," he laughed, "your customers have to have it, so they can't complain about price."

I was disappointed that Jesus would be willing to sell heroin. I tried to explain to him that grass was a good thing and opened people's minds to things they might never have experienced otherwise, while heroin was a downer and made people sick and ruined their lives. He listened patiently to what I had to say and nodded.

"Are the laws against heroin that much more severe than for grass?"

My moral reasoning had made no sense to him and he assumed there must be some other more pragmatic reason why I wouldn't smuggle heroin.

We agreed to twelve dollars a pound and as we were about to leave the ranch, the campesino came up and offered me the artifacts he had shown us earlier. I thanked him and told him I would treasure them forever. I sneaked a last glance at his beautiful daughter and we left.

The pickup went smoothly and on a whim I decided to take the bus back to the border instead of flying. I was in a nostalgic mood and wanted to see all the familiar sights the Bub and I had come to know from our many trips down and back. As I boarded, I noticed an older American man toward the back of the bus and immediately looked away, not being in the mood for company. After the bus got rolling, though, the man came up to me and asked if I was an American. I admitted I was and he asked if he could take the vacant seat next to me. Bruce wouldn't have tolerated this guy for an instant, I thought to myself, but couldn't bring myself to be rude to the old guy. He brought his suitcase forward and settled in.

"Yessir, I pegged you for an American the moment I saw you. You're wearing Mexican clothes and you're pretty tan, but your eyes are a dead giveaway. You'll see some Mexicans with green eyes and even a pale blue, but not deep blue like yours. Now Culiacan," he went on in the same breath. "There's a strange town. You don't see too many Americans in Culiacan." And he turned to me pointedly.

I made up a story to the effect I had spent the last week in Mazatlan, then tried hitchhiking home and got a ride this far but couldn't get another ride and decided to take the bus.

"No, the Mexicans won't pick you up," he nodded, apparently satisfied with my story. "And in a way, maybe you're better off. Who knows what might have happened if they had?" He raised his eyebrows at me.

It was a twenty-two-hour ride to the border and I got to hear this guy's entire life story. I tried to tune him out, but when he mentioned he was a retired customs officer, I was suddenly all ears. Gold! I thought to myself. I've struck gold! But when I encouraged him to talk about his work, it came out that in forty years of service he had never advanced beyond rooting through people's luggage and didn't know the first thing about planes or radar. He droned on about his straight, inconsequential life.

"Yessir, in twenty-three, I was working as a security guard in Ogden, Utah, and had two women in love with me. I didn't know what to do, so I flipped a coin and married Lydia. Forty-three years we were together. She passed away two years ago and I've been traveling ever since. Lydia never did like buses much. My friends tell me, 'Gee, Pat, don't you get lonely traveling around by yourself like that?' But I tell them no, you always meet someone. Like you, for instance!"

He stuck with me the whole trip. I couldn't even shake him during the rest stops. He would tell me in advance what restaurant we should go to—he knew them all—so I would purposely head for a different one. "No, the good one's this way!" he would holler after me. "I like this one!" I would holler, not bothering to look back. Next thing, he would be running up beside me. He was like a puppy and a part of me couldn't help growing fond of him.

We finally rolled into Nogales and I got out my travel bag and began sprucing up. I was a little worried about crossing the border because I knew the figurines the campesino had given me were pre-Columbian and illegal to bring back. While I had my travel bag open, the retired inspector's instincts for peering into other people's luggage didn't fail him. He spotted the figurines and asked what they were. "Just some artifacts," I said, closing my bag. He was quiet for a while. Then, in a very official voice and staring straight ahead, he said, "I'm afraid it's my duty as a retired U.S. customs officer to advise you that it's illegal to bring those artifacts back to the States. Anything that old is considered part of Mexico's heritage and belongs to the Mexican government."

I saw red. If he thought he could bore me for the entire ride and now keep me from bringing back these artifacts, I was going to throttle him! But then he turned to me with a coy look.

"Tell you what, though. If they ask you what you're bringing back, don't call them 'artifacts.' Call them 'curios.' And stick close to me. They're liable to be buddies of mine."

And that's exactly what happened. The customs agents knew him and waved us on through.

Which just goes to show everyone's a smuggler at heart!

CHAPTER 38

AFTER EVERY RUN I ALWAYS MADE THE ROUNDS of all my friends, telling them about my latest adventures. I knew this was unprofessional, but my friends loved my stories, and the glory of telling them was as important to me as anything. Arf heard more about the runs than anyone. Over coffee in the mornings and during breaks between studying, he would listen in a subdued way as I related success after success. I was completely forgetting about the promise I had made not to make him feel bad.

For me, the runs were so unbelievably exciting that it wasn't even enough to tell people about them; I wanted to show them to someone. And the part I wanted to show them was the pickup. This was the high point for me. By now we had gone through a number of different strips. For a while we used the highway between Altata and Navolato. The roadway there was paved, ran straight for twenty-one kilometers, and was elevated from the surrounding countryside, making it an ideal strip. There was little traffic on it in the early morning, and the tall red and white smokestack of the sugar refinery at Navolato made it easy for Bruce to find from the air. Bruce would scan the entire length of the highway and when no vehicle was coming from either direction, he would rock his wings as a signal and come in to land. At the signal, Miguel and another hired hand would pull cars out at either end of a stretch of highway to form roadblocks. No one ever came along, but if they did, and there was trouble, Miguel and the hired hand had machine guns.

This was such an ideal strip that other smugglers began using it too and Jesus worried that it was getting hot. So for our next run we used the governor's strip at his very own country villa! When I asked Jesus how he came up with this plan, he simply said he had read in the papers that the governor was going to be at a meeting in Mexico City. He must have had inside knowledge, though, to feel confident there would be no relatives or caretakers around. And what a fun pickup it was! While waiting for Bruce to appear, Miguel and I walked about the premises with our noses in the air, ordering each other to bring tea, fetch the paper, and so forth—each trying to outdo the other's impersonation of the governor himself!

Eventually we found a strip that seemed ideal and figured we would be using it forever. It was an abandoned crop duster strip off the road from Navolato to Altata. It was wide and long with no bushes or trees close to it, and an abandoned yellow tractor at one end made it easy for Bruce to find from the air. Some heavy vegetation nearby made a perfect place to hide the truck with the grass.

On a typical pickup, Jesus, Abelardo, and I would head out while it was still dark and arrive at the landing strip right at dawn. Miguel would be following in a truck with the grass and would park it in the nearby dense foliage. As the sun rose, the strip would begin to sparkle from all the dew-laden cobwebs blanketing it, and we would pace its length, kicking aside stones and pulling up large weeds. Sometimes there would be cattle on the strip and we would chase them off, whooping and waving our sombreros like cowboys. After clearing the strip, we would compete to see who could be the first to spot Bruce. Depending on the wind, we sometimes heard him before spotting him. After he landed, we would rush to turn the plane around, taking care to stay clear of the propeller. He would taxi to the other end of the strip and we would run after him to turn the plane around again. Then he would stand with one foot on the wing and Miguel and I would hand up suitcases. When they were all packed, he would hand me money to give to Jesus and take off, barely clearing the vegetation at the far end of the strip because of the weight he was carrying.

A strange phenomenon occurred on one of these pickups. We were standing around waiting for Bruce when we spotted a tiny point of gold light in the far distance to the south. I thought it must be the sun shining on the window of a distant building though I couldn't imagine where the building might be as there were no cities anywhere near. The point slowly rose and we saw that it was the tip of a golden spike shining brilliantly in the sun. By now we realized it was too big to be an earthbound object and for several moments the run no longer mattered, nor did anything else, because we were witnessing an apocalypse and there was no telling what life was going to be like or if there was even going to be life at all after the spike got through doing whatever it was going to do. But as the spike rose higher yet, it acquired a slight curve, revealing it to be the tip of a fingernail moon gleaming in the sun. The fact that it looked vertical at first must have been due to some unusual conjunction of the sun, moon, and earth.

I wanted someone to see the pickup so badly that on an impulse one day I invited Arf to come along. He thought I was joking at first, but seeing I was serious, he chuckled and murmured something about being low on cash.

"I'll pay your way."

He chuckled again. "Naw. Anyway, I can't afford to take time off school."

"We can do it over a weekend. I've got these runs down!"

"No, I really can't."

That same day I saw Bruce, and he surprised me by acting enthusiastic when I happened to mention Jesus's offer of heroin.

"Say, that's what we ought to get into. I mean to say, it would be a cinch to get rid of in an emergency. If I saw someone following me, I could just pitch it out the window."

"You mean you'd smuggle heroin?"

"Shore. Why not? It's not as if we'd be forcing it on anyone. People take it of their own free will."

"Yeah, but you know it's bad for them."

To this he simply rolled his eyes.

"Don't you care what happens to other people?"

Bruce shook his head slowly and deliberately for emphasis.

"People can bloody hurl themselves off cliffs for all I care, chap."

School resumed and I concentrated on my studying. One night Arf tapped on my door and asked if he could speak to me. I put my book down and told him to come on in. He said he had a proposition for me. "I've been thinking about your offer to show me the next run," he said. "I'd really like to come, and I can even pay my own way, but it all depends on a big favor." He wanted Bruce to bring back two ounces of heroin for him.

"Don't look so shocked. I mean, it's not like I'm going to be standing in front of junior high schools selling dime bags if that's what you're thinking. It's for a friend of mine. He's an addict, but you'd never know it. He's in complete control. In fact, he's a respectable businessman. He owns a couple laundromats in town. He also gives piano recitals. He just wants it for a long-term stash so he won't have to sweat scoring off the street all the time."

"Bringing back heroin's out of the question. I really want you to come, though. I'll pay your way. You won't have to pay a cent."

"No, I would want to pay my own way. And the only way I can do that is with the heroin."

I thought that was the end of it, but over the following week Arf kept trying to get me to change my mind. Heroin wasn't as bad as it was made out to be, he told me. I was just prejudiced because of the hysterical attitude people had toward it in this country. In England, the government distributed heroin free to addicts, he said. The biggest problem with heroin was that it was illegal. That was what caused people to commit crimes for it and that was why they died from it—because they didn't know what they were getting when they bought off the street. Addicts who had a stable supply could lead normal lives just like anyone else. As far as these two ounces went, the only difference they would make is whether or not his friend had to score off the street.

"Why don't you just let me pay your way?" I asked him and he sighed.

"You know, with the price you said Jesus quoted, I could turn these ounces over to my friend and make enough money to pay my own way and also live for the next couple months. As it is, I'm really pressed."

Arf continued to try to persuade me during odd moments when we were cooking in the kitchen or on the way to school, and in the end, and against my better judgment, I agreed. I bought into the idea that two ounces wouldn't make any long-term difference and I really wanted Arf to see the run. "Only you've got to promise never even to ask me to smuggle heroin again."

Arf raised his right hand as though giving testimony and laughed. "Don't worry. I promise I'll never ask you again."

I checked with Bruce and he said he didn't mind carrying the two ounces although he didn't see the point of it. "Just have the Mexicans hand it to me separately so I can get rid of it in a pinch. I still say that's what we ought to get into, though."

So this was it! I was finally going to show someone a run. Arf and I flew to Culiacan, giggling and cracking jokes the whole flight. It felt just like our very first run all over again—that time with Bill Gretsch and my yellow pickup. Things changed, though, as soon as Jesus picked us up at the airport. I hadn't anticipated how Jesus would react to a fellow Latin. Within minutes, he and Arf established a rapport that seemed to rival what I had spent months cultivating. Anyone witnessing their conversation would have supposed they were lifelong friends. All my smuggling instincts went into full alert. Normally, in talking to me, Jesus slowed his speech and took care to enunciate clearly. This was one of the things I appreciated about him and probably accounted for the fact we had pulled off so many successful runs with no misunderstandings. Around Arf, though, Jesus lapsed into his normal, rapid rate of speech, so that, good as my Spanish was, I had trouble following him at times. The limit came when Arf started interpreting for me.

"I'm not deaf!" I told him.

Normally I stayed at Jesus's home during the runs, but I was determined to separate him from Arf as soon as possible and told him to take us to the Motel Tres Ríos, offering the excuse that this would "look cooler." Jesus didn't seem to think anything of this and once we were at the Tres Ríos and Jesus had left, I felt a lot better.

There were hardly any guests at the Tres Ríos and we had the pool to ourselves. A liveried waiter brought us drinks poolside, and from our lawn chairs we looked out over freshly swept packed-earth walkways, thick-bladed lawns, and cottages half smothered in bougainvillea. I took a swim, rolled over on my back, and looked up at tall, converging palm tops set against a perfectly blue sky.

"Isn't this the life?" I told Arf.

Later I took Arf to dinner at the Hotel San Luis, an elegant hotel set on a hill overlooking all of Culiacan. The hotel was new and I was convinced it was built to cater to the Culiacan Mafia. It seemed unusually luxurious for a dusty agricultural town, and the couple of times Bruce and I had eaten here, the patrons were mostly well-dressed men dining in twos or threes and conversing in quiet tones. I couldn't wait to show off some of the savoir-faire I had picked up from Bruce and got us one of the best tables in the house, next to a full-length plate glass window overlooking the town. I ordered a vintage Graves, which was brought to us in a silver ice bucket.

"I like it when they keep your glass filled," Arf said after the waiter had left.

"Yes, but it's not good when they hover over you."

"No, if it's a good waiter, you hardly even know he's there."

We laughed at the notion of ourselves as sophisticated connoisseurs.

I ate *calamares en su tinta* and Arf had lobster tails. I was intending to treat, but when the bill came, Arf insisted on paying and produced a roll of twenties thick as his fist. Evidently his friend had paid him in advance for the heroin.

Back at the Tres Ríos I set my travel alarm for five in the morning. "Are you sure you want me to come along?" Arf asked and I turned to stare at him.

"Are you kidding? That's the whole reason I brought you down here."

"Well, you know. As long as you're sure we're not going to get busted or anything." He gave a short laugh to cover his faux pas, but my spirits sank with the realization that he couldn't care less about the pickup. All he cared about was the heroin.

CHAPTER 39

THE RUN PULLED THROUGH AND I PICKED UP the load from the Bub in Berkeley. As so often happened, one of the cheap suitcases had ripped open and there were loose bricks lying about. I knew these loose bricks would be a temptation for the Bub and to keep him from pilfering, I made sure to create the impression I had an exact count on every load. In fact, I never did. That may seem strange, but when I examined the bricks at the Mexican end, whether it was in a warehouse or our recently created cavern, I could never bring myself to painstakingly count every brick. Just the same, when the Bub delivered the load to me in Berkeley, I would say things like, "Our biggest load yet! Four hundred and thirty-seven bricks!"

At the flat, Arf and I devoted most of our time to studying. Another run was coming up and I worried that Arf might ask me to bring back more heroin, but he didn't. I flew to Culiacan and Jesus showed me several sacks of Michoacan that he had acquired. I dipped my hand into the loose colitas, rubbed some between my fingers, and inhaled the wonderful piney smell that Michoacan has. Jesus was packing the bricks again, now that Miguel had shown him our technique for packing them without sugar, and I told him to pack the Michoacan in a different color from the rest. He packed it in green. The run pulled through and this time the Bub wanted his full payment in cash. On every previous run he had taken part of his payment in bricks. "At least get some of this Michoacan," I told him, but he just wanted cash. This struck me as strange, but I peeled off thirty hundred-dollar bills to him and didn't give it further thought.

Two days later a long-haired hippie came to my door asking for the Bub. "He doesn't live here," I told him and the hippie shifted about on my porch.

"Well, do you know if he has any more of those green bricks he was selling?"

My mind went berserk. I got rid of the hippie and checked the clock. It was six in the evening. I knew the Bub often mooched dinner at his parents' home, and I jumped in my Mustang and drove there, breaking speed limits the whole way. Looking back, I would have handled this development differently, but at the time I was in a blind rage.

The Bub's parents' home was just a few doors up the street from my parents' home, the Bub and I having known each other since we were toddlers. As I approached, I spied the Bub's red Econoline van parked opposite his parents' house. I pulled up and there he was, walking down the front steps. I guess the expression on my face said everything, for he took one look at me and broke into a run for his van. I yanked the parking brake on the Mustang and jumped out while it was still rolling. The Bub got in his van and slammed the door, but I was already at the open window and reached in to grab his neck. I almost had him, but he was rolling the window up quickly and I had to jerk my hands out. He fired the engine and as he took off, I kicked my bootheel hard against the side of his van. About twenty yards away he stopped, rolled down his window, and stuck his head out.

"So, I suppose you're all pissed off 'cause I helped myself to a few bricks."

"You stole from me!"

He rolled his eyes. "Man, you must have known I was taking a few bricks here and there. I thought you had a perfect count on them. I figured you looked at it as a tip."

"You mean you stole off every run?"

He sighed. "I probably took twenty bricks over all the runs. BFD. You and Bruce can afford it. You're making plenty of bucks."

"Bullshit! Twenty bricks is over two thousand dollars. You owe me that!"

He made a snort and then his engine died. Blanching, he reached for the key. I made a rush for him, but he pulled away before I could get to his open window. This time he stopped a good fifty yards down the street and kept the engine revved. He leaned his head out the window again.

"So, I suppose this means I'm out of a job?"

"Fuck you!"

He took off, leaving me screaming and flipping the bird in the middle of the street I grew up on.

The next day our whole crowd was abuzz over this incident, with everyone speculating what might happen the next time the Bub and I crossed paths. Meanwhile, Bruce and I hired Harold again to transport the grass. Harold had gotten his confidence back and Bruce was determined to do everything in a thoroughly professional manner this time. He bought a brand-new white van and had "Harold's Painting" stenciled on the sides. When Harold drove the grass back, he would be wearing paint-spattered overalls and a painter's cap and the grass would be covered with a paint-spattered tarp, a stepladder, paint cans, rollers, and so forth.

Things fell back into a routine. Midterms were coming up and I devoted my time to studying my math texts. One afternoon I was alone at the flat and went out to get the mail. In it I noticed a large manila envelope addressed to Arf and the return address caught my eye: Coast and Geodetic Survey. I knew they made maps. Then, penciled in the lower right-hand corner, I saw "Tijuana section." A surge of adrenaline coursed through my veins. So that's why Arf hadn't asked me again to smuggle for him!

I couldn't even think about studying and paced back and forth in my room. What was Arf smuggling? Probably heroin. If that was the case, it was wrong and against code and I would simply tell him he had to stop. What if he was smuggling grass, though? I would strangle him.

He showed up around dusk. He was wearing a brand new sports jacket and carried a bag of groceries into our kitchen. He greeted me cheerfully, pulled a large filet mignon out of the bag, and gave an abashed laugh. "How do you cook these things anyway? In a pan or what?" He began rooting through our collection of pots and pans. I said, "You've got some mail here," and handed him the envelope.

"Oh, thanks." He tossed it on our kitchen table right in full view as though he had nothing to hide. I tried to control the emotion in my voice. "I couldn't help noticing it's a map of the border. What are you doing with a map of the border?"

He put down the pan he was holding and held his palms up in a gesture that was almost flip. "I mean, what can I say? What do you think I'm doing with a map of the border?"

"I think you're smuggling!"

"Well, I am."

"What? Pot or heroin?"

"Heroin."

"Then you're getting it from Jesus!"

"That's right."

"You can't do that! You didn't ask me for permission!"

"Oh, I'm a big boy now. I don't need your permission."

"That's contact jumping!"

"Well, if it makes you feel any better, Jesus offered me his number. I didn't ask him for it."

That hit me like a blow and I took a second to compose myself.

"How much have you brought up?"

"Two more ounces."

"OK, I want it stopped right there. Jesus is my contact and you have no right to deal with him."

Well, I'm not going to stop." Arf's eyes narrowed. "You know, Tom, you must be crazy if you think you can go around bragging about all the money you're making and then take me down there and show me how you do it and not expect me to want to get in on it." He stared at me as though failing to understand me and shook his head. "You really must be crazy."

I felt abashed because his words rang true. I was beginning to see what an ass I had been.

"OK, I'm sorry I took you down there. And I'm sorry I bragged around you so much. I've made a lot of mistakes. But I'm not going to let you smuggle heroin."

"I don't see how you can stop me."

I stared at him. His tone wasn't defiant. He was simply stating a fact.

I left the flat and drove to a pay phone. By the time I got a line to Culiacan, it was around eleven o'clock there. Jesus's sleepy voice came on the line and I apologized for the late hour. "I'm calling about Rafael. Did you sell him some of 'the other thing'?" Pot was always "merchandise" and heroin was "the other thing."

"*Sí,*" he responded sleepily.

"Why didn't you contact me first?"

"Because so many times I asked you and you said you didn't want any."

"Yes, but I don't want anyone else selling it. It's bad for people."

"Oh."

This line of reasoning was going nowhere. I had to switch tacks.

"The reason I'm calling is because a problem has come up. You see, Rafael is a good person, but he is not very good at *los negocios*. He doesn't know who to sell to. Already with what you just sold him, he has attracted the attention of the police. He and I live together, you know, and this could bring heat down on me. It could even get back to you possibly. If you were to sell to him again, it could jeopardize the entire operation you and I have built together. *¿Entiendes?*"

"*Sí, sí,* Tom," I understand. "I won't do any more *negocios* with him. It was just a small thing, you understand. I didn't even make that much off it. Don't worry, OK?"

"It's not worth risking what you and I have built up together."

"*Sí, sí,* I understand."

"Also, do me a favor and don't mention this conversation to Rafael, OK? Just tell him your source dried up and you can't get any more."

"OK, Tom."

We hung up and I waited for the operator to tell me how much I owed.

CHAPTER 40

SEVERAL WEEKS WENT BY. I FELT SURE Arf would suspect I was behind the sudden end to his heroin business, yet he didn't seem the least suspicious or resentful. Final exams were coming up and we spent most of our time studying. Things seemed almost the same as before, except there was a certain tension between us. We no longer talked in the carefree, spontaneous way we had before. I felt I would never be able to trust Arf again.

The following weekend I was at Bill Gretsch's place, watching him work on his motorcycle, when he said, "Say, do you know if Arf's run pulled through yet?"

"Oh, he's not doing that anymore."

"Yes, he is."

"What makes you think that?"

He put his wrench down to laugh. "Well, he better be. I just fronted him six hundred dollars!"

I hung around for another few minutes to create the impression this news didn't mean much to me, then jumped on my Hornet and sped flat out to the nearest pay phone to call Jesus.

"I thought you weren't going to sell any more to Rafael."

"Oh, it's OK, Tom. I asked him about the police and he said everything is perfectly safe. He doesn't even handle 'the other thing' anymore. He sent his partner down to pick it up. He assured me there would be no problem with the police."

I had been screwed by my own ruse. All I had left now was the truth.

"Listen, Jesus, I don't want you to sell 'the other thing' to Rafael because it is bad for people. My reasons may seem strange to you and they are hard to explain, but on the basis of all you and I have done together, could you please do me the favor of not selling any more to Rafael?"

There was a pause. "Well, if it is that important to you . . . "

"Believe me, it is. Tell him your supplier got busted or something."

"OK, Tom."

"I really appreciate this. By the way, how much did he get this time?"

"Six."

I sped to the Bear's Lair to see what I could find out. There I learned that Arf's partner was Jake Miller, one of the gamblers. Jake was warm and personable and very intelligent but completely amoral. He was one of several gamblers who specialized in "cutting up fish." "Fish" were suckers and "cutting them up" meant playing secret partners against them in a card game. To do this, he and his partner used an elaborate set of signals involving sniffing, scratching their shoulder, shifting in their seat, and so on to convey what cards they held. After the game, the secret partners would split the take. I remembered that he had once been busted when the police stopped him and found a kit in his car. Word was that Jake was handling Arf's entire operation for him: picking up the heroin from Jesus, smuggling it, and selling it. All Arf did was call Jesus to arrange the score. This sounded like the type of operation Arf would set up. Evidently he was counting on Jake's inability to speak Spanish not to get cut out.

I felt reasonably sure Jesus would be true to his word and not sell Arf any more heroin. I kept in close touch with the Bear's Lair grapevine and nothing seemed to be happening. Meanwhile, Bruce and I were ready to do another run. I called Jesus, and his wife, Alicia, said he was out of town. That didn't make sense as he knew we were ready to do the run.

"Where did he go?"

"Nogales." I thought I detected a note of disapproval in her voice, as though she wanted to say more.

"Does this have to do with Rafael?"

"*Sí*, Tom, it does."

So Arf's runs now took precedence over ours!

I quizzed Alicia about Arf's runs and it was like unleashing a flood.

"I am so worried, Tom. What you and Jesus do is all right, I guess—at least everyone here in Tierra Blanca does it. But this new thing is bad. It will lead to trouble, I can just tell. And what am I going to tell our children? That is what I ask Jesus. What am I going to tell our children when they get older and begin to ask questions?"

I told her I understood and was doing everything I could to stop these runs. "You can keep me informed. Do not tell Jesus what we have just talked about and I might phone you again to see what is going on."

I felt strange colluding with Jesus's wife against him like that, but I was determined to stop Arf. I had steadfastly refused to make money off heroin, but now that Arf was doing it off my contact after I had introduced them, it was almost as if I were running heroin myself. He was contaminating the entire operation I had built up. And as far as Jesus went, he wasn't being entirely square with me. Everything was suddenly getting mixed up and sordid.

It was dusk. I left the pay phone and drove home—and there was Jake Miller's Volvo parked right in front of our house! This was like a total slap in the face. Evidently Arf now felt he could conduct his heroin operations right in our own home!

I opened the front door and heard Arf and Jake laughing in the kitchen. I walked in and found them seated at the table drinking Heinekens. They went quiet for a second and then Jake greeted me affably, seeming genuinely pleased to see me. I had been planning on playing things close to the vest, but seeing Jake there rocked back in his chair as though he owned the place caused me to flip. I wheeled on Arf.

"I happen to know you're still smuggling and I want it stopped! And if you think you can keep on doing it behind my back, you're wrong because I've got a way of finding out you'll never guess in a million years!"

Arf looked shocked. He held his palms up and shrugged.

"I'm not trying to do anything behind your back. I told you I intended to keep on smuggling and I am. I just didn't mention it because I knew how you felt about it."

We exchanged words and Jake cut in.

"Listen, Tom," he said in his soothing, con artist's voice. "I know exactly how you're feeling now. I've been in the same situation myself. You've got an operation you built up from scratch. No one turned you on to Jesus. You went out and found him yourself. You took the risk to find out whether he was reliable. You made him reliable. He's your baby. So naturally you're pissed off when you see someone else come along and take advantage of the situation. But listen, we don't want something for nothing. We're willing to pay you for the work you've done. We'll give you a cut. There's enough in this for all of us. We'll give you a percentage off each run and you won't even have to do a thing for it. That's like free money. How can you pass up free money?"

"Easy! You don't think I could run heroin myself if I wanted to?"

"Sure, but this way we're saving you all the hassle. It's not like selling pot, you know. You're dealing with a whole different category of people—guys that wouldn't think twice about knifing you for your stash. Plus the laws are much stiffer."

"Well, all that's beside the point because I don't want anything to do with it and I don't want you guys dealing off my contact!"

"Well, we're not going to stop," Arf put in firmly. "After all, I don't go around telling you to quit smuggling pot because I'm morally opposed to it."

Arf was sitting on my left and Jake was sitting opposite him. I was standing in front of an empty chair. I had the sudden urge to pick that chair up and bring it crashing down on the table between them. That would show them how serious I was! Instead I pretended to calm down a bit as though I still strongly disapproved of what they were doing but recognized I wasn't going to be able to stop them. If this was going to be all-out war, there was no sense in warning them. Arf's last comment kind of scared me, too. It seemed he was almost saying, interfere with his operation and he would interfere with mine.

Things between Arf and me were tense for the next several days. Then, on an impulse one evening, I stopped him in the kitchen and said I wanted to talk. "You know I'm opposed to what you're doing," I told him, "but I hate to see it come between the friendship we've had all these years. Maybe there's some way we can overlook the different ways we think."

I felt very strange saying this because it came from my heart, yet at the same time I knew it could also work in my favor as a con. If he let his guard down and gave me an opening, I wouldn't hesitate to foil his operation. For his part, Arf seemed eager for things to go back to the way they were.

"I know we've been kind of estranged lately. I was thinking of telling you the same thing."

We began sharing meals again and went on a shopping trip together to San Francisco, where we bought near-matching hand-knit wool sweaters made in Iceland, Arf paying for his with his heroin money while I paid for mine with pot earnings. Arf began confiding in me just like the old days, even telling me about his experiences with Jesus. "Every time the weight is off, you know what he says? He says in Mexico an ounce has only twenty-five grams in it. Can you believe it?"

I could just see Jesus saying that and forced a laugh.

Arf was spending money on new clothes, steaks, and imported wines. He confided that he suffered terrible guilt, though, and began seeing a psychiatrist. He became enthralled with the psychiatrist, who kept him on pins and needles for several weeks trying to decide whether it was ethical for him to accept Arf's heroin dollars. In the end he did. Arf went out and bought tweed jackets with leather elbow patches and took up smoking a pipe. One day he showed me a list of resolutions he had made. "You're looking at the New Arf!" he declared, striking a jaunty pose with his pipe. Every couple of weeks there was a New Arf.

As I didn't object, Jake began spending time at our place and confided in me too. He told me about their first run when they ran two ounces. He said he simply taped them underneath his balls and walked across.

"You know the feeling. You're hanging around Tijuana, you get your shoes shined by some little kid, you knock off a couple quick shots at a bar, and then there's no more stalling around and you've got to do it. I was in the pedestrian line and this old bastard pulled me over to the side and frisked me. I felt his hands work up my legs and saw my whole life pass before my eyes! But when his hands bumped the ounces, he didn't even react. I'm telling you, these ounces were packed so tight with tape, they were like rocks." Jake made a fist and laughed. "He must have thought I had cast-iron balls or something. Ha-ha! Not to mention the size!

"I'll tell you, though, Tom, having money has really changed my life. When I think back to the way I was living just six months ago, I realize I didn't like myself very much. Like that time I got busted for having a kit in my car. I was dealing dime bags on the street and cutting guys up in card games just to stay alive. Now I don't have to mess with any of that. That's what money can do for you: it can allow you to become a better person."

He rocked back in his chair and laughed. He was a keenly intelligent guy who saw the irony in everything he was saying and loved it. He had his hands clasped behind his head and was grinning.

"Yep," he concluded. "It's nice to be able to afford morals."

CHAPTER 41

ANOTHER RUN PULLED THROUGH AND I MET Harold at a Safeway parking lot, took over the van, drove to a rented garage on Milvia Street, and unloaded the grass. The garage was the middle one of three in a row behind a two-story wooden apartment building and felt safe. I quickly emptied all the bricks out of their suitcases and threw the limp plastic suitcases in the back of the van. This was our biggest run yet, a little over half a ton. Right before I closed the door, I looked at the mountain of bricks and thought, How am I ever going to sell all this stuff? Grass never failed to sell, though. At the nearest dumpster I got rid of the Mexican suitcases, which, if found with the bricks, could possibly convert a possession for sale charge into the more serious charge of smuggling.

I returned the van to Harold, got my Mustang back, and drove to Thorpe's house to let him know the run had pulled through. He was one of my biggest customers and I knew he would end up selling a large portion of the load. Bill Gretsch was there and looked relieved to see me. He drew me aside.

"I've been looking for you. I can't answer any questions, OK? I just want to tell you there's a plot out to steal your dope."

It took me a few moments to assimilate this. I was beat, having just gotten back from Culiacan earlier in the day.

"Well, do you think it could happen tonight?"

"No, I don't think so. But it could happen really soon."

I drove home and thought over this news. The Bub had to be behind this plot. I hadn't seen him since our falling out and word was that he had moved though no one seemed to know where. The garage where I had left the grass was one I had rented months earlier, and I recalled mentioning it to the Bub one day as we happened to drive past. I couldn't remember whether I told him which of the three garages was mine, though. To be safe, I resolved to move the grass first thing in the morning.

Dawn came and I drove to Milvia Street, checked to make sure no one was watching the area, then pulled into the driveway that led to the garage. As the garage came into view, my heart jumped when I saw that the doors to it were partly open. I must have forgotten to close them, I tried to reassure myself, but my broken lock lying on the pavement told a different story. I parked, jumped out, and looked in. There were just a few loose bricks lying about where there had been a mountain the night before. I felt sick with remorse for not having moved the load when I had the chance.

I was hurting and needed to confide in someone. Thorpe lived a few blocks away and I drove straight to his home. He came to the door in a bathrobe, looking sleepy-eyed.

"Someone stole my dope!" I told him and he put his fingers to his lips.

"Shh! There's neighbors, you know. Come on in. . . . So someone stole your dope?"

I stared at him, unable to ignore the trace of a grin on his lips. What did the good Frenchman say? In the adversity of our best friends, we often find something that is not exactly displeasing? I left Thorpe standing there and sped home.

On pulling up, I didn't see Arf's car. I went inside, got out the crummy pistol the Bub and I had bought on our trip back east, and fired three shots into the floor. "That's what's going to happen to the motherfucker who stole my dope!" I shouted, not expecting anyone to hear. I stepped into the kitchen and there was Arf, slumped in a chair looking white—at least to the extent a Puerto Rican can look white.

"Sorry. I didn't know you were here."

Arf seemed unable to speak for a moment. "God, you scared the shit out of me."

"Sorry. I didn't see your car outside."

I told him what happened.

"Someone stole your dope?"

I stared at him. I didn't like the way he said it. It was the same as with Thorpe; he didn't really care. I knew someone who would care and that was Wade Maddox.

He came over expecting to buy several suitcase loads and his face fell when I told him about the theft. He immediately laid out two heaping lines of coke for us to snort, then pounded his fist on the table. "They'll never get away with it! We'll track 'em down!" I knew I was never going to see that grass again, but it was good to be around someone who felt the way he did. This was the first run Bruce and I had financed entirely ourselves, too, having grown tired of paying out double for front money. We were out a fortune.

I had classes, but there was no question of going. I was too shook up. Wade and I went to the Bub's old address and his Honda 250 scrambler was there, but when we peered through the window, we saw that most of his belongings were gone. There were just a few pieces of heavy furniture. As we left, I made a mental note to come back with my pickup and appropriate his scrambler when I felt up to it. Next we drove to Ron's place. Ron was the Bub's best friend—the two were like twins—and I felt sure Ron must be in on this. The Bub was too much of a follower to pull off a job like this alone. The fact Ron was Bill Gretsch's brother would explain why Bill knew about the plot but didn't want to reveal his source.

Ron lived in a trailer in back of Bill Gretsch's place, and Wade and I walked up and peered inside. No one was home. We wedged a tiny twig in the doorjamb and left.

Wade had to see a bunch of people about deals in San Francisco and Marin County and invited me to come along. I was grateful for his company and felt too despondent to do anything else. While he visited different people at their homes, I waited in his car. Around evening I finally got up the courage to call Bruce. He was staying in Mill Valley with a friend. I told him the news and he criticized me in a tone he had never used before.

"Why the bloody hell didn't you tell me as soon as you heard there was a plot afoot? We should have moved the stuff right away. I would have helped you. And why the hell did you put it where the Bub could find it in the first place?"

He ended by saying he wasn't sure when he wanted to do another run—if ever. He had other deals going. He mentioned diamond mines in Angola, gold in Qatar. He would have to think about it. I felt devastated. These plane runs had become everything to me; I didn't know what I would do without them. After my phone call, I learned later, Bruce went straight to the No Name Bar and tossed off three stiff drinks. And he didn't even like alcohol.

Wade and I ended up at his place in Corte Madera, where he lived with his wife, Janet, and their one-year-old daughter. They had a cottage on the edge of town, near the woods, and Janet prepared a delicious meal to help us feel better. Wade got out a bottle of twelve-year-old Scotch his father had given him and which he had been saving unopened for years. He opened it, poured a glassful, and handed it to me along with the bottle. "Here, drink all you want!" And he laid out some more lines of coke.

Around midnight we drove back to Berkeley. We checked on the Bub's place and it was no different from the way we had left it. We drove to Ron's trailer and his blue VW bug was parked in Bill's driveway. Wade quickly pulled over and cut his engine. We stepped out and I whispered, "Now, I'm not positive Ron was in on it." Without proof, I worried what we should do if he said he wasn't involved. Wade frowned.

"Are you kidding? You said yourself the Bub would never attempt this without a partner. Who else would it be besides Snively?"

"Snively" was short for "Snively Shit," Wade's nickname for Ron. From the moment they met, Wade had taken a dislike to Ron because of his self-deprecating manner and the floppy, unmacho way he carried himself.

"Now don't let him bullshit you," Wade whispered as we crossed the street. "He's going to deny everything, of course, and we'll just have to get tough with him. You tend to be too easy on people."

The lights were off in Bill's house and we crept down his driveway to Ron's trailer. No lights there either. By the starlight we could see that our tiny twig was gone. I gave a short rap on the door and moments later there was rustling inside and a light went on. Ron opened the door cautiously and peered out. "Oh, it's you, Tom." He looked relieved and opened the door wide. "You scared me. What time is it anyway?"

"It's late, but we have something important to talk to you about."

His expression turned serious and he glanced at Wade. "Sure. Come on in."

The trailer was sparsely furnished. There was a mattress on the floor with an Indian print bedspread, and a picture of Meher Baba hung on one wall. Ron apologized for the lack of chairs. "You guys can sit on the mattress if you want."

"That's OK. This shouldn't take long." I waited till he had closed the door and we were facing each other.

"Listen, Ron, I know you and the Bub stole my load of grass and I want it back." Ron looked shocked.

"But I didn't—"

"Bullshit!" Wade cut in, moving to slug him, but I held him back. Ron regarded Wade with alarm.

"Come on, Ron. Don't make me do something I don't want to do."

"But I'm telling the truth!"

Without warning I grabbed him by the shoulders and propelled him backward till he smashed against the wall of the trailer. A picture somewhere clattered to the floor. I had my hand at his throat. "Come on, Ron, I'm not messing around! I want answers and I want them now!"

I could hear my words as though they were coming from someone else and they sounded like the words of a bad actor in a B movie. I was having a lot of trouble doing this.

Ron caught his breath. "Hey, man, you're out of line! I heard about a plan to steal your dope and as soon as I heard about it, I left the room 'cause I didn't want anything to do with it. Maybe I should have told you about it and I'm sorry I didn't, but you got no right to push me around like this!"

"That's a crock o' shit!" Wade's fist caught Ron on the jaw and sent him spinning to the side. Ron wheeled to face Wade with his fists raised, surprising me by his defiance. Wade must have had fifty pounds on him. Ron's eyes were blazing as he turned to me.

"Hey, man, get this goon off o' me!"

Wade went to slug him again.

"Wait! I think he's telling the truth."

Wade dropped his fists in disbelief. "You got to be kidding! He's lying through his teeth! Can't you tell?"

"I don't think so. Anyway, we've got no proof."

Wade pleaded with me. "Just give me five minutes with him. You can wait outside if you want. Take a walk down the driveway. I swear I'll find out where that dope is."

"I don't want to do it."

I turned to Ron. "Either I owe you the biggest apology of my life or I ought to beat the living shit out of you, but I'm not going to do either till I'm sure." The words sounded lame to me the moment I said them. Ron rubbed his lip and we left.

"Man, I think you're blowing it," Wade told me as we walked back out the driveway. Behind us I could hear the bolt to Ron's door close with a sharp clack.

CHAPTER 42

BILL GRETSCH WAS AT MY DOOR FIRST THING the following morning, looking tense. "Ron told me about last night," he said in a controlled voice. "On the night your grass was stolen, Ron was with his girlfriend at her parents' house in Aptos. Her parents are witnesses. He couldn't have had anything to do with the rip-off."

"God, I am really sorry. I am so, so sorry. I'm going to go to Ron right now and do whatever I have to do to square things with him."

"Well, if he wants to meet you somewhere, that's up to him. But I don't want you going back to the trailer. And I don't want Maddox ever to set foot near my property again."

This stung badly. Bill and I had been friends since high school. All I could do was stand there and apologize. Bill left and I straightaway phoned Ron. We met at a café and I told him how sorry I was. His lip was swollen, but he otherwise looked OK. He surprised me by seeming eager to remain friends. I told him if another run ever pulled through, I would give him an especially low price on bricks and even front them to him.

Things seemed to be falling apart. My best friend had jumped my contact and was smuggling heroin, I had let Bruce down, we had each lost a fortune, and I had alienated my good friend Bill Gretsch. And there was a chance the runs might never happen again. I felt desperate. I was so anxious that I couldn't even take a bath, unable to lie still for that long. I kept imagining jumping back to some previous point in my life and doing a retake.

All I had left was my school work and I tried to throw myself into it. To my surprise, I was able to concentrate pretty well. After a week I was really into it. Maybe all this bad luck was a sign I should give up smuggling, I thought. It had been a wild ride while it lasted, but now maybe it was time to get serious about a career and move on. Wade kept telling me we should track down the Bub before the grass was all sold, but I knew that grass was as good as gone. Finals came, and I was amazed how easy they seemed thanks to all the studying I had done. Wade was there to meet me after my last exam, and we had "tall darks" at the Pizza Haven across the street from campus. He was still eager to track down the Bub.

"That grass is gone."

"It's not, I'm telling you." He pounded his fist down. "I've got people from here to Seattle looking out for those bricks and no one's seen a single one. They must be sitting on them."

I knew the grass market couldn't be tracked that easily but didn't bother contradicting him.

I was at loose ends and we took my Mustang for a drive down University Avenue to the marina. On the way, we spotted a girl walking along wearing shorts so short you could see the bottom of her cheeks poking out below like two white crescent moons. "That's Prime 1-A eating pussy!" cried Wade. "Round the block!"

I did as told and pulled up next to the girl, who turned to look. Wade leaned out the passenger-side window.

"Hey, we were just wondering if you had a razor blade and a mirror we could borrow."

The girl was hip and caught on even before Wade pulled a packet of coke out of his pocket and flapped it suggestively. She laughed.

"I'd love to, but I've got to meet my boyfriend in five minutes."

"He'll wait."

"Another time."

She walked on and Wade threw me a mock hurt look. "Well, T.J., I guess we're just going to have to snort this stuff ourselves."

We snorted while parked at the marina overlooking the water. It was a typical gray Berkeley day with just a few sailboats out. The sky looked like tarnished silver. Wade quizzed me again about any leads I might have on the Bub. I told him I remembered visiting him once at an older Victorian apartment in the Haight.

"Do you remember where it was?"

"Not really."

"Anything about it?"

I shook my head. "About all I remember is that one of the guys at the apartment was a Sergeant Pepper freak."

"Well, let's go track him down!"

I had nothing better to do and thought, Why not?

217

We went to the Haight and walked up and down the street, hoping to spot the Sergeant Pepper freak. Wade was taking our mission very seriously. He had on a long, dark blue pea coat that gave him a Sherlock Holmes look and had his hands thrust deep in his pockets as he peered over the crowds of hippies camped along the sidewalks. Sergeant Pepper costumes were the rage and from time to time Wade would nod his head in the direction of someone wearing one. "No, wrong freak," I would tell him. We were approaching the Drogstore Café and I happened to remember that one of the Bub's friends had gotten a job there as a soda jerk.

The Drogstore Café was a café with a soda fountain and tables and was one of the hippest scenes in the Haight. It was originally called The Drugstore, but since it wasn't a licensed pharmacy, authorities forced it to change its name. We walked in and it was like a contest to see who could look the freakiest. One guy had red hair sticking a foot out from his head in every direction and, backlit as he was where he was sitting, his face appeared surrounded by a red glow. A teenage girl was wearing clothing so sheer that you could see her nipples and the dark triangle of her love box. The place reeked of pot and patchouli oil. Hardly anyone was talking; everyone seemed focused on checking out the next person to walk in. It seemed a pretty sorry scene to me and I told Wade, "You know, we're contributing to the way these people are. Doesn't that make you feel a little guilty?"

"Fuck no, I don't feel guilty. The way I look at it, they were destined to be losers. If it weren't for drugs, they'd probably all be bikers." Wade had a thing against bikers for some reason and frequently referred to them in disparaging tones.

We got in line and two guys were working the soda fountain, one tall and one short. For no reason I could identify, I thought the shorter guy looked more like the type who would know the Bub. Our turn came and as luck would have it, we got the shorter guy. I described the Bub and the Sergeant Pepper freak and he said, "Sure, I know those people," and gave us directions to their flat. I thanked him and turned to leave when Wade stepped up, serious as Humphrey Bogart, and handed the guy a folded twenty-dollar bill. "Thanks, man."

Outside I told Wade, "You've flipped."

"Twenty dollars to get back a half ton of dope? I don't think so."

I still thought there was no chance we would ever see any of the grass but told Wade, "Well, on the off chance we get any of this stuff back, you're welcome to half of it."

He turned to face me as we walked.

"Thanks, man!"

The apartment was an older Victorian with peeling white paint and newspapers stuffed in the window frames. As we climbed the interior stairs to the third floor, I reviewed our cover. If the people in the apartment didn't want to tell us where the Bub was, we would intimate that we had a big deal going and the Bub would be really bummed if he missed out. This ruse wasn't needed, though, for the Bub's friends turned out to be very trusting and let us in before we even finished explaining who we were.

The room seemed humid and I noticed steam wafting in from the kitchen. "That's Herschel," explained a girl in fishnet hose. "He's boiling down his draft card so he can shoot it up as a protest." They remembered the Bub but didn't know where he was. One of them thought he might be staying with a friend who had a cabin in Mendocino County. He didn't have an address but said the cabin was in Annapolis.

Outside on the landing I gripped Wade by the shoulders. "I know the guy they're talking about! His name's Denning. What better place to stash a half ton of dope than a cabin in Annapolis!"

"Let's go, man!"

At the bottom of the stairs Wade hesitated. "But we'll need guns."

"I've got a pistol in the trunk."

"Let's go!"

It was just getting dark. We sped across the Golden Gate and up Highway 1. I didn't know Denning that well and had never been to his place, but Annapolis was a small town and if the Bub was there, I figured we could find him by spotting his red Econoline van. In Marshall we stopped at a market and asked the proprietor for his best bottle of red wine. He sold us a 1962 Gamay Beaujolais and loaned us a corkscrew so we could step outside and open it. We traded hits heading up the highway. Beyond the guardrail to our left, the ocean lay hundreds of feet below, looking like obsidian in the moonlight. I was powering the Mustang through the curves, feeling the controlled slide of the tires sideways, but when I came to a hairpin turn, I realized I wasn't going to make it and spun out. "God, sorry!" I told Wade as I jerked the Mustang back to the right direction.

"What are you apologizing for, man? You're doing great!" He handed me the bottle. "Here, have another hit!"

We reached Annapolis around nine at night. All there was to the town were a few yellow-lit cabins hidden among tall redwoods. There were no stores and the road going through was the only paved road. We made a quick pass through but saw no sign of the Bub's van. At the edge of town we pulled over and conferred. I told Wade about the Bub's uncanny ability to identify cars by their engine sounds and said I didn't want to go back through again for fear of alerting him. Across the road from us was a neat, brightly lit home with a carved wooden sign over the door that read "The Hendersons." We decided this home was unlikely to be Denning's and went up to ask. An older man answered the door and laughed when we asked if he knew where Denning lived. "Well, I guess I ought to. I rent to him!" We listened carefully as he gave directions.

With our lights out, we followed a dark dirt road and slowed when we spotted Denning's cabin ahead. Denning's battered VW van was parked in front, but there were no other cars around—no sign of the Bub's van. Aside from the light coming through the shades of the cabin, it was pitch dark. We stopped noiselessly and as we stepped out, the whole forest suddenly lit up with flashing orange light. I dropped to a crouch and wheeled, my heart pounding, but it was only the Mustang's turn signal lights—I had evidently bumped the lever stepping out.

I got the pistol out of the trunk and we approached Denning's cabin, creeping from tree to tree till we couldn't get any closer without entering the semicircle of light cast by Denning's porch light. While we debated what to do, the door opened and we held our breath. Nothing happened for a moment and then Denning's voice said, "Go on," and a cat stepped out, seemed to sense us where we were hiding, and skittered off in a different direction. The door closed and I handed the pistol to Wade.

"I'm going in there. If I'm not back in ten minutes, come get me."

I ran to the cabin and flattened myself against the wall. One at a time I crept up the stairs, stepping on the nail heads so the boards wouldn't creak. Slowly I brought my eye up to the window of the door, the only window without a shade. Inside I could see Denning reading a magazine by a wood stove. He seemed to be alone. I looked around and didn't see anything I recognized as belonging to the Bub. I decided to play things straight and knocked on the door.

"Wow, Tom, you're about the last person I expected to see standing there. Come on in."

I told Denning why I was there and he sucked in air through his teeth. "Well, I guess we all knew the Bub wasn't the most honest guy in the world, but I never thought he would steal from a friend. That's pretty cold."

"I'd really like to find him. I'm not out to hurt him. I just want to get my stuff back."

Denning nodded. "The last time I saw the Bub was about two months ago. I guess that must have been right before he did it. He was up here visiting. He told me he was thinking of moving to Santa Cruz. He said he found a house for rent there."

"You don't have an address, though?"

"No. But I remember he said the only thing he didn't like about it was that it was across the street from a police station. Oh, and he said it had a big yard."

I thanked Denning for the information and told him that if it led to getting the grass back, I would repay him with $500 or three bricks, his choice. We chatted a while and then I suddenly remembered Wade. I hurried to open the back door and found him stealing up the steps, pistol in hand, looking grim-faced and murderous.

CHAPTER 43

WE HAD THE SLIMMEST OF LEADS, YET we talked as though we had the Bub in our hands. Wade said we should swing by Berkeley and pick up a friend of his who specialized in collecting debts. "You need to see this guy. He's a fucking gorilla. He doesn't even need to say anything. He just appears at the door and people run to find money."

"Is he Black?"

"No, man, he's Italian!"

Wade was waving his hands excitedly. "Check this. I had about ten grand worth of bad acid debts in Seattle. These were debts that had been going on for over a year, right? I wasn't expecting to get a cent out of them. Well, I went up there with this guy and in two days we got eight thousand of it back. We probably would have gotten the rest, too, only the guy who owed it to me was already in the hospital from a motorcycle accident." Wade said his friend went by the name of Rent-a-Heavy.

We caught some sleep at a motel in Cotati and were in Berkeley first thing the following morning. We picked up Rent-a-Heavy and I was surprised to see he wasn't very big, not nearly as big as Wade. What impressed Wade evidently was the fact Rent-a-Heavy had black hair protruding from every pore of his body save for his palms and a small space around his forehead and nose. It was the Charles Manson effect. His fee, Rent-a-Heavy explained, was a flat $500 for which he would do "whatever's necessary."

We dropped by Wade's house briefly, then swung by my flat to pick up a rifle I owned. Arf was there and in my excitement I forgot about our differences.

"Hey, we found out where the Bub's hiding and we're going after him with guns and stuff! Want to come along?"

Arf chuckled in his above-it-all way. "No, thanks. I think I'll pass." He saw me get my rifle and looked concerned. "Hey, be careful, you guys. I mean, somebody could get hurt." He followed us out to the porch and watched us take off.

We reached Santa Cruz in the late afternoon. The city police station was likely to be downtown in a dense area with high rents and small yards, which led me to believe the station in question must be a Highway Patrol station. We stopped at a service station and the attendant told us the Highway Patrol station was on the other side of town. We followed his directions and soon found ourselves in a semi-rural area with older homes on large lots. We topped a rise and there, parked in the driveway of a home two blocks ahead, was the Bub's red Econoline van! I quickly turned down a side street and Wade and I let out whoops and hollers. I pulled over and we debated how to proceed. Rent-A-Heavy said it would be easier to take the Bub by surprise if we waited till dark. Also, the Highway Patrol station would be closed by then.

We found a small diner far from the Bub's place and filled up on hamburgers and fries. Wade flirted shamelessly with the waitress. I envied the way he and Bruce had with women. The waitress was wearing a wedding ring and as we stood up to leave, Wade told her, "You know, you're pretty cute. If you weren't married, I'd ask you out." The waitress was carrying some dishes and stopped to face him.

"Well, thank you! A woman likes to hear that. If I weren't married, I'd go out with you!"

We waited till it was completely dark, then drove to the Bub's house. This time his van was gone. The house was dark. We pulled up and saw two sheds along the side of the driveway. "I bet it's in one of those sheds," Wade and I said simultaneously.

We got out and I opened the trunk and handed Wade and Rent-a-Heavy my rifle and pistol and some tools Wade had thought to bring. They melted into the shadows in the direction of the sheds, and I drove the Mustang several blocks away, parked it on a side street, and jogged back. Wade's broad-shouldered form materialized from the darkness. "Both those sheds have brand new locks on them!"

The sheds were next to the fence line and on the other side was a two-story home with lights on behind the shades. We stopped at the first shed and Wade took an immense screwdriver big as a pry bar and levered it through the padlock of the shed. He waited for a car to pass, providing noise, and gave a fierce tug, ripping the entire lock and hasp away from the wood. We slipped in and saw the shed had a single window facing the neighbor's house. While Rent-a-Heavy held his jacket over it, Wade and I lit matches. All we found was a rusted lawn mower, some cans of paint, and an old wheelbarrow. We broke into the second shed the same way, but there was only more paint and some empty boxes. That left the house itself.

We circled it, checking the doors and windows, but they were all locked. Wade tried jimmying each of the three doors with a credit card, but they all had deadbolts. The side door was the only one with a window, and even though it was facing the neighbor's house, Rent-A-Heavy said this was where we should break in. Wade had thought to bring masking tape with him and began applying it to the window in a crisscross pattern. This was a trick he had learned somewhere and was meant to keep most of the glass from falling and making a racket. He wrapped a cloth around the head of a hammer and held it poised, waiting for a car to pass by. One passed and he gave the window a sharp rap but nothing happened. Another car passed and he gave the window a sharper rap but again nothing happened. For a long time no cars passed by. Finally one passed and Wade gave the window a really sharp rap and this time the glass broke, clattering to the floor inside so loudly I felt sure the neighbors would hear, Wade's trick having accomplished nothing. Wade reached in and turned the door handle and he and Rent-a-Heavy slipped inside. I hesitated on the porch, scanning the neighbor's windows at the same time that I was calculating sprint distance to the back fence. "Get in!" Rent-a-Heavy was hissing. "You're safer inside where no one can see you!"

Most of the windows lacked shades and we were able to see by the faint light coming in from outside. The house had only a few furnishings and there was no phone. Right away we found two boxes of the stolen bricks on a shelf in a closet. That was all we found, though, even after searching the attic and the crawl space underneath the house. We were going to have to wait for the Bub to tell us where the rest was.

At my suggestion, we went around and unscrewed all the light bulbs in the house. Then the three of us sat ranged along the living room couch facing a large window that looked out over the street. Wade had my rifle, Rent-a-Heavy had my pistol, and I had somehow ended up with the hammer. It was like a game of Clue! Some time passed and I said I wished we had a bottle. Wade snapped his fingers. "The dope!"

There were some green-wrapped bricks in the boxes and we rolled a fat joint of Michoacan and passed it around. It was stony grass and made us talkative. Rent-a-Heavy described what it was like growing up in Little Italy. He said he first got into the debt collection business as a young kid doing small jobs for low-level Mafia types. Most of the time he had to rely on his fists or maybe a knife. "Man, I'm sure glad you guys got guns," he commented, glancing down to admire my crummy .22. "I hate using knives. I had to stick a knife through a guy's hand once. It was a real bummer. I could feel the bones crunching and everything." He made a face. "I didn't dig it at all."

A couple of hours passed and we got so involved telling each other our life stories that when headlights swept across the front window, we were caught by surprise. We lurched to our feet in a panic.

"He's at the front!"

"No, he's at the side!"

We were bumping into each other like a scene out of the Three Stooges. I ended up alone beside the front door. It opened and a little guy I had never seen before stepped in and began flicking the light switch up and down repeatedly when the lights failed to go on. I stepped up with the hammer raised and told him, "Don't move!" as I kicked the door shut with my boot.

It was awful! The poor kid practically wilted in front of me from fright. "It's OK, it's OK," I rushed to reassure him, lowering the hammer. "Everything's OK. Just do what we say and you'll be all right."

I took him into a hallway where there were no windows and had him lie facedown on the floor. Wade and Rent-a-Heavy came in leading the Bub and I had him lie on the floor too. For some reason he and his friend had come in by separate doors, which was what had caused the confusion.

"Fancy meeting you here," I told the Bub.

He snorted.

"OK, Bub, where's the dope?"

"What dope?"

I had to laugh. It was the same brazenness he and I used to pull on customs.

"Come on, Bub. We already found those two boxes in your closet."

"Those? I bought those off a guy." In a way I was almost hoping for this.

I turned to Wade and told him to take the little guy into one of the closets and guard him. "Rent-a-Heavy, you—"

"Alright, alright. Don't get all uptight. I'll tell you where it is."

It seemed Rent-a-Heavy's name was possibly the best thing about him.

The Bub said the grass was in a rented garage in Berkeley. "It's practically all there, too. Hardly any of it's missing. Only you're going to have to break in 'cause I don't have the key."

"Where's the key?"

"My partner has it."

"This guy here isn't your partner?"

"No! I didn't have anything to do with it!" piped the little guy. "I swear!"

"Is that true, Bub?"

"It's true."

"Who's your partner then?"

"I can't tell you."

"I'm not out to hurt him. I just want to get the key from him."

"Take my word for it, it'll be easier to break in."

I thought this over. "You mean you expect me to believe you stole this stuff and now you don't even have a key to it?"

225

"That's the honest-to-God truth. Why would I lie to you now?"

It sounded only too true, too. The Bub was such a follower. I could just imagine a more strong-willed partner keeping the only key and controlling things much the way I used to control things in the old car-running days. I could have beaten the Bub to get him to name his partner, but I respected his principle not to fink. Also, I assumed his partner was some friend of his I might not know and didn't feel like getting involved with an unknown adversary.

We led the two out to the Bub's van. Rent-a-Heavy had the pistol and was supposed to be guarding them, but on the way he began talking to Wade and let the Bub get a good twenty feet ahead of him. I ran up to the Bub with the hammer raised and he regarded me with a withering look. "Don't worry, I'm not going to make a run for it." He nodded in the direction of the pistol Rent-a-Heavy was holding. "As if that thing could stop me." He recognized it as the same piece-of-shit pistol we had bought in Utah on our trip back east, a trip that now seemed so long ago.

The Bub glanced down and his mood seemed to soften. "Actually, I'm kind of glad it's all over with. I should have known I would never get away with something like this against you."

We put the Bub and his friend in the back of the Bub's van with Rent-a-Heavy guarding them. Then Wade drove the van while I followed in the Mustang. During the drive to Berkeley, I don't think the word "kidnapping" even once crossed my mind. I was just doing what I had to do to get something back I considered rightfully mine. In Berkeley we transferred the Bub and his friend to the garage beneath my flat and left Rent-a-Heavy there to continue guarding them. It was now one o'clock in the morning.

The Bub had described the garage where the grass was stashed and warned us that it was only a half block from the Berkeley police station. The Bub seemed to have a thing for police stations these days. Wade drove and we took the Bub's van to the address he had told us and found the garage. It was at the end of a driveway that ran between a pair of two-story older wooden homes. We looked down the street and saw the bright lights of the police station just a half block away. No one was about. Wade quietly backed the van down the driveway till it was close to the garage. We got out and there was a brand-new, heavy-duty lock on the garage. Wade had his oversized screwdriver and put some pressure on it, but it was solid. The wood didn't even creak. I looked around and noticed a light on behind a shade in a second-story window of the home nextdoor. The only sound was the purr of the van's engine. I was studying the light, trying to remember if it was on when we first pulled up, when Wade abruptly planted his foot against the garage door and yanked the screwdriver back with the full weight of his six-foot-plus frame. The lock along with the section of plywood it was bolted to tore away with a screech that was bound to wake up the entire neighborhood.

"Man, you're nuts!"

"Why?"

Inside were three large trunks, just as the Bub had said. Wade lit a match and quickly checked to make sure they had bricks in them. I felt sick with fear. It would take the cops less than a minute to get here. Each of the trunks weighed about 400 pounds and we got two of them in the van before a light went on in a window directly above us. I headed for the passenger seat.

"Wait, we need to get the last one!"

I wheeled. Wade was standing there looking resolute in the moonlight. It was going to take less time to load the trunk than to argue with him. We got it in and Wade took the wheel and cautiously poked the van out toward the street. Nothing was happening at the police station to our right, and Wade turned left into the street and took off. At the first opportunity he turned left again and soon we were safely distanced from the police station and I felt I could breathe again.

Wade drove to a rental garage he maintained in Oakland and we stashed the trunks there. Back at my place, I gave the Bub back his van keys and let him and the little guy go. I paid Rent-a-Heavy the $500 we owed him and he left. Wade asked to use my phone and I told him to go ahead. Moments later I overheard him saying, "Hey, old lady, I'm just waking you up in the middle of the night to let you know we're considerably richer than we were just a few hours ago."

CHAPTER 44

WADE ENDED UP WITH A QUARTER TON of grass without having to pay anything for it and with the money he made selling it, he rented a palatial home in the Berkeley hills, which had a redwood deck that offered a sweeping view of the bay. To furnish the home, he became a regular at Butterfield & Butterfield, where he bid on Persian rugs and antiques. His wife was good with plants and provided the rooms with potted palms and exotic cactuses. In the living and dining rooms, Wade placed little Chinese lacquered bowls containing mounds of cocaine. When I asked him about these, he explained that he wanted his guests to be able to indulge without having to ask all the time.

Wade began going on what he called "consumeathons," where he would drop by various shops and buy whatever he liked. When I first met him, he was tight with his money and often tried to bargain with shopkeepers. "Better to open your mouth than your pocketbook" was a favorite saying of his. Now he considered it gauche to even mention price. I was with him once when he paid an antique dealer his asking price of $800 for a leaded glass lamp. Outside the shop, Wade gave the bizarre explanation that he thought the lamp was a Tiffany and the shop owner hadn't realized it. We looked over every square inch of that lamp but couldn't find Tiffany's signature.

Wade hung the lamp over a pool table he had bought and one night in the excitement of making a difficult shot, an acid dealer named Murray jerked his cue up and struck the lamp, which before this didn't have a single crack in it. This happened again and Wade set out a Mason jar on a shelf near the pool table: anyone who cracked the lamp had to drop a twenty-dollar bill in the jar. Before long the jar was filled with bills while the lamp was little more than a lead skeleton with shards of colored glass clinging to it.

I didn't fare nearly so well on this run because I had paid money for that grass. Also, I knew I should give half my proceeds to Bruce though part of me felt like keeping more than half, considering all the risks I had taken to get it back. While I was debating this in my mind, Bruce found out through the grapevine that we had recovered the grass, which severely embarrassed me. I took all the cash I had made off the run, drove over to his place in Mill Valley, and told him to take as much as he wanted. He took half.

"I mean to say, chap, why didn't you ask me to help you recover the grass? As it is, you've given half to Wade."

God knew Bruce had guts, but somehow I couldn't imagine him tracking the Bub down in the Haight, kidnapping the Bub and his friend at gunpoint, and breaking into a garage near the Berkeley police station in the dead of night.

"We can keep on doing these runs as before," Bruce told me, "but I want Harold to deliver the grass to me so I can keep track of it and give you portions to sell."

This felt like a slap in the face, but I supposed I deserved it and didn't argue the point. At least the runs were going to keep on happening. I was going to be transporting large quantities of grass from Mill Valley to Berkeley and thought I better get a car with a big trunk. Once when I was a kid, a friend had remarked that the new '57 Plymouth was bigger than the Cadillac of that year. I went to a used car dealer and was excited to find a '57 Plymouth on the lot. Most car buyers probably look under the hood first, but I asked to see the trunk. The dealer opened it and I could hardly conceal my delight. You could throw a party in here! I thought to myself. I paid cash without even trying to bargain, set the radio buttons to all my favorite stations, and took off in my new purchase. This was probably the entirely wrong way to buy a used car, yet that Plymouth ended up being one of the most reliable cars I ever owned.

Denning appeared at my door one day and before he could even say anything, I apologized for having forgotten about him. I asked if he wanted $500 or three bricks and he said he wanted three bricks, which I went and got for him. He left and I happened to glance out the window as he was taking off. Who should be sitting beside him in the passenger seat but the Bub! The very guy he had finked on! It seemed there were no hard feelings in this business. I could just see the Bub encouraging him to come see me, saying, Don't worry, if he said he'd give you three bricks, he will.

A new quarter began and in addition to my math courses, I excitedly signed up for a course titled "The Interpretation of Dreams" and another titled "The Sociology of Capitalism." Wade wasn't even a student but he accompanied me to my lectures out of interest. The classes were fascinating, but after a couple of weeks I grew restless and dropped out, telling myself this time it was for good. Just as I had taken the theft of the grass as a sign I should quit smuggling, I now took the recovery of the grass as a sign smuggling was my destiny.

With total free time I began smoking grass again and also dropping acid and doing PCP. I bought a .45 semiautomatic pistol off a Hells Angel and threw away my crummy .22. Arf and I no longer had much in common, it seemed, and things between us became more estranged. He still confided in me, but the old, excited feelings we used to share were gone. He told me he wanted to get out of the heroin business soon and settle down and get married. He said he even had a girl picked out, a student in one of his classes named Leslie. He told me she was blonde, attractive, and intelligent, wrote poetry, and played piano. Also, she came from an upper-class family, a fact that seemed important to Arf. He told me so much about her that I assumed he was seeing her, so when he admitted he hadn't even spoken to her yet, only spying on her from afar, I figured this was just another New Arf pipe dream. That weekend, though, he brought her home after a date, and a month later they were making plans to live together. Arf told Leslie about his heroin dealings and she loved him anyway.

This provided a natural end to our living together. Arf moved in with Leslie on the North Side and, partly inspired by Wade, I rented a large home in the staid, wealthy community of Piedmont and moved in with a girlfriend named Vickie and also Fred Swaha and his girl and another couple. This was the beginning of a brief phase I think of as my bourgeois phase. I was enamored of Bruce and wanted to put into practice what I had learned from him. I bought straight-looking blazers and ties and began frequenting expensive establishments in The City—the more expensive, the better. For company, I dragged along all my housemates. They didn't have money, so I paid their way. They didn't have sports jackets and ties, so I loaned them sports jackets and ties. We would slick back our long hair in an attempt to look straight, but the staff at these places recognized that we didn't fit in and gave us poor service, which only spurred me to try all the harder.

Someone told me The Purple Vixen was the most expensive restaurant in all San Francisco, so I had to go there. The atmosphere was ponderous, the food unremarkable, the service abominable. Throughout our meal the waiters ignored us in favor of a party headed by a loud business type who kept hollering to the manager, saying things like, "You remember that night, don't you? Bing Crosby was sitting right where I'm sitting now and Joey Bishop had the table in the corner." Despite this, I went back the very next night and couldn't wait to impress Bruce with my find. Yet when I took him there, he balked at going in. "Are you sure you want to eat here, chap? It seems a bit solemn. Wouldn't you rather go to a place where young people hang out? Someplace more lively?"

One day Bruce told me he had bought a plane, a twin-engine Beechcraft D-18. It had been built during the war and used to belong to the Royal Canadian Air Force. Currently it was hangared in Salinas and he rented a light plane and took me down to see it. I was stunned to see how big it was. The cabin had seats for twelve passengers and the two Pratt & Whitney engines were so big you wouldn't be able to get your arms even halfway around them. It was a taildragger, meaning that its nose stood up in the air while the tail rested on a small wheel at the stern. Bruce admitted it was too large for our runs and would likely stand out on radar.

"So why did you buy it?"

He flashed one of his gummy grins. "I can't really say, chap. I've always wanted my own plane and thought it would be a good thing to have around."

To register the plane, he had created a shell corporation of which he was very proud. "Anyone who tries to find out who owns this bird is going to wind up with a post office box in the Bahamas!"

Another run pulled through and Bruce said he had run across a boat he felt we should buy. "The ocean is the wave of the future," a friend had once quipped and I suspected it was true. Word was that the government was developing a better system of radar along the border and the only way to escape it was to take advantage of the curvature of the earth and go around the border via the ocean. The boat was a forty-foot, steel-hulled cutter named The Saga and was anchored off Sausalito. The cost was $8,000 plus incidentals, and Bruce, Wade, and I each put up $3,000 to buy it. It needed some repairs and outfitting, and we hired a guy Bruce knew from St. Ives to do the job. His name was David and after inspecting the boat, he presented me with a list of hardware he said it needed. I looked at his list and saw terms like "shrouds," "stays," and "blocks" written out in a neat, laborious hand. In his plodding St. Ives accent, David proceeded to explain why each of these parts was needed, but I cut him off, asking how much he needed, and peeled off hundred-dollar bills.

Walking along Telegraph Avenue one afternoon, I ran into Arf and Leslie. I hadn't seen or even spoken to Arf in the several months since we quit living together. He seemed ill at ease around me and we struggled to make conversation. He and Leslie were shopping for material to make curtains for their new place, he told me. While he spoke, Leslie hung adoringly on his arm. Arf wore his hair cut very short now, and together they were the picture of a happy, straight, bourgeois couple. A heroin smuggler buying curtain material!

I kept track of Arf's operation through the Bear's Lair. Word had it he was in a lull right now. Maybe he was even quitting, I told myself. Meanwhile, I remained on the lookout for any information about his operation that might enable me to put an end to it once and for all.

CHAPTER 45

FOR A WHILE NOW BRUCE HAD TALKED about hiring another pilot to fly the runs so he could take more of an "administrative position" as he put it. He was afraid the Law of Averages was due to catch up with him. I put the word out and got in touch with a dope pilot who went by the name of Airplane Mike. He lived in a rented room in an area of Oakland that was so rundown and depressing that even hippies didn't live here. It was the kind of semi-industrial area where old men who never married went to rent cheap rooms and die. I walked in and there were male bodybuilding magazines strewn all over the floor and dishes piled up in the sink. "Bummer of a divorce," Airplane Mike commented by way of explanation. He wanted to fly a run for us, but I was so put off by his circumstances that I decided not to use him. Several months later I heard that Airplane Mike had crashed a light plane somewhere in southern California, killing himself and two passengers.

Bruce and I decided to train a friend of his to take over the runs. Jerry Jones had flying experience but lacked the 200 logged hours and the instrument rating required to rent a plane. Jerry was eager to take over the runs and Bruce lined up an FAA instructor to train him. To save on plane rental costs, Bruce bought an old Citabria for him to train with. Citabria, which is a corruption of "aerobatic" spelled backward, was the name of a lightweight fabric plane with tandem seats and an actual stick for steering. It looked like the kind of plane Snoopy would fly chasing the Red Baron. Bruce and I took it for a spin one day and buzzed Bill Gretsch's house, but Bill didn't seem to be home, so I said we should check out the Berkeley campus. This was during the height of the People's Park riots when Governor Reagan called out the National Guard. We flew over the park and it was so torn up from riots, it looked as though it had been napalmed. A chain-link fence surrounded it and with National Guard vehicles lined all along Haste Street and rifle-toting guardsmen everywhere, the scene looked like something out of Vietnam.

A huge demonstration had been taking place at Sproul Plaza and we looked down at the crowd of demonstrators as they headed down Telegraph Avenue toward People's Park. At the same time, we spotted a contingent of Blue Meanies lying in wait for them behind the windowless Bank of America building at Telegraph and Durant. These were the Alameda County Sheriff's deputies who wore blue uniforms and were famous for their brutality. I watched them don gas masks in unison and felt awful knowing they were about to ambush the demonstrators yet there was nothing we could do about it. They rushed out, lobbing tear gas and swinging their batons, and the demonstrators in front shrank back, sending a ripple back through the blocks-long crowd that was like a wave passing over seaweed.

"We need our walkie-talkies!" I shouted to Bruce above the wind and engine noise. "We could warn the demonstrators next time there's a demonstration! We could be the People's Plane!"

Bruce gave a sort of snicker at the idea and next thing we heard a loud chopping noise and saw a National Guard helicopter bearing down on us from above while a fixed-wing aircraft with military markings was approaching from our left. We got the hell out. So much for the People's Plane!

Jerry Jones began accumulating hours on the Citabria and Bruce took advantage of the break to get acquainted with the Marin County social scene. His skill at social maneuvering continually amazed me. In a short while he was getting invited to cocktail parties thrown by ambassadors and wealthy industrialists. At one of these parties he met a well-to-do art collector who was interested in acquiring some Mayan artifacts recently discovered in the jungles of Guatemala. The artifacts were called stelae and were slabs of stone about five feet high, three feet wide, and a foot thick with the profile of a warrior carved on one face in bas-relief. A UC Berkeley archeologist had discovered the stelae and Bruce showed me a book the archeologist had produced with photographs of the stones. They showed profiles of warriors wearing headdresses with serpents and plumes. Penciled in alongside some of the photographs were prices the art collector was willing to pay for particular stelae. I saw figures like $15,000 and $17,500. Bruce saw this as a chance to put his D-18 to use and was excited about the possibility of "spiriting out" these stelae as he put it. When I told him this was stealing, he scoffed.

"No, it isn't, chap. They don't belong to anyone. They were only recently discovered. Hardly anyone even knows they're there."

"They belong to the people of Guatemala. They're part of the people's heritage."

Bruce rolled his eyes. "That's a lot of rubbish. Anyway, you're a fine one to talk—a bloody dope smuggler!" He broke into one of his gummy grins. To Bruce, breaking the law was breaking the law. He wasn't much for subtle distinctions.

Bruce wanted me to go with him to steal these stelae, saying he needed me to interpret for him. He described it as a fun trip to a place I had never been before and said he would pay me $500 in addition to expenses. I told him I wanted nothing to do with stealing artifacts this important and valuable, but he kept pressing me. One day I looked up the density of rock and calculated how much the stelae would weigh. They would weigh a ton. I asked Bruce how he intended to get the stelae from the middle of the jungle to a strip big enough for the Beech and he said he might have to have them flown out by helicopter.

"Where are you going to find a crooked helicopter pilot?"

"Oh, people can be bought easily enough. That's no problem."

I looked at him askance.

"Anyway, I'll build a crude road if I have to. You're such a doubter."

I eventually agreed to go with him because I couldn't believe Bruce was ever going to get these stones out of the jungle. I even bet him an additional $500 that he wouldn't.

Jerry Jones still had ninety hours to go on his training, but Bruce grew impatient and went to meet Jerry's instructor to see if things couldn't be speeded up. He came back and proudly showed me Jerry's new pilot logbook with the required number of hours filled out. I stared at it, slack-jawed.

"You bribed an FAA instructor?"

Bruce just grinned.

"I keep trying to tell you things, chap, but you never listen."

Bruce rented a Cherokee Six and the three of us took off for Guatemala. Bruce's plan was to get his stelae-stealing operation going and on the way back Jerry would use the Cherokee Six to fly a run. I had only met Jerry a couple of times but got to know him well on this trip. He was short, solidly built, and used to box. He had been a radio operator in Vietnam and asked me about my draft status. I told him about the amazing trick for avoiding the draft I had pulled off by accident. For over a year now I had registered for classes at Cal every quarter, but half the time I had dropped out and evidently when I registered, a letter would be sent to the Selective Service System verifying that I was in school, but when I dropped out, no letter would be sent notifying them of my change in status, so that to the Selective Service System it appeared I was attending school four out of four quarters. At least this is what I assumed was happening, for while all my friends were getting Notices to Appear, my 2-S classification had remained untouched. Jerry listened to this and chuckled.

"They'll have your ass over there before you know it. You'll see."

"No, they won't. I'll go to Canada if I have to."

He chuckled again. "They'll have your ass over there to get shot at same as everybody else."

Nothing came of Bruce's stelae-stealing plan. Just as I had predicted, the stones were way too heavy and the surrounding jungle way too dense. We headed back north and I called Jesus and told him to meet us at the Mazatlan airport. We landed and a commercial flight had come in just before us, so that the terminal was packed with travelers. We spotted Jesus and Miguel at the far end of the terminal and began making our way toward them but were unable to find them. They seemed to have disappeared. People began leaving, and eventually we were the only ones left in the terminal save for a janitor, who had begun mopping the floor. Later, I was able to reach Jesus by phone at his home and he gave the bizarre explanation that he and Miguel had taken one look at Jerry, decided he was narc, and fled. In all my dealings with Jesus, this was the first time he had done something less than rational. The result was that Jerry backed out of the run, calling it "shaky."

"Shaky?" Bruce erupted. "How can you call it shaky when I've already done it eleven times?"

Jerry refused, though, and for months afterward Bruce would refer to his friend as "that bloody coward, Jerry Jones."

CHAPTER 46

THE HOUSE IN PIEDMONT BROKE UP and I found an apartment on University Avenue. There were rumors that the narcs were on to me, so I lay low and told only a few close friends where I was living. One afternoon I picked up a girl hitchhiking and she told me she had just broken up with her boyfriend. "I've had it with men!" she said, adding that it would be months before she ever got into another relationship. "If ever!" We ended up sleeping together that night. Her name was Gloriana and she was half Mexican and half Apache and spoke fluent Spanish.

A couple of weeks later, I got a phone call from Arf. In a circumspect voice, no doubt knowing how I would feel about the call, he told me Jesus and Abelardo were coming to visit and gave me the name of the hotel in San Francisco where they would be staying. We hung up and I felt like throwing the phone through the window, I was so angry. So Jesus was now closer to Arf than he was to me! I managed to calm down and told Gloriana, "The Mexicans are coming! We need to entertain them!"

Jesus and Abelardo arrived and Gloriana and I went to meet them at their hotel in the Mission. Just as we walked up, Jake came skipping down the hotel stairs. The sight of him visiting my contacts before I had even had a chance to see them caused me to lose it, and I ran toward him with murder in my heart. He began running, and I was just about to catch up to him when he darted between two parked cars into the street and was nearly run over by a truck. Jesus and Abelardo rushed up and convinced me to let him be.

"If it means this much to you, Tom, we will quit doing *negocios* with Rafael and Jake," Abelardo told me. And I believe he truly meant it even as I knew it was never going to happen.

I called Wade and we took the Mexicans sailing on a rented Catalina. We purposely took them to Hurricane Gulch, where the winds were strongest, and got the lee gunwale awash. The deck was so steeply tilted that we had to hang on to the stanchions to keep from sliding off our seats. For some reason I felt compelled to impress Jesus and Abelardo with the scary things I could do even though this was the exact opposite of the way they treated me in Culiacan, always wanting me to feel at home and comfortable. Later I took Jesus for a ride on the back of my Hornet and scrambled up a hill so steep that if my front wheel had weighed an ounce less, I think we would have flipped over backward.

I didn't know what to do with the Mexicans. I drove them around, showing them different sights in San Francisco even though I knew the sights wouldn't really interest them. Just to be doing something, we kept stopping to get things to eat and drink. Food piled up on the back seat. In Culiacan the Mexicans were content to let me blend in with their lives, but what kind of life did I have here that they could blend into? I was holed up in an apartment in semi-hiding and, save for Gloriana, hardly any friends came by. What was my life anyway? I sometimes imagined myself on a large ranch in Mexico with a beautiful wife and kids who would grow up riding horses, and in fact, Abelardo and I had often talked of buying adjoining *ranchos*. Other times I saw myself in an elegant home in the Berkeley hills throwing parties attended by UC professors and other intellectuals. These dreams were so far from reality, though, as to be pathetic.

The Mexicans left a day earlier than planned and it was sad. On their last night here, Abelardo asked me if I could provide him with a vieja and I said sure. At least this was something I could do for him. I drove him to the Tenderloin district in The City and found a block where prostitutes were standing about showing off their legs. Abelardo seemed rather shocked and I had to explain this was the way it was done here and felt bad knowing the Mexican way had so much more class. Abelardo pointed to one he liked, but in that very moment police cruisers screeched up with lights and sirens and the girls scattered. We beat it out of there and I turned to see Abelardo looking pale. I told him there were other places where we might find viejas, but in his gentle and polite way, he told me how much he appreciated my efforts and didn't want me to think otherwise because I was such a wonderful host to take him here, but that he had lost the desire.

The next morning we said goodbye. Jesus and Abelardo were at my apartment along with Jesus's mistress, who had come with them on the trip, and I was with Gloriana. Abelardo asked me if grass prices were going up and Gloriana immediately cut in, telling him in her fluent Spanish how dry it was and how grass prices were skyrocketing. *"No puedes creer—"*

"Shut up, stupid! You want to double how much I have to pay for this stuff?"
Even I was surprised by my own vehemence.

*

Bruce wasn't inclined to fly any more runs and it was Wade Maddox who finally found a pilot for us. The pilot's name was Nelson Mitchum and his qualifications for the job were remarkable: he had over 10,000 hours total flying experience, including 600 hours on Cherokee Sixes. Wade had known him since Jesuit school and vouched for his trustworthiness.

Bruce spent an entire afternoon with Mitchum, explaining exactly how we did the runs and showing him the locations of our clandestine strips on his aeronautical charts. Bruce then stunned me by saying he was going on a two-month trip around the world. He had already bought tickets and hadn't even told me. He had become like family to me and I expected him to let me know everything he was planning. He saw how shocked I looked and tried to pass the trip off as a belated honeymoon, saying he was only doing it to satisfy his wife. However, I suspected he was going in order to investigate other deals he might segue into.

"Don't worry, chap. We wouldn't be able to get any decent grass this time of year anyway on account of the dry season. By the time I get back, the new harvests should be just coming in."

"Well, where are you going?"

"Lots of places."

"Such as?"

"Well, Africa, for instance."

"Oh, Africa. Well, it shouldn't be too hard to find you in Africa."

He grinned briefly before turning serious.

"Really, chap, there shouldn't be any need for you to get in touch with me. Just have everything ready and as soon as I get back, Mitchum can do a run."

He left and I made out a list of things I intended to do with my free time. First on the list was getting my Hornet in perfect condition. I made a list of parts I needed and drove all over the Bay Area hunting them down. Three days later, though, there were still problems with the bike. There was something wrong with the wiring I couldn't get right and the mufflers kept rattling loose no matter what I did to secure them. I broke out in that sweaty feeling again that I was wasting time, wasting my life.

It was strange because when a run got delayed and I ended up having to hang around a motel in a strange town for days on end with nothing to do, I felt fine. Actually, I felt better than fine. Having a run pending was a way of making time stop still, almost like a mystic experience. I could wander around the town, noticing little details and letting my mind drift, and not feel the least need to accomplish anything because the run was what was being accomplished. Without a run going, I didn't know what to do with myself. The Rolling Stones tune "What To Do" kept running through my mind.

I began spending a lot of time at Wade's place. He was going through the same sort of existential crisis. We would stand in front of his bay window looking out over the city below and marvel at all the people out there running around and getting things done as though it was perfectly clear to them what they should be doing.

"Who would have believed it?" Wade cried, pausing for effect. "Money doesn't make you happy! . . . I mean, I always figured that was just a line to keep poor people happy, right? Who would have guessed it was actually true?" He shook his head. "I'm just glad I found out now rather than later. Can you imagine how I would have felt if I worked thirty years as an engineer to find out?"

Wade asked his wife, Janet, what she thought we should do. She was peeling carrots and stopped to consider.

"Maybe you guys should get some exercise. You could throw a ball around at a park."

Wade and I looked at each other. Neither of us felt like it and anyway, Wade had terrible eyesight.

Some days passed and I guess it was inevitable that Wade and I would get around to considering a run without Bruce. The idea scared me at first, I was so used to counting on Bruce. I looked at him almost like a father. But with Mitchum I didn't really need him anymore. I often thought of smuggling as requiring three cards: a contact, financing, and a method. I had the contact, Wade and I had the financing, and Mitchum was the method. I felt a little guilty planning a run behind Bruce's back, but then he was off checking out deals that didn't involve me. Mitchum was game and Wade and I stuffed $7,000 into our boots and headed for Mazatlan.

Jesus and Miguel met us at the airport and we sped north to Culiacan. It was July and the hills were only just starting to turn green. The air was thick and humid. I thought to ask after Abelardo and saw Jesus and Miguel exchange looks in the front seat.

"*Está en la sierra,*" said Jesus.

"Buying merchandise?"

"No. . . . Hiding."

"Hiding? From what?"

"The law. He killed the chief *judicial* of the state of Sinaloa."

"Oh, sure."

Jesus held my eye in the rearview mirror. "It is true. I have the newspapers at home. You can read the headlines."

"It is true, Tom." Miguel turned to face me.

239

Jesus went on to explain that the chief judicial was *muy cabrón* — a real prick. He killed people just for the pleasure it gave him. One night he accosted Abelardo's brother at his home. The chief drew his gun and Abelardo's brother stepped in front of his wife instinctively to protect her. The chief shot him once with a .357 magnum and the bullet passed through Abelardo's brother and hit his wife, killing them both.

When Abelardo found out, he drove to Tucson, bought a used Mustang, drove it back to Culiacan, and lined up a driver, a *pistolero*, and two machine guns. The pistolero was under strict orders not to shoot unless Abelardo first missed. On a sunny afternoon, as the chief was walking to his car, Abelardo cut him down with a spray of machine gun fire. A chase ensued and the three managed to get away, but the Mustang was now hot and they doused it with gasoline and set it on fire. The fire, however, did not obscure the vehicle identification number and the police were able to trace the car to the used car lot in Tucson and from there to Abelardo. Abelardo was tipped off and fled.

I gave a low whistle. Abelardo was such a gentleman, it was hard to imagine him killing anyone. "Is he very upset?"

Jesus shrugged. "No one has seen him. He is deep in the *sierra*. Even his own family do not know where he is."

"Can't he pay his way out?"

"Not now. It is too soon. He will have to wait for a change of governor. The current governor was a good friend of the chief, *¿Entiendes?*"

I thought to ask when Abelardo gunned down the chief and Jesus named a date shortly before he and Abelardo came to visit me in the Bay Area. I could hardly believe it. He seemed so relaxed. But then I remembered how pale he turned when the police showed up during our visit to the prostitutes.

I interpreted all this for Wade and his eyes went wide. Well, I had wanted to impress him with the excitement of these runs and now I had. I stared up at the hardscrabble hills to our right and tried to envision Abelardo's new life as a fugitive. So much for our plan to live together on adjoining ranchos.

Jesus wasn't able to get us quality grass. He spent the evening bringing us different samples, but they were all immature. Every growing season pot farmers were faced with the stressful decision when to harvest their plants. With each extra day their grass became more potent, but there was the chance their fields would get ripped off or busted. The government, of course, timed its anti-grass campaign to coincide with the final stages of the season. It was a high-stakes gamble. Some farmers would inevitably chicken out early and cut their plants down before they had even developed seeds. This was the type of grass Jesus was showing us: grass without seeds. I asked him if there was any grass left over from the previous harvest and he said he didn't know of any.

"In a pair of months there will be good *mercancía*," he told me. "Maybe only a month and a half."

Wade and I didn't want to go back empty-handed and when we were alone, I suggested we give Meche a try. Wade frowned.

"Didn't that guy burn you once?"

"Not intentionally. He's just a middleman. He's not in control of things. He might be able to introduce us to his suppliers, though. We'll pay him a cut. We won't shell out any money either till we've seen all the grass. That way we ought to be safe."

"Outtasight."

I didn't want Jesus to know we were going to see another supplier and told him we were going to Mazatlan to do some body surfing. He told me to call him before going back to the States, just in case he found something. "It is not very probable, though."

CHAPTER 47

IN MAZATLAN WE CHECKED INTO THE Hotel de Cima and got a room on the second floor with a balcony that overlooked the beach. I had never stayed here before, considering the place to be hot, but chose it this time for that very reason. I was beginning to think I was invincible and felt like flaunting what we were doing. I saw myself a little like the thirties Chicago mobsters who were known to the police but were so powerful, they couldn't be touched.

A copy of *The Last Supper* hung on the wall and we hid our money behind it, then went to find Meche. He was at his home and brightened on seeing me. We hadn't seen each other in nearly a year. I introduced him to Wade and we went up to the roof where we could talk freely without his wife overhearing. I explained our situation and he set us up with two men named Carlos and Ricardo. Over the next two days, we met with Carlos and Ricardo several times but could not come to terms. They wanted $3,000 in advance to set up a run and we wanted to see the grass first. When I talked about the type of strip we needed, they paid little attention. As a test, I talked a little about the next run, saying it would be much bigger because we would be able to afford a larger plane. This was one of the most reliable ways I had found for deciding whether a supposed supplier could be trusted. The true supplier takes a genuine interest in future runs because he stands to profit from them, whereas the con artist takes little interest in runs he knows will never happen. Carlos and Ricardo showed little interest.

I told Meche I didn't think Carlos and Ricardo were good people and he agreed, saying they were *mala gente* — bad people. I knew Meche well enough not to bother asking why he would set us up with bad people. We were standing along the beach road next to a restaurant and fell quiet while a waiter wheeled out a rolling display of pastries for the flies to sit on.

"What about Manuel and Modesto?" I asked after the waiter had gone back inside. I had heard these names several times and was under the impression they were big suppliers. I asked Meche if he had heard of them.

"Of course," he said in a tone as if to say, Who hasn't?

"They are big suppliers, right?"

"The biggest."

"Well, what about them? Can you get us an introduction to them?"

Meche paled, turning to face me. "Oh, no, Tom. You would not want to have dealings with them."

"Why not? Are they *rateros*?"

"No, they are not *rateros*." He paused. "It is just that they are very powerful, very dangerous men. They have many men working for them. They have killed many men. If you were to have some sort of misunderstanding with them—"

"I'm not worried about misunderstandings. Can you get us an introduction? You wouldn't even have to be there. You could just set it up."

I managed to convince him and Wade and I watched him hobble off down a rutted alley. I turned to Wade. "This could be the start of the ultra-Big Time."

Meche met us the following morning at a small café near the downtown bus terminal. He nervously handed me a scrap of paper with an address written on it. A meeting had been arranged for two o'clock this afternoon, he told me. I glanced at the address.

"Do you know how to get there? It is in the Colonia Reforma."

"Sure. If I have any trouble, I will ask a cab driver."

"No, no, no! Do not show this address to anyone. If you were to bring heat down on Manuel and Modestillo, they could kill you."

I assured Meche I would not show the address to anyone and slipped it into my shirt pocket. Meche took off and Wade and I wandered to the central plaza to pass some time. We had our shoes shined and made eyes at a couple of American girls heading toward the marketplace. I could hardly believe we were an hour away from meeting the biggest dealers in all Sinaloa. "These guys are probably going to come off real macho," I told Wade. "The thing to do is act just as macho back. Don't ever let them know you're scared."

"Oh, I'm not the least bit scared. I've got complete confidence in you."

The address applied to a modest stucco home in a row of similar homes in a modest neighborhood. I had been imagining a villa with palms and caged parrots but then realized Manuel and Modesto would never invite two strange gringos to their homes for a first meeting. This was likely just a safe house they used for conducting business. As we were looking up a narrow flight of concrete stairs, the door above opened and a man stepped out and beckoned us up. He was lean, good-looking, and had green eyes.

"Pásense."

He ushered us in and bid us sit in some folding chairs arranged around a metal table like the kind you find in outdoor cantinas. I looked around and saw this was the only furniture in the room. A single window faced the street and was covered with a sheet. A pinup advertising spark plugs hung on one wall. We could hear men talking and laughing in another room and then the laughing stopped and three men filed in. Each carried a pistol at his belt pointing to his balls. One by one they removed their pistols and laid them on the table in front of us, stepped back, and stood with their hands clasped in front of them. I counted two .38s and what looked like a .32. Then a man who wasn't wearing a shirt came in. He was short and powerfully built, and all over his chest and left shoulder were large knife scars. You could actually see scars where the knife had entered and was repelled and places where it had been drawn through the flesh. A gold crucifix dangled in the black hairs at his chest and a pearl-handled .45 was tucked at his waist. He laid the .45 on the table, we exchanged *Buenas tardes* and there was silence for several moments.

"You are Manuel?"

"No." He let some moments go by. "Modesto." He nodded toward the man at the door. "He is Manuel."

The scene unfolded like a study in macho cool. Modesto pulled up a chair and sat down with a sort of snigger. I casually draped my hand on the table near the guns to show I wasn't intimidated by them. Wade scored points by drawing up a fourth chair and propping his boot on the rung. Modesto scratched absently at his left teat.

I tried making conversation but got only monosyllables in return. We couldn't seem to get past this study in machismo, so I got straight to the point and asked Modesto if he could get us large quantities of mature merchandise. He said he could. I asked if he could show us a sample and he nodded to one of his men, who stepped into the other room and came back with a plastic sack full of grass. Modesto took the sack and tossed it to my side of the table. I examined the grass inside, then handed it to Wade.

"Is this the shit they want to sell us?" Wade murmured.

"Yeah. They must take us for fools."

I pushed the sack back across the table to Modesto. "This grass is immature."

"Immature?" Modesto burst out with a harsh laugh as though I had said something preposterous. One of his men, apparently thinking Modesto had made a joke, laughed too. Modesto silenced him with a look.

"It has no seeds."

"You do not want it then?"

"We would not be able to sell it."

Modesto tossed the sack to the man who had brought it in and he took it back to the other room. Modesto then got up, turned his back to us, and began talking in low tones to his men.

"What's going on?" Wade frowned.

"I don't know, but I think it's time to split."

We got up, I murmured *"Con permiso"* to Modesto's back, and we headed for the door. Manuel blocked our path fractionally before stepping aside. The stairway was narrow and we took it single file.

"Strange vibes," Wade commented as we crossed the street.

"You can say that again. Don't ask me what was going on up there."

We agreed the run was off. Neither of us felt up to trying yet another contact. "We ought to go swimming," I said then to which Wade replied, "Far out!" and we headed back to our hotel room to change. With the run off, all my smuggler's instincts fell away from me like so much heavy baggage. Later we would recall that we never once looked back to make sure we weren't being followed.

CHAPTER 48

THE SUN WAS OUT AND THE WATER was clear and warm. No sooner had we jumped in than Wade lost his glasses despite having spent twenty minutes back at our hotel room fashioning a string and tape to hold them. I jumped out and announced to a group of kids that there was a hundred-peso reward for the glasses, then watched as a dozen brown bodies plunged into the water. No one could find them, though. The sea had claimed them. Without his glasses, Wade had to scrunch his eyes into a squint to see, which gave the impression he was frowning all the time.

We swam out past the surf and noticed two American girls swimming just south of us. They wore matching pink bathing suits, looked like sisters, and appeared to be about fifteen and sixteen. Their long hair made lazy blonde manes where it floated as they trod water. Slowly, as though the current were carrying us, we worked our way over to them and struck up a conversation.

They said they were from Oregon and we impressed them with our knowledge of Mazatlan and Mexico in general, mostly made up on Wade's part. Wade then asked them if they wanted to have dinner with us and they said sure but they would have to ask their parents first. I figured that was that, but Wade said, "Where are your parents?"

The girls pointed to the beach. "Right there."

"Let's go!"

I couldn't believe Wade was doing this. The girls weren't even legal age and I figured their parents would make short work of us. They turned out to be a young-looking couple, both slim, lying on a blanket and wearing swimsuits. The girls introduced us, their last name being Hansen. Mr. Hansen, it turned out, was a logging contractor and Wade instantly hit it off with him based on his logging experience, throwing out terms like "stumpage" and "gyppo loggers." When Wade asked if we could take his daughters out to dinner, I cringed inside, but to my surprise, the Hansens said OK. They were staying at the De Cima too and we traded room numbers.

Back in our room, Wade held up a bottle of tequila he had bought and grinned. "You know what they say, 'Candy's dandy, but liquor's quicker.'"

"Well, let's not push them into anything."

Wade took umbrage. "Why, Tom, I've never pushed anyone into anything."

I took a shower and as I was washing the salt off, Wade called to me through the bathroom door, his voice strangely somber. "Hey, Tom. You better come out. There's two policemen here to see us."

I threw my clothes on without bothering to dry off and stepped out. Wade was standing between two Mexican men dressed in civilian clothing. The men wore short-sleeve shirts and cheap slacks and I ran my eyes over them looking for bulges and didn't see any. They were average sized for Mexicans and Wade towered over them. One of them was a little taller than the other and he explained in Spanish that they were detectives sent to investigate reports of marijuana smoke coming from the balcony to our room.

"That is impossible. We do not smoke marijuana."

"Just the same, we would like to search your room with your permission."

"Of course. Go ahead." They would search anyway and trying to prevent them would only further their impression we had something to hide.

They began with the closet, then searched through our dresser drawers. I wasn't worried till the thought struck me that the reports of smoke coming from our balcony might be true. I wanted to ask Wade but didn't know whether the men understood English. I didn't want to whisper, either, as that would seem suspicious. From my own experience learning Spanish, I knew that it was almost impossible to understand a foreign language when it is spoken rapidly and slurred. In a normal tone of voice I asked Wade, "Hey, youdin'byanychancesmokeweed ou'onth'balcony, djoo?"

"No," Wade replied earnestly.

"Djoobringanywi'you?"

"Yeh,bu'they'llne'erfineit."

"Wherzit?"

"'Sfoldedinmysocks."

The two men were just now going through our suitcases. My heart was in my throat as I watched the shorter detective pick up Wade's folded socks one by one and squeeze them in his fist before dropping them back. When he shut the lid of Wade's suitcase carelessly over Wade's shirttails, I felt a wave of relief.

The taller detective now turned his attention to the bathroom, still steamy from my shower. Against one wall there was a louvered vent with five spaces between the louvers and his hand dove straight into the middle space and pulled out a folded piece of newspaper. I had the bizarre thought there might be a used tampon inside but of course, there was pot.

"That is not ours!" I burst out.

"What is it doing in your hotel room then?"

"I do not know. That you might know better than I!"

"Well, you must admit the circumstances are very suspicious. First we get reports of marijuana smoke coming from your balcony and then we find marijuana in your room."

I wanted to ask him how he knew to reach into the middle space between the louvers instead of starting at the top or bottom but didn't quite know how to phrase this in Spanish.

"Look, we are being framed and you know it. Who turned in the reports of marijuana smoke?"

"That I would not be at liberty to tell you even if I knew."

"Well, they are the ones who planted marijuana in our room!"

The detective seemed rather taken aback by my vehemence and tried calming me.

"Do not worry. This is merely an informal investigation. You will, however, have to accompany us to the police station. There you can explain your story to the chief and if you are telling the truth, you will be released."

I didn't like this idea one bit. Wade wanted to know what was going on and I interpreted for him. The four of us were standing close together in the space between the bathroom and the first bed. Again, I noticed how much bigger Wade and I were than the two men. "Whaddyathinkabouthittin'emoverth'head-an'split?"

"Theydon'appeartobearmed."

"I know. Youtaketh'tallerone?"

"Wha'ftherzmorepoliceou'side?"

The taller man grew impatient and cut in. *"Vámonos"*

We didn't quite have the guts to knock these guys out, which, for all we knew, could have gotten us life in a Mexican prison. Sheepishly, we headed for the door. I was in front and opened it just as the two girls from Oregon were about to knock. They were wearing lip gloss and had on freshly ironed dresses.

"These men are police!" I blurted. "Someone planted grass in our room and now they're taking us to the police station!"

"Vámonos!" The taller man began prodding us down the hallway. I glanced back to see the two girls standing there, their mouths making two round Os of utter astonishment.

The lobby was filled with tourists carrying towels on their way back from the beach. Seeing so many Americans emboldened me and I insisted on stopping at the *Administración*. The young clerk there looked up from the mail he was sorting and I quickly explained what was going on.

"It is merely an informal investigation," cut in the taller man. "They are not being arrested."

"Just the same, if we are not back by eight o'clock tonight, could you please contact the U.S. Consulate on our behalf?"

The clerk said he would and the detectives guided us in the direction of the door. I glanced back and saw that the clerk had already resumed sorting mail.

The detectives led us to an older model pickup with battered fenders. Wade got in but I balked. "Are you sure you are police?"

"*Sí, sí.* We drive this truck for undercover purposes." He pointed to a no parking sign next to us. "We park wherever we want and do not get tickets."

I got in and they sat on either side of us. The taller detective drove, heading toward downtown. I planned what I intended to say to the chief of police, conjugating verbs in advance. I asked the detectives how to describe the louvered vent where they had found the grass and they helped me come up with the right terms.

They parked in front of the police station and led us through an archway to an interior courtyard. We passed a group of *policías* shooting baskets at a bent, netless hoop, holsters flapping at their sides. After waiting briefly in an anteroom, we were ushered into the office of the chief. He was an older man with graying hair and the impassive look of someone used to disappointing people. He sat behind a gray metal desk with a Mexican flag hanging to his right and a framed photograph of President Echeverría on the wall behind. While Wade and I stayed back, the taller detective stepped forward and showed him the newspaper with the grass and they conferred in low tones. The chief asked me to step forward.

"Excuse me, *señor jefe*, but that marijuana is not ours and I can prove it if you would like."

He nodded for me to go ahead.

"Your men found this marijuana in a louvered vent in the bathroom of our hotel room. When they came, I was in the bathroom taking a shower. My friend called through the door and said two policemen were here to see us. For the time it took me to get dressed, the door remained closed. Now if I had known about the marijuana, surely I would have taken the opportunity to flush it down the toilet. The fact I did not flush it down the toilet proves that I did not know it was there."

"Perhaps," the chief nodded. "Is there anything else?"

"No, *señor jefe*."

I stepped back and the chief conferred again with the taller detective. "Take them to a cell," I heard him say.

CHAPTER 49

THE TWO MEN LED US DOWN a flight of stairs to a floor below ground and turned us over to a jailer, who locked us in a squalid cell that smelled like a latrine. Oddly, Wade and I weren't that bummed. This was all part of the Grand Adventure and we naively believed the men when they told us this was still just an informal investigation. We checked out the cell. It was about ten by twelve feet with concrete walls covered with scratched-in graffiti. A concrete partition jutted partway into the cell parallel to the bars, and behind it was a knee-high concrete block with a hole in the middle: the toilet. There were no furnishings in the cell. No washbasin, no water, no cot—not even a sheet or blanket.

The ceiling was high, maybe fourteen feet, and near the top of the back wall, above the toilet, was a rectangular hole that seemed to open out to the street. Sunlight filtered through and we could hear traffic sounds and the sound of people walking by, the sunlight flickering when they did. Standing as far back from the hole as possible with our backs to the cell bars, we still couldn't see all the way through the hole because the wall it passed through was too thick. We could only see as far as a set of recessed vertical bars.

We walked around reading the graffiti, which was thickest around chest level and faded around a height of seven or eight feet. Much of it was in English. One message read, "The first duty of the revolutionary is to not get caught!" Another read, "You should have done what your good mama said." The prize, we agreed, went to an elaborate figure carved into the front face of the partition, where it was one of the first things you saw as you entered the cell. It was a caricature of a fat Mexican judge done in meticulous bas-relief— you could actually see the folds in the judge's robes. The judge was grinning broadly and held up a stubby forefinger next to a balloon caption that read,

"Your fine is $1,000,000. Cheap!"

We decided to add our own graffiti, pulled out pesos, and began scratching at the walls. I actually hurried, thinking they might let us go soon. The concrete was harder than it looked, though, and I had to press with all my strength, which made it hard to get smooth curves. After twenty minutes I stepped back and was barely able to recognize my own initials. Wade hadn't done any better. We stood again in front of the finely detailed judge. "Do you realize how long it must have taken to carve this?" I said and we exchanged expressions of mock horror and laughed. We still couldn't believe anything truly bad was happening to us. We would be out in a few hours or maybe a day.

The floor was shiny with grime and had stains that might have been vomit and a couple that looked like blood. Scattered everywhere were the bodies of squashed cockroaches. We were wearing our best slacks for our date with the girls from Oregon and didn't want to ruin them by sitting down. After several hours, though, our legs grew tired and we picked a relatively clean spot and sat down on the floor with our backs against the wall. Above, shafts of sunlight slowly twisted across the top of the cell. Who could have planted that dope in our room? we kept asking ourselves. It seemed the two detectives had planted it since they knew exactly where to look. But why? Darkness fell, the municipal offices above us grew quiet, and we realized we were going to spend the night in the cell. It was a hot night and we took our shirts off and rolled them up for pillows. At least our faces wouldn't have to touch the grime.

The next morning a man with dark eyes and a severely pockmarked face came to our cell and directed the jailer to open the bars. He identified himself as an investigator for the state and led us to a small room down the corridor. Inside was a metal table and several folding chairs. He told us to empty our pockets and I emptied my pants pockets but didn't happen to think about my shirt pocket. Between us we had over $200 in cash and I worried we might never see it again, but after recording the amount in a small notebook, the investigator surprised me by giving it all back.

He told us to sit and proceeded to ask rapid-fire questions about our stay in Mazatlan. How had we arrived? Where did we first stay? What was the purpose of our visit? How long had we been here? I wove a story around the basic premise that we were two students on vacation. At the first opportunity I tried to make the same point I had made with the chief of police: that if I had known there was grass in the bathroom, I would have gotten rid of it when Wade announced there were police there to see us. The investigator abruptly cut me off.

"What concerns us is not so much the relatively small amount of marijuana that was found in your room." His small, dark eyes bored into mine. "What concerns us are reliable reports we have received to the effect you came here to buy large quantities of the drug."

My stomach went light, but I concentrated on acting incredulous, repeating that we were just students. The investigator gave me a "Come off it" look, rose, and stated the interview was over. I rose to face him.

"What is going to happen next?"

"There will be an investigation."

"And then?"

"Everything will depend on whether you are telling the truth." On the word "truth," he eyed me pointedly. I decided it was time to act.

"Apparently we are in a worse situation than I thought," I began delicately. "If there is anything you could do to help us, we would be very appreciative. Specifically, if you could get us out, we could pay you $3,000 in cash. No one else would have to know about it."

The investigator surprised me by showing almost no reaction to my offer. "We will see," was all he said.

Walking back to the cell, I asked him, "If by some terrible mistake we are found guilty, is there any chance we could go to prison?"

"Of course."

"For how long?"

"Five years."

"*Five years?*"

He stared at me, affecting surprise at my distress. "Why, yes. That is the usual sentence for trafficking."

I stepped into our cell in a daze. The investigator turned to leave.

"Wait! What about a phone call?"

The investigator hesitated, frowning.

"Didn't you already make one?"

"No."

"Hm. Well, the time for making a phone call has already elapsed." And he turned on his heel.

Two more interrogations followed, one by an investigator for the federales and one by an investigator who didn't say for which branch of the government he worked. These interrogations were short and seemed perfunctory. I made the same offer of $3,000 cash to each of the investigators and neither displayed interest. I asked each of them how much time we might do if we were found guilty, and the investigator for the federales said three years, while the investigator who hadn't said for which branch of the government he worked said seven.

"Seven years," we repeated to ourselves back in the cell. We couldn't imagine doing that much time. It wasn't thinkable. The jailer seemed like a friendly sort and I asked him if he knew of any Americans who had been convicted of trafficking in grass.

"*Sí, muchos,*" he grinned.

"What kind of sentences did they get?"

"Oh, maybe six months."

"Six months? But the investigator said we could get seven years."

"*Sí.* Some get seven years."

I stared at him. "Well, what makes the difference whether you get six months or seven years?"

He framed his shoulders into an elaborate shrug and grinned. "*¿Quién sabe?*"

We hadn't eaten in nearly twenty-four hours and I asked the jailer if meals were served in the jail. He said no, but if we had money, he could send out to a restaurant for food. All we had were hundred-peso notes and I gave him one, assuming I would never see any of it again. He soon came back with two plates heaped with enchiladas, rice, and beans and two Cokes, then handed me back more change than I would have expected for such a meal. I gave him a ten-peso note as a tip. Later we needed to use the toilet and the jailer gave us some pages from a comic book to use for paper, then opened the bars and handed us a bucket of water.

I decided to offer money to the jailer too. Why not? He was the one with the keys. He was a big guy with broad, hulking shoulders, looked young, and spent most of his time sitting on a three-legged stool in the corridor reading comic books. I asked him if he was married and he said he was and that he had two daughters, which surprised me as he didn't look over eighteen. I told him that and he seemed pleased. I asked if it wasn't hard getting by on a jailer's salary and he said it was, adding that he had another job on the side, hauling bricks. By afternoon I felt I had established a pretty good rapport with him and beckoned him close to the bars.

"Listen," I whispered. "We don't belong in here. It is a mistake. If you can get us out, we can pay you $3,000 in cash. With that kind of money, it wouldn't even matter if you lost your job. You could move to a different town, start a new life, use a different name if you had to. Think of your two daughters."

He glanced down the corridor nervously like a schoolboy contemplating mischief. "I will see what I can do," he grinned and took up where he had left off reading.

The afternoon wore on and the pockmarked investigator for the state came back and led us down the corridor to the small room again. This time there was a typewriter on the table. In a bored voice he informed us that his detectives had discovered conclusive evidence we were large-scale marijuana traffickers and that we might as well confess. I saw no future in confessing and feigned shock, sticking to our story that we were just students. "Fools!" the investigator burst out, dropping his bored look. I decided there was no sense holding back.

"Apparently our situation is very bad," I told him. "We are prepared to offer you $6,000 cash if you get us out. We can get it to you in a matter of hours. We have wealthy friends at our hotel. If you don't trust us, just let one of us out and he will get the cash. No one will have to know."

The investigator frowned. "Who are these wealthy friends of yours?"

"Just some friends."

He made no further response to my offer and led us back to the cell. While we were waiting for the jailer, two officers needed to get by and we moved to one side to let them pass. This put the investigator so close to me that he could see down my shirt pocket and his hand dove in and pulled out the scrap of paper Meche had given me with Manuel and Modesto's address. I couldn't believe I had forgotten it! Meche's admonition rang in my mind: "If you were to bring heat down on Manuel and Modestillo, they could kill you."

The investigator studied the address, frowning. "Who lives at this address?"

"Two Mexican girls we met on the beach."

"You are lying!" He became so excited, spit was flying. "I think known marijuana traffickers live at this address! I will send detectives to this address right now! If I am right, you may soon have company!"

He left and the jailer closed the cell bars behind us. I felt my spirits plummet. I imagined Manuel and Modesto getting thrown in the same cell with us and coming after us with knives. I apologized over and over to Wade. "God, I'm really blowing it," I told him. Wade didn't seem that worried.

"Do you seriously think Manuel and Modesto would let the police take them alive?" he offered hopefully.

For the rest of the afternoon I waited in dread. Each time we heard footsteps approaching, my heart jumped, worrying it was Manuel and Modesto being led to our cell. By evening, though, I had all but forgotten about it. The whole experience was taking on the disjointed and surreal quality of an acid trip. What happened a few hours ago no longer seemed relevant.

That night a commotion woke us up around two. We got up and saw police officers leading a group of ten or twelve drunks down the corridor. They shuffled to a stop in front of our cell. As the jailer opened our cell bars, I asked one of the officers if the drunks couldn't be put in another cell. He told me there were no other cells available. "What about that one?" I pointed to a cell across the way, the only other cell we could see, where a lone prisoner had spent the day staring blankly. The officer turned to see which cell I meant.

"Not a chance," he laughed. "That man is dangerous. He killed his wife last night."

The drunks filed in and quickly staked out spaces for themselves on the floor. They had been through this before. In a minute, the floor was covered with ragged bums and the cell reeked of beer breath. Soon, all were asleep save for two indios squatting near the opposite wall. One had a bruised cheek and was loudly reliving an argument he had been having with a bartender before his arrest. In self-righteous and bitter tones, he described to his companion what he was going to do to the bartender when he got out.

The indios paid no attention to us. They had heard me speaking Spanish to the officer and evidently assumed we were Mexicans. Then Wade happened to ask me something and at the sound of English, they turned to stare.

"Fucking Americans!" the one with the bruised cheek muttered. "They have all the money! They will be out tomorrow while we, the citizens of Mexico, stay here till we starve!"

They began rousting the other drunks, trying to promote a riot against us. A few woke up and took the trouble to swear at us. One sat bolt upright and raised his fist in the air. "Son of a fucking whore! . . . I fucked her good, he-he . . . behind a barn . . . " And he collapsed back on the floor.

I called the night jailer over, slipped him a twenty-peso note, and told him to get us two Cokes and keep the change. The Cokes came and we quickly emptied them, then held the bottles upside down by their necks. The indios saw how we were holding them and went sullen and shut up.

We decided to sleep in shifts. We flipped a coin and Wade got first watch. I squeezed out a place for myself between two drunks and fell straight to sleep. I had vivid dreams, including a dream that someone was poking something in my face. I would put my hands up, but this thing kept poking at me, usually hitting my hands but sometimes my nose and mouth. The thing was damp and had a foul smell, like toenail clippings. I woke up and saw that the drunk lying next to me was having fits and flailing about with his arms. So the dream was real. Then I saw there were no hands at the ends of his arms, just filthy bandages where his wrists ended. These were what had been poking me in the face! I grabbed my shirt and wiped my face in a fit of revulsion. I no longer felt sleepy and scooted over to Wade.

"Why didn't you do something when that guy started poking me in the face?"

Wade squinted at the guy. Without his glasses he could barely see. "What's he got anyway, leprosy?"

We both shuddered.

Neither of us felt like sleeping and we just sat there for a while against the wall and talked. The night had cooled off a little and a breeze drifted in, carrying the smell of the sea. A truck with a blown muffler rumbled by outside leaving a vast silence in its wake. For a couple of hours we just talked, talked about what we would do when we got out of here, our lives, and what we truly, deep down felt about things. It was one of the best conversations we ever had, too. For a couple of hours we had escaped the cell.

The drunk with no hands began stirring again and we nicknamed him Stumpy. I wondered how he had lost his hands and Wade suggested he may have stolen something from Manuel and Modesto. Stumpy sat up, rubbed his eyes with the backs of his bandaged wrists, and crawled over to the bars. On the other side, the night jailer was sitting on a stool reading *Novelas de Amor* and beside him was the bucket of water we used for flushing the toilet.

Stumpy asked the jailer for water, but the jailer ignored him. Stumpy asked him several times more and when the jailer didn't respond, Stumpy reached through the bars to try to get the water himself. His arms weren't quite long enough, though, and when he tried to press his stumps against the sides of the bucket, he succeeded only in pushing it further away. "*¡Agua-a-a!*" he called out pitifully. The jailer never even looked up, just kept turning the pages to his *Novelas*.

"*¡Agua-a-a-a-a!*" Stumpy proceeded to call out at intervals, pacing himself to endure. He lay there with his arms poking through the bars. "*¡Agua-a-a-a-a!*"

"It's the unstoppable force encountering the immovable object," Wade commented. This was some concept he had learned in Jesuit school. Stumpy kept on calling out. From time to time one of the other drunks would holler for him to shut up if he didn't want to get beaten to a son-of-a-whore pulp, but Stumpy never even broke rhythm, just kept on calling. The jailer got up, grabbed another *Novelas de Amor* off a shelf, and sat down again.

I never intended to get involved, but after an hour or so of this I suddenly found myself asking the jailer, "Why don't you give him some water?" The effect was electric: the jailer sat up, regarded Stumpy as though noticing him for the first time, got up, grabbed a pink plastic bowl off a shelf, scooped it into the bucket of water meant for flushing the toilet, and slid it along the floor underneath the bars. With no hands, Stumpy couldn't bring the bowl to his lips reliably and had to lap at the water like a dog. "*Gracias. Mil gracias,*" he thanked the jailer between slurps. "*Gracias. Mil gracias. Es muy amable. Dios le bendiga.*" I thought he might thank me too, but his only acknowledgement of me was a brief, uneasy glance.

Stumpy knew which side of the bars was which.

CHAPTER 50

THE DRUNKS WERE CLEARED OUT FIRST THING in the morning and Wade and I had the cell to ourselves again. The friendly day jailer came on and took up his position reading comic books. For some time now we had been interested in checking out the hole near the top of the back wall, and when the jailer got up and disappeared down the corridor, we saw our chance. Wade gave me a boost, but even kneeling on his shoulders, I couldn't quite reach the hole. He was going to have to stand on the concrete toilet. The toilet had a layer of green scum on it and on our first try Wade nearly slipped while I struggled to stay balanced on his shoulders. But after scuffing at the scum with his boot, Wade was able to get a better footing and this time I caught hold of the lip of the hole with my left hand, pulled myself up, and used my right hand to reach in and grab one of the recessed bars. "OK!" I murmured and Wade hurried back to the cell bars to keep a lookout.

I stared out and it was a giddy feeling seeing free life go by. There were people, cars, pushcart vendors, shops—the whole makeup of a typical Mazatlan street. It was a street I knew well too, one I had walked down many times.

The wall I was staring through was about two feet thick, so that the hole was really like a short tunnel or shaft and opened directly onto the sidewalk at about knee level. Aside from four vertical bars spaced about six inches apart, there was nothing between my face and the street. Someone passing by would have a hard time seeing me, though, as I was at the dark end of the shaft. I had barely taken all this in when Wade hissed that the jailer was coming and I had to drop down.

Wade and I discussed what I had seen and tried to think how to best take advantage of it. Our problem was that no one knew we were here. We needed to get a message out. Under the guise of wanting to play tic-tac-toe, I asked the jailer for a pen and paper and he provided us with several sheets of paper but said he didn't have a pen. As we debated what to do next, a ballpoint pen bounced to a stop in front of our cell. I reached between the bars and grabbed it while calling out *"¡Mil gracias!"* to a prisoner I would never see.

Pretending to play tic-tac-toe, we wrote out a message for help, jotted down Wade's wife's name and phone number, and promised a $250 reward for placing a collect call to her. We then folded the message into a glider and wrote "READ INSIDE!" across the top of the wings. The message had to be delivered to an American, we had decided. Only a fellow American would take our message seriously enough to place an international collect call to a complete stranger and anyway Wade's wife didn't speak Spanish.

Around midmorning the jailer wandered down the corridor and Wade gave me a quick boost up to the hole. I used my left hand to hang on to one of the recessed bars and hooked my left elbow over the lip of the hole. With my right hand I held the glider and made several tentative passes between two of the vertical bars. A long wait followed. The street was busy with people, but they were all Mexicans. I knew Americans had to pass by here, though, because the marketplace was only a block away. Wade coughed, our signal that the jailer was coming, and I dropped down.

Footsteps sounded and we were visited by a man who said he was our lawyer. He had fine, smooth features that seemed vaguely Asian, spoke good English, and introduced himself as Mr. Martinez. The jailer let him into our cell, where he made a brief show of not wanting to put his briefcase down on the grimy floor. There was something insinuating and affected about him that made me suspicious. He asked if we knew his son. "He's a well-known surfer here. . . . No? . . . Hm. I'm surprised. Practically everyone knows him."

He went on to say his son had been busted for pot several times and had even been in this very same cell. Once when he was bailing him out, he said, his son asked him to help some Americans who were in the same cell with him. He was happy to do it and found the experience so rewarding that he decided to devote himself full-time to representing Americans busted in Mazatlan for pot. "It's a good Samaritan thing I do." He said his wife owned a chain of radio stations, so he didn't have to work. "You'd be amazed how many Americans I've helped get out of jail. Every Christmas I get a flood of cards. A couple of them are really big smugglers. If I mentioned their names, I'm sure you'd recognize them."

We said we didn't know any big smugglers.

"No? . . . Hm. . . . Because the police are pretty convinced you guys are big pot smugglers yourselves. You can tell me, you know. I'm your lawyer."

Through barely audible grunts and throat clearings, Wade and I communicated our mutual suspicion that Mr. Martinez was just another cop sent to get information out of us. We stuck to our story that we were just students on summer vacation. Mr. Martinez kept trying to get us to admit we were big smugglers and we began treating him with thinly disguised sarcasm and disrespect. I finally told him, "You're an agent, right? Why don't you just admit it?" He seemed so genuinely hurt by this remark, though, that I began to think we could be wrong. Plus, part of me wanted to believe he really was our lawyer. We eventually reached an understanding in which we would assume for the time being he was our lawyer and he would assume we were two students on vacation who happened to get framed.

He reviewed the details of our case and I told him the reasoning I had used with the chief of police. He said, "Yes. . . . Hm. . . . Well, I might get a chance to talk to him later this afternoon." My hopes shot up.

"You know the chief of police?"

Mr. Martinez brightened. "Well, yes. Of course. We have lunch together."

This was crucial. Jesus had often told me that if I ever got busted, I should go straight to the man of highest rank and offer money. That's why none of our offers was working—because we weren't making them to the man at the top. And the man at the top in Mexican towns like this was the chief of police.

"Can you get us an interview with him?"

"Well, that's what I'm going to try and do, of course. Hopefully I'll get a chance to speak with him this afternoon. I'll drop by and let you know before I go home. By the way, when were you arrested?"

"Two days ago."

He frowned. "Two days already? Someone should have called me sooner." By Mexican law, he explained, anyone still in jail after seventy-two hours is presumed guilty and transferred to prison. "I'll be sure to get back to you later on."

After he was gone, I asked the day jailer if he knew the occupation of the man who had just left. He shrugged. "Just some man who comes here."

"But what is his title?"

He shrugged again. "*¿Quién sabe?*"

Wade and I discussed Mr. Martinez's visit and didn't know what to believe. Everything seemed surreal. Narc or not, Mr. Martinez's remark about the seventy-two hours sounded true. I had heard similar comments about the Mexican justice system. A prison wouldn't have a convenient hole facing the street. We had to get a message out now.

Our next chance at the hole didn't come till afternoon. This time the jailer stayed away for a long time. I clung to the bar, my left elbow hooked over the concrete lip, my right hand holding the glider poised, praying and praying for an American to pass by. My hopes rose when I spotted a young, light-skinned guy wearing Levi's heading our way. My hopes sank, though, when I saw him stop at a pushcart vendor and buy an *agua de arroz*. No Americans drank non-bottled liquids off the street and the smooth way he had effected his purchase was further proof he was no American. More time went by and my left arm grew so weak with fatigue that it was trembling. I held on with my right arm for a while but worried that I wouldn't be able to throw the glider as well with my left. My right arm got tired and I shifted back and forth. Eventually both arms were trembling and in order to hold on, I played mind games with myself, imagining I was in the Olympics with the whole world watching—vast crowds on their feet shouting with their fists raised, rooting for me to hang in there. A mango pit lay on the sidewalk in front of me, and to get my mind off the excruciating pain, I focused all my attention on it, trying to decipher the existential meaning of a mango pit. As it happened, this distraction proved so effective that I missed Wade's cough and he had to yell at me to get down. In a panic I let go, landed off balance, and tripped backward over the concrete block that was our toilet. Pain shot through my left calf as I jerked to my feet and attempted an expression of innocent boredom. It was too late. Our friendly day jailer was at the bars, his face flushed with fury.

"You were trying to escape!"

"No, I only wanted to see out."

"Don't lie to me, *hombre!*"

I tried to reason with him, but he ordered me to shut up. He felt we had jeopardized his job. "And after all I did for you. See if you get another favor out of me!" He pulled his stool up and planted it pointedly in front of our cell. Wade and I sat down against the wall and I pulled my pants leg up to see what was going on with my calf. There was a wide green stain where the corner of the toilet had ripped through my pants and drops of blood dotted the abraded skin. I knew I should beg the jailer for some water to clean it off but didn't feel up to it. I was beginning to lose heart.

The day dragged on. The jailer remained true to his word and refused to get us anything to eat or drink. Finally it grew dark, the night jailer came on, and we were able to order a meal. Mr. Martinez never showed.

"I'm beginning to feel kind of down," Wade admitted. I did too. We talked about all the things we would do differently if we ever got out.

"I'm going to start treating Janet and Sarah a lot better," Wade said. "I've been treating them kind of shitty, actually. I just take them for granted."

I said I was going to appreciate things more—little things like playing guitar or going for a drive to Sausalito. I promised when I got out I would take a drive to Sausalito for no other purpose than to remind myself what it was like to be free. We thought of the times we had spent hanging around Wade's place feeling down and shook our heads. To be free and unhappy seemed unimaginable. We recalled the last time we had felt blah. It was just a few days ago, between meetings with Carlos and Ricardo. We were drinking fresh orange juices at the Olas Altas on a glorious morning with a beautiful blue sea in front of us—pelicans diving, children laughing, fishing boats heading out to sea—and yet we had both felt detached and blah—so much so that we had even commented on it. How could we have felt that way? we wondered. It seemed crazy to us. We kept talking like this when a terrible insight hit me.

"You know what? I bet we're full of shit. I bet if we got out of here tomorrow, we could go straight to the Olas Altas and feel just as bummed as we felt the other day. Nothing's going to change. Everything will be just like it was before. It'll be like this whole experience never happened. It just won't count."

"Ha!" Wade let out a laugh over the horrible irony of it all. "You really think so?"

"I'd bet on it."

Wade shook his head in rue. "You're probably right. . . . You're probably right."

We stood around the cell not talking much and I began to face the prospect of doing time. The jailer had originally mentioned six months. Six months was something I could do. All my friends would still be around when I got out and the runs could pick up right where they had left off. I began to fasten on the idea of doing six months. I offered a tentative deal to the administrators of fate: grant me a sentence of six months and I will give up all rights to whatever chance I have of getting out sooner. I am willing to do six months, I told the administrators, and the more I thought about it, the more it didn't even seem that bad. I turned to Wade.

"You know, if we only get six months, it won't be that bad. Prison is bound to be better than this. We'll have beds and an exercise yard and everything. As long as our health holds out, that's the main thing. And as long as they don't separate us. I don't see why they would, though. You could pick up some Spanish. I'll help you. There'll be plenty of guys to practice with. We'll come out talking like Mexicans! We could probably get guitars. I could teach you some guitar. We'll work out some songs together. We could even try writing. We've been talking about writing some of this—" I stopped when I realized Wade was staring at me in horror. He was standing across from me and threw his arms wide.

"I can't do any six months!" he wailed. "I already miss my wife and kid!"

After that we didn't talk for a long while. Wade's words had plunged me into deep thought. Why didn't I have anyone to miss? Or anyone who would miss me? All my friends were either married or at least living with women. I had never spent more than a few weeks going with a woman and my strongest bonds were with other men. In fact, I spent most of my time in the company of other men.

261

Was I homosexual? I wondered to myself. I looked deep into my desires and tried to find evidence that I might be attracted to the male body. I couldn't find any. No, I wasn't queer. The real answer, which I knew in my heart all along, seemed even more shameful to me at the time: I was afraid of women. Why, I didn't know. But I was. It was a strange fear, too, in that sometimes I would meet a woman like Gloriana or Mary and not be afraid. But I couldn't tell in advance whether I was going to feel confident or not. So until I got to know a woman, I didn't want to be thrust into an intimate situation with her. That's why doing six months' time didn't seem all that terrible to me. It would be a six-month break from having to pretend I wasn't terrified when my friends and I ran into girls or when they wanted me to come with them to chase chicks. And thinking all this led me to wonder: Could a fair proportion of prisoners be men who had a strong fear of women?

CHAPTER 51

OUR RELEASE THE NEXT MORNING WAS SO unexpected and abrupt, it was almost anticlimactic. Mr. Martinez appeared at our cell, saying we had to hurry to meet with the chief of police. As we passed down the hallway, Wade and I tucked our shirts in and ran our fingers through our hair. "Let the chief do all the talking," Mr. Martinez was saying. "Don't speak unless he asks you a question." I nodded as if in agreement, thinking the whole while that I wasn't about to lose this opportunity to offer a bribe. I decided to start at $5,000. At the first sign of hesitation on the chief's part, I would jump to the entire amount we had in our hotel room: $7,000.

We were ushered into the same office as before. Mr. Martinez held a brief conversation with the chief, then stepped back, indicating for me to step forward. The chief asked how much money we had on us and I told him $200. He frowned as though disappointed, and I was just about to make my offer when he asked if we could get a hundred dollars more. I was stunned for a moment.

"A hundred dollars more? Why, yes. Certainly, *señor jefe*. We have that much back at our hotel."

"Bueno." He made a brief notation in a ledger. "Your fine is three hundred dollars. You will pay two hundred dollars now and Sr. Martinez will accompany you to your hotel to obtain the additional hundred dollars. If you are unable to pay it, you will go back to jail. There is one additional condition: You are to leave the city of Mazatlan within twenty-four hours and never return."

"That is fine. Of course, *señor jefe*. You are very kind." I paid him the $200 and practically bowed to him as we left.

Stepping out into bright sunlight, I got that same joyous feeling you get on your first step outside after recovering from a long illness. Mr. Martinez led us to his car, an older model Ford station wagon. During the ride to the De Cima, we passed some teenagers playing basketball and I stared at them, thinking that's what it meant to be free. We entered the De Cima and I began to worry how we were going to get our money out from behind the copy of *The Last Supper* without Mr. Martinez seeing us. If he saw all that cash, he would know his first impression of us had been right. Wade must have been thinking the same thing, for he was giving me meaningful looks as we climbed the stairs. It wasn't a problem, though, for as soon as we entered our room, Mr. Martinez asked to use our bathroom. He closed the door and I quickly slipped my hand behind the picture. The money, of course, was gone.

I flipped the picture around, nearly ripping the backing off in a frenzy of desperation, then stared down at the floor, hoping the money might have fallen out. It was gone. Mr. Martinez stepped out to find us pretending to rummage through our suitcases. Meanwhile, I was racking my brain for some kind of plan. Mr. Martinez paced briefly, then turned to stare. "What's going on?" We had to admit we didn't have the money.

"But that's impossible. You promised the chief!"

I always carried a blank check in my wallet for emergencies and offered to write it out for a hundred dollars.

"No, it has to be cash. You heard the chief say it had to be cash."

I asked Mr. Martinez if he would be willing to accept my check and pay the chief cash but he refused, threatening to take us back to jail. I could think of only one way out: the Hansens. I didn't even know if they were still around but I remembered their room number. I said we should go to their room, which was on the floor above.

"Really, you shouldn't expect me to have to run around like this," Mr. Martinez objected as he followed us up to the next floor. I knocked on the girls' door and felt joyous relief when their father opened it. He saw our three-day beards and rumpled clothes and looked startled.

"We just got out of jail!" I blurted. "Someone planted grass in our room! We thought we were going to do seven years!" Mr. Hansen held his palms up to calm me. "Well, you're all right now," he said and opened the door wide. "Come on in and tell us all about it." Mr. Martinez hung back, saying he would wait outside.

Mrs. Hansen greeted us warmly and insisted we have a seat on the bed despite how grimy we were. The girls weren't here, for which I was just as glad. I explained our circumstances—leaving out the incriminating parts, of course—and finished by asking if they would take my personal check in exchange for a hundred dollars cash. Mrs. Hansen started to say something but her husband held up his palm.

"I'll handle this, dear.

"We'd be glad to help you boys out on two conditions. First, I would like to have a word with Mr. Martinez. Then I would like to go downstairs and place a call to the U.S. Consulate to see what they have to say." This was fine with us and we stepped outside.

Mr. Martinez seemed put out at having to meet Mr. Hansen. "Really, this isn't at all necessary," he murmured as they shook hands. Mr. Hansen asked him a few questions, basically verifying our story, and we headed downstairs to the lobby, where the phone booth was. While Mr. Hansen was in the booth placing his call, Mr. Martinez fretted. "If I had known it was going to be this much trouble . . . ," he murmured, which, considering our freedom was at stake, struck me as a tad ungracious. He stepped away for a moment and Wade and I compared notes. We were both impressed by the mature and capable way Mr. Hansen was handling the whole affair.

Mr. Hansen came back and drew me aside. "The consulate has heard of Mr. Martinez," he told me. "Apparently he's helped Americans out before although they're not sure if he's acting on his own or performs some kind of liaison service for the police. They recommend that you pay the hundred dollars. If you don't, they won't be able to guarantee safe passage out of the country. They said you might be able to sneak out, but if you got caught and sent back to jail, they wouldn't be able to help you. Also, from a humanitarian standpoint, if you pay the hundred dollars, it might go easier for Americans who get arrested here in the future. It's up to you. If you want to pay it, I'll be glad to give you the money in return for your personal check."

I told him we had every intention of paying and wrote out a check on the spot.

Once we handed Mr. Martinez a hundred dollars in cash, his mood brightened considerably. Wade and I thanked him and he left. I never did find out anything more about him, but I believe he was probably who he said he was. Mr. Hansen invited us back to their room and his wife served us each a Cuba Libre. It was the best Cuba Libre I had ever had, too. They were really wonderful people.

"So," Mrs. Hansen smiled, "now that it's all over, are you really big-time grass smugglers like the police thought?" She was so sweet that I hated to lie to her, but I didn't have to.

"Of course, they're not, dear," interjected her husband. "You can tell just by looking at them. Real smugglers wouldn't have long hair. They probably wear three-piece suits and carry attaché cases."

We were finally free. Our only problem now was how to pay off our hotel bill and get home. I phoned Jesus, and when he heard we had lost $7,000, he was beside himself. "Seven thousand dollars? Why didn't you tell me you were carrying seven thousand dollars? I would have guarded it for you." I remembered hiding our intentions from him and realized how badly I had underestimated him.

"Tom, if you ever want to buy *mercancía* from someone else, I'll help you. I'll go with you. I can guard your money for you and make sure you don't get ripped off."

I knew he would, too. He cursed and groaned over the loss of the $7,000.

"Well, it's gone now. There's no way to get it back."

"Tom," he said then very solemnly. "It's seven thousand dollars. *Hay que tratar* — You have to try."

He asked where we were staying and said he would be right down. I hung up the phone and told Wade, "We're not giving up that money without a fight!"

Jesus was at our room in less than three hours, which is probably some kind of record between Tierra Blanca and Mazatlan. Miguel was with him and grinned ruefully, shaking his head. "*¡Qué Tom!*" He thrust a bottle of Old Parr at me and we passed it around. Wade and I sat on one bed facing Jesus and Miguel on the other as I explained everything that had happened. Jesus nodded.

"Manuel is a good man but Modesto is bad. He used to be a cop in Culiacan. Those knife scars you saw? He got those in a fight one night, trying to arrest a drunk."

Jesus was convinced Manuel and Modesto had stolen our money, then planted the grass in our room just to get us out of the way. "Of course, the police were in on it too. The police and Manuel and Modesto work hand in hand."

"But the investigator for the state was going to have Manuel and Modesto arrested."

"Pure games. They were just playing with you."

"He seemed so serious, though."

Jesus shrugged. "It is possible that he was serious, but he would not be able to do anything without the permission of the chief of police, and the chief and Manuel and Modesto—they have dinner together."

I told them about the two detectives who picked us up, asking, "Were they real police, do you think? Or just Manuel and Modesto's men?"

Miguel held up two fingers pressed together to make a point. "Manuel and Modesto, the police—they are one and the same, Tom. It is not worth trying to tell them apart."

I asked why none of those investigators seemed interested in my offers of a bribe, and Jesus confirmed my supposition that only the chief had the power to act in these matters.

"Well, why do you suppose he didn't ask for more?"

Jesus shrugged. "This was not his case. It was Manuel and Modesto's case.

Maybe he even knew they had already taken all your money."

We killed the Old Parr and now it was time to go after Manuel and Modesto. I could hardly believe Jesus was willing to attempt this for us. I felt wild and exhilarated, envisioning the dope battle of the century. Our first stop was the *Administración*, where the same bored clerk was on duty. Jesus demanded to see the cleaning woman in charge of the second floor during the afternoons.

"Is there something I can help you with?"

"No, I must speak to the cleaning woman herself."

"Well, that is not permitted and anyway, she has already gone home for the day. Now if there is some question—"

"The question is, Who let thieves into the room of these two *jóvenes* so that seven thousand dollars could be stolen from them!"

Adrenaline filled my veins. Jesus was speaking loud enough for other people to hear and the memory of jail was still fresh in my mind. The clerk gave Jesus a withering look. "Seven thousand dollars? Come now, *señor*."

"I saw it with my own eyes!"

This wasn't true but Jesus knew it was as good as true. I grabbed Wade and we ran upstairs and got our bags. By the time we came down, Jesus and the clerk had quit arguing and Jesus loaned us money to pay our bill.

Outside it had grown dark. The four of us slipped into Jesus's banana-yellow Barracuda and he took off, burning rubber. As he was driving, he reached over to the glovebox, took out a .38, and spun the cylinder to make sure all the chambers were loaded. "So where does this Meche live?"

"Oh, I don't think he had anything to do with it."

"I know, Tom. Just the same, he may be able to give us information."

I knew it was bad smuggling etiquette to take a supplier to meet another supplier without first asking, but these seemed to be special circumstances. We arrived at Meche's home and I went in alone and found him sitting shirtless and using a fly swatter to alternately fan himself and swat flies. He beamed on seeing me and asked how our meeting went. "Not very well," I told him and said I had a friend outside who needed to speak with him. His face turned serious and he threw on a shirt. We stepped out into the alley and on seeing Jesus standing there with the .38 tucked at his belt, Meche blanched.

"Go back to the car, Tom," Jesus said, and his tone was so stern that I did as told. Back in the car I thought how Meche had only done what we pressed him to do and felt awful for siccing Jesus on him like that. A long time seemed to pass before Jesus came back, got in the car, and fired up the engine without saying anything.

"Did you hit him?"

"I treated him with the greatest respect."

Jesus turned onto a street that passed through an upscale residential district with grillwork fences in front of the homes. The evening was hot and humid and we had our windows down. Jesus was creeping along at twenty kilometers per hour staring straight ahead when he abruptly gunned the Barracuda to a hundred kph. This was his way of thinking.

The street ended in front of a large swath of swampland and Jesus stopped and cut the engine. The rumble of the Barracuda's V8 was instantly replaced by the sound of a million crickets chirping. In the distance to our left, we could see the lights of the Avenida del Mar, and to our right, the yellow lights of outlying colonias. Between lay the black void of the swamp. A few moments passed with no one saying anything.

"*Pues*, there is nothing we can do tonight," Jesus sighed. "We cannot take Manuel and Modesto with only a pistol. We will have to go back to Culiacan and get more guns and hire *pistoleros*. It could be expensive."

"That's OK. We will pay you back."

He nodded. "The *pistoleros* could cost as much as $500 apiece."

"We will pay it."

"And then there is the cost of the machine guns."

I frowned. "Don't the *pistoleros* come with machine guns?"

"No. Only pistols."

This struck us both as funny and we laughed. Miguel, ever eager to help, said, "I think Lupe has a machine gun we can borrow, *compadre*."

"Is that so?" Jesus murmured without enthusiasm. I could feel the momentum of the evening slipping.

Jesus turned to face me. "What I am trying to say, Tom, is that it could be very expensive to take on Manuel and Modesto and there is no guarantee you will get anything back."

"That is true," put in Miguel. "The money could be half-spent by now. On *cervezas, las viejas*." He said it as though it pained him to cause me the least disappointment.

"There is no telling how many ways the money was split," Jesus went on. "The chief of police must have gotten a cut. There could be others."

"What's going on?" Wade asked and I interpreted for him.

"Actually, I'm kind of anxious to get home and see my old lady."

I felt like the last person to leave a party after everyone else has paired up and gone home.

"Don't worry, Tom," Jesus told me, firing up the Barracuda. "The new harvests will be here soon. We will become millionaires yet!"

He took us to a quiet motel far from the De Cima and lent us money to get home.

In the morning we had a couple of hours to kill before our flight and made a point of going to the Olas Altas to drink fresh orange juices. Our juices came and we drank them and stared out over the water.

"Well, T.J., do you feel any different after all that's happened?" Wade asked me. I watched three pelicans flying in formation and sighed.

"Not really. How about you?"

Wade shook his head ruefully no.

"You were right."

CHAPTER 52

WORD AROUND THE BEAR'S LAIR WAS THAT Jake had cut Arf out of their heroin operation and was dealing directly with Jesus himself. This was eminently predictable as all Arf was providing to the operation was his ability to speak Spanish. So Arf now felt what it was like to be contact jumped! Not long afterward I learned that Jake had somehow managed to jump Jesus and was dealing directly with Jesus's suppliers. At this point I saw the operation as being out of my control, and since it no longer involved my contacts, I quit worrying about it.

Bruce got back from his round-the-world trip and we met at an International House of Pancakes. Bruce loved using IHOPs as meeting places, feeling they were quintessentially American and anonymous. "So, I hear you tried to do a run without me," he grinned. He didn't seem at all sore about it, but I could tell he had made note of it, and in the complex calculus of our relationship, he seemed just a little more wary of me. I asked him about his trip.

"It went good, chap. Quite good. I met a lot of interesting people, got a lot of new ideas. You know, the really big money is in straight business, I've discovered. Or at least the gray areas surrounding straight business. That's what I intend to devote myself to—those gray areas. I mean to say, smuggling's great for raising some working capital, say one or two million, but if you want to start making real money, you've got to get into some kind of ostensibly legitimate business. I personally won't be satisfied until I've made fifty or sixty mill. But that's a good goal for these runs, don't you think? Make one or two million, then move on to something else?"

Jesus called to let me know the new harvests were coming in and what followed was probably the most amazing of the many amazing coincidences in this story. Fred Swaha had a friend named Al Frank who flew out from his home in New Jersey to visit Fred from time to time. Al was an Air Force pilot and on a couple of occasions I had tried to get him to fly a run. He liked to smoke cigars and would chew on one while listening to me describe what the runs involved. "I don't know," he would say. "It's damn tempting. If I got busted, though, I wouldn't even be able to collect my Air Force pension, not to mention the time I'd do." *Chomp, chomp.* "I don't know. . . . " I didn't think he would ever fly a run as he truly had a lot to lose.

Things changed for him, though. His job was to fly reconnaissance over Vietnam, and one day he made the bold decision to quit flying on the basis of conscientious objection. No Air Force pilot active in the Vietnam War had ever done this. Al was one of their best pilots and his commanding officer was loath to lose him. "This place gets to everyone," he told Al. "You just need a break." And he gave him a desk job. But after a half day of signing requisitions for materiel, Al decided this was contributing to the war effort as much as flying recon and declined to sign any more. This time his commanding officer was less sympathetic. Nevertheless, he gave him two weeks' leave to get some R&R and hopefully a new attitude. Al flew home to New Jersey and contacted a civilian lawyer who formally petitioned the Air Force for an honorable discharge on conscientious objector grounds. His lawyer warned him that if the Air Force decided to fight the case, it could get costly. Al decided the time had come to fly a run.

By now Al had only a week left of leave. He tried to contact me, but I had just moved and changed my phone number out of concern that I may have gotten hot. Even Fred had no idea where I was now living. Al decided to fly out and try to find me. Meanwhile, I had just arrived at the San Francisco airport after lining up a half ton of newly harvested grass in Culiacan and called Bruce to see if he could pick me up.

"Chap, I'm afraid you've caught me at a bad time. I've got two birds here and we're sitting out on the lawn drinking champagne. They've just taken half their clothes off"—giggling in the background. "Say, why don't you come by and have some fun? You could take a cab."

Feeling frugal, I decided to take an airport bus into the city and catch a cab from there. I got on the bus, took a seat next to an open window, and as the bus was about to take off, I heard my name being paged to a white courtesy telephone. I almost ignored it, but curiosity got the better of me and I jumped out. It was Bruce. He said the "birds" had left and he might as well come pick me up. I settled in to wait, then heard my name being paged again. I assumed it was Bruce changing his mind, now that I had lost my bus, and headed for the phone feeling irritated. But when I picked up the receiver, a different voice came on the line. "Is this the Tom Jenkins who owns a dog named Ogre?"

It was Al Frank! He had just arrived, heard my name being paged, and thought he should try paging it too. And if it weren't for this amazing coincidence, I don't know if he would have ever found me!

Bruce arrived and we planned the run over drinks right there at the airport lounge. And it was one of the smoothest runs ever! Al had no trouble finding our clandestine strips on the way down and picked up a half ton of grass from three strangers with whom he had no common language. Jesus later told me he handed them all cigars. Bruce was extremely impressed with Al's skills.

"I mean to say, you tell him to do x, y, and z, and he does precisely as you say. It's his Air Force training. You can see what a good pilot they made out of him."

With the help of the three grand we paid him, Al was able to get the honorable discharge he sought.

Nelson Mitchum wasn't at all pleased seeing Al Frank swoop in and fly the run he had been waiting to do all summer. Bruce and I explained to him that Al had only a week left on leave and that it was just a one-time deal. Mitchum could now do a run, only we needed financing. Both Bruce and I were short on cash, having made some bad investments recently. For my part, I had dumped thousands into the Saga and had given most of my remaining cash to a British mechanic friend, who was to go to Britain and buy used Morgans, Austin-Healeys, and other British sports cars, have them fixed up in Britain where the labor was cheap, and then send them to me to sell in the States. All he ever sent me, though, was a single Lotus Elite. When I saw he wasn't going to send any more, I went to a garage in Mill Valley, where he had left an Aston Martin DB5 in storage, and appropriated it. This was the same model of car James Bond drove. It was a convertible and had right-hand drive, which was convenient for picking up girls who were hitchhiking as I didn't have to lean across the seat to speak to them.

Bruce and I met at Wade's palatial home to figure out how we were going to finance the next run. Mitchum was there and so was Duncan, a crazy chemist who was involved in some way in the acid trade. Malcolm Murray, the big acid dealer who had ruined Wade's leaded glass lamp, dropped by too. He had a brown paper bag with him, which he tossed onto a shelf. He heard us talking about front money and asked how much we needed. "About fifteen grand," Bruce told him.

"I've got that much here," he said and proceeded to pull fifteen grand out of the paper bag he had brought in.

We agreed to doubling his money back, standard terms for front money in the trade. To make sure there were no misunderstandings, I explained that if the run pulled through, he would get back $30,000, but if it failed, due to a bust or a theft or whatever, he wouldn't get back anything. He understood this, but Duncan butted in, saying, "No one's ever lost a penny of front money with me! If I took money on a deal that turned bad, I'd pay it back if I had to spend the next ten years peddling lids up and down the Haight to do it!"

"Well, that's not the deal we're offering," I said, hoping to put an end to the subject.

"Then you're a dishonest businessman," put in Mitchum.

Mitchum was an OK guy but had a bad habit of opening his mouth without thinking. I had worked so hard to develop a reputation for impeccable honesty in the smuggling world that for Mitchum to imply otherwise caused me to lose it. Before anyone knew what was happening, I had Mitchum slammed up against a wall with my left hand splayed across his throat and my right fist cocked back. He turned purple and apologized.

The next day President Nixon announced plans for Operation Intercept, a massive anti-smuggling campaign that would include a dense radar net designed to detect light planes flying across the border. Our run was scheduled to happen two days before the official start of Operation Intercept, but we worried that the radar net might already be operating by then. Considering this, Bruce came up with a new plan for the run involving two planes. He would use one plane to pick up the grass as usual in Culiacan and bring it to a deserted strip in Baja near the border. Then Mitchum would sneak across the border into Mexico, flying low and without a flight plan, meet Bruce at the deserted strip, pick up the grass, and sneak back. One advantage of this plan was that Mitchum would have a lot of fuel on board and could fly well north into California before having to refuel. We calculated that he could make it as far as Fresno, which was in a much cooler area compared to the area we had been using between Ramona and Escondido. This plan violated Bruce's longstanding policy to remain as aboveboard as possible by always filing flight plans, and I didn't see how it addressed the issue of Operation Intercept, but Bruce had confidence in the plan and I trusted his judgment. Mitchum approved of the new plan and we ran it by Murray and offered him a chance to withdraw his front money, but he said he wasn't worried about Operation Intercept and gave the new plan a green light.

The pickup went without incident and I flew home the same day. Mitchum was due to arrive in the Bay Area the day after but failed to show. Bruce hadn't returned either. Wade and I stayed close to our phones, but there was no word from either of them. When another twenty-four hours passed with no word, we knew something serious must have gone wrong.

The fact neither of them had phoned meant they were in trouble together. This put the problem at the remote landing strip in Baja. I saw two possibilities: either they were busted and being held in a Mexican jail without phone privileges or they had been ambushed by Mexican bandits, in which case they could be dead. In the meantime, Operation Intercept had begun and was dominating the evening news on TV. Nixon was putting on a real circus with task forces in different major cities purporting to monitor the price of grass as it rose in supposed response to the campaign. Typical TV footage showed a couple of spokes-narcs behind a workstation with the supposed local price of kilos prominently displayed behind them. As they ballyhooed the success of Operation Intercept, a monitor would silently step in and replace the already inflated price with an even higher one.

Another day passed with no word and Wade and I were in a sweat. We were at my apartment trying to decide what to do when his wife, Janet, called. She said Bruce had just called and left the following message: "Be in Puertecitos with a four-wheel-drive pickup by midnight tonight without fail." He had given her the name of a motel and a room number. So he was still alive! We pressed Janet for details, but that was all Bruce had told her.

It was already two in the afternoon and while I packed my travel bag, Wade used my phone to call a rental agency in San Diego and reserve a four-wheel-drive truck. He then called Pacific Southwest Airlines and got us reservations to San Diego. We jumped in Wade's Healey and he averaged ninety to the San Francisco airport while I craned my neck around, keeping a lookout for cops. The flight gave us time to relax for a few minutes and knock off a couple of drinks. Then we elbowed our way to be first off the plane and paid a cab driver twenty dollars to speed the two miles to the truck rental agency. Wade signed the forms and we sped off in the Willys pickup they had reserved for us.

We crossed the border at Tijuana and here I became confused and thought we needed tourist cards to enter the interior of Baja. I had Wade double-park in front of Mexican Immigration, ran in, cut in front of a line of startled tourists, and began waving twenty-dollar bills at the Immigration official. He tried to explain that we didn't need tourist cards, but in my excited state I interpreted this as bargaining and pulled out more bills. Abruptly realizing my mistake, I pocketed the bills and turned to leave, but by now the official had become furious and forbade me to enter Mexico. To make sure I returned to the States, he left a line of dumbfounded tourists and followed me out to the pickup, his hand resting on his holstered .45. What followed was like a scene out of the Keystone Cops. Wade pulled out and pretended to start a U-turn, then floored the gas pedal straight into Mexico and swerved right at the first corner, nearly rolling the Willys. I glanced back and saw the official shouting and waving his pistol.

We beat it out of town and headed south on Highway 5. Dusk fell and we hunched forward, straining to spot cattle on the road. Little hills half chopped by road cuts grew gradually larger, loomed briefly, and receded into purple darkness as we hurtled past. We made Puertecitos by 12:48 a.m.—not midnight, but close enough, we imagined, and a time we were pretty proud of.

As it was, we had to rouse Bruce and Mitchum out of bed. There was no great urgency but in typical fashion Bruce had exaggerated his message in order to ensure we took it seriously.

Bruce explained that he had lost his engine while flying over the Sea of Cortez. With a half ton of grass on board, the plane sank like a stone and he was barely able to make the Baja shore, where he managed to land the plane on the beach without damaging it. No one was around and in hundred-degree heat he unloaded the suitcases of grass, moved them away from the beach, and hid them behind bushes. While he was doing this, he spotted Mitchum flying overhead. When Bruce failed to show at the preassigned landing strip, Mitchum began searching for him, tracking back along Bruce's intended path. Bruce used his radio to communicate with Mitchum, and Mitchum advised him to hike to a town he had spotted below, the town being Puertecitos. Mitchum then landed in a nearby uncontrolled strip and the two met in town. All they needed now was a vehicle to transport the grass from the beach to the uncontrolled strip. They asked around and several ranchers were willing to rent them their pickups but expected to come along. Before long the whole town was abuzz over the two gringos who wanted to rent a truck to do something but didn't want anyone to come with them.

Bruce asked if Operation Intercept had gone into effect and I told him all about it. He asked if there had been any plane busts and I told him none so far. That didn't mean planes were getting through, though. Probably everyone was lying low. We considered lying low ourselves, but this would require stashing the grass and we had no place to stash it. Furthermore, grass, even when it's well stashed, has a Houdini-like tendency to disappear. We decided to go ahead with the run despite Operation Intercept. If Mitchum flew through a canyon low to the ground, he should be able to avoid even the densest radar net.

Early in the morning, Wade and I headed south of town in the Willys. The road became little more than a pair of tire tracks in the sand and we stopped, got out, and locked in the four-wheel drive. It wasn't even nine, yet the sun felt like a hot iron next to my face. We drove until we came to a small cairn Bruce had arranged by the side of the road. The suitcases were supposed to be hidden behind the bushes on our left, but when we looked out the window, we couldn't see any trace of them. I was afraid the grass had been discovered, but when we got out and walked into the desert, we began finding suitcases behind every bush. It was like an Easter egg hunt! The bushes weren't that dense, yet Bruce had done an amazing job of ensuring the suitcases wouldn't be visible from the road.

We found all thirty-three suitcases and got them loaded into the bed of the Willys. We hadn't brought anything to cover them and they lay there stacked in the back for anyone to see. We now had to drive for an hour to reach the uncontrolled strip outside Puertecitos. Thankfully, there was little traffic on the road, but every time we spotted a vehicle in the distance heading toward us, we died a little inside. No matter how hard I tried to limit my risk, it seemed, situations like this kept coming up.

We made it to the strip, and while Bruce and Wade helped Mitchum load the plane, I kept the strip's caretaker occupied. He was a young indio, who lived here in a tarpaper shack with his luscious india wife, who was dressed in little more than shorts and a bra because of the heat. I envied their simple life and imagined they probably spent half their day making love. The indio stared at the quantity of suitcases being loaded while I made idle conversation to fill time. I told him Mitchum was a world-famous botanist who had spent the last six months collecting plant specimens in Mexico and those were his specimens being loaded as well as his books, notebooks, typewriter, tools—I went on, naming every possible thing I could think of. I couldn't make it, though. There seemed to be no end to the suitcases and I ran out of things to list. The two of us stood there dumbly watching. "Your friend has much luggage," the youth remarked in the understated way of the country indio.

CHAPTER 53

I FLEW HOME AND THAT EVENING Bruce called me and gave me the number of the pay phone he was calling from. I went out to a pay phone and called him back.

"Listen, chap, something very strange is going on. Mitchum called me from Bakersfield and said the fuel pumps were closed for the night and wouldn't reopen till six in the morning. He wasn't supposed to land in Bakersfield! He was supposed to land in Fresno! Then he told me he wanted me to meet him at the strip tomorrow instead of LeGrande. He said he didn't trust LeGrande. Well, he never said anything like that before. I tell you, chap, he sounded very strange over the phone. I didn't commit myself in the slightest. I told him, 'Listen, Mitchum, I don't have the vaguest notion what you're talking about.' He said, 'You know. I need some help moving my furniture.' 'Just give me a call when you're in town,' I told him and hung up. Chap, I don't know what the hell's going on here, but I smell a fish."

Gnoss Field was an uncontrolled strip in Marin County and the following morning a driver we had hired—LeGrande—drove there in a rented van to meet Mitchum and pick up the load. At the last minute Bruce drove out there too, his curiosity getting the better of him. At the field they were dismayed to find four men in suits waiting in an unmarked Ford. The men approached them and struck up a conversation, saying they were waiting for a friend to pick them up to go duck hunting. Bruce and LeGrande didn't bother asking why they were going duck hunting in suits. The men pulled out cameras and began taking pictures of themselves, making sure to include Bruce and LeGrande in the background. Bruce left, but LeGrande made the bold decision to wait for Mitchum, planning to rush out onto the strip and warn him off.

Mitchum never showed and LeGrande eventually gave up and headed back to Berkeley. On the way he was surprised to see the four men following him. He drove in a crazy pattern until he was sure he had lost them—only to see them pull up on a side street just ahead. At that point he realized they must have planted a tracking device on the van and remembered stepping away from it for a minute to take a leak while back at the strip. He then drove to Hink's department store in downtown Berkeley, jerked to a stop without bothering to park properly, ran into the store and out a back way, successfully ditching them. As a courtesy, we phoned the rental agency and told them where they could find their van, which, fortunately, we had rented under a phony name.

Murray was the first to confirm what we were all suspecting. He had two dope lawyers on retainer, and they learned that Mitchum had been busted with the planeful of grass and was being held at a facility in southern California. Bail was $100,000. I could hardly bring myself to believe it. I drove around for a while in a daze, then stopped at a pay phone and dialed the number of the facility where Mitchum was being held. A male voice came on the line and I asked if Mitchum was being held there.

"Who's calling?"

"An interested party."

"And just what's your interest in the matter?"

I hung up.

The next morning Mitchum's bust made headlines across the country. The bust was portrayed as a spectacular success for Operation Intercept, which, sadly, it was. It would be the largest bust and the only plane bust during all of Operation Intercept and must have made Nixon's day.

Mitchum's strange call to Bruce was on everyone's mind. It seemed he must have made that call after he was busted and that it was an attempt to set Bruce up. Considering the camaraderie the two had just shared in Baja, this seemed particularly cold. Bruce was devastated. "Never, never—no matter how much time I was facing—would I do what Mitchum did." Meanwhile, we were all wondering who Mitchum was going to fink on next.

Five of us were involved in the run besides Mitchum. Bruce and LeGrande were in it the worst, having been witnessed by narcs at Gnoss Field. Bruce could be placed in Mexico at the time of the run by his flight plans and probably by the motel owner and other residents of Puertecitos if the narcs chose to look that far. He was in deep. Wade could be implicated by the truck rental papers he had signed in San Diego. I reviewed the evidence against me and concluded there were only the two calls Wade placed from my home phone, one to the truck rental agency and one to PSA. By itself, this evidence was nothing. Coupled with Mitchum's testimony, it could bring a conviction.

Of the five of us, Murray was the only one with no solid evidence against him. All he had done was to put up money. As there was no record of this,

Mitchum's testimony against him couldn't hurt him. Oddly, Murray seemed more worried than any of us. He gave his lawyers a $5,000 retainer and told them to do everything possible to lower Mitchum's bail. "We've got to get him out," Murray told Wade and me. "He's probably sitting in jail all bummed out and thinking we've forgotten about him. We've got to get him out so we can talk to him and let him know we're going to help him."

Murray's lawyers had Mitchum's bail reduced to $50,000 and then $15,000, which was as low as it was likely to go. Murray put up $10,000 and appealed to the rest of us for the remaining $5,000. Bruce wasn't about to help Mitchum and Wade was now broke. LeGrande didn't have that kind of money and was just a small-time player in the run anyway. That left me.

"I know you don't like the guy," Murray told me, "but we've got to be practical." Five thousand dollars was nearly all I had left, though, and I wanted to hang on to it in case I needed a lawyer myself. Meanwhile, Murray's lawyers learned that the grand jury had handed down indictments against Bruce and LeGrande. We got to both of them in time and Bruce went into hiding while LeGrande hired a lawyer and surrendered to the police. The district attorney's office recognized that he did not have a large part in the run, and when they saw he had no previous record and held a responsible job as a medical technician, they released him on his own recognizance pending trial.

I contacted the phone company and learned that phone records were kept for six months and then destroyed. If the D.A.'s office subpoenaed my records before that time, I could find out they had done so, but I would not be able to stop them. I paid a visit to the phone company office and asked to see my records, just to see how feasible it would be to bolt with them though I wasn't ready to resort to that just yet. As there seemed to be no alternative, I provided the remaining $5,000 for Mitchum's bail.

Several days later I was in San Francisco and had a reason to phone Wade. Janet answered and said, "The police are here." It took me a moment to absorb this shock.

"You mean it's a bust?"

"It looks that way."

"Then I better hang up."

"You probably better."

I hung up and felt the blood drain from my face. If they were on to Wade, were they on to me?

I remembered a brick I had in my apartment, hidden up underneath the kitchen sink. I was now going with a Black girl who lived in the apartment below mine and she had a key to my place. I phoned her, told her where to find the brick, and said if she got it out of there, she could have it.

"Margo, don't do it, though, unless you're absolutely sure it's safe. Look all around before you go in."

I avoided my place and spent the afternoon at friends' places and driving around. I was on familiar terms with Murray's lawyers and called them every few hours. By the end of the day, they were able to tell me Wade had been busted by state agents, not federal agents, which meant it had nothing to do with the Mitchum case. They weren't sure what it was about but hoped to bail him out the next day.

It was around midnight by the time I finally got up the nerve to return to my apartment. I lay on my bed staring up in the dark, worrying, when there was the sudden thud of something landing on my bed.

"There's your dope, kid."

I looked over and saw Margo's voluptuous figure silhouetted in the door-way. She was always calling me "kid." I picked up the brown paper bag that had landed and felt the full weight of the brick of Michoacan inside.

"No, it's yours. I said if you got it out of here, you could have it."

"You sure? That's a lot of dope." She sauntered up to me.

"Sure, I'm sure."

She leaned over and soul-kissed me, letting her breasts brush against my chest through the thin shift she was wearing. She went to lift off the shift.

"Wait! First get this thing the fuck out of here!"

CHAPTER 54

WADE WAS OUT THE NEXT DAY and told me he had been set up by a teenaged girl he had had an affair with several months back. Since their affair, the girl had apparently gotten busted and started working for the police. As a result of Wade's dalliance, his family was put through the trauma of a bust. Janet, he confided, was beyond pissed.

Mitchum's bail was arranged and he was released. He came to Berkeley and Wade put him up at his palatial home. Everything was turning out the exact opposite of the way it was supposed to. In the movies Mitchum would have been snuffed for having finked on Bruce, but instead, we were treating him like a returning hero. The fact was, we were all afraid of him. I could hardly believe it when Wade told me he was throwing a "Welcome Back" party for Mitchum at Wade's home.

"It's Murray's idea," Wade explained wryly. "He doesn't want Mitchum to feel like we're abandoning him."

"Do I have to go?"

"Well, you're invited."

I put off going and was the last to arrive. I hadn't seen Mitchum since the bust and resolved to act neutral toward him, neither hostile nor falsely friendly. I walked in and found him lying on one of Janet's large paisley cushions in the living room. We greeted each other and he made no move to sit up, which gave me the welcome excuse not to shake hands with him. I asked how they had treated him in jail and several other safe questions and moved on at the first reasonable opportunity.

Everyone was there—except Bruce, of course, who had gone into hiding and would have throttled Mitchum if given the chance. Besides Wade and Janet and their daughter, Sarah, there was Murray, Murray's girlfriend, LeGrande,

Duncan, and several groupie types who thought it was cool to hang out with big dealers. I slipped into the kitchen, where I was greeted by the strange spectacle of Wade preparing food. He was about to toss a large salad.

"This is my penance," he laughed and went on to confide that two nights ago Janet had come downstairs in the middle of the night to find him going down on a strange girl right in their own living room. His womanizing had more than caught up to him.

"I'm really in the doghouse around here."

Footsteps sounded and we turned serious as Janet walked in scowling. Wade commenced tossing the salad with quick, vigorous strokes.

I wandered back to the living room, where people were hanging out with forced smiles, trying to think of something to say. Everyone felt constrained by the unmentionable fact that Mitchum was a fink and here we were throwing a party for him. Duncan, the crazy chemist, would spout off from time to time, but his remarks were so inane that it was difficult to follow them up with anything. Mitchum, I noticed, seemed to be getting a perverse satisfaction out of our discomfort. He studied everyone from his paisley cushion. "Gee, I never knew I had so many friends," he remarked with what I took to be pure irony.

The long silences were growing excruciating. We were a dozen people hanging around with nothing to say. People who were already wasted out of their minds rolled more joints just for something to do. Duncan went into a long monologue about his latest chemical discovery and everyone felt grateful for the opportunity to pretend to be interested in something. He said he had developed a non-toxic substance that could be mixed in small amounts with LSD and would foil the police field test for LSD, causing the test to come out negative. He called his product "Merlin Bust-Proofer" and envisioned making a fortune selling it to acid dealers. Ironically, Duncan's product would have the exact opposite of the desired effect and would result positive to an LSD field test all by itself. A week later Duncan would be arrested with over a pound of the substance, prompting a local paper to declare, "BIGGEST LSD BUST EVER!"

"Yes, strictly self-taught," Duncan was saying to one of the dealer groupies. "Learned everything I know from going to libraries and studying abstracts. Never went to college. Never had time really."

Wade's two-year-old daughter suddenly burst into the room, pedaling her tricycle and screaming, "Quick! Hide the dope! It's the pigs!" She had no idea what the words meant, but she had heard Wade utter them when he was busted and they had left a deep impression on her.

Dinner was ready and we sat lotus-style out on Wade's redwood deck. People struggled for something to say. Someone thought to compliment the meat and everyone followed suit, trying to think of different nice things to say about the meat. Mitchum, I noticed, hardly ate.

Afterward Murray's girlfriend, Charlene, drawled, "Now, nobody move. Stay right where you are."

Charlene fascinated me because she was the most affectatious person I had ever met. She was from Fort Lauderdale and moved in a slow, languid way, wore beads, and liked to glance down in an Aw-shucks way and say, "Yes, I'm a hippie." At the same time, she only went with wealthy dealers and spent their money on designer dresses and trips to Puerto Vallarta and Nepal. Wade liked to joke that if she missed shopping at Saks Fifth Avenue for a week, they sent her a get-well card.

She went to the kitchen and came back with a chocolate cake she had baked. "This is for you!" she gushed as she laid it in front of Mitchum. The icing on the cake read, "Welcome home, Nelson!" Charlene then knelt down and threw her arms around Mitchum, giving him a bear hug. I thought how she was the only person I knew who could have pulled this off.

The sun was going down and people drifted back inside. I took the opportunity to steal upstairs and be alone for a while. I was in a room with dark ceiling beams and a spectacular view of the bay. This was a proud older Berkeley home and I wondered if it had ever witnessed a scene as sordid as the scene it was witnessing now. I took a deep breath and went back down.

Everyone had settled in the living room. Mitchum was back on the same paisley cushion as before, talking about his experiences in jail. "They wouldn't let me take a shower till the third day. Then, right when I had soap all over me, they turned the water off and made me go back to the cell." When he began talking about the bust itself, I cringed. He was getting close to the unspeakable.

"I had this feeling I was being followed so I flew into a cloud and did a one-eighty and came back out, but I didn't see anyone. It was just getting dark and I decided to land at Bakersfield. I landed and all of a sudden two planes came in right after me with their lights out. They didn't even notify the tower. I was taxiing to the parking area and one of them practically lost a wing swerving to cut me off. A bunch of agents jumped out and pointed guns at me. They yelled, 'You so much as fart and we'll blow your head off!' I saw their planes and realized why they were able to follow me like that. They had a Beechcraft Baron and a Cessna push-pull and on the nose of the Baron there was this huge Bendix transponder."

The room was silent. This was way too close. Yet Mitchum went on.

"They had me put my hands up to the roof of the plane. I had a gun in my lap, a thirty-two I'd brought, and I told them about it and asked them what they wanted me to do with it. They asked if there was a bullet in the chamber and I told them no. They told me to pick it up very carefully by the butt and drop it out the window. After that they took me to a pay phone outside the terminal. They plugged in this portable recorder they had and that's when they had me call Bruce."

So there it was. Not only had Mitchum finked, but he was now blandly admitting it. No one stirred. I picked a point on the carpet and concentrated on staring at it. Mitchum looked around and grinned. "Gee, it sure is nice of all of you to throw this party for me."

Mitchum's comments grew even more ironic as the evening dragged on. I found Wade shooting pool in his billiard room.

"Mitchum isn't on anything, is he?"

"Yeah, he dropped some blotter acid."

"You've got to be kidding! Who gave it to him?"

"Murray."

I found Murray and drew him aside. "What the hell did you give Mitchum acid for?"

The big acid dealer raised his palms up in a gesture of helplessness. "He asked me for it. What was I going to do? Tell him I don't have any?"

I left. I was the last to arrive and the first to leave, but I didn't care. If Mitchum was going to fink on me for leaving his party early, I would just have to deal with it.

In the weeks that followed Mitchum continued to stay at Wade's place, hitting us all up for favors: rides, money, meals, drugs. Meanwhile, Murray's lawyers were doing their best to find out just how much Mitchum had told the narcs. We all waited in a state of dread. Mitchum knew he had power over us and seemed to enjoy making ironic comments just to see us cringe.

I passed time hanging out with Margo while Bruce lay low in Salinas outfitting his D-18. He drove up to visit and we met at an IHOP. He asked me what I knew about hash and I shrugged.

"It's like pot only more concentrated. Takes up less volume."

He nodded and took a sip off his tea. "That pretty much tallies with what I've been able to find out. I've been thinking, maybe it's time we shift our operation eastward if you know what I mean. The Beech is about ready. It might do us both good to get out of this country for a while."

We visited the Beech and Bruce showed me a large hollow space he had discovered beneath the floorboards. We measured it and I calculated there was enough space to hold approximately 400 pounds of hash. At a wholesale profit of $600 per pound, this meant a single run could bring in a quarter million. Bruce's plan was to buy the hash in Afghanistan and fly it through Iran, Turkey, Greece, Italy, Spain, Portugal, and across the Atlantic to Newfoundland via the Azores. None of these borders was particularly hot and there was no reason to expect a rigorous customs check. From Canada it would be a simple matter to smuggle the hash into the States by car.

To finance this run we needed at least $15,000. None of us had this kind of money and I went to the Bear's Lair to see what I could find. Everyone there said the same thing: the man with the big bucks these days was Jake Miller. Seeing no alternative, I approached him. This had to be one of the strangest partnerships ever conceived: he had jumped my contact and I had nearly caused him to get run over by a truck. Yet he was eager for the deal. He knew my reputation, knew people had made fortunes providing me with front money, and knew I would honor our agreement regardless of any personal distaste I might have for him. We worked out a deal in which he provided us with $15,000 front money in return for a substantial cut of the proceeds. He even told me there was more where that came from in case we ran into unexpected expenses.

Winter was approaching. I got a passport, sublet my apartment to a friend who agreed to look after my dog, and packed my things. My last day in Berkeley I spent with Margo. We ate hamburgers at Buddy's Café, then hung out at a park. In the several months we had spent together, we had never said anything mushy or serious. Margo was a ghetto Black, not the type you would expect to see with a white guy, and very proud. Things between us were casual. If we had something serious to say, we said it through jokes.

Margo showed me a piece of writing she had done. She was an unusual girl. God knows where she learned to write, but she had somehow acquired the knack of perfectly mimicking de Maupassant. She especially liked his story about a man who seduces a young maiden for the sole purpose of stealing her wooden leg.

The morning I departed, Margo did a funny thing. She took off the red bandanna she was wearing and tied it around my dog Ogre's neck so that Ogre looked like a waif. Then as I walked out with my bags, she knelt on the porch with one arm around Ogre and holding her other out to me like a figure out of a Thomas Hart Benton painting, crying, "No! Don't leave us like this! You can't do this to us! We'll starve! We'll have to beg in the streets!"

We both laughed at this little skit and then I soul-kissed her and left. Riding out to the airport, though, I felt sad suddenly thinking maybe I had fallen in love with Margo without even realizing it and never said anything to make her know this.

CHAPTER 55

STEPPING OFF THE PLANE AT JFK, I looked around at the throngs of Easterners dressed in their dark winter clothing—hundreds of people who didn't know me and never would—and felt wonderfully anonymous and safe, worlds away from Mitchum and any legal problems he might be causing.

Bruce met me and we drove to Connecticut, where the D-18 was being prepared for our Atlantic crossing. The twelve passenger seats had been removed and replaced by five fifty-five-gallon drums for holding fuel. An electric pump moved the fuel from the drums to the wing tanks and in case it failed, there was a manual backup. The drums were held in place by guy wires that slanted out into the narrow aisle that led from the only door at the back of the plane to the cabin up front, and it was so awkward trying to squeeze between the drums with their guy wires that I found it easier simply to clamber over the tops of them. To get at our hiding place would involve undoing the guy wires and removing the drums, which would be particularly difficult if they had fuel in them. Unless they had a solid tip, we couldn't imagine customs ever attempting such a task. The ferry company that had installed the drums also rented us an inflatable life raft and Bruce and I meant to learn how to use it but never got around to it.

On a crisp winter day we took off and I looked down to see the New England woods in their red and purple splendor. Our first stop was Montreal and here Bruce insisted on spending some of Jake's money on a room at the Queen Elizabeth Hotel—the "Queen E" as he called it—which he said was the classiest hotel in all Montreal. Passing through the opulent lobby, Bruce looked around. "I bet half the men in here are private dicks." During the elevator ride to our room, Bruce sniffed, wrinkling his nose. "A woman on her period's been in this lift. I don't know about you, chap, but I can't stand being

286

around women when they're on their period."

No sooner had we gotten to our room than Bruce pulled out his little black book and phoned a Cuban model he knew who lived here. I was beginning to see he was the original girl-in-every-port guy. The model came over and was exotic-looking and beautiful. I tried to make conversation with her, asking if she knew any Americans who had come to live here in order to escape the draft, but she couldn't have cared less about the draft or the Vietnam War. She was all glamor and glitz. She and Bruce left and he didn't come back till the following morning, having spent all of ten minutes in the room we paid dearly for.

We flew on to Gander, Newfoundland, which is the easternmost point of North America and our takeoff point for crossing the Atlantic. We landed at the airport and a cab driver drove us between twelve-foot snowdrifts to the tiny town. We found a room in a pine-paneled hotel and had dinner there, then bundled up and made a dash across the street through freezing cold to a brightly lit saloon, where we were surprised to find four ferry pilots. These were pilots who made a living ferrying other people's planes across the ocean for a fee. They were an unusual breed of high-stakes gamblers who flew planes they had never flown before, maintained by people they rarely knew. As there would be no point in splitting the fee, they worked alone. They had no one to see them off and no one to greet them on the other side, these lonely heroes of the sky. When they heard this was our first crossing, they insisted on buying us a round.

I was slightly shocked to see pilots drinking. The one that drank the most was a young blond who was ferrying a Piper Twin all the way to the Belgian Congo for the CIA. He complained about the people who had hired him. "It's a fucking crime the condition the engines are in. They're both leaking oil by the quart. I ought to take it back and tell 'em to fly it themselves! . . . Aw, what the hell," and he ordered another Scotch. He said a typical fee for crossing the North Atlantic was $600, but because of the extra distance and the hazards involved, he was getting $800.

I asked if there was ever ice on our route and one of the pilots laughed. "You know what to do if you get ice, don't you? . . . Just fly low over the water till you're clipping the tops of the waves. The salt'll dissolve it right off!" He and the others were full of pilot jokes like this.

One of the pilots was older, about middle-aged, with big eyes that bulged way out. When he stepped away to the men's room, Bruce asked about him. "That's Dutch," the others told us and said he was the king of the ferry pilots, having completed over 300 Atlantic crossings. "That's why his eyes bug out," quipped one of them, "from so much time spent staring for land!" Dutch came back and we learned that he was taking a Cherokee Six across, a plane Bruce and I knew well. Bruce asked if he wasn't a bit nervous crossing all that water with just a single engine and Dutch shook his head.

"No, I'd rather fly this single than a lot of twins I've seen. I happen to know the owner and the plane has been very well maintained. That engine won't fail me. Plus I've got radar and Loran."

The talk kept circling back to the risks we all faced. One of the younger pilots, a quiet, sad type, told us, "Along the route you guys are taking, if you have to ditch, you can expect to last twenty minutes in the water this time of year. Your only chance is if you can ditch near a ship or if you have time to get an Air Sea Rescue helicopter to follow you down. They can drop paramedics with wetsuits into the water and they pack these bags of chemicals around you that turn warm when they get wet. A few guys have been saved that way but not many. Personally, I'd rather go down on the northern route. There you're only going to last a couple minutes. It's over quicker." The northern route involved flying to Baffin Island, Greenland, Iceland, and Ireland but wasn't an option for us as the Beech lacked de-icing equipment. Our route involved flying to the Azores, refueling, and flying on to Lisbon.

Dutch asked us what our cruising speed was and Bruce told him. Dutch nodded.

"That's about the same as mine. If you want, we can fly together. What's your estimated time of departure?"

"About eight o'clock in the a.m."

Dutch frowned. "That would put you in Santa María after dark. You don't want to do that. That strip's difficult enough in daylight."

"No, we should have light left. I just worked out the computations a couple hours ago."

"I don't think so. Maybe I better have a look at your calculations."

"Do you have the time? I don't want to put you out."

"I have as much time as it takes to make sure you boys have a safe trip."

Dutch crossed the street with us to our room, took a look at Bruce's figures, and right away saw the problem. Bruce had neglected to account for the fact we were flying into the sun.

"You're going through three time zones this flight. You're going to lose two hours." Dutch stared at Bruce and Bruce turned a deep red, the first time I had ever seen him blush.

"Maybe I better have a look at the rest of your figures."

Dutch spent the following hour with us reviewing the flight in detail. He had designed his own form for transatlantic flights and gave us a copy and helped us fill it out. "How about your point of no return, have you calculated that? . . . No? . . . That's important. Say you develop engine trouble. You're not going to want to waste time calculating whether you have enough fuel to turn back or not." He had Bruce work it out and checked his figures.

"Now Santa María's a tough airport. There's a tall mountain near the runway and it's a bitch in bad weather. I've got a transponder, so I don't have to worry as much but you don't. If the visibility is bad, err to the north. Also, they've got their transmitter right next to the mountain for some reason and you tend to get funny readings off it, homing in. If it's a choice between following your compass or your ADF, think twice before choosing the ADF. I've got Loran, so I won't have a problem. With luck, you might be able to follow me. The weather reports are good for tomorrow, so you've got a chance. By the way, where did you leave your plane? . . . Outside? . . . It'll be covered with ice in the morning, so you better get up an hour early and have the ground crew spray it off. I've got mine in a hangar."

After Dutch left, Bruce just sat for a moment in awe. "Now, there's a pilot for you, chap. You can see why he's made so many successful crossings, can't you? Everything he does is perfectly thought out and methodical. And did you notice, while all the others were downing Scotches, he just nursed his tea?"

We got to the airstrip the following morning just as it was getting light. Dutch was right; the Beech was covered with ice and we had to pay $150 to have it sprayed off with a mixture of steam and alcohol. The ground crew then placed large electric blankets around the engines to warm them so they would be easier to start. Bruce paid for these services with a Shell Carnet card, considered the most prestigious card among aviation circles. He was very proud of this card, having managed to get it just in time for our trip. With it you could charge thousands of dollars at a time for fuel, oil, and other expenses.

Dutch arrived and showed us his Cherokee Six in the warmth of the hangar he had rented for twenty dollars. The passenger seats had been removed and a single fifty-five-gallon drum was mounted crosswise on the floor. That was all he needed; his plane used far less fuel than ours. We walked out to the Beech and Bruce showed Dutch our ferry system. Dutch examined it, frowning.

"Who did it?"

Bruce told him.

"Well, the materials look good, but they've got the ferry lines going into the bottom of your wing tanks when they should have hooked them in at the top." He pointed. "Say that line starts leaking. You're going to lose fuel from your ferry system and whatever you've got in your wing tank as well. . . . Well, there's nothing you can do about it now."

I glanced at Bruce. He gave a resigned look and sighed quietly. It struck me he had no real idea what he was doing.

We went to the small tower and checked the latest Pan Am reports. Clear weather was predicted all the way to the Azores. "There's a good chance you'll be able to follow me the whole way," Dutch told us. He wished us luck, shook our hands, and went to his plane. We got in the Beech and then Bruce did something that caught me by surprise. With a look that was almost fatherly, he told me, "You know, chap, you don't have to come along on this portion of the trip if you don't want to. There's no reason you should risk yourself. I can fly the plane alone. You could take a commercial flight and meet me in Europe. Or when I get to Afghanistan."

"No, I want to come along." I figured we were in this together.

"Well, I just hope you don't end up regretting it," he said and began revving the engines.

We taxied toward the strip, stopped, and watched as Dutch lined his Cherokee up with each of the three runways in turn in order to calibrate his compass card. This was a maneuver he had taught us the night before and said it was important because of the strong magnetic deviation in the area. By now it was completely light with blue sky all around save for a lone cloud that hung over the runway. Dutch took off and disappeared into the cloud. By the time Bruce calibrated our compass card and ran his checklist one last time, a good ten minutes had passed. We took off and flew through the cloud, but when we reached clear air, there was no sign of Dutch. "I'm rocking my wings," he told us over the radio. Even so, we couldn't spot him. There were some large clouds in the distance and a while later he radioed, "I'm heading for a cloud that looks like a dog's head. I'm heading for his nose." We couldn't see such a cloud, though. There were clouds ahead but none that looked like a dog's head. Until this trip I had no idea of the vastness of the air. A cloud that looks like a dog's head could be as big as the state of Connecticut and could change appearance every few minutes as you approach it. Dutch tried several more times to get us to see him and then his transmissions grew fainter until there weren't any more and we realized we were alone. All we had for navigating was our compass, an ADF, and a VOR. I didn't like being separated from Dutch and had to fight down fear that was welling up inside me. I consoled myself with the fact there were two lightships between us and the Azores. Lightships are ships stationed permanently in the water to aid in navigation, like floating lighthouses.

The air around us was clear and I stared down at the fishnet patterns the waves made 8,000 feet below. We came to a cloud and Bruce deviated to the left fifteen degrees to avoid it, kept track of the time, then deviated to the right fifteen degrees for an equal amount of time. We homed in on the first lightship and it was comforting to spot it lying there below us, knowing we were right on course. We raised the ship and they said Dutch had passed by eighteen minutes earlier. So he was making a little better time than we were.

I broke out some sandwiches our landlady had prepared for us and Bruce got on his favorite topic of conversation, namely money.

"PMA and OPM—that's all you need, chap. . . . A Positive Mental Attitude and Other People's Money." He turned to grin.

"After we pull off these hash runs, I'd like to start an insurance company. That's a bloody clever trick, don't you think? Get a bunch of people to pay you money so you can turn around and invest it? You need capital, though, and that's where these runs come in useful." Again he seemed to see these runs as just a stepping stone, while I now saw them almost as a way of life. He adjusted the throttles ever so slightly to bring the engines into perfect sync.

"I can tell you a good way to get rich, though. In fact, I can tell it to you in three simple words." He turned to me, pausing for effect.

"Screw the poor."

He grinned, knowing how I might react to such a remark. I rolled my eyes but didn't say anything. Bruce had gone off on tangents like this before and arguing with him, I had learned, just dragged things out.

"That's right. I mean to say, you would expect it to be the exact opposite. You would expect if you wanted to make money, that you should look to the rich. But the fact is, the rich are too bloody smart and know how to hang on to their money, whereas the poor are a pack of fools and don't have much choice anyway. Furthermore, they come in much larger numbers. Take a little bit from each one and before you know it—bingo!—you've got a million."

He adjusted the throttles again. I kept quiet and didn't rise to the bait.

"I've got a friend in London who's made a fortune buying rundown apartment buildings and packing them full of Pakistanis. He never does a lick of work on the places, just drives up once a month in his Rolls Royce and collects rents. Half the apartments don't even have running water but the Pakis never complain. They're happy to have a place at all. They're a bit like your Blacks in the States."

"What you're saying is very perceptive, Bruce. Have you ever thought of lecturing at Berkeley?" I hadn't meant to say this. It just came out.

Bruce was staring at the clouds ahead and ran his eyes over the instrument panel. His brow was knit. This was the first time I had been sarcastic toward him and I was afraid I had hurt his feelings. He continued staring straight ahead.

"Your problem, Mr. Jenkins, is that you've spent too much time in that bloody town. You have no conception of the world at large. I mean to say, the rest of the world is *not* like Berkeley. Why don't you take a couple years off and spend some time traveling? By the time I was your age, I had already been around the world twice." He adjusted the throttles again and sighed. "Oh well, maybe this trip will do you some good."

His words plunged me into a funk. How could he suggest I take a couple of years off? Weren't we partners? I considered us partners for the long run, but he was giving me a lot of signs he didn't feel the same way. With the Mexico runs ruined, I didn't know what I would do without him.

CHAPTER 56

WE FINISHED EATING AND SETTLED INTO the routine of the flight. More clouds appeared and we made more detours. At one point we made a detour within a detour. Eventually the clouds grew too thick to avoid and we held our course and flew into them. The light around us flickered rapidly, then went gray. Occasionally there would be a gap in the clouds and we could see the dark, shadowed water below. We were flying IFR now, something we had hoped to avoid. Drops of water collected on the windshield and it began to rain. Somehow we had gotten into a storm. Bruce frowned. "I wonder why this wasn't in the Pan Am reports." He checked his watch. "Well, we just passed our point of no return."

It grew dark around us and we hit turbulence. I didn't like flying blind and felt vaguely nauseous. Every time one of the engines varied slightly in pitch, my heart froze imagining the worst. Cars and motorcycles had broken down on me so many times that I could hardly believe I was trusting my life to an internal combustion engine. If the left engine went, I knew we could still fly, but if the right one went, it would be harder because of the torque. We hit a pocket of turbulence and lightning shot out beyond our right wing. I asked Bruce if lightning ever struck planes and he said, "Hardly ever."

"What happens if it does?"

"I wouldn't worry about it, chap. Probably all it would do is maybe knock out the instrument panel."

We began to pick up ADF signals indicating the second lightship was off course to the north. We homed in on it and established radio contact. They said the bad weather had just blown up and that Dutch had made it through forty minutes earlier while it was still clear. It felt strange communicating with the lightship but not being able to see it. They gave us a fix and Bruce calculated a crosswind component nearly twice that predicted by the Pan Am reports.

We flew on and the storm grew worse. Turbulence that would have terrified me an hour earlier was now routine. Then for no apparent reason we began losing altitude. Bruce frowned as he eased forward on the throttles. We watched the needle of the altimeter slowly drop. "Maybe there's a problem with one of the engines," I said. Bruce waved his hand curtly.

"No, the engines are running fine. Look at the RPMs."

Finally he eased the throttles all the way forward. "That's all she's got." Still we continued to lose altitude. It was as though the hand of God were slowly pressing us down toward the sea. I felt sick with dread. "Maybe it's ice," I said then, voicing one of my worst fears.

"Not in all this rain, for Christ's sake."

At last the plane leveled out at 6,000 feet. With full throttles like that, it should have been cruising at 15,000. We stayed at 6,000 for a miserable several minutes and then the plane slowly began to rise. We got to our cruising altitude of 8,000 feet and Bruce was able to back the throttles off gradually to their original positions. He shook his head and shrugged. "All I can reckon is it was some kind of tremendous hundred-mile-an-hour downdraft."

After that the weather got better and finally cleared. We could see the water below and a clear horizon ahead. Our relief was short-lived, though, because another problem now faced us in that our ADF was beginning to pick up faint signals suggesting the Azores were off course to the north. We held our course and it seemed the signals were getting slightly stronger though we couldn't be sure. An awful choice faced us: either we followed our compass or our ADF. We didn't have enough fuel to make it to mainland Europe, so if we chose wrong and missed the Azores, we would fly until we ran out of fuel and drowned.

Bruce decided to follow the ADF. He swung the Beech into a bank and altered course to the north. An hour passed, and we began scanning the horizon, straining to spot land. I thought of the way Dutch's eyes bugged out. We spotted a freighter below, which made me feel better thinking at least if we ran out of fuel near a ship, we could try to ditch next to it and they might be able to rescue us. More time passed, and I thought I spotted the tiniest defect in the broad curve of the horizon ahead. Bruce thought I was imagining things, but after a while he saw it too. We held our breath. It seemed too big to be a freighter. It was the first in the chain of islands!

I felt limp with relief and wondered if this was anything like what Columbus felt when he first spotted land. Soon we were passing over the small island. Bruce flew low and we could see a farmer tilling the side of a hill with an ox-drawn plow. Seeing this earthbound scene warmed my heart. Now all we had to do was fly from island to island until we reached Santa María. We were halfway there when the next storm hit.

At first there was just a bank of clouds ahead. The clouds were white and didn't look like storm clouds. As we drew closer, though, the sky turned dark and the clouds welled up, turning dark green and purple, like an angry welt across the sky. There was no choice but to fly straight into them. Before we knew it, we were in a storm far worse than the first. Everything around us went black and all we could see was the rain streaming across our windshield, illuminated by the red glow from the instrument panel. We hit downdrafts so fierce they made our stomachs go light while pens and other loose items rose up in the cockpit like ghosts. The whole plane shuddered. Lightning struck to our right and I got a split-second view of the tip of our wing flexing by several feet. I didn't know metal could flex that much. Suddenly there was a horrific din as though we were being hit by machine gun fire from all sides. I thought it was the end, but it was only the rain having turned briefly to marble-sized hail.

Using the ADF, Bruce managed to home in on Santa María, raised the tower, and requested permission to land. In a nervous, Portuguese-accented voice, the controller informed us that visibility was a hundred feet and there was a crosswind component of thirty knots. These were essentially impossible conditions for landing. I began to feel sick with dread. Bruce pursed his lips and lined the Beech up according to our fan marker, which was our one landing aid. A radio transmitter located at the strip emitted a triangular beam like a fan, which we could use to home in on. Three lights on the instrument panel indicated our relationship to the fan: green meant we were in it, purple meant we were off course to the left, and orange meant we were off course to the right. The goal was to keep the green light on, meanwhile losing altitude, until we came to the fan's point and landed.

From twelve miles out, Bruce was able to get into the green part of the fan easily. He cautiously lost altitude in the darkness, knowing there was a mountain to the right of the strip. The purple light flashed and he made a rapid, slight correction to get us back into the green. As we drew closer to the strip, the fan grew narrower and he had to correct more often. Turbulence made it all the harder. I focused on the lights. They flashed green, purple, green, orange, green, orange—and then there was no more green, just purple and orange. Bruce cursed, banking the plane sharply to the left as he pulled back on the yoke to gain altitude, meanwhile informing the tower we were executing a missed approach. Now we had to backtrack ten miles to get back in the wide part of the fan and start all over again.

This was a waste of ten or fifteen minutes of precious fuel and seemed like something we should avoid at all costs. Yet Bruce couldn't keep the Beech in the fan marker and began executing missed approach after missed approach. I didn't think there was anything I could do and kept quiet. I reminded myself of the many tough scrapes Bruce had gotten himself out of before. Then I thought of Margo. I wished I were at home with my arms around her. I had had it good. Why did I have to come on this stupid trip? I thought to myself. I thought of my parents, too, and kept having the bizarre urge to pull over at a phone booth so I could give them a call.

I sat back in the copilot's seat and tried to endure. Meanwhile, the controller had become hysterical and was babbling in what seemed a mixture of English and Portuguese. English is the universal aviation language but he could barely speak it. He knew there was a good chance we were going to crash and his freaking out only made us feel worse. We grew sick of hearing him and turned our radio off. Looking back, this seems an insane thing to do but that's how bad he was making us feel. I peered down into the darkness and it seemed so strange to know that there was a town down there where people were eating dinner and enjoying themselves yet all we could see was blackness. If it weren't for our instruments, we wouldn't even know the town was there. Bruce and I didn't speak much as he continued his attempts to land. When we did speak, it was with a special tenderness. We both knew this might be the end and didn't want to make the other feel bad. Bruce failed his sixth approach and turned to me with a sigh. "I can't seem to keep it in the fan marker, chap. Do you want to give it a try?"

This was insane!! Bruce was a highly skilled pilot and I didn't even have my license. His words jarred me into the realization that he wasn't going to get us out of this. I could no longer sit back. I had to act.

"Why don't we go out over the ocean and slowly lose altitude till we're nearly at sea level? Maybe there's a sandwich of clear air and we can stay in it and home in on the strip visually."

Bruce didn't like this idea. "The turbulence is too severe. We could easily wind up in the drink."

"Maybe we should tell them we're going to ditch. Maybe they could get boats out before we run out of fuel."

Bruce shook his head. "I doubt they'd find anyone willing to go out in this shit, chap."

Just the same, I said I was going to go back to check the life raft.

I grabbed our flashlight and crawled back over the tops of the fuel drums. A sudden downdraft hit us, throwing me up against the ceiling. I crawled on more cautiously, using my right hand to hang on to the guy wires that held down the drums. At the back I opened the loo as Bruce called it and got out the box with our raft. Wedging myself into a space between the last fuel drum and the loo, I opened the box, found the instructions, and began reading them by light from the flashlight. It was hard because of the constant turbulence. I was trying to make sense of parts labeled A, B, and C when a sudden gust hit us and some metal parts to the raft went flying. I tried to feel for them in the darkness between the drums but couldn't find them. This was hopeless. We were never going to get this raft blown up. I left it there. I was tired and didn't feel like fighting a hopeless battle for my life in icy waters anyway. This plane is a flying coffin, I thought to myself, clambering back over the drums. At the last drum, I stopped for a moment and considered drinking aviation fuel to get things over with but there was no way to get the fuel out of the drum and anyway, that was no way to go.

Bruce executed another missed approach. I thought of my parents again and asked Bruce if I could turn the radio back on. Maybe I could get a message out that I loved them. My entire attention was now focused on this final task.

"Do whatever you like, chap."

I raised the controller and he began babbling again.

"*¿Acaso habla Ud. español?*" I cut in.

"*Sí,*" came the welcome response.

"*Bueno,*" I continued in Spanish. "I want to speak to someone at the airport who speaks English. I don't care if they are an employee or not. Just anyone who speaks English." Just like that time in the Mazatlan jail, I suspected only a fellow English speaker would take my request seriously enough to follow through.

A moment later a voice addressed us in perfect English. It was Dutch! I was never so happy to hear someone's voice in my life! He had been standing by all this time, no doubt imagining the worst as the controller tried over and over to raise us.

"I guess you boys got into a little more than you bargained for!" he said with a laugh, then turned serious without waiting for an answer. "Bruce, count your fuel."

Bruce counted. "We've got just a little over an hour." And if it had been any less, Dutch would have had the unenviable job of telling us we were likely done for.

"Good. That's just enough to make it to Graciosa a couple islands back. There's a U.S. Air Force base there where you can land. I just checked the weather reports and the storm isn't as bad there. Plus, it's a much easier strip and they've got Precision Approach Radar to bring you in.

"You'll have to declare an international emergency in order to land there, so raise them on the radio as soon as possible. Set your course right now to three-one-zero. That's only approximate. You can calculate the exact heading on your way. Have your buddy fly the plane while you work out the details. Good luck!"

Bruce swung the plane around. "Here, fly this thing!" I had never flown

IFR before, let alone a twin in a severe storm, but we had a chance now and I was going to do it! Dutch had said we had just enough fuel. Any wobbling off course, either up and down or sideways, would lengthen our trip and possibly cause us to come up short. I determined to fly as true a course as possible and focused my entire concentration on the compass and altimeter. Bruce got out his charts and calculator and began plotting our course. Lightning continued to strike all around us while thunder periodically drowned out the engine sounds. I was managing to keep the oscillations of the compass needle to within just a few degrees and our altitude wasn't varying more than fifty to a hundred feet. The attitude indicator showed we were flying through the air with the wings at a thirty-degree angle to the horizontal, but the plane felt perfectly level to me, so I ignored it, figuring it had been knocked out by lightning.

Bruce glanced up and saw the attitude indicator. "What the hell's going on? You're flying this thing fucking sideways!"

"No, I'm not. Lightning knocked out the instrument!"

Bruce jerked the yoke around till the attitude indicator said we were flying level. "Lightning did *not* knock out the instrument, chap! You're bloody fucking disoriented. You've got to believe your instruments, otherwise you're dead."

Now I felt as though we were flying through the air slantwise. After a few minutes, though, it felt right. I continued to stare back and forth between the compass, the altimeter, and now the attitude indicator. Bruce raised the tower at Graciosa and declared an international emergency.

The Air Force picked us up on their radar and began guiding us in. Already the weather was easing up a little. It was still pitch dark and raining but the turbulence wasn't as bad. Bruce finished with his charts and took over the controls.

From time to time the Air Force controller would direct him to descend another hundred feet in altitude or make a slight correction in course. This seemed to go on for a long time. Then light suddenly flickered around us as we broke through the underside of the clouds, and there below lay the twilight blue ocean and in the distance, Graciosa, with its military airstrip aligned perfectly with our course. And what tore me up was that the strip was flanked on either side with innumerable fire engines and ambulances, all with their red lights flashing—just for us! My country loves me! I thought to myself and fought to hold back tears.

Even so, it was a difficult landing. There was a strong crosswind, which was especially difficult for the Beech with its dual tail fin. On the first two tries, Bruce bounced off the runway literally thirty feet in the air and had to execute missed approaches. By the third try, our fuel gauge was on "E." Bruce shook his head. "I'm going to put this thing down this time if I have to slam it into the ground." And that is practically what he did. The Beech bounced so horribly I thought sure the landing gear would fail, but the bounces dampened out and soon we were on land again thirteen hours after we had started out. We stepped out in a daze. A terrific wind was blowing. There was handshaking . . . papers to sign . . . an officer showing us where to bunk . . . the mess hall.

We were beat.

CHAPTER 57

THE STORM MOVED EASTWARD AND WE FLEW to Santa María the following morning in near-perfect weather. Dutch was still there, waiting for the storm to clear Lisbon. We thanked him profusely for having saved our lives and treated him to a drink at a small bar overlooking the town's whitewashed houses with their tall chimneys, each topped with a stork's nest. Dutch said he had made it to Santa María before the storm got really bad. The fact he had a transponder and a glideslope receiver had helped. We mentioned our mysterious loss in altitude and he said he had experienced the same thing, though not as bad, and agreed it must have been a fierce downward current of air.

I ordered an ouzo because I liked pouring water into it and watching it precipitate. Dutch made a show of studying me and turned to Bruce. "I'm waiting to see if he ends up screwing a cat!"

Bruce laughed. "Speaking of that, what are the chances of getting laid on this island?"

Dutch roared. "Bruce, I've been flying through here for fifteen years, and if you can get laid on this island, I'll buy you a transponder. The only way you could get a woman here into bed is by marrying her. They're all Portuguese."

We lingered a while and Dutch began asking in a roundabout way what we were doing with the Beech and where we were headed. After a couple of evasive answers, Bruce simply treated him to a blank grin, one of several ways he had of getting people to quit asking questions. Dutch took the hint with a chuckle and stared out over the Santa María streets, still dark from rain. "The way I see it, you guys are smuggling something. I just can't figure out what."

The waiter came and Bruce paid for our drinks with his Shell Carnet card. Dutch spied the card and shook his head.

"A Beechcraft D-18 and a Shell Carnet card. If that isn't a smuggler's ticket to paradise, I don't know what is!"

The weather cleared and in the morning Bruce and I dead reckoned across 400 miles of water, hitting Lisbon dead on. It had colorful hills and a bay spanned by golden bridges that reminded me of San Francisco. I sent a telegram to my parents, letting them know I was all right, then let Bruce con me into detouring south to Faro so he could look up an old girlfriend he hadn't seen in years. "Carolyn may be the only bird I've ever truly loved," he told me to justify this crazy side trip. I didn't care. This was my first trip to Europe and I was eager to see new places I had never seen before.

We landed at Faro in the late afternoon and Bruce was immediately curious about three Lockheed Super Constellations parked at the far end of the strip. Wherever we went, Bruce always took notice of the other planes around and could identify all but the most obscure makes. These Super Connies stood out with their long, eel-shaped bodies and triple tail fins. We had a drink at the airport bar and in a matter of minutes Bruce was able to get the story on the planes. They belonged to two Irishmen who were using them to smuggle guns and salt into Biafra. They flew into crude jungle strips at night, maneuvering the immense planes over the tops of trees with their lights off. Twice they had been shot at and a previous pilot lost his life when he came in too low and crashed. All of Faro knew what the Irishmen were doing and regarded them as heroes. After each run the pair would go on a spree for several days straight, hitting every bar in town and buying rounds.

"You see," said Bruce, "there's no end to the number of things you can make money on smuggling. Take toilet paper into Spain, for instance—there's a good scam. The toilet paper in Spain is like sandpaper. You'll see when we get there. Guys used to bring in high-quality toilet paper in speedboats from Gibraltar. Perfume too. You seem to think drugs are the only thing."

Bruce's old girlfriend had since moved and we headed east by way of Barcelona, Rome, Naples, Athens, Istanbul, Ankara, and Diyarbakir. My excitement on seeing these new places was tempered by near-daily frights. Over the Mediterranean on our way to Rome, the ferry tanks suddenly began making loud, metallic pops as we descended in altitude. Bruce wrote it off to a change in atmospheric conditions, but we had already been through some extreme changes in atmospheric conditions and the tanks had never done this before. At Istanbul there was a thick rain and we had to come in under IFR over the tops of minarets barely visible through the haze. Then on the way to Ankara, we were buzzed by Turkish military jets. Two of them played a game with us, trying to see how close they could come to our plane. We could actually see their maniac grins as they flashed past. They were so much faster than us and the way they banked suddenly, exposing their bellies to us, made them seem like sharks. Suddenly there was a loud cracking sound and the whole Beech shuddered violently. I thought they had shot us.

"No, it's the jet vortex coming off their wings," Bruce said. "Buggering assholes! If they keep this up, they're liable to knock our wings off!" He raised Ankara control but they said they had no way of communicating with the military. The pilots hit us a couple more times with their jet vortices before streaking off.

The worst, though, came when we tried to cross the rugged mountains between eastern Turkey and Iran. As we approached them, we saw that their tops were shrouded in a layer of white clouds. At our maximum cruising altitude of 15,000 feet, we couldn't quite get above the clouds. We could fly through them, but our charts showed there were several peaks in the area taller than 15,000 feet and the closest one was only twenty miles off course. We couldn't count on our course being that accurate either as the mass of all these mountains was likely to affect our instruments. If we flew through the clouds, we would be running the risk of slamming into one of these tall peaks.

Bruce then tried something that was like the aeronautical equivalent of taking a running jump at the mountains and made about as much sense. He backtracked ten miles to get some distance on them, then headed for them while maintaining steady back pressure on the yoke. Gradually we gained altitude but at the expense of airspeed. The stall warning gave a beep and I startled. "Don't worry about that," he told me. "It's set way high."

I was tired of feeling frightened for my life every day and watched in dread as the altimeter needle slowly climbed till it was pointing to 16,000 feet. By now the stall warning had become a continuous shriek. It looked as though we were just about even with the top of the cloud layer, but in the meantime our airspeed had fallen below a hundred knots. Our pitch attitude was so high, it felt as though we were flying through the air belly first. The wings kept trying to dip into a dive and Bruce was making rapid, precise corrections to keep them level. We could hear the engines straining against the thin air and the lack of oxygen was making us both giddy. I glanced down and saw rocky crags just a thousand feet below. If the Beech went into a dive, it could take us two or three thousand feet to pull out of it. On a sudden impulse, I pushed the yoke in and in seconds we lost half the altitude Bruce had worked so hard to gain, but our airspeed was up to 110 and the stall warning was off. Bruce stared at me.

"What the fuck did you do that for?"

"We were going to stall."

"We were not going to stall, for Christ's sake!"

"What, you were going to fly all the way across the mountains like that?"

In a curt motion Bruce banked the plane around through a one-eighty. His anger was more show than real, though. He knew if we had stalled over those clouds, we would have lost thousands of feet before recovering, and there was no end of terrain we could have hit at thirteen or fourteen thousand feet.

We backtracked to Ankara and asked some of the local pilots there for advice. They said those mountains were always shrouded in clouds and to get over them safely, we needed a turbocharger and oxygen. We considered detouring around the mountains, but to the north was the Soviet Union and to the south there was a war going on. If we carried less fuel, we would have a higher cruising altitude, but we wouldn't be able to reach Tehran. We could reach Tabriz but the pilots told us there was no fuel available there.

I knew a girl named Carol who had scored large quantities of hash in Morocco and suggested we try scoring there. I phoned her and she said she was pretty sure she could get the quantity we needed. Bruce was agreeable to this new plan and we paid for Carol's plane ticket and flew back through the Mediterranean to Casablanca. At the airport there, we were treated like royalty. All we had to say was *"avion privé"* and we had complete run of the place. Bruce was immediately excited.

"I mean to say, this is the sort of country you want to do business in. You can tell money talks here. Not like these bloody repressive regimes, such as Greece and Spain, where the officials are always worrying over petty details and regulations."

Carol came, but her contact was nowhere to be found. She was cute and had a sexy way of giggling, and in a reckless effort to impress her, I dashed across the busiest intersection in all Casablanca and scored some hash off a cabbie. Bruce was now smoking and the three of us got high. That night I ended up sleeping with Carol in our hotel room with its two beds, and in the morning Bruce drew me aside.

"Harrumph! Now see here, chap, you can't expect me to sit idly by while you're screwing that bird. You should give me a piece of the action. Share and share alike, you know."

I was flattered that Bruce with his great prowess with women was appealing to me for help, but when I passed his request on to Carol, she made a face. "Eew, that dirty old man? No thanks!" Bruce ended up having his wife fly out to meet us. As a Pan Am stewardess she could fly anywhere for free. Holding hands, the four of us wandered through the Casablanca night redolent of cumin, past neon signs in Arabic that looked like tangled snakes. Meanwhile, the run was going nowhere.

The girls left and I asked Bruce if he remembered the young Avis clerk at the airport who had rented us our car. This clerk had impressed me. He had green eyes and lighter skin than most Moroccans and his English was excellent. He had struck me as intelligent and aspiring. I said we should approach him and Bruce agreed. We found him behind the Avis rental counter and after a few pleasantries, I told him what we wanted. He responded without hesitating.

"I don't know why you came to me but you came to the right person. As strangers you would not have a chance of finding what you want. I live here. I know the right people to see regarding this type of matter. The amount you are asking for is large but I can find it. Do not approach anyone else. You could get in trouble that way. Just relax and have a good time. See the city. I will take care of everything."

The next day he visited us twice at our hotel. He assured us he had made contact with the right people but seemed unable to come up with a sample. Finally, he agreed to show us a gram but wanted ten dollars in advance to pay for it.

"A gram? We don't want to see a gram," I told him. "Anyone who has four hundred pounds ought to be able to show us bricks. And they shouldn't have to charge either."

He got heated. "That is not the way business is done here. Suppose you want to buy pencils wholesale. You don't ask to see four hundred thousand pencils. You start with one pencil." He held up his finger. "One."

Things seemed to be getting tense. We told the clerk to check back with us later, hoping he wouldn't show. He did, though, and I looked out the window to see two burly Moroccans waiting in a car as he skipped up the stairs to our room. We told him we had decided to call the deal off and he erupted.

"Call it off? Do you realize how much work I've put into this? I've got people waiting! You can't just back out like this!"

He began jabbing his chest. "Do you know what I am? . . . I am a Jew! Do you know what it means to be a Jew in an Arab country? . . . Of course not! You have no idea! You guys have it made!"

We left the next morning, cringing as we passed the Avis rental counter on the way to our plane. And that's what this run had come to: slinking out of Casablanca in fear of an Avis car rental clerk!

CHAPTER 58

BRUCE AND I PARTED WAYS IN FARO. He headed back toward Afghanistan, figuring he might be able to get over those mountains without my weight on board, and I caught a flight home. Before boarding, I called one of our lawyers and he said he knew of no indictment against me though that didn't mean much as the grand jury often handed down indictments in secret. I asked him about the big books Immigration had and he didn't think I was important enough to appear there. "I think those books just have undesirables and maybe really serious criminals, like murderers," he told me. Just the same, I knocked off the two-drink limit during the flight and still trembled when I handed the immigration officer my passport.

Back home I learned that Margo was no longer living in the apartment below mine. No one seemed to know where she was. I had met her mother once and drove to her home. She answered the door and took a moment to look me up and down. "Well, you're still blue-eyed and white. Guess there ain't much you can do about that," she chuckled. "Come on in." Over coffee she told me that Margo had joined the Venceremos Brigade and was in Cuba helping Castro with the sugarcane harvest. She wouldn't be back for six months.

I found Wade and his family living in a rundown flat in Emeryville. Nearly everything they had was gone—the palatial home, the pool table, the antique furniture. On the day I showed up, they were debating which of their remaining Persian rugs to sell in order to pay off Wade's lawyers. Oddly, Wade didn't seem that bummed by all his legal problems. He had a way of throwing his full energy into things and his first step was to master the terminology of the particular field involved. He spoke optimistically about his case, dropping terms like "reasonable expectation of privacy" and "motion for disclosure"—terms I wasn't familiar with and hoped never to have to learn.

In addition to his bust, he had also been indicted in the Mitchum case. Mitchum, it turned out, had finked on both Wade, the person who put him up in his home, and Murray, the person who put up most of his bail—this in addition to finking on Bruce and LeGrande. The only person he didn't fink on was me. I remembered slamming him up against a wall that time and wondered if he was afraid of me.

Wade had a court appearance and invited me to come along. This turned out to be one of the more bizarre experiences of my life. A gaggle of Berkeley narcs was there to testify, and during a break they approached me in the hallway, where I had gone to stretch my legs. Without a word, they surrounded me and began staring at me, jutting their faces to within inches of mine. I didn't know if they were intent on memorizing my features, hoping to intimidate me, or what.

Determined not to let them rattle me, I stepped over to a window, where I would at least have one direction in which to look and not see narc faces. They followed me in unison maintaining their close distance to me as smoothly as if the scene had been choreographed and rehearsed. I spent a minute or so staring out the window before the thought struck me that I didn't really need to be here and left. I had often wondered whether the local narcs were on to me and now I knew.

I needed a place to live and moved into the basement of a communal home in Montclair, where some friends from Wichita, Kansas, lived. They had come west to check out the hip scene and were in many ways hipper than folks from California and New York. They were loosely arranged in three couples but there were always intrigues going on. At home they spent much of their time naked, even answering the door that way. Nudity was common in communes I had visited but it was generally considered uncool to look. Here the girls felt insulted if you didn't look. If a girl was wearing clothes, the guys would say to her, "Gityer bush out," and if a guy was wearing clothes, the girls would giggle and say, "Gityer dick out." They were like a bunch of kids whose parents were permanently away.

Sharon was the one I knew best. She was a cute blonde who drove a Triumph 650 and worked three evenings a week as a topless waitress at the Hotsy Totsy Club in Albany while taking dance classes at Mills College. I asked her how her job was going and she giggled and said, "Oh, it's odious." But it kept her from having to work as a secretary. One evening I happened to tell her about my failed attempt to get Abelardo a prostitute.

"Why didn't you call me? I know a bunch of horny Mills girls who would have balled him. Is he handsome? . . . A handsome Mexican dope dealer? . . . God, I would have balled him myself."

I checked on the Saga and there was so much rust damage to the hull that it was unsalvageable. We had had the boat surveyed before buying it and I got out my copy and read where it said the hull was in "fair and sound condition." But when I examined the copy further, I discovered that it wasn't really a survey but just a "One Page Report" with a fine-print disclaimer at the bottom releasing the surveyor from all responsibility. I began asking around and learned that the surveyor was a close friend of the man who had sold us the boat. The Berkeley harbor master laughed when I asked him if he had heard of the Saga and said it was a well-known joke around the bay, having been sold several times over to various suckers. He said it was even part of a scam once involving a free cruise to Tahiti.

That crooked surveyor had cost us thousands and Wade and I went to pay him a visit with no clear plan in mind. At first he claimed not to remember the boat, but after we showed him his report, he was able to come up with an amazing number of details in his defense. Wade got heavy with him and he began whimpering, even mentioning that he had a wife and kids, at which point Wade and I lost heart for this poorly thought-out endeavor and left.

Grass was scarce, but some was still getting up and I tried to figure out how. Operation Intercept had officially ended, but much of the radar net was said to be still in place. Supposedly, the trick now was to fly out over the ocean in order to get around the net. I sounded people out about putting together a plane run but in the wake of Mitchum's bust, no one wanted to take a chance. Grass prices were high, too. Just by throwing a few bricks over the fence you could make an easy grand.

One day I was watching Bill Gretsch work on his motorcycle and we happened to get on the subject of my half ton of grass that was stolen. "Well, you know who the Bub's partner was, don't you?"

"No."

"It was Arf."

My mind reeled. "No way."

"Yeah, it was Arf. You didn't know that? I'm surprised you didn't sense something was wrong. He was practically incapacitated with guilt. That's why he sat on that stuff for so long without selling any of it."

Of course, I had sensed something was wrong but I thought it was just his guilt over having contact-jumped me to smuggle heroin.

"Remember that time you fired some rounds off into the floor? Right after you found out about the rip-off? Well, Arf was so consumed with guilt, he thought you had shot him and just sat there waiting to die."

I remembered how pale he looked.

Bill laughed and took a swig off a beer he was drinking. "That wasn't the first time he tried to rip you off, either. Remember that time someone messed with the lock on that dope garage you were renting from me? That was Arf and Jake. They tried to saw through it with a hacksaw, but it was too hard. They came back the next night with a huge pair of bolt cutters, but you'd already moved your dope. If you hadn't, you would have lost it."

"How do you know all this?"

"Arf told me about it. He was so consumed with guilt, he was confessing to everyone."

I couldn't believe it—Arf, my best friend since tenth grade. Why would he try so hard to steal from me when he was already making a fortune selling heroin? I wondered. Pure greed was Bill's guess.

"He was extremely jealous of you, you know. He even cheated you at cards. You know those poker games on Addison Street? Arf would sit out so he could wander in and look at your hand and give signals to Jake."

I remembered Jake once calling my jack-high bluff with only a king high. I began connecting dots.

"I can't believe I invited Arf to go capture his own partner. The Bub didn't have a phone at his place in Santa Cruz, but Arf could have raced there to warn him. Or at least moved the dope."

"By that time he felt so guilty, I think he was just as happy to see you get it back."

Bill killed his beer and crumpled the can. "You know what surprised everyone, though, was your reaction to it all. Everyone assumed you would flip out. But you didn't."

My friendship with Arf was already pretty well shot but if I had any thoughts of rekindling it, Bill's news ended them. Yet for months afterward I had frequent dreams in which I found some reason to excuse Arf's rotten treatment of me so we could become best friends again.

*

For a while now, I had heard of a flamboyant smuggler who went by the name of Roger the Dodger, and a mutual friend arranged an introduction. Roger stood about six foot three, had broad shoulders and mutton chop sideburns, and liked to wear vests and overcoats that made him look like a riverboat gambler out of a Mark Twain novel. He had the right accent too, coming from Mississippi.

His smuggling method was to cross in West Texas through the Rio Grande. He had started by wading sacks across and graduated to driving large quantities across in a four-wheel-drive dualie. On a typical run, he and his partner would score in Michoacan, then drive all the way back to the border without stopping, popping bennies to stay awake. Recently, he had taken a bust when they got confused in the night, picked the wrong place to ford, and got their truck stuck in the river. They tried to winch out but couldn't, so they unloaded the grass and stashed it in bushes on the Mexican side, and as soon as it got light, they found a farmer and offered to pay him to tow their truck out with his tractor. Under the pretext of getting his keys, the farmer went inside his home and phoned the Border Patrol. Agents arrived and had no trouble finding the hidden grass.

Roger was out on bail but his partner was still sitting in a West Texas jail cell. I asked Roger if he thought he could beat his case and he laughed. "Not a prayer." He had no intention of sticking around, though. His plan was to make as much money as possible while postponing his trial and then split with his girlfriend to Brazil.

He and I compared notes and realized we were about as different as two smugglers could be. Whereas I tended to be cautious and methodical, Roger acted on impulse and sheer balls. In all the time he had spent smuggling, he had scarcely learned two words of Spanish. "What does *mira* mean?" he asked me when he learned I spoke Spanish. "The Mexicans are always going, '*Mira, mira.*'" "*Mira*" meant "Look," I told him and his face lit up with sudden understanding. I couldn't believe he had never bothered to look this up.

I was dubious of Roger's method because it seemed so easy. Also, I felt his bust must have made the area hot.

"Sure they know grass is coming through there," he told me. "They've known it all along. There ain't a thing they can do about it, though." He got out a map to show me. The border between West Texas and Mexico follows the Rio Grande and for about seventy miles east of El Paso, the border is closely paralleled by Interstate 10.

"There's any number of places you can cross here. There's bushes all around and the river takes a turn every quarter mile. They'd have to have a hundred guys out there every night to keep people from crossing and I bet they ain't got more'n two. And once you make it to the interstate, you've got it made. Interstate 10 carries all the traffic from Miami to Los Angeles, you know."

Roger felt he was too hot to take an active part in the run and we worked out a plan involving his younger brother, Les. I would be responsible for delivering the grass to the Mexican bank of the Rio Grande and Les would be responsible for transporting it home to Berkeley. The split would be fifty-fifty. We decided to start with 500 pounds. Roger's dualie had been confiscated and for this first run Les would simply wade the grass through the river and bring it home in a rented van. This way we wouldn't have to worry about finding another truck and there would be no chance of getting stuck. Later, when we had more money and wanted to move larger amounts, we could consider getting a truck. I phoned Jesus and he was eager to get the runs going again. He felt confident that he could move the grass up through Mexico and deliver it to the river. Essentially, Jesus would be handing the grass off to Les and I envisioned my risk in this run as minimal.

Roger was waiting for some money to come in and I spent time hanging around his place. He lived in a stately three-story home not far from the UC Berkeley chancellor's house. Roger was interested in photography and had a large darkroom, a couple of Hasselblads, and a room full of photographic equipment. While he spent time in his darkroom, friends streamed in and out and were entertained by Roger's beautiful girlfriend, Dinah. Dinah seemed Roger's opposite. She was petite, refined, and sophisticated. She confided to me that she didn't know if she would like Brazil. She worried about culture shock and being away from her friends.

Roger was the only smuggler I knew who was a true criminal. Other smugglers I knew were mostly middle-class guys who saw a chance to make a chunk of money without hurting anyone. Roger told me how he had grown up dirt-poor in Mississippi and had to drop out of school in order to pick cotton. One day he threw his sack down, said, "Fuck it!" and took off with his brother to Chicago, where they got by stealing cars and burglarizing warehouses. Roger grinned as he recounted breaking into a warehouse and using the company's own forklift to load color TVs into a moving van stolen for the occasion. They took a bust, did some time, and when he got out, Roger visited a friend he had made in prison whose grandfather owned a ranch along the Rio Grande, which is how Roger got into smuggling.

Les drove down from somewhere in northern California, where he lived in a cabin in the woods. He was smaller than Roger, didn't seem as bright, and lacked Roger's charisma. But he seemed honest and trustworthy, which were the main things I cared about. We discussed the run and he told me, "Well, yer gonna help me carry them sacks through the river, ain'tcha?" I told him I would rather not.

"You're taking all the risk driving out of there anyway. There's no sense in both of us risking a bust." I had no idea what his arrangement with Roger was but told him if it was a question of the cut, I was sure we could work something out.

"I don't give a shit about the money. I just figure we're both in this together."

I could see my answer hadn't sat well with Les, but I wasn't ready to volunteer to help carry the sacks. I really didn't want to take any risk on the American side.

Several days later I happened to be at Roger's when a truck pulled up and lowered two large wooden crates onto the front lawn. Roger and Les eagerly broke open the crates to reveal two Bultaco dirt bikes Roger had ordered. By afternoon we had them running and headed up to the hills behind Berkeley, Roger and Les on the Bultacos while I rode my Hornet. The ground was muddy and slick from recent rains and Les nearly spilled when he used his front brake going down a hill. Roger saw this and grinned. I caught up to Les and tried to yell to him above our engine noise. "Don't use your front brake going downhill! Use compression!" He turned to me with a blank look that was uninterpretable. A short while later he went down a hill too fast, used his front brake again, and went flying headfirst over the handlebars. Roger and I caught up to find him sitting in the mud cradling his left arm.

At the hospital I was amazed how many friends Les had considering he didn't even live in the area. By the time the doctors were through casting his arm, about eight or ten hippie chicks had arrived to console him. They mothered him and drew pretty hearts and flowers on his cast. The scene felt more like a party than a hospital waiting room. I wasn't feeling the least bit festive and left. Thanks to Les's idiot motorcycling skills, I saw that I was now going to have to carry those sacks through the river and even load them into the van.

CHAPTER 59

LES AND I FLEW TO EL PASO, RENTED A VAN under Les's name, and drove out to the Rio Grande. I took one look at the river and it was almost as though all those plane runs I had done with Bruce were a waste of time. I couldn't believe how easy this place looked. There wasn't a soul around. No buildings, no cars, nothing. Just a levee road next to the river and enough tall bushes around that we couldn't be seen by anyone unless they were within a few hundred yards of us. The river itself was so still you couldn't tell which way it was flowing. "God, you could probably cross here in the daytime!" I exclaimed and Les grinned.

"I believe Roger's done it a few times."

I wanted to drive along the levee road, but Les advised against it, saying we might run into a patrol.

"So what? We're not holding. If there's any heat on this road, I'd just as soon find out now."

We drove down the levee road, stopping every so often to check out possible crossing sites. The water wasn't clear enough for us to see the bottom, so we looked for places where the river was wide, indicating that it was also shallow. In two hours we saw one patrol, a farmer driving a pickup, and a couple making out in a '56 Chevy. The patrol was on a side road and didn't even look our way. It seemed there was just enough activity in the area that a passing vehicle wouldn't attract attention.

We picked a crossing site and planned how we would do the run. There was a natural hollow along the bank here, where I could stash the sacks as I was bringing them across. The levee road ran above the hollow and Les could crouch there keeping a lookout while I was crossing the sacks. The van meanwhile would be parked where we had it now, in a cleft in some bushes.

At my signal, Les would bring the van up onto the levee road, and in less than a minute I could have all the sacks loaded and he could take off. He would immediately get off the levee road and take a dirt side road to a county road that led back to the interstate. Meanwhile, I would wade back to the Mexican side and get a ride out of the area with the Mexicans.

The main risk with this plan lay in Les's seven-mile drive back to the interstate. The route we had picked passed through scrubland with no farmhouses, but there was still the slight risk of stumbling across a patrol. Roger had said that the patrols in this area had little orange lights attached to their front bumpers, which illuminated the roadway just ahead of them, enabling them to travel at fairly high speeds without using headlights. They used these lights to sneak up on smugglers. If there was any way possible, I wanted to eliminate even this small risk.

Near our dirt road was a large, open field flanked by bushes on three sides. A dry arroyo cut across the field in the direction of the interstate, and where it passed through the bushes, there was a natural tunnel formed by overhanging willows. The tunnel looked just big enough to accommodate the van. If Les could use this natural tunnel to get all the way to the interstate, he would have it made. I wanted to check it out, but Les objected.

"Roger and them guys—they never went to this kinda trouble to do a run."

I convinced him it was for his own good and we drove the van across the field to the arroyo. After checking the bed to make sure it was hard, we drove up it and entered the tunnel of willows. The air here was cool and smelled of roots. Les drove, stopping every few yards so I could jump out and move a rock or fallen branch. There was no sign that anyone had ever been through here before: no footprints, no tire tracks, no trash. The odometer said we had gone two and a half miles when the tunnel opened up briefly as we crossed a county road going perpendicular to our path. Then at about five miles there was another county road. We got stuck right on the other side of it. I got out and saw that our left rear tire was spinning. I jacked up the van and put rocks and branches underneath and had Les ease out on the clutch, but after a couple of tries the wheel had sunk up to the axle in sand. Les got out to look.

"Damn! Why do you hafta make everything so fucking complicated?"

Obviously the arroyo idea was out and I agreed Les should just use the road. In the meantime we had to figure out how to get out of here. I was prepared to hike out to the interstate to get help when a jeep suddenly appeared, speeding along the county road heading toward us. We flagged it down and the occupants turned out to be two hunters, both clean shaven with crew cuts and wearing identical brand-new hunting vests filled with shotgun shells. They stared at us with cold, suspicious looks. For a moment I thought they were going to drive on, but without saying anything, one of them got out and got a chain out of the back of their jeep. In the ten minutes it took them to get our van out, they hardly spoke. The one who had gotten the chain out then turned to me.

"You're not from these parts, are you?"

"No, I'm from Berkeley."

No sooner had I said this than I felt like slapping myself across the face. I liked to think I was professional and yet I kept on making mistakes like this. I should have had a cover prepared involving a less controversial town that I happened to be familiar with: San Jose, Salinas, Monterey—any place but Berkeley! The hunters left and Les chuckled.

"Them hunters knew exactly what we're doing here."

In the morning I crossed into Juarez and met Jesus and Miguel. I hadn't seen them since the ill-fated Mitchum run and we slapped each other on the back as we traded abrazos. From Juarez we drove east to a tiny town called El Porvenir and from there it was a short drive to the river. I was able to find our crossing site from the Mexican side and we memorized landmarks in the area. All that remained now was for Jesus to transport the grass north from Culiacan. Jesus guessed this would take about a week. Back in El Paso Les said, "I ain't hangin' around here that long. I hate this place. Call me when you want me to come back." He caught a flight back to the Bay Area and I found an inexpensive motel and settled in.

I quickly established a routine in which I spoke to no one save to order food or say hello to the woman who ran the motel. After breakfast each morning, I would read the newspaper, then take a long walk around town or out into the countryside. El Paso was flat with barren purple mountains that rose up behind it so abruptly that they looked unreal to me, like papier-mâché props. There were few trees in the town and it looked so barren that I took to thinking of it as "El Sparso." Marty Robbins' song kept running through my mind, butchered in my own way with "El Paso" becoming "El Sparso" and "beautiful Mexican girl" becoming "beautiful Mexislowan girl."

One night at this motel I had the worst dream of my life. I dreamt that I was wading sacks of grass through the Rio Grande and was suddenly confronted by a Border Patrol. I looked up and saw that it was my father. He said, "Even though you're my son, you know that by the oath I've sworn to, I'm duty-bound to arrest you." I pulled out the .45 I had bought off a Hell's Angel and told him, "If you're going to play by your code, then I'm going to play by mine." I woke up in a fright, my heart pounding as though it were going to burst out of my chest.

Days passed and I had a lot of time to reflect on the strange turn my life had taken. As a kid I was always hiding things. I once had a crush on my little sister's best friend and wrote a love letter to her, then sealed it in an envelope, placed the envelope in a can, placed the can in a jar, placed the jar in a bigger jar, and buried the whole works three feet deep in our backyard.

My parents liked to think we were a normal, happy family with no problems and I learned to hide anything that didn't fit this view. I even learned to lie because they seemed happier that way. I spent much of my childhood dissembling, so in a way it was only natural that I became a smuggler.

There are probably many reasons I became a smuggler. The one thing I knew is that it felt unbelievably right to me, as though there were nothing else I could have become. Still, it was hard to reconcile with the life I was supposed to lead. I often thought I must feel the way a gay person feels: raised with the expectation that you will be a certain way—only to discover that you are very different.

A blizzard hit and it became an ordeal to phone Jesus from exposed pay phones. I bought a ski cap and gloves but still had to keep my bare ear to the freezing receiver during the fifteen or twenty minutes it took the operator to get a line. The blizzard hit northern Mexico too, and Miguel got stuck with the truck full of grass somewhere out of Chihuahua. Christmas was coming and I hoped we could do the run on Christmas Eve, reasoning there would be less Border Patrol on duty, but Christmas Eve came and went. We weren't even able to do it on New Year's Eve. To celebrate the New Year, I bought a bottle of Beaujolais and spent the evening in front of the TV in my humble motel room with its lamina of St. Francis on the wall and the smell of Rosa Venus emanating from the bathroom. It wasn't just the end of the year either. It was the end of an era. The end of the sixties.

Miguel finally made it to the border, Les flew in, and the run was set. At two in the morning, Les and I set out in a van rented under his name and headed east on Interstate 10. Les nodded as I reviewed the details of the run one more time. No one was behind us and we turned off at the Fabens exit and killed our lights. I crawled to the back of the van and disconnected the brake lights. Anyone watching would have seen us abruptly vanish. Les could see just well enough to make out the road thanks to the light from a fingernail moon—a "smuggler's moon." The darkness tended to distort things and some of the landmarks I remembered looked smaller while others loomed larger. I put on hip waders.

We came to the levee road and Les parked the van in the cleft in the bushes as planned. I walked up over the levee road and down to the river and gave two short whistles. Two short whistles responded from the darkness on the Mexican side. I waded in and felt the water press up tight against the waders. The footing was solid and there were no rocks. On the other side Miguel and I traded abrazos. He had seven sacks lined up along the bank and I began hauling them across the river one by one, slung over my shoulder. On the other side I would double over, letting the sack fall off my shoulder into the hollow. But when I crossed the fifth one, I saw there were only three left in the hollow. Les must have removed one. This wasn't the plan.

I scanned the darkness and called softly, but there was no sign of him. I crossed the remaining two and now there were only five in the hollow. I got up on the levee road, looked around, and saw something white swinging in the darkness: Les's cast. He approached, saying, "You gonna help me with these sacks?"

"But you're supposed to bring the van up here so I can load it!"

"I ain't bringing the van up here in the open." He said it as though it were unthinkable, as though we hadn't already agreed on it and gone over it a half dozen times.

"I found a better place for the van. Back in them bushes." He pointed.

"But I'm not supposed to be carrying sacks on the American side. I've done my part."

Les grabbed a sack by the neck with his good arm and leaned forward to begin dragging it. "You gonna give me a hand with these sacks or not?"

I grabbed a sack and followed him to where he had parked the van. I didn't like being on the American side one bit. If a patrol came, I would have to lose myself in the bushes. But unless I could get back to the river and then Mexico, they could call in other agents with dogs and flush me out.

We got all the sacks loaded and I wished Les good luck and waded back through the river. Miguel was waiting on the other side, wondering what had taken me so long. He lit up a Raleigh *con filtro* and despite having quit smoking, I allowed myself one exception. I wanted to savor the Mission Accomplished feeling you get when a run works out and wanted to dream a little too about what this new method of crossing could lead to.

We stood there on the bank, smoking and staring out over the inky ribbon of water shining faintly in the moonlight. The night was dead quiet, the only sounds being the sounds we made ourselves. Halfway through our cigarettes we heard a faint, high-pitched whine coming from the American side and froze, cocking our ears. It stopped—only to start again a short while later. It stopped and started again. My heart sank and I turned to Miguel.

"I've got to go help him. Wait for me no matter how long it takes, OK?"

"Wait! I'll go with you!"

I stared at him, taking in his street clothes. "How will you get across?"

"On your back!"

"OK, let's go."

"Wait! Let me get the jack out of the car."

He got the jack and I carried him piggyback through the river. He was a good 180 pounds, too. We hurried up the dirt road and found Les dragging a sack over to some bushes where he already had half of them stashed. It was going to be a perfect reenactment of his brother's bust: the patrol would find a stuck vehicle and a pile of grass hidden nearby. In his unemotional way, Les seemed glad to see us. "Give me a hand with these last sacks!" The van, I noticed, was a good twenty feet off the road. Why Les would have driven off the road here, I couldn't imagine but wasn't going to waste time asking.

"Fuck the sacks! Which tire is spinning?"

He indicated the right rear and Miguel slapped his jack up to the bumper and began pumping while I grabbed branches and rocks to throw underneath the tire. I remembered a tarp in the van and threw that underneath, too. On the word "Go!" Les eased forward on the accelerator while Miguel and I threw our weight behind the van. The van moved forward about a foot or two before losing traction. Meanwhile, the stars were beginning to fade.

We kept jacking the right rear tire up and throwing rocks and branches underneath, each time gaining one or two feet. The road was another fifteen feet away and by now it was light enough that a patrol passing by would probably see us. Miguel and I traded back and forth on the jack, our arms aching, our hands smarting from grabbing vegetation with stickers. With enough time we were going to reach solid ground, but with each attempt, the van was sliding to the right toward a gully, following the natural contour of the slope. We got the van about ten feet from the road, but now it was right next to the gully and we didn't dare try anymore. We racked our brains what to do.

"There is only one way!" cried Miguel. "We must jack the back of the van up and then push it over to the left!"

I didn't like this idea. I was afraid the jack might break and the hydraulic jack that came with the van was useless. I couldn't think of anything else, though, and told him to go ahead. He slapped the jack up to the middle of the van's back bumper, began pumping, saw the van start to tilt to one side, and let the jack down to center it better before starting over again. By now it had dawned. I felt sick with dread. The back end of the van began to rise and I steadied it to keep it balanced. Miguel kept pumping. The jack began to curve precariously and he held his face away from it, grimacing as he kept on pumping till he got it all the way to the top. As he backed away, I pushed the side of the van and felt its bulk swing slowly away from me at which point the jack sprang out with a tortured metal cry that sounded as though it could be heard clear across Texas. I ran to grab it. It was OK! We jacked the right rear tire up several times more and made it to solid ground.

We grabbed the sacks Les had hidden and threw them into the van and Les took off. Miguel and I ran back to the river and I carried him through again piggyback. We left, following the levee road on the Mexican side, Miguel driving. I let my body go limp with relief.

"We never would have made it if you hadn't helped," I told Miguel. "Or if you hadn't thought to bring the jack." Praise always embarrassed him and he blushed.

"God watches over me," he laughed, quoting a common Mexican saying I knew he didn't believe.

I had $300 in emergency money on me and offered it to him. He didn't want to accept it and I pressed him.

"Well, actually, I could use the money for my wife and daughter."

And if he hadn't had a wife and daughter, I doubt he would have taken it—that's the kind of saint he was.

We rode for a while in silence and I stared out at the gray mist rising from the river on our right. The hip waders! I suddenly remembered them and began peeling them off. They were just evidence now. I tossed them out the window and watched them flap down the embankment like a pair of shot crows.

"Some wetback will find those and say God watches over him too," I told Miguel.

CHAPTER 60

ROGER AND I MADE PLANS FOR THE NEXT RUN. He wasn't the type to have heart-to-heart talks, but he did acknowledge his brother's mistake in not staying on plan and said it wouldn't happen again. This time we decided to bring back 800 pounds, a reasonable limit for wading through the river. After that we would get a truck.

While waiting for Jesus to get the grass up, I spent a lot of time at Roger's house. Roger was often in his darkroom and I passed the time talking with Dinah. People were always dropping by and there was the feel of things happening. A girl named Carrie began living there and I paid no attention to her until Dinah happened to mention she was part of our next run. Carrie was quite pregnant, spoke with a drawl, dressed slovenly, and generally looked and acted like a hick. "What's she doing in the run?" I asked Dinah and she shrugged.

"I think she's going to ride back with Les and pretend to be Les's wife. You better ask Roger."

I went upstairs and found Roger handling a pistol while talking to some guy with long hair. "I'll take a .38 any day," he was saying. "Ever seen the trajectory on a .45? . . . Sinks like a fuckin' stone." He made a diving motion with his free hand. "*Pffft!*"

The longhair left and Roger tossed the gun on his desk, sat down, and propped his feet up. "What's up?"

"What's this about Carrie being part of the next run?"

"Oh, she's going to ride back in the van with Les, you know, to make things look cool. They're gonna pretend to be married and all."

"Cool for what? You said yourself, once Les makes it to the interstate, he's home free."

"Well, there's them agricultural checks."

"But we never worried about them before."

"People get busted in 'em. I've heard of it."

"Let's find a way around them then. There's no sense in risking an extra person."

"But Carrie could use the money. She's pregnant, don't you know. It's a chance for her to make a thousand dollars. Anyway, I owe my partner a favor."

So that's what this was all about: returning a favor.

"Why not just give her the thousand dollars then?"

Roger put his feet down and sat up. "Why, Carrie's a proud person. She would never accept charity like that. She wants to earn the money. Besides, I'm the one who's paying her, so why don't you quit worrying about it?"

"Because I don't like having an unnecessary person along. As far as I'm concerned, she's just one extra witness and one extra person to get busted."

Roger stood up and approached me. He had a good four inches over me and let me know it. "It seems to me when we first got together, we made a deal. You were going to take care of the Mexican side and I was going to take care of the American side. Them's two separate things. You just see to it that the Mexicans do their part and let me handle the rest, OK?"

"Well, if you want to look at it that way, the American side didn't go too well last time. If I hadn't gotten involved, your brother would be sitting in a West Texas jail cell right now."

"Well, the Mexican side didn't go too well either. Look how long it took them guys to bring that shit up!"

I had a bad feeling about Carrie and quit spending time at Roger's place. I didn't want her to learn my last name or anything about me. I was also thinking this would be my last run with Roger. Now that I knew his method, I could replace both him and his brother.

Roger had a court appearance in El Paso and the four of us flew there together: Roger, Les, Carrie, and I. On leaving a Texas airport, you always had to pass a six-foot-plus Texas Ranger standing at parade rest while he observed the crowd. I supposed this was Texas's way of letting you know you were entering a law-and-order state. Roger split from us, thinking the Ranger might recognize him from his bust, but he didn't, and we regrouped outside and caught a cab. The driver dropped Roger off at the courthouse, where he was to make a routine appearance, and I watched him skip up the steps in his robin's egg blue dress shirt, tan slacks, hand-tooled cowboy boots, and a full-length sheepskin coat that billowed out behind him like a king's robe. It would be the last I ever saw of him. When he failed to show at our motel that night, I went out to a pay phone and called Dinah. She told me to wait while she went out to a pay phone to call me back.

"He's in jail!" she told me and went on to explain. Even though his appearance was just a formality, a motion to delay trial, the D.A. convinced the judge to revoke Roger's bail. The D.A. said Roger was living too high off the hog and produced photos of Roger's Bultacos and other possessions as well as the elegant home where he lived. Dinah sounded stressed.

"Can you believe he actually said that in court? Too high off the hog? Well, that's Texas for you!"

Roger's only chance now was to hire a lawyer with local influence and that was going to take money.

"It's more important than ever that this thing goes through, if you know what I mean. It can still happen, right?"

I said there was a problem in that Roger hadn't yet paid me for his share of the merchandise.

"How much is that?"

"Three grand."

"I've got that much. I can wire it to you."

"Don't wire it to me. Wire it to Les or Carrie."

"OK, I'll wire it to Carrie. I'll do it right now."

"By the way, was I in any of those photographs the D.A. had?"

"Roger didn't say. I'll ask him when I see him in person. I'm coming down as soon as they decide where they're going to keep him."

The money came and I crossed over into Juarez and paid Jesus, but then the run was delayed for three days when bandits tried to hijack the grass as Miguel was transporting it from Juarez to El Porvenir. The area just south of the border was extremely dangerous, not only because of the heat but because of bandits who lurked there in order to prey on smugglers. As a male driving alone in a car with the back end riding low and Sinaloa plates, Miguel made a perfect target. He said he was on the road when three men in a car pulled up alongside him and pointed a pistol at him. He got away by driving off the road and spent the night hiding in a garbage dump. The upshot of all this was that Les and Carrie and I spent three days together in the same motel room.

The evening before the run, I began to realize how badly I had compromised myself. I never should have flown with the others and never should have stayed at the motel with Les and Carrie. The safest thing would have been for me to fly down separately from them and spend my time in Juarez. The only justification for spending time on the American side was to make sure Les got up at two in the morning and made it to the score. I would have done better to buy him a reliable alarm clock.

I had a sense of foreboding and tried to think how to extricate myself from my mistakes. Discreetly, so as not to alarm Les and Carrie, I went about the motel room wiping fingerprints off of everything I might have touched. I then gathered my belongings, borrowed the van, and after driving in circles several times to make sure I wasn't being followed, I drove to the Greyhound station and stashed my belongings there in a locker. This way I wouldn't have to return to the motel room after the score.

Two o'clock came and Les and I got up and drove out to the score. Shortly before the Fabens exit, I noticed headlights about three miles behind us and told Les to pull over and kill our lights. We waited a good ten minutes, but no car ever passed. I figured the car must have exited. This time the run went exactly as planned with Les following instructions to the letter. I rode back to Juarez with Jesus and Miguel, crossed into El Paso without getting hassled, caught a cab to the bus station, picked up my belongings, caught a cab to the airport, and arrived in the Bay Area in the late afternoon. I drove straight to Roger's house and Dinah opened the door. "Les and Carrie are busted," she said before I could even open my mouth.

"How do you know?"

"Les just called me. He couldn't go into the details obviously, but it sounds like you guys got hot somehow."

I was devastated. I had gotten away with so much and now everything I touched, it seemed, turned bad.

Dinah flew to El Paso and made a tour of the West Texas jail system, visiting Roger, Les, Carrie, and Roger's former partner. She spoke with Roger's lawyer and phoned me to let me know what she had learned. Apparently agents had been watching Les and Carrie and me at our motel for the entire three days we were there. The night of the run they followed us out the interstate, then lost us when we took the Fabens exit and killed our lights. They waited there by the exit and picked up the van again when Les came back to the interstate. They saw that the passenger seat was now empty and thought I was probably in the back of the van taking a snooze. They followed it back to the motel, watched Les pick up Carrie, followed them as they headed west, then busted them just short of the state line. The agents were quite surprised not to find me when they opened the back of the van. One of them turned to Les and said, "Where's your friend from Berkeley?" Les took a second look at him and recognized one of the "hunters" who had helped us get our van out of the sand.

My mind reeled hearing this. If I hadn't thought to stash my belongings at the Greyhound station, I would be in jail right now. I wondered whether they tried to follow me to the Greyhound station. The elaborate circles I made might have forced them to back off for fear of tipping their hand.

I wasn't in jail, but I was about as close as you could get. Agents had witnessed me at the motel room and riding out to the river, and the "hunters" had seen me face-to-face in that same area. All they needed was my name. Dinah was in a similar position. When she wired the $3,000 to Carrie, she made the mistake of sending it under her own name. That evidence coupled with Les's or Carrie's testimony could get her convicted. Everything now depended on Les and Carrie.

A couple of weeks passed and Carrie got probation. The D.A. went easy on her, not wanting her unborn child to become a ward of the state. Her lawyer's fees were $3,000 and she wanted to be reimbursed. All this was communicated to me through Dinah.

"I already sent my fifteen hundred. If you want, I can send your share for you."

I told her I didn't want to pay. "I didn't even want her in the run in the first place. Why should I get stuck paying for her now?"

"Well, of course, I see your point. But as a practical matter, don't you think it might be kind of wise to pay her if you know what I mean?"

Looking back, I know Dinah was right, but at the time I was outraged at the thought of paying for someone whose involvement I had argued so vehemently against. I met with Dinah again and she said she had spoken to Carrie by phone. "She got really upset when I told her you didn't want to pay. She feels it's the least you can do, considering you're the only one who got away. Also, she says her lawyer saw some of the agents' notes and there's things in them like, 'Suspect drove to Raley's, bought a Newsweek and a six-pack of Millers, returned to motel.' She says they even watched you in Juarez, talking to the Mexicans."

I wondered if Carrie could have made this up, but after thinking about it, I concluded she wasn't bright enough.

I paid a visit to one of Murray's lawyers. "I've never handled a blackmail case before," he told me frankly. "All I know is what I've seen on TV. I mean, you never pay them, do you? They'll just keep coming back for more.

"Why don't you try stalling her for a while? I've got a friend who's a federal prosecutor in the Sixth Judicial District—that's the district that includes El Paso. I'll try getting in touch with him. I won't mention your name, of course. I'll just say, Oh, . . . I've got a client who is worried about getting falsely implicated in the case. . . . One of the defendants holds a grudge against him. . . . Can he find out if the D.A. is planning to hand down any more indictments?"

Two days later Dinah handed me a letter with an I-told-you-so look. It was from Carrie. After skipping through some newsy stuff, I read, "And tell the doggie that if he doesn't start behaving soon, I'm going to have to send him to the pound."

That did it for me. There was no way I was going to pay her.

Following the lawyer's advice, I got word to Carrie that I intended to pay her but didn't have the money right now. I implied that I was working on a deal and would pay her as soon as it pulled through. Carrie responded by demanding a way of keeping in touch with me. I asked Bill Gretsch if he would serve as an intermediary and he agreed to do me the favor.

And what a perfect intermediary he turned out to be! Carrie would call every month or so and he kept her strung along with stories of deals just about to pull through, minor delays, unexpected setbacks, and so forth. When Carrie confided how pissed she was, Bill actually commiserated with her, claiming I owed him money too. Once when she threatened to go to the D.A., he told her, "We'll never get our money back if you do that. He's down and out right now, but he'll get back on his feet, you'll see. Then we'll get our money out of him."

I never did hear from Les. I learned later that the D.A. came to him several times and offered him a reduced sentence in return for naming me. He refused. I had saved his butt when he got the van stuck at the river and now he was saving mine and paying a price to do so. I wonder how often you see this degree of integrity in the straight, non-criminal world. He was given eight years as were Roger and Roger's partner.

December rolled around and Carrie gave me an ultimatum through Bill Gretsch. She needed money for Christmas presents and if I didn't pay her $200, she was going to the D.A. It was the dark underbelly of Christmas! I paid her the $200 through Bill and it was the last I ever heard from her.

In hindsight I realize that Murray's lawyer was wrong to characterize my situation with Carrie as blackmail. I believe she was an honest person and only wanted the $1,500. Even though I was technically correct in not paying her based on the strict separation of Mexican and stateside responsibilities Roger and I had agreed to, Roger was in no position to help her and I wish I had handled things differently.

CHAPTER 61

BRUCE CALLED ME FROM CANADA TO TELL ME the hash run had finally pulled through—sort of—and I flew to Toronto to meet him. He was still wanted in the Mitchum case and didn't want to risk entering the States. I stood waiting on the balcony of the twentieth floor of the Tower Building when I heard, "Hullo, chap!" and turned to greet him. He flashed a gummy grin, then glanced around, lowering his voice.

"I swear, the maids in this hotel are randy as bloody hell. At first I thought they were simply being pleasant as part of their job. I was just in my room, though, and one of them pulled her blouse down to show me her teat. Can you beat that? She just stood there smiling. I swear, they're all running some sort of business on the side. I've got a good mind to take one of them up on it. They're all Bahamians. A couple are damned cute, too."

We took seats in his room and he brought me up to date on the run. In Athens, one of the Beech engines had to be rebuilt, which set things back two months. Once that was taken care of, he had no trouble getting past the mountains between Turkey and Iran. He brought oxygen with him and said the weather was perfectly clear. "Those Turks who told us there were always clouds over those mountains were full of shit." He arrived in Kabul, then had trouble finding a reliable contact. After spending a couple of weeks getting nowhere, he had a friend from the States fly over to help. The friend supposedly knew a lot about hash but attracted attention wherever he went because of his long hair and beard. I couldn't believe Bruce was telling me this.

"Why didn't you ask *me* to come over? I wouldn't have brought heat down. I would have gotten a crew cut if I had to. I'm the one who got financing for this run. You couldn't be doing it without me."

I felt pretty hurt and angry.

"I know. I should have, chap, and I'm really sorry about that. I mean to say, all Trevor did was hang out in coffeehouses and get high. Anyway, I sent him back. Look, if I need any help on the next run, rest assured, I'll call you over. I promise."

Bruce said he eventually found a contact on his own. Now the problem was getting the hash aboard the plane. The Afghan airport officials had become suspicious of him and were searching everything he carried out to the plane. As a last resort, he taped bricks of hash to his body and made multiple trips to the plane, pretending to be making repairs. To support this pretext, he carried tools with him and made sure there was grease under his fingernails. He got twenty-six pounds on board this way before the Afghans began following him out to the plane to see what he was doing. He decided it was time to leave Kabul.

He flew back through Iran, Turkey, and across Europe, making it through customs each time with only a brief search or no search at all. Because it was spring, he was able to take the northern route across the Atlantic—through Ireland, Iceland, Greenland, and Baffin Island. When he entered Canada at Frobisher Bay, the customs official didn't even go out to the plane.

We brought the twenty-six pounds into the States using the old Mustang method. Jenner had taken a couple of busts and was too hot to get involved with the hash, but he introduced me to a close friend named Camdyn. Camdyn was able to borrow a fastback Mustang and had his wife bring the hash in via the Rainbow Bridge. I sold some in Boston, Camdyn sold the rest, and after paying off Bruce's Shell Carnet card and other expenses, there was just enough money for Bruce to go back to Afghanistan and try again. He hoped the Kabul airport officials would have forgotten him by now, so that he could bring back a full load.

I flew back to the Bay Area to my basement apartment in the Montclair house. I contacted Jake, told him what was happening with the run he had financed, and he took the news reasonably well. Time passed and I began selling off possessions to get by. I sold my Mustang, an Austin Healey I had bought, and my Hornet. The Aston Martin was already gone, the legal owner having managed to steal it back from me. The Hornet took the longest to sell. I had to advertise for weeks before finally selling it to some poor kid who stood about five foot four and had never even ridden a motorcycle before. I felt like a murderer selling him that bike, but I needed the money. With a little luck the bike would break down before he killed himself on it. It was a BSA, so there was a good chance.

A couple of months passed and Bruce's wife called to tell me she had just met Bruce in Mexico City and that he was flying to Mexicali in order to meet with me. Despite being a fugitive, he was still able to fly all over the world for free using his wife's Pan Am privileges. "He's really aged, Tom," she told me. "He looks haggard. Being on the run is really wearing on him."

I flew to Mexicali and met Bruce in a seedy hotel two blocks from the border that he was afraid to cross. I didn't think he looked that bad and his spirits seemed OK. It was around eleven in the morning and his small, dark hotel room felt like an oven. "God, it's bloody hot and repressive in this town," he said. "What say we rent a car and drive to the coast? It'll be a fun drive!"

We rented a VW bug and it felt just like the old days when we used to hang out together and do things on impulse. We took Highway 2 toward Tijuana, the same highway the Bub and I had traveled so often in the days of the car runs. We came to the bridge where Catholic girls run up holding out cans and gave them money. Then a short while later, we were pulled over at an impromptu checkpoint manned by Mexican agents. They were extremely suspicious of us and waved on other drivers so they could devote themselves to searching every square inch of our car. Bruce and I stood just off the road and I could hear Bruce sigh and knew he was worried they had somehow identified him as a fugitive. After a while, I asked one of the agents, "Why are you so suspicious?" He wheeled on me.

"Why are *you* so suspicious?"

After a long half hour they let us go. Things were so much hotter these days. I thought about the days when the Bub and I used to drive through here with grass stuffed in the back seat and shuddered.

Bruce told me what was happening with the hash run. When he got to Kabul, he said, the airport officials were even more suspicious of him than before and he realized he wasn't going to be able to load anything onto the Beech. His contact said he had access to expert welders who could hide the hash in a false compartment welded into the gas tank of a car. Apparently a lot of smugglers were transporting their hash this way. Seeing no alternative, Bruce flew to Germany, bought a used Mercedes limousine, drove it back to Kabul, and had the contact weld a hundred pounds of hash into the limousine's large gas tank. When it came time to head west, though, Bruce balked when he learned the penalty for smuggling hash through Iran was death.

There was no way around Iran either, at least by car. Instead, he drove to Karachi and had the Mercedes loaded onto a freighter bound for Genoa, Italy. From Genoa he intended to drive it to Germany, then ship it to Montreal. A classic older Mercedes being shipped from Germany to Canada shouldn't attract much attention at customs, he reasoned.

We came to Ensenada and found a restaurant on a hill overlooking the ocean. Next to it, a bank of oleanders was sending out shock waves of pink. We ordered tacos and they were the most delicious tacos we had ever eaten. We were the only patrons in the place and the señora who owned it came over to see how we were doing. Using me for an interpreter, Bruce told her how wonderful her food was but that she needed to advertise. She lingered awhile and chatted with us. Outside, the sun beat down and from somewhere in the distance we could hear the sound of children playing. For a moment everything seemed as wonderful as it used to be in the old days.

The señora returned to her kitchen and Bruce said, "If you want, chap, you can fly over and help me drive the Mercedes to Germany. It's going to take a long time to get to Genoa, though. The freighter will have to go all the way around the Cape. I mean to say, if the Suez Canal were open, it would be a breeze, but with the war going on, it's liable to take months. This run will pull through sooner or later, but if I were you, I would try to get something else going in the meantime."

I knew I wouldn't be able to get anything else going and waited the three months.

CHAPTER 62

GENOA WAS AN OLD PORT CITY WITH narrow streets and tall, ornate apartment buildings that crowded right up to the water as though they were thinking of stepping in. I was sitting on the stone border of a moss-stained fountain when a long lacquered-gold Mercedes pulled up and the tinted window zoomed smoothly down. "Hullo, chap!"

As I slid onto the red leather seats, Bruce pressed a button and a glass partition behind us rolled down to reveal jump seats and a fold-out bar. "Not bad for three grand, eh?" He said it used to belong to the Tunisian ambassador to Germany. "I wouldn't be surprised if it was even bulletproof!"

We proceeded north toward Germany, and while Bruce's driving had never been great, behind the wheel of the Mercedes he seemed to have gone mad. Italian sports cars shot past us doing 120 mph and he would try to race them. I knew if I said anything, it would only make things worse and tried to keep quiet. During a preposterous race with a Maserati, the Mercedes engine began missing and Bruce pulled over and popped the hood. "It's just a clogged fuel filter," he explained as he undid the filter and shook sediment out of a fine brass strainer. "The same thing happened to me in Pakistan."

That night we got a room at a small inn near Como. The landlady there looked us over. "One bed or two?"

Bruce laughed. "Two. We're good friends, but not that good!"

In the morning we zoomed through the pristine Swiss Alps, stopping briefly to see the village where my Italian Swiss grandparents grew up. Once more the fuel filter clogged up. When it happened yet again, I asked to see the sediment. Caught in the fine mesh of the strainer was a light brown paste. I tried smelling it, but it smelled only of gasoline. "What if this is hash?"

Bruce waved his arm curtly. "It can't be. The hash is welded into an airtight compartment, for Christ's sake."

"What if there's a leak? Did you actually see them weld it?"

"No, but I've got complete faith in this guy. He's been doing this sort of thing for years."

We drove on, but the fuel filter was now clogging up every hundred miles or so. Bruce eventually had to admit there was a chance gasoline was getting into the compartment where the hash was. It wouldn't take much gasoline to ruin the entire load.

That night we were detained by Swiss authorities when we tried to cross into Germany. No explanation for the detention was given and we were directed to sit in a bare, fluorescent-lit room while a Swiss guard holding a rifle upright by the butt stood at the doorway. We sat in metal folding chairs and waited. By the wan lighting, Bruce looked old and careworn and he was only twenty-nine. He turned to me with a look that said, Well, this may be it, chap. It seemed crazy that his indictment would show up at an outbound Swiss border check, but then Bruce had often commented that the Swiss police were some of the most efficient in the world. I wondered if there might be an indictment out for me, too, and felt nervous and trapped. After an hour the Swiss authorities abruptly let us go. It was like that time out of Mexicali several months back. The police seemed to be tuning in to our guiltiness.

At the German border, a guard and I exchanged a few words in German and he waved us on. Bruce stared at me. "I didn't know you spoke German, chap!" I told him I didn't know I did either, not having thought about it since the two semesters I took of it back when I was studying math.

After that Bruce seemed to fall into a deep funk. The constant fear of living as a fugitive was getting to him. His driving was downright vicious and I tried to take the wheel as often as possible without offending him. Meanwhile, we had to decide what to do about the fuel filter getting clogged. The only way we could find out whether the hash was getting ruined was by tearing into the gas tank, and then if the hash was good, we would have ruined our method for smuggling it. On the other hand, if we continued with our original plan and the hash was ruined, we would be risking money and a bust for nothing.

We went back and forth, trying to decide what to do. If we tore the tank apart and the hash was still good, Bruce said he might be able to rent a Piper Cherokee in London and fly the hash into Canada via the northern route. It was hardly a sure thing, but he knew some people who had rented him a plane in the past. If we did tear the tank apart, we would need another one to replace it, and the logical place to get one would be the Mercedes factory out of Stuttgart. We resolved to make our decision when we got to Stuttgart.

We made Stuttgart the next morning. Bruce was at the wheel and all his pent-up fears and frustrations seemed to come out in his driving. I hadn't said a word, but when he nearly ran down a poor old German woman trying to cross the street, I couldn't help myself. "God, Bruce, you're driving like a fucking maniac!" He turned to me with a hurt look.

"I am not, chap!"

And in that very instant he ran a stop sign and slammed into the side of a passing Volkswagen bug.

We watched in horror as the young driver struggled to keep the bug from rolling. The impact had knocked him clear across two lanes and he ran up over a curb onto the grassy center divider and managed to stop short of two small trees. He jumped out and seemed so happy to be alive that he rushed up and shook hands with us.

A German policeman arrived and the whole matter was taken care of courteously and efficiently. Bruce had international insurance that covered damages to the VW but not the Mercedes. The Mercedes still ran, but the grille and the left front fender were smashed in. Importing a wrecked car like that would attract attention, yet fixing it would cost thousands. Effectively our decision was made for us: we might as well tear the gas tank apart and find out whether the hash was any good.

At a hardware store we bought tools and at the Mercedes factory we spent nearly our last marks on a new gas tank. It was afternoon and we drove out past Hansel and Gretel villages to a secluded area of the Black Forest. Screened by some trees, we dropped the gas tank, dragged it behind some bushes, and chiseled it open. The hash was good. The individual bricks were wrapped in cellophane, and in order to protect them from the heat of welding, the Afghans had insulated them with a layer of light brown paste that appeared to be clay. We supposed some of this paste must have gotten into the main part of the tank and was the cause of the fuel filter getting clogged.

If it weren't for the accident and if we had made the correct decision to proceed with our original plan, we probably would have been rich in a few weeks, but there was no going back. We installed the new tank, placed the hash in the trunk, and drove back to Stuttgart, where we took a room at a small guesthouse, wondering how we were going to pay the bill. By now we were broke. We had already hit Jake up for an additional $2,000 for our failed trip to Morocco, and I didn't feel right asking him for more. I made several overseas calls to friends, but no one wanted to front money in the run. It seemed we had no choice but to sell some of the hash.

We broke one of the bricks into chunks and stuffed them in our pockets. We couldn't even afford cab fare and walked the several miles to the Konigstrasse, where the street was closed off for Oktoberfest. Night had fallen and the streets were filled with strolling crowds. We stopped at a booth and spent our last change on a beer for me, lemonade for Bruce, and a large roll of bread. It was like that time we roamed Mazatlan looking for contacts only this time we had something to sell. We stopped to check out likely customers but couldn't get up the nerve to approach anyone. When we spotted a Volkswagen van with a peace symbol painted on the front, I thought we had it made, but before we could get to it, the driver drove off. How had I gotten into this strange situation? I wondered to myself. Trying to sell hash to strangers in a foreign town? My own life was beginning to feel unfamiliar to me.

It was fun being with Bruce, though, in the warm German autumn night with smells of sausage and beery laughter. We ended up at a German imitation of the Fillmore West, a huge warehouse with light shows splashing across all four walls, deafening music, and no one dancing. An obvious dealing scene was going on toward the front near an espresso machine, but the two guys running it were swarthy Mediterranean types who spoke God-knew-what language and we chickened out of going up to them. We walked back to the Konigstrasse, where the crowds were starting to thin out. By fishing in our pockets, we came up with just enough change for me to buy one more beer in a plastic cup. We headed back to our guesthouse and on an impulse I pulled a piece of hash out of my pocket and crumbled it into my beer. I was beginning not to care anymore.

I slept like a rock that night but woke up wired from a hash overdose. Straight away I knocked off seventy pushups—more than I had ever done before. I needed company and rousted Bruce. We went downstairs to the dining room to have breakfast, thinking the food might help calm me down, but the dining room was filled with dignified German types reading newspapers over wire-rimmed spectacles, and I immediately became paranoid. We took a table, our coffee came, and I took a sip, but when I went to put the cup back down on its saucer, my hand shook so badly that there was a loud clatter and coffee spilled all over the tabletop. Immediately every eye in the place was on me—Freudian types with goatees, peering over their spectacles. The landlord was passing by and wheeled to see what the clatter was about. For a second I thought I was going to finally lose it right then and there and all would be done, but I managed to pull some German out of the deep recesses of my mind and said, *"Gestern abend, viel bier trinken."* There seemed to be a collective sigh of understanding and the landlord smiled sympathetically as he wagged his finger toward my coffee. *"Ja. Bier und Kaffee, nicht gut."* He moved on and I tried to explain to Bruce how close I had felt to freaking out, but Bruce only shook his head.

"You just have a bloody guilty conscience is all. Sometimes I wonder how the hell you ever got into this business."

After our complimentary breakfast we had to decide what we were going to do for money. I had noticed there were a lot of GIs in town and said we should try to sell hash to a GI. A few years earlier this would have been unthinkable, but the Vietnam War had changed all that and now a GI was as likely to want drugs as anyone—maybe more so. We decided to walk to the train station to see if there were any GIs there.

Sure enough, there were a number of them milling about as they waited for trains, and we walked up to a mezzanine where we could get a better look. Most of the GIs were traveling in pairs and I thought it would be easier to approach a GI who was alone. I spotted one who was by himself and had a small mustache, which I took as a subtle clue he might be hip. I decided to approach him and told Bruce to wait where he was. With his straight mannerisms and stilted accent, I was afraid Bruce might put the guy off.

The GI wanted to know how I happened to pick him out of all the GIs there and I told him. He shook his head in wonder. "That's amazing because I'm probably the biggest hash dealer on the base." He wasn't even interested in our hash. "You couldn't get it to me cheap enough. I've got Turks bringing it in for $200 a pound."

He thought for a moment. "You just want to sell a few ounces for expense money, right? . . . I'll tell you what to do. You're lucky because tonight's Saturday. Go to the House of Three Colors—that's the whorehouse where all the GIs go. Any cab driver can tell you how to get there. Go through to the back and there's this wall where the guys hang out and take leaks after they've been with the girls. It's like a big outdoor urinal. Just go up to them and tell them what you've got, like you did with me. You shouldn't have any trouble. Good luck!"

We went to the House of Three Colors and it was everything you would expect of a German whorehouse. The building itself appeared to be a former factory and on the inside the three floors had been partitioned into rooms on either side of a long hallway, like a hotel. And that was it—no band, no dance floor, no bar, no colored lights—nothing to make you feel that the experience was anything more than the paid encounter it was. Sex on an assembly line.

We wandered in and saw that each girl had her own room. Between tricks they would leave their door open so prospective customers could check out their wares. We joined the crowds of GIs roaming from open doorway to open doorway. Most of the girls wore tube tops and miniskirts or else negligées. A few wore only a bra and panties, but that was considered "trying too hard" we learned. While guys stared, the girls walked back and forth, offering different profiles of themselves, like runway models. I was impressed by the different motifs they had thought up for decorating their rooms. One room was done up in pink with roses and lace hearts while another was psychedelic with paisley patterns and a small black light. We passed a girl who wore wire-rimmed glasses and seemed to be playing up the schoolgirl look with a shelf full of books and a desk. Another girl had a framed photograph of President Kennedy overlooking her bed and grinning.

We hooked up with two GIs who said they were from Colorado. "I've developed a real relationship with her," one of them was telling me in reference to a girl he saw on a regular basis. "I'm not just another trick to her. We lie in bed and talk and stuff. She takes all her clothes off for me."

"They don't usually take all their clothes off?"

He stared at me as though I were weird. "Hell no. They just lift up their skirts. You want to feel their breasts and stuff, you got to pay extra."

We toured all three floors. At each stairway landing, a large, muscle-bound German woman stood guard and collected money for transactions. The three women were all that was required to maintain order apparently and we saw no men working in the place. At one point a GI began complaining loudly about a blowjob he had paid for and never got, and in seconds the three women were on him and hustled him out.

The GI from Colorado kept talking about his girl. "As soon as she makes enough money, she's going to quit working here and we're going to get an apartment together in town." I asked him if he had ever seen her outside the House of Three Colors and he said he hadn't. "We've talked about it, but she's afraid she'll get caught. She wants to wait till she's ready to quit." I wondered to myself if that was ever going to happen.

We stopped before a group of GIs crowded around an open doorway. We had to wait a couple of minutes before there was room to wade in. Inside the room was one of the most breathtakingly beautiful girls we had ever seen. She was about five-ten, blonde, with cute freckles across her cheeks and long, perfectly shaped legs. She wore a pink mini-skirt and matching halter and looked as though she had grown up around apples and cheese and snowy mountaintops. Guys had their heads literally pressed together inside the doorway, trying to get a better look as they gave soft whistles and made comments. The girl just smiled, turning slowly with the grace of a colt. A little guy who looked like Mickey Rooney burrowed his way to the front, his head barely on a level with her breasts. "How much for a blowjob?" he demanded, staring. The girl smiled demurely and named a price. The little guy said nothing and continued to stare as though the fact he could have her was satisfaction enough.

We found the urinal out back, which was just a concrete wall with a trough at the base and water trickling past. Above the wall glowed the starless city sky. GIs knotted in groups, discussing the girls.

"Anyone make it with the chick in three thirty-six?"

"Naw, she wants too much. She's stuck up."

"Two forty-eight's got this cream that makes your orgasm last longer."

The two GIs from Colorado took us around and in short order we sold all the hash we had brought with us. Our pockets were now stuffed with bills and as we stepped away from the GIs, Bruce broke into a leer. "Well, what do you say, chap? Think we should follow our business up with a little pleasure?" We were both thinking of the beautiful blonde with the long legs. I didn't think we should spend our money on something so frivolous and instead we decided to treat ourselves to our first real meal all day. "You're right," Bruce told me as we hailed a cab. "I mean to say, why pay for it when it's so easy to get for free?"

CHAPTER 63

BRUCE FLEW TO LONDON TO SEE ABOUT renting a plane and I flew to the States to wait for him in Buffalo, where the hash would ultimately come through. Camdyn was caretaking an old twenty-seven-room mansion on West Ferry Street at the time and said he could put me up. The owner of the mansion was an older woman artist who had recently entered a nursing home. Camdyn knew her because he was an artist himself, having recently been described in a newspaper article as "Buffalo's most promising young artist." He was the only person the owner trusted to care for her place.

Camdyn picked me up at the airport. "Wait till you see this place. It's got gables within gables. It's like something out of a Halloween poster." We came to a six-foot-high stone fence surrounding the grounds and turned in down a long driveway. The front lawn was big enough for playing soccer and the back lawn was just as big, extending all the way back to the next street. The house itself was three stories high, shingled in dark wood, with a broad front porch and wrap-around balconies. Camdyn said it was built in the mid-1800s.

We went in and Camdyn played the magnanimous host as he showed me different rooms. "You're welcome to the third floor," he laughed in his wry drawl. "We never use it." He showed me a bed he had set up for me. "I put it here because I thought you might like the southern exposure, but you're welcome to move it wherever you like." Later he took me down to the cobwebbed basement and showed me where he thought we should hide the hash when it came in. "I mean, this is just one idea. There's no end of nooks and crannies where you could stash the stuff. Can you imagine the narcs trying to search this place? Ha! They'd take one look and throw their hands up!"

The entire first floor, I noticed, was furnished with a style of furniture that came from Mexico. The furniture was made of torched pine and had a heavy, baroque feel to it—the kind of furniture that goes with felt paintings of bull-fighters and varnished plaques with crossed swords. The last time I had seen Camdyn, he was starting a Mexican furniture store and I asked him how it was going. "Oh, that," he said with an abashed laugh. "Well, you knew that store used to be a pharmacy, right?"

He went on to say he used to get mail addressed to the former pharmacy and normally threw it away, but one day he happened to notice an order form from a pharmaceutical company. He looked it over and saw checkboxes for things like Seconal, Valium, and Dilaudid. A friend had a PDR and together they went through the form and ordered massive quantities of pain pills and downers, adding things like laxatives and talcum powder to make it appear legitimate. Camdyn mailed the form and for the next week he and his wife, Dawn, waited nervously, imagining agents bursting in any moment. The delivery came and when an hour passed with nothing happening, Camdyn whisked the drugs out to a safe place, came back with a rented truck, and removed all their furniture from the shop, which they had rented under a fictitious name.

"This is our inventory," Camdyn laughed, waving his hand to take in the blood-red velvet sofas and ponderous armoires. "I made more money selling those pills than I would have made in a year selling furniture. I never even had to pay for them either. It was all charged to the old pharmacy." He shook his head in wonder. "I mean, you'd think the government would have some kind of check on drugs being delivered like that, wouldn't you? . . . Anyway, let me know if you need a laxative. I've got enough laxatives here to start a nursing home."

Things quickly settled into a routine around the mansion. Dawn was suspicious of me at first but seemed amazed and delighted when I offered to help with the cooking. "Camdyn never lifts a finger around here. If I didn't feed him, I think he'd just wither away and starve." Dawn had dyed blonde hair, tattoos, and looked like a tough biker's girl but was really warm inside. We had long talks in the kitchen, which seemed scarcely changed since the house was built. There was an ancient eight-burner range, an old ice chest made of mahogany with nickel hinges, and a dumbwaiter that led to the floors above. Dawn confided that she wasn't sure she could stay with Camdyn. "He's got great talent, but he never paints anything. All he does is sit around. Meanwhile, I don't know how we're going to buy food." One day I walked in as she was sighing. I asked her what was wrong and she shrugged. "I don't know. I guess I just feel like I'm missing out on life."

She was right about Camdyn. He was in a slump and couldn't bring himself to paint. It seemed an effort for him just to enter his studio, which was on the second floor. Occasionally, he would make a few tentative sketches before heading downstairs to sit and brood in front of the television set. Most days he simply poured himself coffee and went straight to the TV without trying to work. He didn't really have any interest in TV and simply used it to provide a bland background to his brooding. Half the time he didn't even know what he was watching.

I soon got to see an example of Camdyn's talent. A friend dropped by and asked him if he could paint a mural for an Italian restaurant he was about to open. Several hours later Camdyn came down from his studio to show me a sketch he had made. It was done in charcoal and showed an Italian pushcart vendor selling clumps of grapes in front of an arbor with winding tendrils. It was beautiful. Camdyn never did anything more with it, though, and his friend had to hire someone else.

Several weeks passed and Bruce contacted me to let me know he was having trouble finding someone to rent him a plane. Meanwhile, the hash was stashed in the trunk of the Mercedes parked at the Stuttgart airport. I passed the time playing guitar and going for long walks around town. Buffalo was the most racially divided city I had ever seen. It was like a pie split in three: one-third Polish, one-third Italian, and one-third Black. In the center was a small pocket of Iroquois. The bars seemed filled with frustrated young factory workers who had built up their muscles and were looking for a fight.

I kept pretty much to myself as I wandered along strange streets past people I would never know, people no one I knew would ever know, and so on in endless nauseas of isolation. The Buffalo skies were a dull gray, the humidity oppressive. Overly lush foliage leapt out from behind chain-link fences and if I brushed against it, great clouds of insects rose up. The muted greens and grays of the neighborhoods made the bright red and yellow plastic toys lying in people's yards look somehow false.

After coming home from these walks, Camdyn was often waiting for me, eager to talk. He especially loved trading dope stories. One of his favorites involved a friend named Stanley who drove all the way to The City to score a kilo and ended up fronting ninety dollars to a Puerto Rican he met in Central Park. The Puerto Rican said he would be back in fifteen minutes and Stanley waited two hours. The punch line to the story was that the guy finally showed with the kilo. This was a source of profound fascination to Camdyn. He was like a scientist who had seen gravity defied. "You're always figuring out the odds. Say you give a strange Puerto Rican in Central Park ninety bucks to score a kilo. What are the odds you'll ever see him again? . . . Stanley's the only guy who could have pulled it off, too. Only Stanley would have waited two hours. You'll see what I mean when you meet him. He's a little on the dense side. Well, he's Polish. You've been around Poles, right? . . . The grass wasn't bad, either. I smoked some of it."

One afternoon while we were hanging out, I happened to notice a photograph lying on Camdyn's coffee table. It showed a young man with muscles built up to Charles Atlas-like proportions. I asked Camdyn who it was and he chuckled. "You don't recognize that? . . . That's me." I stared at him. He was average in size, had a vaguely dark complexion, and always wore baggy sweatshirts, so that I never noticed what sort of build he had.

"Of course, that was back when I was with the Road Vultures and working out every day. I don't look like that now."

He began talking about his past. He said he was the only child of an Iroquois prostitute. He could remember the sounds of his mother entertaining men in the next rooms of the tenements he grew up in. When he was eighteen he left home to join the Road Vultures, which was the western New York equivalent of the Hells Angels. He built his muscles up to bone-crushing strength and was elected sergeant-at-arms despite the fact he was only five foot nine. His job was to take care of any disputes that developed between the club and other groups. He said he and a buddy once held off fifteen Air Force jocks with only their fists and a couple lengths of chain.

Code was very important to the Road Vultures, Camdyn told me. If a group of Vultures got busted, the newest member to join was expected to take the rap. It was a way of minimizing time. If the cops stopped a bunch of guys in a car and found drugs, the newest guy had to step forward and say, "That's my dope and I'll swear in a court of law no one else here knew about it." Some guys were in the club for only a few weeks and got five years.

I felt even closer to Camdyn after he told me his story and we sought each other out in odd rooms of the mansion and talked about life. He showed me stretch marks on his biceps and said one of his balls was shriveled to the size of a peanut from getting kicked during a fight. Tattooed across his knuckles, one letter per finger, were the words "HARD LUCK." I asked him if it felt good being all muscled out the way he was and he laughed. "Almost too good. I was full of nervous energy all the time. If I wasn't doing something, I would go nuts. And the guilt, Christ, if I missed just one day of training, I would feel terrible for the rest of the week!"

I asked Camdyn to show me some tips on fighting and he considered. "Well, it's mainly experience, you know. The main thing is to lead with your left. You'd be surprised how many guys who think they can fight will haul straight off with a right. In the Road Vultures, with the little guys or the guys who hadn't fought much, we used to tell them to use their teeth. This was like in big gang fights. We used to tell them to bite a guy's nose or his ear and not let go." He chuckled. "You'd be surprised how hard it is to fight with some guy hanging on to your ear."

He put his coffee down to show me a few judo holds and various ways to break a guy's arm. "Now just because I've shown you these things, don't go rushing out to pick a fight or anything. I'm just showing them to you in case you have to defend yourself someday."

We talked about everything, but the subject often came back to dope. Once Camdyn fell to reminiscing about a time he scored a brick off two kids through Jenner. "This was in the absolute dead of winter and these two kids with long hair had driven all the way from the west coast with a load of bricks hidden in their car. Every time they needed more bricks, they would go get them out of their car. Swear to God, it was the loosest thing you ever saw."

I jumped out of my chair. "That was me! Me and my partner, the Bub!" I suddenly remembered selling a brick to a guy who came to the door wearing a baggy sweatshirt and carrying a cup of coffee.

"That was you? You're shitting me."

The awful circle was groaning to a close.

*

I spent three months waiting at Camdyn's place for the hash to pull through and by the end Dawn was sick of us both. In all that time Camdyn didn't produce a single painting. He told me a story one day by way of explaining why he couldn't paint. There was a Japanese master, he said, who was hired to produce a painting of a duck within a week. For six days all the master did was meditate and wander about his garden. The people who commissioned him grew nervous, but on the seventh day the master approached his easel and with a few deft strokes executed a perfect painting of a duck. Asked to explain, the master stated, "For the first six days I didn't feel like a duck. On the seventh day I *was* a duck."

Dawn stopped dusting to throw up her arms. "Oh, great! Now all we have to do is wait around for Camdyn to turn into a duck!"

Camdyn paid her no mind.

Dawn would yell at Camdyn to paint. "How are we going to eat?" she would ask him. I didn't like being a witness to their arguing and spent most of my time out of the house. There was a stump in back cut off at the perfect level to sit on, and I spent long hours there playing a '64 Martin 000-18 I had acquired for $100 and a chunk of hash. When I wanted to learn new pieces, I took my guitar to a park. Invariably someone would come up and listen for a few minutes before asking if they could play my guitar at which point they would knock out a dazzling series of riffs. Everyone was a great guitar player, it seemed. In return for playing my guitar, they would feel obliged to show me a few riffs and in this way I learned an amazing variety of styles.

Sometimes to pass time I would play solitary Frisbee on the lawn out front. By throwing the Frisbee up at just the right angle, I could get it to come back to me. After playing this for a while one afternoon, I simply lay down on the lawn and fell asleep. I woke up and went inside to find Camdyn amazed. "You must be the most relaxed guy in the world. I couldn't fall asleep out on the lawn like that if my life depended on it." He even called Dawn in, he was so awed. She listened to him, frowning.

"I don't think he's relaxed. I think he just keeps it all inside."

I could feel my welcome here wearing thin.

I stayed away more and more, taking long walks across town and wishing I had a girl. To stay in shape, I used the pool at the University of Buffalo. Camdyn and Dawn argued nearly all the time now. There was a cabinet near the kitchen where they kept a bottle of codeine-based cough syrup and they were always stopping to take hits. "Yeah, you'll never hear a cough in this house," Camdyn laughed. Then came the phone call that was to change everything. An administrator from a local hospital called to ask Camdyn if he would be interested in painting murals along the hallway of a new wing they were just finishing. It was a children's wing and they wanted paintings of friendly-looking lions and bears. I heard Camdyn talking to the administrator and his lack of enthusiasm bordered on rudeness. The administrator must have chalked this up to artistic temperament, though, for he kept calling back. Dawn would answer the phone in honeyed tones, then rush to the living room and scream at Camdyn to take the job. Camdyn finally agreed to go see the place. "Don't worry," he confided to me as he threw on his jacket. "I'm only going to keep Dawn happy. I'm going to name terms they can't possibly accept." Several hours later he came back looking chagrined. "I might really have to do this job. They gave in to all my demands!"

He had demanded a hundred dollars a day, top pay for muralists at the time, and at the end of eight days the job would be considered finished, regardless how much work had been done. "That means," Camdyn drawled, "when five o'clock rolls around on the eighth day—say I happen to be painting a bear, but I haven't finished its paw. Well, that's the way it stays." I had a sudden vision of a sick kid being wheeled down the hallway and looking up to see a bear cheering him on with an amputated paw.

Dawn was a new person now that Camdyn had agreed to the job. She cooked all his favorite meals and ran errands for him. The first day of the job, though, Camdyn did what he always did, which was to pour himself coffee and settle in front of the TV. Dawn screamed at him so fiercely it scared me just to be in the same house. It was no use, though. Camdyn had witnessed the existential futility of life and was beyond employment.

CHAPTER 64

THE HASH RUN FINALLY PULLED THROUGH, BUT again it was a disappointment. During their long period of confinement in the Mercedes trunk, many of the bricks had rotted, turning into a smelly goo. Bruce had to throw half of them away. The ones that were left had a musty smell to them and I was lucky to get $600 a pound for them. I kept $3,000 for my efforts, which left just enough for Bruce to turn around and go back to Afghanistan. He was obsessed. Most people who get in a rut go back and forth, say, from their home to their office. Bruce's rut ran from Toronto to Kabul.

I flew back to the Bay Area and found Wade, Malcolm Murray, and Duncan all excited about a new company they had founded named Ecology Syntechnics. The ecology movement was just getting underway and they envisioned themselves at the forefront. They intended to establish their own ecological seal of approval that would apply to all consumer goods and expected it to become as famous as the Good Housekeeping Seal. To raise capital, they sold ecology flags, which were American flags colored in green and white instead of red, white, and blue, and they sold decals too, depicting the same flag. Their office was a small shop on California Street and they got permission to change the address from 1982 to the Orwellian 1984, which was more in keeping with their predictions of imminent ecological doom. I arrived as they were looking for a secretary. I visited Wade to find him adjusting his tie and splashing cologne over his face. "It's my turn to interview secretaries today," he explained with a knowing grin. I told him he was becoming just like the straight businessmen we all looked down on when we first turned hip. "No way," he told me, brushing dust off his wingtips. "We're for the right cause."

They placed ads in the papers and soon found a secretary who suited their needs perfectly. Her name was Sandy and she had the body of a young Sophia

Loren. She spent her time lounging around the Ecology Syntechnics office drinking Southern Comfort and giving the three partners blowjobs. Most of the people who visited the shop were either lost or wanted change for the meters, but every now and then a legitimate customer would walk in. Often they would be greeted by the strange spectacle of Sandy hurriedly tucking in her blouse as she leapt up from behind the counter.

No work got done at Ecology Syntechnics and it lost a considerable amount of money, considering there was rent to pay plus Sandy's $800-a-month salary, which no one dared suggest cutting. This was evidently a sore point with Murray, for when I mentioned it to him, he gave me a withering look. "Well, you knew Ecology Syntechnics was just a front for laundering money, didn't you?" He was only saving face, though, as no one had any money to launder.

I moved into a big house on Henry Street with Wade; his wife, Janet; their daughter, Sarah; Murray and his girl; and crazy Duncan and his beautiful girl, Kathleen, who looked sharp enough to be a model. LeGrande moved in too, bringing a Les Paul and a set of drums. We made a little stage in the living room and jammed every night, playing Chicago-style blues. Duncan joined in—he had a Les Paul too—and Murray would get drunk and beat on the furniture. People came by to party, including Sandy, who enjoyed showing off her luscious anatomy by letting her top fall off one shoulder or forgetting to wear panties under her miniskirt. Oddly, none of the other girls resented her and in fact, they became fast friends.

I contacted my lawyer and he said as far as he knew, both the Mitchum case and Les and Carrie's case had died down with no more indictments expected from either of them. When I thought how narrowly I had missed getting busted, it gave me shivers. I sounded people out about a possible Mexico run, but things had gotten so hot that no one was interested. I had absolutely no idea what I was going to do but was in reasonable spirits having just gotten back from my three-month exile in Buffalo. I made the rounds of all my friends, telling them what I had been up to and catching up on the latest happenings.

One group of friends I always visited lived in a commune on Regent Street. They included Mary, the girl who turned me on to PCP; her boyfriend, Gary; and Melanie, who was like the den mother for the whole group, weighed ninety pounds, and had the energy of a buzz saw. There were others too. Except for Mary, all of them had tried heroin and liked it, and one day they came up with a plan to keep themselves from getting strung out: they would only shoot up on Sundays. It would be like a family thing. Whereas some families go to the park on Sundays, they would all shoot heroin together.

This went on for a few weeks and then, in keeping with their pact, they began staying up Saturday nights until the clock struck twelve at which point they would all shoot up. More weeks followed and one Saturday night when it was only ten o'clock, Gary said, "This is ridiculous. I'm not going to wait another two hours." Over Melanie's screamed objections, he got out his kit and shot up. Following that, all discipline was lost and everyone in the commune but Mary became strung out.

Furious barking erupted from the other side as I knocked on the large oak door to their place. "Calm down, Hash Pipe!" came Mary's voice from inside. As she opened the door, she had to stoop to restrain Gary's phenomenally ugly bulldog, thus treating me to a pleasant view down her blouse. "Wow, I was just thinking of you the other day. I don't know who you came to see, but I'm the only one here. Come on in."

We passed through the living room, which was strewn with cushions, pop bottles, and ashtrays spilling butts. She made an apologetic wave. "Sorry for the mess. We had one of our group gropes last night."

"Group gropes?"

"It's Melanie's idea. We all take our clothes off and roll around on top of each other in a huge pile. Even the dogs get in on it."

"You should invite me next time," I said and she laughed.

"It's not all that risqué really. Everyone just rolls around and then the people that are already couples go off to their rooms and the people that aren't go back to whatever they were doing before. Sebastian always ends up jacking off Gary's dog. Gary doesn't dig it but he never says anything. I mean, what can you say? Please quit jacking off my dog?" She laughed. "Tea?"

"Please."

We talked and I asked her out the way I had done several times since that time I made it with her, but this time, instead of reminding me she had a boyfriend, she considered. "That might be kind of fun, actually. Things are getting pretty boring around here with Gary nodding out in front of the TV ninety percent of the time."

She looked at me sidelong. "You're always asking me out. What makes you so sure you want to go out with me?"

I shrugged. "I think you're interesting. We always have a lot to say to each other."

Feigning reproach, she said, "Oh, you just like me because I said I went to Cal. I remember that. The first time you met me, you thought I was just another dingy hippie chick till I happened to mention I went to Cal and suddenly you got all interested."

"That's not true! I kissed you five minutes after we first met, remember?"

"Well, that's true. God, that was pretty ballsy too, with my old man right in the next room."

"I didn't know you had an old man. Anyway, it was your fault. You got me high on PCP. I didn't know it was an aphrodisiac."

She grinned. "It's a pretty intimate drug, I have to admit."

"Anyway, suppose I am impressed that you went to Cal. That's what I'm supposed to like you for—your intelligence, right?"

"Well, just because someone goes to Cal, I don't think that means they're all that intelligent necessarily. Anyway, forget intelligence. I'd rather a guy liked me because I was sexy."

"Oh, I do," I said, running my eyes pointedly over her body. She laughed. A car door sounded outside and she turned serious.

"I tell you what. I've been spending a lot of time at my mother's lately. I'm thinking of moving back there for a while. I'll be there tonight, so why don't you give me a call and we can go sailing or something. Barbara might want to come too."

Barbara was a stunning five-foot-nine model Mary knew from when she used to model herself. I sped home and told Wade, "Man, I know these two outtasight-looking chicks who want to go sailing with us!"

"Outtasight!"

A date was set, but Barbara never made it. Wade didn't care; instead, we competed for Mary. We took her sailing in Wade's International 110, one of the few dope purchases he had been able to keep. It was berthed at Richmond and we threw on foul weather gear and took off on a clear fall morning with a mild breeze. As we left Richmond, the breeze picked up and we were able to tack all the way across the bay to Sausalito, where we decided to dock at the Trident restaurant. This was the ultimate in class: to luff to a perfect stop and dock in front of the terrace full of diners, then appear casually trailing water across the redwood decking like real sailors—not the would-be sailors and other phony types trying to be part of the hip Sausalito scene. We dined on luscious crab-and-avocado salads and drank beers, but when the bill came, Wade and I suddenly realized we had left our wallets back in Richmond, not wanting them to get wet. Mary could hardly believe it. We sheepishly appealed to her.

"God, here I thought I was going out with two big dope smugglers! It's a good thing I brought my purse along!"

In hushed tones we tried to assure her we really were big dope smugglers but she just laughed.

"Forget it. Your reputations are blown!"

With the bill taken care of, we crossed the street to spend more of Mary's money on oranges at a corner market. "To prevent scurvy at sea!" Wade cried. This was a corny line he used whenever we took girls sailing. As we leaned over the bins of ripe fruit, Mary let her breast rest against my arm and I realized I was going to make it with her again.

We saw each other again two days later. Wade was crewing in the Perpetual

Trophy race and I took Mary to the San Francisco marina, excited about watching him. We found a stretch of lawn where we could lie down yet still see the water and I spread out a blanket. The boats were so far away, though, we couldn't be sure which was Wade's. All we saw were a bunch of white specks moving around. I cursed myself for not thinking to bring binoculars. We weren't even sure we had heard the gun go off and I sensed Mary getting bored. "Maybe they'll come in closer," I told her.

"That's OK," she said and quit bothering to look as she lay on her back and stared up at a lusterless sky.

I lay on my back too and racked my mind, trying to think of something to do or say. I couldn't think of a thing. It was the kind of Sunday afternoon I had always hated. Families were everywhere, wandering past the marina and saying how pretty it looked, buying their kids candy to keep them quiet, taking pictures so they could look back later and imagine what a wonderful time they must have had. I began to feel as inadequate and miserable as I had ever felt.

I lay perfectly still as though I were one false move away from something terrible. I could feel Mary's bare arm lightly touching mine. The sun beat down, so that we had to squint. Neither of us had thought to bring sunglasses.

Here I am, I thought, lying next to a wonderful girl with no idea what to do. I saw myself looking down at myself, saw myself looking down at myself looking down at myself, and so on in an endless spiral of nauseas. I hated that feeling. I tried to stop it by focusing on solid things like the walkway, the low seawall, the boats berthed at the marina. It was no use. I felt myself getting more and more removed from myself. And the whole time I kept thinking, Say something! Do something! I ought to just go home and relieve Mary of my miserable presence, I was thinking, but then Wade's boat pulled in, and in the excitement of going on board and meeting the crew, all my black feelings lifted. Next thing we were heading through The City and stumbled across Sharon, her boyfriend, Byron, and the entire Wichita crowd. Night fell and the whole lot of us ate dinner at a Chinese restaurant. Later Mary told me she had had a really fun time.

Mary began coming over on her own to visit me at the Henry Street house. Now it was my turn to ask her why she liked being with me. She thought for a moment.

"I tend to judge guys by how long it takes before they say something stupid. The average is eight minutes. We've been seeing each other for over a week now and you haven't said anything stupid."

I felt bad that I was stealing her from Gary, a guy I knew and liked and had sold grass to. Then one morning Gary and I both appeared at the same time to meet Mary at her mother's house. Gary sat parked on one side of the street in his '55 Mercedes Gullwing and I was on the other side in my red fiberglass

Lotus Elite. It was like a contest in automotive cool. Mary stepped out, hurried over to my car, and got in. "This is really embarrassing," she murmured. "Hurry and let's get out of here." I sped off and for a long time Mary just stared ahead, biting her lip. "Well, maybe it's better this way," she sighed. "At least now he knows it's really the end."

Mary moved into her mother's place and we saw each other every day. She loved my old yellow truck and said riding in the cab way high like that made her feel like a pachuco girl. On warm nights we drove up to Grizzly Peak, parked overlooking the view, and slept in my truck's bed in two sleeping bags zipped together to make one. While Mary arranged our comfortable bed, I serenaded her on guitar. Then we held each other tight and searched the warm Indian summer sky for shooting stars. Without realizing it, we were falling deeply in love.

Weird blacknesses kept bothering me, though. Neither of us had anything to do and we spent endless hours together. I felt somehow responsible for Mary's happiness. If she seemed the least bit somber, I took it to be my fault. Then I would fall into one of my weird, self-conscious moods where I couldn't stop analyzing myself. It was like a trap. Sometimes I felt as though I carried some unspeakable awfulness deep inside me, and if I wasn't careful, I would infect others because this hopeless way of looking at things was so compelling that once anyone saw it, they would be incapable of seeing things any other way. That's why when Mary felt bad, I assumed it was my doing. So when I felt these moods coming on, I did everything I could to try to hide them, acting falsely lighthearted. If Mary could see the way I was truly feeling, I imagined, she would leave me in an instant.

Part of the problem, too, was that I was no longer free. Mary had expectations of me. She wanted me to join her family for Sunday dinners and meet her friends and go to plays. The first time she said we ought to go to a play, I thought it was a great idea. But when we got there and took seats and people started filling in the space all around us, I felt panicked, realizing that once the play started, there was no way I could get up or move about without creating a disturbance. My heart pounded and I broke out in sweats throughout the entire first act. The thought struck me that for several years now I had never been tied down for so much as an hour. I hadn't worked and had kissed off all social obligations. For several years I had been free to get up and walk away from whatever I was doing any time I felt like it.

One day Mary pulled out a joint she had been saving. "Hey, let's get high! Do you realize we haven't even gotten high together yet?"

I hadn't smoked grass in a while and worried it might bring on one of my weird moods. I told her I was afraid I might get bummed out.

"Around me?" She feigned umbrage, then laughed and squeezed my arm.

"Don't worry. I won't let you get bummed out."

So we got high and I got bummed out and had to go through the intense struggle to act lighthearted when I was really feeling black and hopeless inside. By myself I didn't care that much if I felt bad. I could go somewhere, do something. I had a million ways of dealing with it. Around others, though, I felt trapped and responsible. After a couple of hours, Mary glanced at me sidelong.

"So, did you get bummed out?"

"Kind of. Dope puts me in a weird, self-conscious mood sometimes."

She reflected. "Well, let's eat. That'll make you feel better. I know what—I'll make a quiche. There's some food at my mom's house. She's not home tonight. We'll have the place to ourselves."

We went to her mother's place, which was a large, old wood-shingle home in the Berkeley hills. Mary put together a quiche using odd leftovers she found in the refrigerator: bacon, onions, cheese, tomatoes, celery—even some hot chili peppers. We drank wine, waiting for the quiche to bake, and when it was done, it was sumptuous. We feasted on it and I felt the blackness slipping away from me. We watched the sun go down over the bay and later the moon came out. We went for a walk.

We walked uphill past stately older homes with well-kept yards. Lights shone behind the shades. Mary ducked into a yard to pick a beautiful white flower and stuck it in her hair, laughing guiltily. She took my arm and we stopped at the top of a hill. Before us lay the lights of Berkeley, the dark blue of the bay, and the stardust lights of The City beyond. I found myself telling her, "There's this thing I do. I think of it as 'abstracting.' It's like I mentally remove myself from my body and look at myself as though I were someone else. I've been doing it ever since I was a kid only I didn't realize it then. I didn't realize it till I started smoking grass. At first when I realized it, it seemed like a neat thing. I could analyze what I was doing and see how I was affecting other people, and I could analyze other people, too. But then it got like a trap. It's like once you start looking at things this way, it's hard to stop. Lately it's been really bad. Like in Buffalo. But even here. Anyway, does that ever happen to you—you start looking at yourself and analyzing everything?"

Mary gave a chagrined laugh. "About ninety percent of the time."

Her answer stunned me. "But you seem so lively all the time."

She stared out over the bay. "I think of my life as a novel. Everything's in chapters. Like when I left my husband, I thought, well that's the end of that chapter. And when I dropped out of Cal, too. And now, leaving Gary. A lot of the time I don't feel as though I'm really here. I just see myself as a character in a novel I happen to be reading."

We stared at the distant lights of The City. Buildings were still giving off heat, making their lights twinkle. In a laughing way, not to sound heavy, I said,

"So, am I going to be just another chapter?"
Mary turned to me and held my gaze.
"I don't know. I hope not."

CHAPTER 65

WITHOUT REALLY TRYING I HAD FOUND a wonderful girlfriend for myself but didn't know what to do. Neither of us had much money so somehow we had to make money, but all I could think of was another run. I told Mary we ought to do a Rio Grande run. She went along with the idea and we fantasized about it. The only reason Les and Carrie had gotten busted was that they had somehow picked up heat. I said we should do a run without telling a single soul. I would get a crew cut and Mary could get some straight-looking clothes. We could just disappear one day and do it. I even discussed the risk of going to jail, telling her, "I wouldn't even care so much if we could share the same cell." She laughed and looked away, running her fingers lightly through my hair.

Then it happened: Bruce was busted in Afghanistan. His wife phoned me in a panic, saying he was under house arrest in Kabul and needed $3,000 to arrange a bribe. This was the exact amount of money I was keeping in an emergency account. I withdrew it and sent the money via American Express. Bruce was freed and made it to Pakistan, where he checked into a hospital with severe dysentery. I had no idea what he planned to do next. It didn't seem to matter. My wonderful times with him seemed to be over and I wondered if I would ever even see him again. I phoned Jake and told him his $17,000 in front money was finally and officially unrecoverable.

I was nearly broke. The house on Henry Street broke up and I had to move. Mary wanted to move too, never intending to stay long at her mother's house, so we moved in with Byron and Sharon, my favorite couple from Wichita. Coming from Wichita, they had no feel for the different neighborhoods here and were always finding amazing deals by looking in areas young people normally never considered. This was one of those deals. It was in Oakland, below Foothill, in a neighborhood of small, two-bedroom stucco houses utterly devoid of character. Absolutely nothing was happening in this neighborhood. Just walking down the street past the trimmed lawns and red-painted walkways was a study in existential boredom.

Byron and Sharon both had jobs and were gone most of the day, but Mary and I were subsisting off odd savings and had nothing but free time. After coffee in the morning, I would rack my brains trying to think what to do. I thought of various small businesses I might be good at. We tried making candles and had a fun time melting wax and adding beautiful dyes, even adding pitch from a pine tree in the backyard in order to give the candles a scent, but they looked sloppy and homemade and we never even tried selling any of them. I thought of trying to make wax-cast jewelry though many people were already doing that. One day we drove to Mendocino County, where I bought a truckload of redwood burl slabs wholesale, intending to make coffee tables out of them, but never got around to it.

I began waking up every night around two in the morning. I would think about our problems and be unable to go back to sleep. "Poor babe," Mary murmured one night as I slipped out of bed and dressed. A blue glow flickering from underneath the water heater in the kitchen provided the only light in the place. Outside there was a late fall chill in the air. I walked aimlessly through our dreary neighborhood, wondering what we were going to do. Several blocks from us was a mammoth older apartment building and I stopped to stare up at it. Old single people probably live here, I thought to myself. It was about six stories high, several units across, and two deep—a giant warehouse for unclaimed souls.

Lights were on behind a couple of the shades and I studied them, trying to imagine what awful regrets might be going on at this hour. Life passed quickly. I felt that if I didn't act soon, I might find myself dying hourly in some place like this.

Something, anything—I had to do it. It was time to do a Rio Grande run, I decided. But when I told Mary this, she reacted with disbelief. She had been going along with the idea as though it were a fantasy, not something she really wanted to do. I quickly backed off, dissembling. It was wrong of me to even suggest it, I immediately realized, and wondered what kind of guy I was that I would expect my girl to risk getting busted with him.

More time went by. One morning I picked up my guitar and started to learn a Big Bill Broonzy piece. Mary walked in with a tight look around her lips. "This isn't working out," she said. I didn't even try to argue with her.

She heaped her clothes in a sad pile on the bed. "It seems like I'm always gathering my clothes out of some guy's closet." We put her things in the back of my truck and drove in separate vehicles to her mother's house. Looking out over the hazy Oakland morning from the freeway, I never felt more disconnected from life in my life.

The day passed in a daze. That evening I was supposed to visit my cousin, who lived in The City near Golden Gate Park. He was studying dentistry and was going to show me how to do wax casting. I didn't know if I had the heart to go. I missed Mary terribly. Then I did something that was unlike anything I had ever done before in my life—something hopeless, something almost irrational even. I phoned Mary. To my surprise, she sounded glad to hear from me. I invited her to come with me to visit my cousin and could hardly believe it when she said yes.

It was one of the best times we ever had, too. My cousin was in his last year of dental school and was happy for the chance to do something besides study. He had a blues harp and a guitar in the house, and we forgot all about the wax casting. We played Dylan songs together and I taught him my guitar adaptation of Ivory Joe Hunter's "Since I Met You Baby." Later Mary and I went for a walk along the Panhandle in the cool San Francisco night. "God, I was missing you," I told her, hugging her over and over again beneath the dewy eucalypti. I asked her if she wanted to give things another try and she said sure.

"I was really missing you too. I think if you hadn't've called me, sooner or later I would have called you."

"I think we can make it," I told her excitedly. "We've just got to find something to do. That's why we're bummed out all the time: we need something to do."

The very next day I got out my old math texts and began studying them. By the end of the week I had decided. I got in my faithful truck and drove to my parents' house. For several years now I had been estranged from them, visiting them from time to time but never really talking to them. I was sick of lying to them and the truth would have only caused them a lot of anguish and worry. To explain the different exotic cars I showed up in, I had told them I was a professional gambler. I doubted they believed this, but they never questioned it.

It was a late fall afternoon as I pulled up in front of the familiar stone steps. I let myself in and found my mother washing vegetables in the kitchen. My father was somewhere outside. I said Hi, then just stood there awkwardly. My mother must have sensed something was up, for she dropped what she was doing and stared. "My life hasn't been going the way I want it to," I blurted and burst into tears.

"I'll run get Dad."

I told them everything: how I had really been smuggling all this time, not gambling, and how I had been incredibly lucky at first to the point where I thought I was invincible and how I was like a folk hero, and then how everything had slowly gone bad. I told them about Mary and said I wanted them to meet her. Then I told them I wanted to go back to school and study math. They offered to help before I could even ask.

CHAPTER 66

WONDERFUL TIMES FOLLOWED. I WENT BACK to Cal and now that I had a girlfriend and had seen something of the world, I had no trouble concentrating on my work and maintained a 4.0 grade point average. Mary got a job as a waitress with an eye toward starting her own restaurant. With some help from my folks, I bought a rundown house just off Telegraph and we moved in and fixed it up. During quarter breaks we drove to the Sierra or to Sonoma, where Wade and Janet were now living in a ramshackle cabin overlooking the Valley of the Moon. I enjoyed being close to my family again and Mary and I had no end of friends.

I studied for four quarters straight, then took a break so we could have some fun. I was dying to show Mary Mexico, and her grandmother loaned us a camper shell that fit the back of my truck. I built a collapsible platform we would sleep on, cut cardboard boxes so they just fit underneath, for our belongings, and made a little cabinet to hold spices and the like. Byron and Sharon had recently returned from Oaxaca and showed us beautiful embroidered dresses they had bought and were selling for five or six times what they had paid for them. Mary and I decided to do the same thing, only on a larger scale, as a way of making money out of our vacation.

We couldn't afford motels and on our first night we pulled over onto a quiet lot behind a warehouse out of Bakersfield. We didn't realize it, but we had parked ten feet from railroad tracks, and in the dead of night the train came, blasting its whistle right next to our ears. Mary literally jumped into my arms in fright. After it passed, we couldn't stop laughing and I got the warmest feeling thinking that another human being had come to love and trust me intimately.

In Mexico I excitedly pointed out places that held significance for me: dirt roads the Bub and I used to use when we wanted to pack bricks, places where we liked to pull over and camp, the toll bridge where we always gave money to the Catholic girls. I couldn't wait to introduce Mary to Jesus and Alicia when we reached Culiacan.

We got there and even though Mary spoke little Spanish, she was an instant hit with everyone because of her exuberance. Alicia especially took a liking to her and drew her aside to ask when we were going to get married and in particular when we were going to have kids, which is generally expected by eighteen or twenty in Mexican families. Jesus took me for a ride and said we should try to get a run going. My old smuggling instincts leapt to the idea though I would have had a hard time justifying it to my parents after they had done so much to help me. I had no way of getting grass across the border, though, and didn't give it much thought.

We spent nearly two months in Mexico, driving all the way to Oaxaca, where we bought the same style of embroidered dresses Byron and Sharon had bought as well as some peasant blouses and shawls. When we got back to Berkeley, we laid them all out on a blanket right in front of the main entrance to UC and in two days the clothes were all sold. We made our trip expenses and several hundred dollars to boot.

Two quarters later I graduated with honors and was offered a place in the graduate math department at Berkeley, a chance to get my PhD. Berkeley had one of the most prestigious graduate math departments in the world, and for me to have gotten accepted was an accomplishment and an honor. This had been my goal for the last year and a half, yet now that I had it, I wasn't sure I wanted it. I loved math, but it was a very introverted and cerebral field and I would be spending long hours every day studying things that none of my friends or family would be able to understand. Mary liked to spend time with friends and party, and I wondered if she would even stay with me. For several months I agonized over this decision, but as the days went by and I did nothing, my decision was gradually being made for me. I never even responded to that wonderful letter of acceptance I had worked so hard to get.

Instead, Mary and I threw the camper shell back on my truck, borrowed some money, and headed south, intending to start our own importing business. We made a great loop through Michoacan, Oaxaca, and Aguascalientes, buying up beautiful embroidered clothes by the boxful and shipping them to Mexicali to be held for us. We stopped to see Jesus and Alicia on the way and spent a wonderful day with them at a beach house Jesus had rented in Altata. By the time we got back to the Líneas Internacionales de Tijuana office in Mexicali, an entire pickup load of clothes was waiting for us. When we tried to cross them, though, we were turned back by customs. We didn't know the first thing about importing and didn't even know that foreign-made clothing had to carry a label stating the cotton content and country of origin. Here Mary proved what a resourceful partner she was. She said there was a type of ribbon we could buy that would stick to cloth when it was ironed and we could use it to make our labels. This was a great idea and I said we should put the name of our company on the labels too. We didn't even have a name yet and I suggested "Tom & Mary's Imports." Mary considered and said she thought "Mary & Tom's Imports" sounded a little better. We flipped a peso and she won.

We had a rubber stamp made up, bought boxfuls of ribbon and an iron, and set up shop in a Mexicali motel room. While one of us stamped lengths of ribbon over and over again and cut them into pieces, the other ironed. By three in the morning we had finally finished. We threw our clothes off and tried not to make too much noise on the rickety motel bed before crashing.

In Berkeley we set about selling our clothes right on the sidewalk on Telegraph Avenue, where throngs of students passed by. To anyone who knows Mexico, sidewalk vending makes perfect sense, yet hardly anyone had ever tried this before on the Avenue. At the time we started, there was only a French couple selling jewelry, a huarache vendor named Bernard, and a blond guy who sold sheepskins occasionally out of the back of his pickup. Students eagerly surrounded our little stand. Word spread to the Bank of America building nearby, and during lunch hour, all the secretaries and tellers rushed out to buy blouses and dresses. It was like a bargain basement sale! In less than two weeks all our clothes were sold.

We made another trip to get more clothes, but this time when we returned to Telegraph Avenue, our eyes popped out to see the entire street lined with vendors. It was a whole new scene with people competing for the best locations—even hiring Hells Angels to save favorite spots. We decided we had had enough of retail and should go wholesale. We packed my truck full of clothes, headed north, and in a short while we had established accounts throughout northern California, Oregon, and Washington, and it was time to go back to Mexico to get more clothes.

The Oaxaca marketplace was the center for buying embroidered clothes, but we eschewed marketplace prices and made arduous treks to the remote villages where the clothes were actually made. The pesos we saved hardly justified this extra effort, but the adventures we had did. We bought clothes from *indias* who couldn't speak Spanish and often didn't even know basic arithmetic. To make sure they weren't getting cheated, they would show our figures to a shopkeeper.

My truck was only two-wheel drive, but I had learned to get it through the most formidable terrain. Once, following a set of tire tracks to a remote village, we passed two indios on horseback, one of them carrying a small coffin awkwardly across his lap. He flagged us down and asked if we could take the coffin to the village for him. We said sure, and he said he would meet us at the *zócalo* at sundown.

We met him, gave him his coffin back, and he invited us to the wake for his two-year-old daughter, which was to take place in an hour. We walked around the small village, which had no paving or sidewalks, and learned that all the inhabitants of the village were indios save for one Mexican family who owned the only store in town. A diarrheal illness had recently swept through the village and many of the children had fallen ill and several of them had died. The daughter of the Mexican family had fallen ill, but her parents gave her antibiotics and she survived. None of the indios had been able to afford antibiotics and this was a source of bitterness in the town.

It was dark when we went to the wake. Ours was the only motor vehicle in the village and we pulled up next to a large thatched-roof hut with mud walls. An older campesino lay in the dust in front of the entrance, a bottle of mezcal in hand, raving. The señora of the hut appeared in the dim interior and motioned for us to step over him. Inside, the women had gathered to one side of the hut, the men on the other. In the middle, the body of the dead girl lay on a bed of flowers. Lit votive candles had been placed on her upturned palms and on her midriff, which was bare, and a lit taper stood on her forehead held in place by a molded base fashioned from melted wax. Behind her stood a crude wooden altar and on it were statues of Christ, Saint Francis of Assisi, and an Indian god. Guests were arriving and each family brought the exact same items as gifts: a basket of corn, an unlabeled liter bottle of mezcal, and a taper. After handing the basket and bottle to the grieving family, they would carefully remove the taper from the dead girl's forehead and replace it with their own. I was in awe of the customs here, which were so different from our own. The señora had enormous breasts and kept rubbing them in front of all the guests. "She must not have weaned that poor girl," Mary murmured. Mary soon excused herself and went back to our truck.

Whites had hardly ever been seen in this village and the dead girl's father made sure to show me off to every man who came in. I was apparently more interesting to them than the dead girl. Each wanted to toast my health with a shot of mezcal. They would pour mezcal into a shot glass until it was overflowing, letting a few drops soak into the earthen floor as an offering, and then hand it to me before pouring their own. After two or three of these I begged off, but the father drew me aside and said it would be a grave offense if I declined to drink with the next man to come in. I saw no way out and kept on drinking.

The father stepped out to go to the store for cigarettes and the men gathered around me, asking questions like, How much can you earn shining shoes in the United States? and What is it like to fuck a blonde? The father returned with a carton of Raleighs *con filtro* and after removing a pack, he lofted the carton onto the altar, where it landed between St. Francis and the Indian god. He shook a cigarette out of the pack, placed it between his lips, bent over, and lit it off the burning taper on his dead daughter's forehead.

Two men with a battered guitar and a violin missing two strings arrived and began playing a strange, mournful dirge. Abruptly all the women began hopping up and down on one foot and wailing. By now I had had ten or fifteen shots of mezcal and realized I was going to get sick. With my palms together in front of me like a cowcatcher on a locomotive, I weaved my way through the hopping women to the doorway, turned the corner, and barfed my guts out. I went and rapped on the door to our camper. "These Indians have poisoned me!" The next day was possibly the worst day of my life. I had a hangover so bad that each minute was an ordeal to be somehow gotten through. At the zócalo we ran into one of the indios who had been at the wake and he asked me what was wrong. "Too much mezcal," I told him and he stared at me.

"No, that was not too much mezcal that you drank."

Every trip it seemed had adventures. When we weren't buying clothes, we spent time on the coast swimming, surfing, and cooking up fresh shrimp curries on the tailgate of our truck. For eight and eleven dollars we bought two used surfboards and tied them to the top of the camper shell, adding to the truck's generally beat appearance with its strapped-on fuel can and water jug. Wherever we went, we camped, avoiding hotels and trailer parks—any place that cost money. We even camped in Mexico City, where we were required to stop each trip to get visas for importing cotton. Right near downtown we managed to find an abandoned construction site where there was a pocket of quiet in the heart of the metropolis. In the mornings we would emerge from the camper shell to finish tying our shoes and brush our teeth, and while I set up our stove on the tailgate and fried up bacon and eggs, Mary would make up a blend of fresh orange juice and grapefruit juice, using a Dazey Speedo juicer that fit into a bracket I had mounted on the truck's dash. The Mexicans walking by never bothered us, some even smiling appreciatively as they passed. We wore the same brightly colored clothes we were importing and lived like gypsies.

Life was a dream for us. When we were on the coastal highway and it got hot, we would look for a set of tire tracks that led to the ocean. We found beaches with pure white sand as far as the eye could see and no one around. Once in our wanderings we found a deserted beach south of Mazatlan. We swam naked and watched the sun go down in a blaze of red and gold. The moment felt magical and the waves seemed to sparkle in the fading light. As it grew darker, we realized the waves really were sparkling. It was due to plankton and any time you disturbed the water, it would glow. We threw handfuls of it in the air and it was like throwing diamonds.

It struck me that I hardly ever fell into the trap of analyzing myself anymore. Life was simply happening. I was just being. It seemed hard to believe things were going so well for us. Still, there were periods when I felt I was wasting time, that I wasn't living up to my potential. We were barely eking out a living and on our trips to Oregon and Washington to show our line, we camped in the back of my truck and went without showers unless we could find a place where we could get them free. There were times, too, when I felt a stabbing longing for my old smuggling days.

I was afraid my life would never be as exciting in that cut-edge way again. Driving through Mexico made me think of old times with the Bub. Living with a woman was definitely better, yet there were things I missed. With the Bub, all we cared about was getting the dope back; we never hassled over anything personal. The Bub—and Bruce too—had a keen sense of intuition and never brought up things I didn't want to talk about. Men respect each other's privacy. With Mary my sense of privacy was trampled daily. She hated secrets and wanted to know everything I was thinking. I felt the pressure of expectations. She wanted me to be more sociable and witty and not have quiet moods. She was teaching me how to get along better with people, and I knew she was tremendously good for me, yet there were times when I longed to be back doing a run with one of my friends.

Things had changed meanwhile in the smuggling world. People were bringing high-quality pot back from Colombia, challenging Mexico as the traditional source. Colombia is where Bruce turned after getting out of jail in Afghanistan. I didn't know this until I heard he got busted and was doing time in a New Jersey prison. I got his address and wrote him letters. He did almost two years and paid me a visit shortly after getting out. I introduced him to Mary and he leered at her with his lecherous grin. We took a walk and every few seconds he would turn to look behind us. He did this so often that I wondered if it was truly a prison habit or just an affectation he thought might impress me.

"Fags kept coming up to me because they wanted to fuck me in the butt. 'Meet my friend, Mr. Gillette,' I'd tell them and hold up my razor . . . We didn't tolerate finks. There was a fink on our cell block but we took care of him. One day we lashed him down to a table up in the library and tied one end of a ball of string around his prick, then ran it down to the rec room and hung a sign on it saying, 'Do not pull on this string!' Ha-ha! You could hear his screams all over the yard."

Bruce seemed to have changed as a result of his prison experience. I would have expected his character to be more durable.

"I'll tell you, though, chap, this time I've spent hasn't been wasted. I've probably met more valuable contacts in the joint than I would have met in a lifetime outside. I mean to say, anything I want done, I know the person to do it. If I want a safe broken into, I can have a man on the job in twenty-four hours. If I want someone rubbed out, I can have a contract on him like that!" He snapped his fingers and glanced at me for my reaction. "Take that prick, Mitchum, for instance. If that whole incident were to happen now, I mean to say, Mitchum would be gone like that—bam!"

Back at my house he showed me a flare gun designed for emergency use on boats and planes. He grinned, aiming it around. "I'd like to see anyone try to mess with this. The cartridge for it is loaded with phosphorus. Once that stuff starts burning, you can't stop it. Can you imagine it burning its way through a guy's stomach? It's perfectly bloody legal, too. The only problem is you can only load one cartridge at a time."

I thought back to the day when Bruce refused to deal with Darnell because Darnell showed him a gun.

"In a way, chap, I'm kind of glad I got busted. Now I know I've got absolutely nothing to be afraid of. I know I can do time. I mean to say, a small amount of time wouldn't even faze me. I could do six months standing on my ear."

CHAPTER 67

I TOOK STOCK OF WHAT WAS HAPPENING with all my friends. Wade's legal problems had dragged on, finally culminating in a trial that took place nearly three years after his bust. All they got him for was a trumped-up charge of offering cocaine to a narc, for which he did sixty days in the Alameda County jail. For probation purposes, the judge asked Wade to submit a "sincere autobiography." Wade took the judge to heart and wrote an eighty-page tome in which he confessed his deep-lying hatred for his overweight mother and made observations like, "I find that my feelings for a woman often change after I jack off" and "Any man who has the guts to go down on a woman he just met shouldn't have to worry about farting in her face." This he submitted to the judge.

Malcolm Murray became a private detective and made a good living working for several well-known dope lawyers. Then for reasons no one will ever know, he drove his car eighty miles an hour down the freeway the wrong way and killed himself, also killing a young Korean and seriously injuring the Korean's newlywed wife.

Duncan moved to Illinois and came out as gay. Years later he would show up on a psychiatric ward in Seattle where Wade's brother happened to be working and recognized him.

LeGrande was senselessly shot and killed by a deranged hitchhiker he made the mistake of picking up.

Mitchum served only a few months for his part in our fated plane run. I presume the judge cut him a deal for cooperating with the narcs.

Roger the Dodger and his brother, Les, were still serving time.

Arf married his girlfriend, Leslie, and moved to Puerto Rico to study hospital administration.

Jake continued to smuggle heroin and bought a ranch in Castro Valley, where his girlfriend could keep horses.

The Bub was getting by doing odd carpentry jobs and small-time deals.

Ron Gretsch got busted for conspiracy to manufacture LSD—his fourth bust. He made bail and then skipped, becoming a fugitive.

Bill Gretsch got his contractor's license and was making a good living remodeling homes.

Fred Swaha was getting by as a freelance photographer.

The last time I saw Dan Miller, his eyes looked bleary and he seemed self-conscious and embarrassed. I heard he was taking a lot of psychedelics. A short while later he committed suicide.

Ray, the crazy paranoid, was managing a shop in North Beach that sold comic books.

Gary, Mary's boyfriend before me, found another woman a lot like Mary but was unable to kick junk. He got depressed and quit getting out of bed. Then one day his Mercedes was found abandoned on the San Rafael Bridge. Two days later a fisherman found his body.

Jenner managed to resolve a number of legal difficulties without doing time and moved to the West Coast, where he resumed dealing. He told me what happened to Camdyn and his wife, Dawn. After I left them, they began doing more and more cough syrup, graduated to junk, and got strung out. They were busted and Camdyn did some time. When he got out, he went to have a beer at one of the toughest biker bars in Tonawanda, a town known for tough biker bars. As he was peacefully drinking his beer, a guy came up to him and said, "Wanna fight?" Camdyn took a long pull off his beer, turned to look at the guy, and said, "Sure. Why not?"

They stepped outside and Camdyn promptly obliterated the guy, where-upon all the guy's friends jumped him. While he was dealing with them and doing a good job of it, a cruiser pulled up and everyone stopped fighting. Two policemen jumped out and wanted to know what the fight was about. They got dead silence. Then Camdyn stepped forward and raised his hand. "I started it. It's all my fault."

He did a couple of weeks' time, got out, and went back to the very same biker bar. As he walked in, the entire place fell silent. He ordered a beer at the bar and as he was reaching for his wallet, a large biker called out, "Hold it! I'm paying for that beer!"

"I've got the one after it!" hollered another.

Camdyn was like God at the bar.

It was on a clothes-buying trip that Jesus told me what happened to Manuel and Modesto. Not long after the pair fleeced Wade and me for our $7,000, they had a falling out with the chief of police. They directed several of their men to dress up as leftist terrorists and had the chief cut down in a hail of machine gun fire as he stepped into the street. The chief took seven bullets but miraculously survived and the next day his detectives gunned down Manuel by the seawall next to the restaurant La Perla. Modesto fled to Hermosillo, later returned, and was knifed at a nightclub called the Capri. While patrons partied, his assailants carried him out as though he were passed out drunk and disposed of his corpse.

Manuel was the *buena gente* of the two and was mourned by the people of Mazatlan—especially all the people he had helped out and lent money to. The day after he was killed, a cross in red paint appeared on the seawall where he had fallen. For years that cross would remain there in honor of his memory; any cab driver could direct you to it and every kid in the neighborhood could tell you the story behind it. A ballad was written about him, "*Corrido de Manuel Salas*," and you could hear it on jukeboxes throughout Sinaloa. I've still got the forty-five.

On the same clothes-buying trip, Jesus told me he was now in touch with Abelardo. He had finally come out of deep hiding in the sierra and was living under an assumed name in Guadalajara. There was more: he wanted to see me and meet my new woman he had heard so much about. This was an amazing honor. Abelardo hadn't yet met with some of his closest friends. If he were to get caught, he risked years in prison or even death.

A rendezvous was arranged and Mary and I waited by a fountain in downtown Guadalajara. Abelardo pulled up in a brand-new Mustang, wearing shades and grinning. I had Mary sit in front as I slipped in the back, and Abelardo immediately showered her with the beautifully phrased compliments he was so famous for. Mary actually blushed. We couldn't wait to treat him to *cabrito a la barbacoa* at the Nuevo Leon, but when we suggested this, he very politely declined, saying his movements were still very limited. He said he had only recently eaten at a restaurant for the first time since his exile and then only after checking the place out for a week in advance to make sure it was cool. It was the only place he felt safe. We went to it and it was little more than a shack with some outdoor tables shaded by jacarandas. Propped over a charcoal fire in front was a huge black vat like a witch's cauldron in which pig parts boiled in an oily broth. Abelardo politely seated us in such a way that his chair faced the street. He was well-dressed and carried a leather case with him, which he set on the table.

We feasted on *carnitas* and afterward Abelardo laid his palm fondly on the leather case. "Many people have offered to buy my *portafolio* but it is not for sale. Not at any price." He opened it briefly to show us a chromed .45. He said it was one of the finest made. "With this you can *tirar el blanco*." "*Tirar el blanco*" means "shoot the white," which I took personally at the time though

I later learned it means "to hit the bullseye" and derives from the fact that in Latin America bullseyes are white. I should have known Abelardo would never use an expression that could offend.

We got back in the car and another idea Mary and I had was to go swimming at Lake Chapala. *"Vámonos,"* I said and Abelardo smiled and said what a great idea this was, that he would like nothing better than to go swimming with us, we were such wonderful friends to be with, but that unfortunately there would be a lot of people around, possibly people from Sinaloa, and someone might recognize him. Instead we drove around. Abelardo told me living in the sierra had been good for him. It had enabled him to meet grass farmers and learn about growing. The latest technique was to grow sinsemilla, which means "without seeds." By removing male plants from a field during the early growing stages, the female plants don't become fertilized and don't produce seeds. Instead, they produce large amounts of resin designed to trigger fertilization and this resin contains a large amount of THC, marijuana's psychoactive ingredient. Ironically, the presence of seeds, which used to be a good sign indicating maturity, was now an indication of substandard quality. Abelardo said he now owned large fields of sinsemilla. "That is how I was able to buy this Mustang," he grinned.

He invited me to come visit his fields. Again I was stunned by his complete faith in me, his fields being everything to him. He said to get to them, we would need to ride burros for two days to get deep into the sierra. In all my smuggling I had never seen a field and could hardly contain my excitement until Abelardo told me Mary would not be able to come along. "It is not a matter of trust, you understand, Tom. Because she is your woman, I trust her completely. However, a woman in this area, especially a blonde, would attract much attention." I was dying to see a pot field but couldn't leave Mary stranded in Guadalajara all week.

In the end there was nothing much we could do. We couldn't go anywhere because Abelardo was too fearful of being spotted. He took us back to the fountain where he had picked us up and we traded abrazos. I was wearing a brightly colored shirt Mary had bought for me with orange, green, and purple flowers on it and Abelardo complimented me on it. I remembered how he and Jesus liked me to bring them U.S.-made shirts and even remembered his size: 15½-34. "I will get you one just like it," I told him. "I will bring it to you the next time we come through."

"It is a very nice shirt," Abelardo replied. "I do not want you to think I do not like it. You have very good taste. However, given the circumstances, you understand, it would be better if you brought me a shirt that does not stand out so much. Perhaps just a solid brown."

CHAPTER 68

I HAD A BEAUTIFUL WOMAN WHO LOVED me madly and we spent half our time on the roads and beaches of Mexico answering to no one. Yet a part of me wasn't satisfied. I still missed the excitement of the runs—all that easy money coupled with the secret thrill of getting away with something. I worried that my life was becoming tame. Every time we passed through Culiacan, Jesus tried to get me to do a run. Part of me wanted to, but I didn't have a way. Meanwhile, Mary and I were tired of being poor all the time. Our clothes business was being threatened by importers who were having similar styles made up in India, where costs were less. Plus we had to contend with smugglers! A lot of people were avoiding the thirty-five percent duty on imported cotton by making multiple trips across the border with only a few pieces each time, claiming they were for personal use. Stores would quit ordering from us and when we went to visit them, we would find Mexican clothes on the racks with no labels in the collars.

We were making just enough to keep up our gypsy lifestyle and no more. When Mary was with Gary, he used to give her a hundred-dollar bill and tell her to go buy a dress on days when she felt blue. Now many of her clothes came from thrift shops. For a bed, we were using a mattress given to us free because it had bloodstains on it where a guy had slashed his wrists. Mary talked about having kids and I felt bad knowing, the way things were going, we wouldn't be able to afford them.

We began to argue over money. One day we had a fight over some bacon at a picnic. I served Mary's eight-year-old sister eggs and bacon and she ran off spilling the bacon on the ground and didn't even notice. I didn't cook up any more and a short while later Mary came over to me.

"How come you're not serving any of my sister's friends bacon?"

"They don't appreciate it. We paid a dollar twenty-nine a pound for this stuff."

We argued and I broke out in a sweat remembering how I had once driven an Aston Martin and dined at The Purple Vixen, and now here I was arguing over some lousy dollar twenty-nine-a-pound bacon.

Postman Joe pulled up in front of our house one day, driving a half-block-long Jaguar. I saw him stride up to the door wearing a suede jacket and custom-tooled boots. No sooner had we let him in than he began flashing money. He was his usual speeded self.

"Hey, we finally made it to the Big Time! Me and the Blade. But then we always knew we would, right? I mean, it's finally come through for all of us. None of us will ever have to worry about money again. I mean, I'm talking big, really big . . . the Brotherhood . . . kilos of base . . . Czechoslovakia.

"Hey, I guess I never told you about that time you sold me a suitcase that was supposed to have twenty bricks in it and when I got home and opened it, it had twenty-one! Ha-ha-ha! . . . By the way, Tom, do you need any cash?" He pulled out a roll of hundreds thick as his fist and began peeling off bills. "Here, take as much as you want. Money is no longer a problem."

He shoved bills at me and I could feel Mary's eyes on me, probably wondering if I would take any, maybe hoping I would. I told Postman Joe we were doing fine.

More and more I thought about doing a run. Two years had passed since I had done one. It was strange too, spending so much time around the border in the course of our clothes business. Shipments often got delayed and we would have to wait for several days in Mexicali. To pass the time, we went swimming in a canal that actually defined the border. Downstream from us, there was a bridge where a service road crossed the canal. The service road had a gate surrounded by razor wire and spikes, but one afternoon we saw a water company employee drive right through because he had the key. I was amazed and told Mary all we had to do was find a crooked locksmith and get our own personal key to the U.S.!

Another time, driving through the border town of Sonoyta, we found the entire area socked in with fog so thick you couldn't see twenty feet ahead. It would have been a snap to walk up to the border and hoist suitcases of grass over the fence. I asked around and discovered that fog was common in the area this time of year.

There were a number of temptations like these. Then one day I got a call from Jimmy Paradise, a guy I used to sell grass to in Boston. He said he had financing and an ideal van driver and wanted to do a Rio Grande run. I stepped out and called him back from a pay phone. It took me about two minutes to realize this was a viable proposition.

I told Mary and she was excited about the prospect of not having to count pennies all the time. I called Jesus and he assured me he could deliver grass to the river as before. Jimmy Paradise flew out and we worked out the details. The van driver was a friend he had known since childhood named Curly. He trusted him intimately. Furthermore, Curly knew the El Paso area and could speak, dress, and act just like a West Texan. Everything would be done in the most professional manner. As few people as possible would know. Curly and I would get crew cuts and wear straight clothes. All phone conversations would take place between pay phones and using code.

What was I going to tell my parents? I now wondered. Mary and I were in the habit of seeing them or at least phoning them every few days. There was no way I could disappear for one or two weeks without their knowing it. I could lie, but it didn't seem right. The day I came clean with them had been a very important day for me and I didn't want to turn it into something false. On the other hand, I couldn't imagine telling them the truth. Not only would I feel like a heartbreaking disappointment to them, but they would worry terribly.

I agonized over this decision. It was one of the hardest I ever made. In the end I felt I had no choice. I told them and my father's face seemed to cave in. My mother wrung her hands, asking, "Why? . . . Why?"

I tried to assure them I knew what I was doing and they shouldn't worry. My father left the room without saying anything and returned wearing his eyeglasses and carrying his account books.

"I've calculated it out and if it's money you need, we can give you five thousand dollars. You could do whatever you want with it, invest it in your clothes business, try something else—whatever you like. There would be no strings attached and you wouldn't have to pay us back."

My heart broke. Five thousand dollars was a large sum by any account and had taken him many hours of honest toil to earn. How could I possibly tell him I already had my sights set on the Big Time?

It was December, a time when families should be together. I told my parents I would keep in touch with Mary and she would let them know I was all right. Then at the last minute Mary got second thoughts and said maybe I shouldn't go. This irritated me. It was like a jinx on the run. I felt too committed to turn back now. She saw me off at the Oakland airport and gave me an old snapshot of herself to take with me on the trip. Soon I was 33,000 feet over the California coastline and remembered how the surf seen from that altitude looks as though it's standing still. The winter hills looked barren and dry. I found myself slipping into all my old smuggling habits: letting my features go lax in order to cultivate a bland, innocuous look; avoiding eye contact without being furtive; spacing the two-drink limit out to best calm my nerves.

That night I was at Jesus's house, seated at a table with him, Miguel, and several other men involved in the grass trade. The problem, Jesus explained, was getting the grass north through Mexico and past the Mexican inspection station. Until recently people had been moving it in tomato trucks. They would buy a truckload of tomatoes, then remove boxes from the interior of the load in order to hide the grass. If the truck got stopped, at most the officials might count how many boxes high, deep, and wide the load was in order to arrive at a total and compare it to the bill of lading. Now things were much hotter and it wasn't uncommon for officials to unload an entire truck in search of drugs.

The men seated around the table murmured in agreement with how hot it was. Miguel then told of a method he had used recently to move grass north. He used it on a highway where the Mexican inspection station was on the east side of the road—the right side as you're heading north. His method took advantage of the fact that passenger buses weren't required to stop at the station and could barrel right past. He was carrying loads in a car and would pull over short of the station at night with no lights. When a bus passed, he would pull out behind it, and as the bus approached the station, he would pull out and slowly pass it, using it to shield him from view of the station. This worked twice, but when he tried it a third time, an oncoming car spoiled his pass and he was spotted by officials at the checkpoint. A patrol car gave chase and he ended up running his car off the road onto the desert and fleeing on foot. After spending twenty-four hours on the desert with no water, he was able to reach an area where the highway was under construction and got water from a road crew.

Everyone agreed this was a clever method but too risky for the job at hand. Then Jesus presented an idea he had recently come up with. Everyone knew the highways were hot, but what about the railroads? No one was yet thinking of the railroads. He said we should pack the grass into the trunk of a car and ship it north by rail.

The men all agreed this was a great idea. Jesus didn't want to risk his late-model LTD for the run, but a friend offered his '50 Chevy coupe if Jesus rebuilt the engine. We went to see it and no two sections of it were the same color. The left front fender was green, the left door was white, the right rear fender was yellow, and there were patches all over painted primer gray. The hood was off and lay upside-down with a puddle of rusty water in the middle, and the engine was out and lay propped on two-by-fours over a glistening pool of oil. My heart sank. "This car is never going to run!" I groaned. A rush of remorse swept over me and I wished I were back home with Mary and had never thought of doing this stupid run.

"*Sí, sí,* it will run," Jesus assured me. "Don't forget, before I started doing *los negocios,* I used to be a mechanic. We will have it running within a week!"

And for him to admit it would take a week, I feared, meant months.

CHAPTER 69

JESUS HAULED THE CHEVY AND ALL ITS PARTS to his backyard and began working on it day and night. Miguel was there most days helping and I hung out and gave advice. Alicia borrowed a guitar from one of the neighbors so I could play while I watched. A neighboring youth who was studying engineering came home for the holidays, and I helped him with physics problems like, If you have ten hobos on a flatcar and they want to get it moving as fast as possible by jumping off the back end, should they all jump off at once or one at a time? (They should all jump at once.)

There were times when it felt just like the old days. Jesus and I got in an animated discussion regarding how the vacuum advance should be hooked up, and in the end his knowledge of auto mechanics trumped my knowledge of the physics of pressure differentials. We took a break over cold Superiores and Alicia brought us fresh mangos. The smoke from charcoal fires drifted over the wet ground and blue discharges crackled off the power lines bringing back wonderful memories of times past.

Other times, though, I felt bored. Bored and ashamed that I was hurting my parents and probably Mary too, trying to do something that was sordid and juvenile and part of a past that could never be relived. Jesus didn't have a ring compressor and I watched him fit the pistons into the block by pounding them through a radiator hose clamp and groaned inside.

It took a week and a half, but Jesus finally got the engine back in the Chevy. The starter was busted, so while Miguel took the wheel, Jesus and I pushed the car down the damp dirt street with help from a half dozen kids hanging out. There was a tremendous drag as Miguel eased out the clutch, then a loud cough, a belch of blue smoke from the exhaust, and the Chevy took off under its own power. I whooped for joy while Jesus stood grinning in the middle of the street, his hand out to accept the hundred pesos I had bet him that the Chevy wouldn't run. He installed a rebuilt starter and we were ready to leave that afternoon.

It was growing dark and we packed 250 bricks in the trunk of the Chevy, shoving them as far forward as possible. The back end sagged a little but not too bad. Jesus threw in a rifle and two pistols and we were ready to go. Miguel was going to drive the Chevy, and Jesus and I and a hired hand named Memo would ride in Jesus's Ford. Miguel was ahead of us as we wended our way along back streets to the highway. He sat hunched over the wheel and the forward-slanting lines of his shoulders seemed to match the forward-slanting lines of the old Chevy, giving the ensemble of car and driver the look of a monstrous cockroach. Because of the dope in the trunk, Jesus said the Chevy was like a bomb waiting to go off and we dubbed it *La Bomba*.

Miguel let us get ahead and we pulled onto Highway 15, heading north. Much of the highway was under construction, and we kept having to drop off the elevated roadbed and drive along makeshift dirt roads graded along the side. Tramp fires burned in the open country to our right. I had my window down and the night smelled of freshly laid asphalt. We kept seeing lights ahead and strained our eyes to sort out the tramp fires and oil pots from lights signifying something we should avoid. Three quick taps on the brake light was our signal to Miguel of possible danger ahead. Just short of Guamuchil we spotted a federales checkpoint ahead and used our signal for the first time. Miguel was able to pull over and back up until there was a place where he could turn around, and we were able to go back and guide him around the checkpoint using back roads.

Around midnight we came to the tiny town of San Blas. There was only one hotel in town and we got a room. We went upstairs and found a sparse room with four cots, each with a ragged sheet thrown over it. Miguel picked up his sheet, which had a hole so big he could stick his fist through it. "We are all going to wake up with *chatos* in the morning!" he groaned and we dubbed the place *el Hotel Chato* — the Crab Hotel.

San Blas was at the western end of a narrow-gauge railroad that cut clear through the Sierra Madre to the state of Chihuahua. A freight pulled in the next morning and the tiny town sprang to life. I stayed in our room as the others crossed the street to the railway station, where Jesus arranged to have La Bomba loaded onto a flatcar to be shipped to Cuauhtemoc. I was the only gringo in town and we agreed it would be better if I lay low rather than take a chance on bringing heat down on La Bomba. From my second-story window I could see the old rural railway station and the yards. La Bomba was loaded onto a vacant flatcar and secured with chocks and guy wires. Memo was to ride in La Bomba atop the flatcar in order to protect her from tramps and Jesus provided him with a pistol and bought blankets and food for him at a general store. During all this time I didn't see a single federal in town, lending credence to Jesus's supposition that the railroads weren't yet hot. In the afternoon a passenger train pulled in and Jesus, Miguel, and I got on board. The freight was still parked on the adjoining tracks and wouldn't leave till the following morning.

The train took off, slowly gathering speed, and we watched dry hills roll by interspaced with fields of withered maize. Later we passed through a semi-tropical area with savannahs, broad-leaved trees, and hills whose folds were filled in with green. We had a compartment to ourselves, paneled in wood with an attention to detail reminiscent of opulent times past. Jesus said the railroad took over sixty years to build. Everything went dark suddenly as we passed through a short tunnel, and Jesus said this was just the first and there would be over eighty more.

The air seemed to grow thinner as we climbed into an area of rocky crags and stunted pines. We passed through more tunnels. The sun went down, turning the sky the color of rose petals and amethyst. Our car rocked back and forth with a pleasant clacking sound as we teetered over canyons that looked as if they were filled with powdered gold. We got up and walked like novice sailors to the dining car, where we ate sumptuous meals followed by fresh-brewed coffee. The whole time, too, I was thinking, This is it! How could I ever think a straight job would be better?

In the morning the train stopped at a promontory overlooking *La Barranca del Cobre* — Copper Canyon. Everyone got out to take a look and someone said it was bigger than the Grand Canyon (it is.) The trees on the opposite rim showed up as bare green specks. A short while later, the train stopped at the logging town of Creel. This was like the Mexican equivalent of Truckee, California. There was snow on the ground, pines all around, and the smell of pine wood burning. Instead of adobe, many of the houses here were made of wood. We got out and took a quick walk through the town, past homes festooned with Christmas decorations, while trucks carrying logs lumbered through the snowy streets in compound low. Jesus said there was good trout fishing in the creeks that ran in the nearby sierra and we made a promise to come back here and go fishing someday and bring Alicia and Mary.

In Cuauhtemoc we got off the train, rented a car, and drove to see a colony of Mennonites who lived at the other end of town. These were the same Mennonites famous throughout Mexico for their *queso menonita*. We had seen a number of them on the train. They stood out with their fair skin and blue eyes, the men all wearing overalls and sombreros while the women wore full-length dresses with floral designs against a black background and broad hats held down with scarves tied under their chins. Jesus said they had originally come from Germany and Holland by way of Canada and had settled in Mexico during the teens. They still spoke their original dialect and didn't drink, smoke, sing, or dance and avoided internal combustion engines whenever possible, riding around town in horse-drawn wooden buses. They were very industrious and produced peaches, apples, and bread as well as their famous cheese. We bought some of their bread and it was delicious. Two thick-wristed blond youths spoke some Spanish and I asked them what they thought of their life. They shrugged pleasantly and said, "This is all we know. We have nothing to compare it to."

The freight arrived early the next morning and we waited for La Bomba to be unloaded. This was done by backing a flatbed truck up perpendicular to the flatcar. The flatbed truck was on a slight hill created specifically for this purpose so that its bed would be even with the bed of the flatcar. After the chocks and stays were removed, Miguel tried to jockey La Bomba around onto the truck, but there wasn't enough room on the flatcar to maneuver. A foreman who was supervising whistled to a group of transients and they jumped up to help. They grabbed the back end of La Bomba, intending to swing her around, but had trouble because of the weight. "*¡'Ta pesado!*" they groaned in consternation. Jesus and I were standing on the ground watching and exchanged grins.

With La Bomba on the flatbed, Miguel got back in and held his foot on the brake as the truck proceeded down a badly rutted road. Both the truck and La Bomba had shot shocks and bounced wildly with the ruts, only they bounced at different natural frequencies, going in and out of sync. One moment La Bomba would appear to hover mysteriously still while the truck lurched beneath her, and the next moment the same side of each vehicle would lurch up so high that I thought sure La Bomba was going to roll off. Miguel clung to the wheel for dear life. I wished I had a video of this moment because it was the most dramatic demonstration of the summation and cancellation of wave forms I had ever seen. The truck backed up to a half-hill the same height as the bed and Miguel drove La Bomba down onto solid ground.

We now headed north—Jesus, Memo, and I in a rental car with Miguel following in La Bomba. We ate dinner in Chihuahua and then night fell, making our timing perfect for the inspection station just south of Juarez. This was the equivalent of the inspection station south of Sonoyta that I knew so well. Just short of the station, Jesus pulled over at a roadhouse and the three of us went in, ordered beers, and watched couples dance to a live *norteño* band. Miguel had dropped from sight behind us but knew to meet us here. After a few minutes, Jesus, Memo, and I took our beers and went outside to look for him. Ten minutes passed and Jesus pointed to a bluff on the other side of the highway and said we should climb up there to get a better view.

We ended up waiting here for over two hours, and I wished I had a tape recorder so I could record every possible way to swear in Spanish. After letting out a string of oaths, Jesus turned to me with a pained look, as though he had hoped never to have to reveal what he was about to tell me. "*Miguel es muy burro, Tom* — Miguel is very dumb. *¡Es burrisísimo!* — He is the dumbest!"

Miguel finally showed up. There was confusion regarding which roadhouse he was supposed to stop at. I never did figure out whose fault it was. It was now one in the morning and we were late.

We drove a few more miles, then pulled over where a set of railroad tracks crossed Highway 45. We could see the lights of the inspection station a little over a mile away. We got the bricks out and packed them tightly into six burlap sacks, each weighing a little over eighty pounds. After stashing two of them in the trunk of La Bomba, we grabbed a sack each and hurried across the highway onto the desert and followed the railroad tracks.

The air was cool and dry and all the stars were out. There was the smell of creosote and the broken glass alongside the tracks glittered faintly in the moonlight. The tracks ran straight and the highway, after crossing them, curved to the left, so that it paralleled the railway. By following the tracks, we would pass directly behind the station and after hiking past it, we would cut back to the highway, which wouldn't be that far away. Following the tracks was a lot easier than striking out across the desert, which had ravines and cactuses. With my sack balanced across my back, I tried walking on the railroad ties, which were firm but required that you pay close attention to each step as they were unevenly spaced. Then I tried walking on the gravel shoulder, which slowed you down a little because of the crunching but required less attention to where you were stepping. Jesus noticed my experiment and told me, "For the next run I will hire a carpenter to make a wooden cart the exact width of the tracks so that we can roll the sacks along. I will have him make it collapsible so that it can be carried in the car." In the cool dark of the night my heart soared. Yes, there *will* be a next run!

I was in good shape and had to hold back not to get ahead of the others— especially Memo, who was panting and slowed frequently to rest. We finally made it past the inspection station and stashed the four sacks in some bushes near the highway, then jogged back to where the cars were parked. Jesus and I grabbed the two remaining sacks while Miguel and Memo took off in the two cars to take them through the station. Jesus and I struck off following the railroad tracks and again I tried to hurry, worrying that it was going to dawn soon, but kept having to slow down for Jesus to catch up. By the time we got to the other side of the inspection station, the stars had begun to fade.

Miguel and Memo were waiting for us and the four of us conferred. La Bomba was parked as close as possible to us on the highway, next to a fence, and the rental car was parked on the other side of the road. We were crouched behind a lone stand of bushes, and between us and La Bomba was a twenty-yard stretch of open ground. The inspection station was about a quarter mile behind us. We couldn't tell if there were federales out front or not. It was that time of morning when objects were just becoming visible as vague, gray shapes. The cars passing by on the highway still had their lights on.

We waited until there were no cars coming, then grabbed a sack each and made a dash for La Bomba. No sooner had we done so than headlights appeared and we had to hit the dirt, flattening ourselves like Marines as we let our sacks tumble in front of us. Every time we made a dash for it, it seemed, another car would appear, and we had to go through this routine several times before finally getting all six sacks to the car. By now it was light and suddenly there was confusion. Someone—I wasn't sure who—thought they saw a federal at the station pointing toward us. Two sacks were still lying next to La Bomba and I moved to throw them in when Jesus yelled at me. "Tom, go wait in the other car right now!" I did as told and he and Miguel got the remaining two sacks in La Bomba and Miguel took the wheel and drove off. Nothing came of this brief scare, but I would never forget that in an emergency, Jesus's first thought was to get me away from danger.

CHAPTER 70

IN JUAREZ WE STOPPED AT A PAY PHONE and I called Curly, who was waiting in El Paso. I was afraid to cross into El Paso, worried that there might be heat left over from the Les and Carrie bust, and told Curly to meet me in Juarez at the Café Sombrero, a large café built in the shape of a hat. We met and I took an immediate liking to him. He was personable, intelligent, and discreet and had a lean, wiry build much like mine. He wore jeans, scuffed cowboy boots, and a cowboy hat and looked just like the ranch hands and construction workers I remembered from the El Paso area. His West Texas accent was perfect.

Our plan this time was a little different from the plan I had used with Les. In order not to contaminate each other with any heat we might have picked up, Curly and I wouldn't even see each other again. I would go out to the river with the Mexicans around one in the morning, wade the grass through, and deposit it in some bushes on the American side. A couple of hours later Curly would come by and pick it up. With these details settled and our breakfasts finished, we shook hands again and left. That night Curly called me from a pay phone and made some innocent remarks that were code to let me know he had gone out to the river and identified the bushes I had described where the grass would be stashed.

Early the following morning Jesus, Memo, and I headed east from Juarez in the rental car with Miguel following in La Bomba. This area was more dangerous than ever now because of increased heat as well as bandits. Jesus had me wear a sombrero and shades and told me to keep a low profile. We made it to Guadalupe Bravos, a squalid town near the river, and got a motel room there to use as a base of operations. By now I was completely into the run, feeling that same nervous but excited feeling I always used to feel as things neared a climax. Jesus left to buy something at a store, and I asked Memo if he could help me wade sacks through the river. I didn't see any reason why he shouldn't; after all, he was Jesus's hired hand. He glanced down and mumbled something about not being able to go on the American side.

"Why not?"

"I did not bring my passport."

Miguel and I collapsed on the bed in raucous laughter over this pathetic excuse. As if you needed a passport to wade grass through the Rio Grande!

Jesus was still gone and I ducked out to a *fonda* to grab lunch by myself, figuring it would be cooler that way. On my way back I was stopped by a friendly cop who introduced himself, extending his hand. He said he was the head officer in the region and wanted to offer me safe passage through the area. I pretended not to know what he was talking about and said I was just a tourist passing through. He smiled knowingly and offered me his card. "Just the same, if you decide you would like to do business here someday, do not hesitate to call me."

Jesus wasn't at all happy when he heard this story. He decided to get me away from the grass and out of the area immediately. I grabbed my sweater, slipped into the rental car, and ducked down until we were out of town. Jesus drove to the place along the river where we were going to cross and left me there to wait. I found a large bush and made myself comfortable in the dense middle of it.

From my bush I had a perfect view of the Mexican levee road, the river, and the American levee road on the opposite side. I suppose most people would have hated waiting in a bush all day but I rather enjoyed it. It gave me a chance to think. I thought how right the run had come to feel. Earlier I had been worried that it wouldn't be the same, that it would be like trying to go back to a lost past. A quote from a great writer ran through my mind: "They say you can never go back, but then most of what they say isn't true." My parents must be awfully worried—that was something I was going to have to work out on future runs. Aside from that, though, it was as though I had never quit.

I remembered the snapshot Mary had given me and got it out. It was an old black-and-white photo taken during her pre-hip days when she used to model for several of the clothing stores on Telegraph Avenue. She had a sweet, innocent smile and her shoulder-length hair curved cutely inward around her neck. I kept it in my shirt pocket, where I could get it out from time to time and stare at it.

In the late afternoon a pickup drove by on the American side heading east. In it were two men dressed in overalls. They stared straight ahead and looked tired as after a day's work. I imagined they worked at a cotton gin I had noticed near the river several miles to the west. They were the only people I saw all day.

Later, a dust storm blew up. Within minutes the river was lost from view and the dust got so thick I could barely see ten feet in front of me. If only we were doing the run now! It would be impossible to get busted under these conditions, I thought to myself. Lights and even infrared would be useless. After about an hour the dust settled and the air became crystalline clear again. I made a mental note to find out if these dust storms occurred with any regularity.

Night fell and the temperature dropped. I put on my sweater—the same Icelandic sweater I had bought that day with Arf. I had worn it on all the runs since and it had become like a talisman for me and caused the Mexicans to grin and say, "*¡Qué Tom!*" By now it was pitch dark save for a flickering red glow beyond some trees to the southeast. I could hear shouts and drunken laughter. Singing began with young male voices throwing in yodel-like *Aiyeee-aiyeee*'s. Just a bunch of ranch hands, I figured, doing what Mexican men do everywhere, which is to get drunk, sing sad songs, and cry.

I dozed a while and when I woke up, the singing had stopped and there was no more glow in the southeast. It was cold. I figured it must be past midnight. I hadn't heard anything but seemed to sense something bulky in the blackness nearby. I stood up. It was La Bomba!

I ran up and greeted Miguel and Memo. Jesus had stayed back at the motel room, they said. Miguel and Memo unloaded the sacks of grass and I slipped into the hip waders they had brought. We moved the sacks down to the river's edge and lined them up. I had given up on getting any help from Memo and hefted a sack over my shoulder. I stepped into the river and felt the cool press of the water around my legs. "Well, this is it!" I thought, wading through. On the other side I doubled forward, letting the sack fall off my shoulder onto the ground. Something was wrong and a jolt of adrenaline shot through my veins.

I jerked up, tensed, all my senses alert to what might be happening. It was Miguel. He was calling to me in a whispered shout. "Tom, come back! Come back! Hurry!"

I tried to get back to the Mexican bank as quickly as I could but the water fought me. It was like awful dreams of childhood where I felt threatened by some terrible menace but was unable to move. I made it to the Mexican bank and found Miguel looking panicked.

"What's wrong?"

"Didn't you see the light?"

"What light?"

"Someone was flashing a light right near you on the other side!"

We stared. No lights appeared. We were in a moonlit open space and ran back and ducked behind a low berm. The five remaining sacks lay at the river's edge.

"Where's Memo?"

"Back at the car."

"Where are the guns?"

"In the car."

"Wait here. I'm going back to get them."

I ran back and found Memo lounging by the car.

"Someone's flashing lights on the other side!"

Memo jerked to life looking concerned, as though this development might require that he do something.

"Where are the guns?"

He opened the trunk and handed me a small pistol, like a .22. It looked like something a lady might carry in her purse.

"This is it?"

He nodded.

"Where's the rifle and the other pistol?"

"Jesus has them."

I thrust the pistol at him and told him to go to Miguel and see what was going on. "I'll be right there!"

He plodded off and I extracted myself from the hip waders and threw on my running shoes. I hurried back to Miguel and Memo. They said the light had flashed around again and they both saw it. The three of us crouched behind the berm and I tried to analyze things with a clear mind. Someone was there; there was no longer any question about that. At this hour it had to be another smuggler, a patrol, or possibly a bandit. Regardless which, they were likely to have pistols and maybe a rifle. If it was a patrol, they might even have infrared.

"What do you want to do?" Miguel whispered.

"I don't know. What do you think we should do?"

Miguel gave a desperate shrug. "I don't know. You're the *jefe*."

I stared at the five sacks dimly visible in the moonlight. Obviously there was no question of going ahead with the run or trying to recover the sack on the other side. What we should do is run grab the remaining sacks and get them out of here. But that meant two trips across an open space in order to lug them back.

I lay there crouched, trying to build up courage. Then I thought of Mary and how much I missed her. I secretly slipped her picture out and stared at it by the moonlight. This is what I'm risking, I told myself. It didn't seem worth it. In the old days I probably wouldn't have hesitated to run grab those sacks. This wasn't the old days, though. Things had changed after all. I had too much to lose.

"What do you think?" Miguel was whispering urgently, interrupting my thoughts.

"¡*Vámonos!*" I told him. "Forget the sacks! Let's get the fuck out of here!"

Having decided this, it suddenly seemed as though we hadn't a second to lose. These were the last moments of what was likely my last run—fate's last chance to catch up with me. I felt myself give way to full-on panic.

We ran back to the car. Miguel took the wheel, Memo rode shotgun, and I jumped in the back. We took off, bouncing over the badly rutted levee road with our lights out. I wasn't going to feel safe till we got to the nearest side road, which was several kilometers ahead. Just as I was thinking this, headlights appeared heading toward us. We couldn't tell how far away they were, but the way they disappeared and reappeared flailing at the sky gave the impression of a car flying over the dips and rises as fast as we were. In the entire time I had waited in the bush, not a single vehicle had passed by on this side, and for this car to appear just now seemed far more than coincidental.

We came to a bad dip and Miguel had to downshift to first to negotiate it. But after we got past, the gearshift remained stuck in first. This was an idiosyncrasy of La Bomba's I hadn't heard about. To fix it, Miguel had to stop the car, cut the engine so he could let out the clutch, run pop the hood, and bang on the shifting mechanism with a tire iron. Meanwhile, the approaching vehicle was getting closer. I was nauseous with fear. The gearshift got stuck again and this time Miguel had trouble getting the engine started. Our battery was running low. I was on the left in the back seat and held my door open so I could stand on the running board, ready to bolt at a moment's notice. We got going again and bushes kept striking my half-open door, mashing it against me. I didn't care. "Get inside," Miguel advised me, but I was too panicked and couldn't just sit. Suddenly there were lights everywhere and I thought we were busted, but it was only the burglar lights of the cotton gin across the way reflected in the window of my wildly swinging door.

The gearshift got stuck again and Miguel killed the engine, ran out, popped the hood, and got it unstuck, but when he went to start the car, the starter hardly had any life left. That was all it took. I was out of there like a shot bullet. After running away from the road about fifty yards full on, I ducked into a bush and froze, listening carefully for any sound.

"Come on, Tom! We got it started! We need to go!"

I ran back and jumped in and this time we finally made it to the side road, which allowed us to enter a whole network of dirt roads, where we quickly became lost in the night, driving as we were with no lights. We were finally safe. (Later I would realize that Miguel never should have killed the engine. Rather, he should have had Memo slide over and hold the clutch down, but we were too panicked to think of that at the time.)

Jesus's face fell when we told him what had happened and he cursed himself for not going out with us and taking the rifle. He briefly considered going out there now but decided it was too late and the grass was a total loss. We groaned over this together, but then he put his arm around me and told me, *"No te preocupes* — Don't worry. The next run will be better. We will become millionaires yet!" I managed a grin but felt bad inside thinking there probably wouldn't ever be a next run.

All I cared about now was getting home to Mary. I was afraid to cross into the States at El Paso and got a ride with Jesus to Chihuahua, where I planned to catch a plane. Christmas was only a few days away, though, and all the flights were booked. I checked into a dreary downtown hotel and waited for an open flight. I called Mary and told her I would die if I didn't make it home in time for Christmas.

"Well, don't worry yourself. If you don't make it back, that's all right."

"What do you mean, it's all right? I'll go out of my mind in this dump!"

It rained—a cheerless sort of rain that clogged traffic outside my hotel room, so that all I heard all day long was horns honking and the squeal of brakes. I didn't even have a book to read but was reluctant to go out and buy one for fear of missing a call from the airlines. I survived on room service. After a miserable two days, the airlines finally called to say there was a flight to Albuquerque available. I took it and from there managed a complicated series of connections that got me home around midday on the twenty-fourth. Mary picked me up at the Oakland airport wearing jeans and one of our Mexican peasant blouses. I thought she was the prettiest girl in the terminal. We got in my truck and right away I made a wrong turn and began swearing. Mary seemed taken aback. "Calm down. We've got all the time in the world." I turned to stare at her. She had said those words in the most natural way and yet something about "all the time in the world" gave me the weirdest feeling.

We got home and I tried to get back into my usual routine. Things didn't seem the same, though. I blamed it on the stupid run and wished I had never done it. A couple of days went by, and when I didn't feel any better, I mentioned it to Mary.

"Yes, I know I've been acting weird around you lately."

I whipped my head around to face her.

"There isn't some other guy involved, is there?"

She looked at me with what could have only been relief.

"Yes, there is."

CHAPTER 71

MY BREAKUP WITH MARY WAS AWFUL and there were times when life without her hardly seemed worth living. We sold off our inventory of embroidered clothes, ending our business together, and to get by I began doing foundation repair work. During the teens and twenties, California exported large amounts of lumber to Japan, and for ballast on the return trip, ships would carry bricks, which were dirt cheap in Japan. The bricks were then put to use to build the foundations of homes throughout the Bay Area. Now, fifty years later, these brick foundations were buckling and I would support homes with jacks I had designed and had built, remove the bricks, and replace them with concrete and rebar. I didn't have a license to do this, which meant I couldn't work on homes where a bank loan was pending, but word of my skill spread and I got as much of this bootleg work as I could handle.

One day I lacerated my finger and had to go to the emergency room, where I had it sewn up and also got a tetanus shot. I forced myself to watch the doctor numb up my finger and sew it and I also watched the nurse give me the shot. It wasn't that bad and it occurred to me that my fear of needles was something I could overcome in the same way I had pretty much overcome my fear of women: by forcing myself to face the fear head-on. Ever since I could read, I had been interested in medicine as a result of poring over my father's medical texts and I decided to apply to medical school.

I went back to Cal and because I had taken so many advanced science courses in the past out of sheer interest, it took me only two quarters to finish my premed requirements. In the meantime I worked at a clinic in Richmond in order to gain medical experience. I aced the MCAT and applied to medical school two years in a row but was unable to get a place. In retrospect, I realized that I hadn't been able to transform my smuggler's personality into a personality that was thoughtful, even-tempered, and doctorly. It didn't help either that I had to inflate my foundation repair and clothes importing experiences to a total of ten years to cover the years I was actually smuggling. Some of the interviewers seemed to see right through me. One said, "I notice you've used the phrase 'to tell the truth' twice now. Am I to understand that you don't usually tell the truth?" Another, out of the clear blue sky, asked me, "Have any of your varied experiences included a brush with the law?"

If I couldn't be a doctor, I decided, I wanted to be a writer. I wrote up some of my smuggling experiences, submitted them to S.F. State, and was accepted to their graduate program in creative writing. I began studying books, especially those written in first person, to see what made them work, and eagerly devoured works by Jack Kerouac, William Burroughs, Flannery O'Connor, Sylvia Plath, Henry Miller, Knut Hamsun, and Ferdinand Celine. While I was attending grad school, Abelardo came up to visit. Sinaloa had had a change of governor, he told me, and for $80,000 he was able to have a meeting with the new governor and get a pardon. Half the $80,000 went to the governor and half to the attorney who arranged it. Abelardo still had grass fields and said he was working on a way of getting the grass across the border. I didn't think much about this, but two months later he called to say, "*Tengo muy buenas noticias para ti, Tom* — I have very good news for you." He said he had just moved two tons of sinsemilla into the States and it was waiting for me in a AAA Self Storage space just south of San Francisco. The key, he told me, was hidden in the gutter directly above the center of the door. I asked him how he got it across and his answer was something I had often wondered about but never thought possible: he had bribed a U.S. Customs officer!

"But how did you know you could trust him? How did you know it wasn't a setup?"

"I got to know him. We had barbecues together. I met his whole family."

Abelardo went on to say he drove the grass across himself in a semi-trailer.

Mary's brother Clint was one of my trusted distributors and I told him where to find the key. Wade and I watched with binoculars from a nearby hill as Clint recovered the key, opened the space, and took some of the grass out without incident. I then gave access to the space to Jenner and another trusted distributor, and within a week all the grass was sold. Another run of six tons followed and another six-ton run after that. All of a sudden I was rich again!

Abelardo's scheme hit a snag and he wasn't able to pull off any more runs, but with enough money to last for years to come, I settled down to writing. From time to time I did fun things like whitewater kayaking, backpacking, and diving for abalone. One day I went salmon fishing with Jerry Jones. We each caught our limit and came back to cook up the fish on Jerry's houseboat, which he kept berthed at Pier Five in Sausalito. Jerry was living with a cute girl named Chris who reminded me of a flapper girl because of the loose way she dressed and her carefree, anything-goes attitude. She was in the cabin changing and through the porthole I saw bare arms fly up and bare shoulders. Jerry was holding a can of lighter fluid at his crotch and squirted it at the barbecue from six feet away so that a huge ball of flame whooshed up.

"Grow up, why don't you, Jerry!" Chris yelled from inside the cabin.

"Shut up and put some clothes on for a change!" he hollered back.

This was the way they talked to each other.

I called my current girlfriend, a cute girl in her own right named Lauren, and she came by to join us. The four of us hung out on the deck and watched the shadows lengthen as the bay turned a deep, rich blue. It was a beautiful summer evening with couples strolling hand in hand along the pier and the slap-slap of water against the side of the gently rocking boat. The last of the sailboats were straggling in under a dying wind. We became aware of someone standing above us on the pier and looked up.

"Hullo, chap!"

And standing there with Bruce was his wife, Jocelyn.

Bruce had dropped by to visit his old friend Jerry Jones, and it was sheer coincidence that I happened to be there. I hadn't seen him in over a year. He was sharply dressed and Jocelyn had on a narrow-brimmed hat shaped like an inverted bowl and wore a scarf. They could have been two characters out of an F. Scott Fitzgerald novel. They clambered down the makeshift ladder made of odd boards nailed to a pier post and joined us. We told them we had plenty of salmon and Bruce said, "Well, if you're going to provide food, the least we can do is provide drink." He seemed to have lost all his yardbird habits and was back to his sophisticated self. Turning to me, he said, "What say we go and get some wine, eh, chap?"

We walked to Bruce's car, which turned out to be a late-model Mercedes he kept in San Francisco for visits to his wife. "I guess you're doing all right," I said as I slid in over the leather upholstery.

"I am, chap. In fact, I've just made my first *one*." He glanced to check my reaction. I thought what an important milestone this must have been for him.

"Off pot? Or coke too?"

"Just pot."

"Colombia?"

"That's right."

We stopped at a wine and liquor shop, where he selected six of the best wines in the house, paying for them with three hundreds he peeled off a thick roll. Heading back he said, "Weren't you studying to get into medical school?"

I waved my hand to indicate it wasn't something I felt like talking about. "That was just a stepping stone to a place I never got."

The fresh-caught salmon was delicious and we drank most of the wine Bruce had bought. The six of us then sat in the cozy cabin of Jerry's houseboat, lit by a hurricane lamp hanging from the ceiling. As the boat gently rocked, the lamp cast spidery shadows across the bulwarks. The wine put everyone in a good mood and we talked for several hours about all the latest happenings: Watergate, the Fall of Saigon, Muhammad Ali, Saturday Night Live. Then during a lull in the conversation, Chris stood up and did a little dance, slightly wobbly from the wine. Jerry rolled his eyes and poured himself some more wine. Chris took off her blouse. "This is Chris without her blouse," she announced in her high flapper girl's voice and tossed the blouse to the side. She wriggled out of the tight jeans she was wearing. "This is Chris without her jeans." She took off her bra. "This is Chris without her bra." She had small, pert breasts that stuck straight out. She bent cutely at the knees and slid down her panties, kicking them off, then stood up with her arms and legs flung out like a cheerleader. "And this is Chris in her birthday suit!"

Everyone stared, transfixed. Bruce grinned lasciviously. Jocelyn looked vaguely threatened. My girl, Lauren, who had never met any of these people before, looked as though she didn't know what to think. Jerry knocked off the wine he had just poured and murmured, "And this is Chris shit-faced drunk."

"Well, come on, everyone!" Chris cried out. "Get naked!" No one moved. I was dying to join her, thinking it would be just like the sixties. But it wasn't the sixties. It was 1975 and we were all getting older. Jerry yelled at Chris to pick up her clothes and get dressed, which she sadly did. It stabbed my heart.

The six of us decided to go for a walk and clambered up onto the pier. We wandered down to a neighboring pier, walked out to the end, and stared out over the dark waters. Bruce did a strange thing then and began holding hands with my girl, Lauren. Lauren knew I wouldn't care and went along with it. Jocelyn and I exchanged looks and shrugged. Bruce leaned over to me and whispered, "I've always wanted to screw one of your birds, chap." There was a strange tension to the night that was brooding and sexual.

Eventually we wandered back to Jerry's houseboat and it was time to go. Bruce drew me aside. "I know you've got a new life now and will probably say no, but I've got a job for you if you want it." I thought for a moment. I had tried to make it in the straight world, but the straight world didn't seem to want me.

"I might not say no," I told him.

CHAPTER 72

BRUCE AND I MET THE NEXT DAY at Jocelyn's apartment on Nob Hill in San Francisco. After serving coffee and tea, Jocelyn left the room and Bruce told me what he had in mind. He needed someone to manage the Colombian end of his operation and said I would be perfect because I spoke Spanish, knew what I was doing, and could be trusted without question.

The action, he said, was happening in the Guajira Peninsula. He showed me a map. The nearest major city was Barranquilla and a little further east was a resort town called Santa Marta. After that it was just small villages and jungle all the way to the Venezuelan border.

Bruce kept his plane in the Bahamas and would fly in low over the Guajira right at dusk, keeping an eye out for Colombian spotter planes. At a remote strip carved out of the jungle, he would land to pick up the grass and refuel, then fly to an island in the Bahamas to pick up two assistants, and finally to a deserted atoll off the coast of Florida, where the assistants would drop the grass over water next to speedboats waiting in a leeside bay. In the morning the speedboats would enter Miami harbor and lose themselves along the inland waterways, which form a vast network that stretches all the way to North Carolina. About forty miles north of Miami, Bruce kept a rented warehouse with a pier, where the grass would be offloaded.

Miami was making the news as a major entry point for grass and I asked him if it wasn't risky entering there. He said not at all, that there was so much pleasure boat traffic there, the authorities wouldn't think of stopping someone without good reason. On a calm day, he said, the boats would come in with water-skiers behind them.

The hard part, he said, was the drop-off over water. He had lost a fair amount of grass working this out. In its current form, his method was to slow the plane down just short of stall speed fifty feet over the water and make repeated figure eights with the X of the figure eight located directly over the drop-off point. Each time he came up on the X, his assistants in the cabin would frantically shove bales of grass out. Bruce referred to these bale shovers affectionately as "dope pushers."

The bales weighed sixty pounds and were made up by the Colombians using a Sears garbage compactor Bruce had brought them. Despite being wrapped several times with plastic and canvas, some of the bales were still breaking up when they hit the water. "Part of your job, should you decide to take it, will be to package the bales in such a way that they don't break up."

He went on to say he had done six Colombia runs now, each time adding refinements. With things well worked out, he was in a position to do a run more than twice the size of his previous runs. He envisioned running a ton. To carry this amount, he was graduating to a Beechcraft D-18, the same make of plane he and I had flown across the Atlantic, only this one was better equipped and had tricycle landing gear, which made it easier to land.

"That would be another part of your job. The D-18 will require a much longer strip—at least fifteen hundred meters. You would have to supervise construction of a new strip."

"I don't know anything about building a strip."

"It doesn't matter. All you have to do is make sure it's long enough and flat enough. The Colombians will take care of the rest. They have access to bulldozers and all sorts of heavy equipment. They have to," he grinned. "Every time a scammer crashes, they have to hurry and bulldoze over the plane before it attracts heat to the area."

I noticed that Bruce was using the word "scammer" to refer to smugglers, which I found jarring at first, but it was the word everyone used in the Colombia-Florida trade and I eventually got used to it.

We discussed terms. Bruce offered me thirty percent of the net profit, an amount well into six digits assuming the run pulled through as planned. This was such a large amount that it had the paradoxical effect of making me think this was just another of Bruce's pie-in-the-sky ideas. I began to think I shouldn't do it. Bruce accused me of being a doubter.

"For Christ's sake, chap, it's not as if I haven't already done a half dozen of these runs. Your problem is that you've spent too much time in Mexico. Forget everything you ever learned in Mexico. Colombians are *not* like Mexicans. I mean to say, you tell a Colombian to do x, y, and z, and he does it. And bloody quick, too. It's a whole different scene."

I told Bruce I would accept ten percent less, but that I wanted $15,000 in advance before I was going to go down to Colombia and risk myself. He scoffed at the idea.

"Why not? You're a millionaire. Fifteen thousand shouldn't be that big a deal to you. Think of the money you'll save if the run pulls through. You'll be giving me ten percent less."

"Chap, you've been in this business long enough to know nobody gives money up front. It's not done that way."

"I've been in this business long enough to know you can do it any way you want."

We must have argued this point for a good half hour. In the end Bruce gave in though he seemed put out about it. Jocelyn came in to see how we were doing and Bruce shook his head. "I don't know what's gotten into Mr. Jenkins here. He thinks he's Melvin fucking Belli." As things turned out, by forcing Bruce to accept my terms, I effectively talked myself out of a quarter million dollars.

Over the next four months, Bruce and I pulled off three Colombia runs in a row. All three went smoothly. I flew to Barranquilla, took a bus out to the Guajira, and introduced myself to Bruce's contacts. He had told me they were very competent and efficient and he was right. They were also rather cool. In the entire four months we never even got on a *tu* form basis. Once, hiking through the jungle, we spotted an Army patrol ahead and one of the contacts grabbed me with him as he dove into the bushes. It was the only sign I had that they cared for my welfare.

Walking through the jungle was a sobering experience. Everywhere we went we saw pieces of wrecked aircraft: small scraps of fiberglass or a twisted strut dangling in the vines. It was daunting to think that each of these fragments probably represented the death of a smuggler. Bruce was right in that you never saw an entire plane; they had all been bulldozed under.

Packing the bales worked out well. Following Bruce's suggestion, I had the Colombians wrap them in three layers of two-mil plastic encircled with duct tape. I then added tape reinforced with fiberglass. I also had the Colombians order bigger canvas bags, figuring the looseness of the canvas would better absorb the impact of the water. We didn't lose a single bale. Building a strip was also easy. The Colombians paid off two farmers for permission to tear down the fence between their lands and bulldoze their cornfields. I paced it off to make sure it was the right length and we spent several days clearing off rocks and roots.

The afternoon of the first run, we built large fires at either end of the strip. Trash fires were common throughout the jungle and not likely to attract attention. We also lined the sides of the strip every twenty paces with tin cans filled with cow dung soaked in kerosene. As the light faded, we scanned the violet sky toward the northeast, straining our ears for distant engine sounds. Surrounding the strip on all sides was thick jungle and the strange noises the birds and monkeys made were as exotic as any Hollywood soundtrack. In typical fashion, Bruce pushed things to the limit, coming in when there was scarcely any light left. We heard him first, then spotted the black speck of his plane flying with no lights. A Colombian youth and I then grabbed a torch each and tore down the strip on either side like Greek runners, stooping every twenty paces to light the cans we had set out. Bruce said the effect from the air was to see the strip gradually light up before him like a Las Vegas casino sign.

This was the high point of these runs. I was pushing thirty while the Colombian youth was eighteen, yet I beat him to the end of the strip all three runs. On lighting the last of the cans, I would toss my torch to the side, tear off into the jungle, and crouch behind a log. The thunder of the twin Pratt & Whitney engines coming in was so loud I could shout into it at the top of my lungs and not hear my own voice. As Bruce swooped in, barely clearing the treetops, the very ground would tremble.

After the first run, Bruce and I met at a houseboat he kept at Paradise Island in the Bahamas. As he counted out a stack of hundreds for me, I said, "You know, if you want to go back to that deal you first offered me of thirty percent—"

Bruce cut me off with a hearty roar. "No, Mr. Jenkins, you'll get your fifteen grand up front and your twenty percent and not a bloody penny more!"

Now I had to figure out how to get this cash back to the States. Bruce suggested I keep it in a Swiss bank instead. He said there was a branch right here on the island and coached me as to how to approach it.

"Forget your conception of an ordinary bank. I mean to say, there are no tellers and no lines. In fact, there isn't even a sign outside; it's just an unmarked suite on the second floor of an office building. You press a buzzer and they study you through a peephole before letting you in. They're very conscious of appearance. Don't go in there carrying your money in a paper bag. Carry it in a briefcase. And get yourself a coat and tie." I did as he suggested and got myself my very own Swiss bank account.

Parts of these runs were exciting, especially the pickup, which had always been my favorite part of the plane runs, but much of the time I felt bored and even a little sad because there seemed to be nothing left of the camaraderie and sense of purpose I used to feel with the early runs. I thought back to the days when we used to clean seeds out of a lid, get high, and psychoanalyze ourselves reading straight from Freud. Now people smoked grass to get "wasted" or "fucked up." We used to feel we were part of a vanguard. Now everyone smoked pot and the revolution we thought was going to happen never materialized. Stockbrokers now smoked pot. People smoked pot and voted Republican. Another reason I felt bad was that I had once again distanced myself from my parents. I had come to visit them much less often so that my several-week absences would not seem unusual.

After the third run, Bruce said he was going to take his wife for a two-month trip around the world in order to make up to her for the fact he was never around. When he came back, he said, he wanted to do a much larger run. He had just purchased a DC-3, which could carry up to four tons, and was having it outfitted and overhauled. He was so pleased with the way things were going that he even offered me a higher cut. I calculated that the next run would net me a third of a million dollars.

Despite the money involved, I wondered if I even wanted to do another run. Maybe now was the time finally to get out. Mary had shown me how wonderful free life could be and the thought of going to jail now terrified me. I asked Lauren what she thought, but she was so awed by this incredible streak of luck I was experiencing that she didn't know what to advise me. My best friend was making nine dollars an hour as a teacher's aide, and to sound him out over my reservations about making a fortune would have been thoughtless. I wished I knew someone wise, impartial, and objective.

On an impulse I phoned Alta Bates Hospital and asked for a recommendation for a psychiatrist. A nurse gave me a name and I was able to get an appointment the following day. I explained to the psychiatrist the difficult decision I was facing and he agreed to see me two more days in a row. By the third day I had made up my mind: I was going to quit smuggling and move on. This was my own decision and I very much appreciated the fact the psychiatrist didn't try to influence me in any way. Rather, he served as a backboard for my thoughts and helped me to get them straight in my mind.

Bruce was furious when I told him. He tried to talk me into changing my mind, even offering me the original thirty percent I had talked myself out of, but I had made my decision and it felt right to me. When he saw he wasn't going to change my mind, his look of entreaty turned to one of disgust.

"So you got nigger rich, eh?"

He eventually found someone else to replace me and in that person's first year, I heard, he made over a million dollars.

CHAPTER 73

I HAD A FEW MORE BRIDGES TO BURN. After consulting a tax attorney, I closed my Swiss bank account, brought my money into the States, and paid taxes on it. Where the IRS form says, "State nature and source of other income," my attorney wrote, "Taxpayer declines to state nature and source of other income on the basis of his Fifth Amendment privilege against self-incrimination." The IRS proceeded to conduct a full-scale criminal investigation of me using reverse accounting, the same method they used to put Al Capone behind bars. They suspected that my stated income might be just the tip of a gigantic iceberg and set about trying to show that I was spending more money than what I had declared. But after visiting my humble home and seeing my '62 Dodge pickup, now battered from hauling concrete when I did foundation work, they quickly lost interest in my case and closed it. At a party one evening I happened to meet the guy who took my place in Bruce's operation. He drew me aside and said, "I guess I owe my success to you, but there's a question I've been dying to ask you. Why in the world did you quit?" I didn't know what to tell him and simply said I was tired of having to go out to pay phones to make phone calls.

I had decided I didn't want to make another penny off pot. I thought of myself as a bit like a recovering alcoholic who can't touch a drop of alcohol for fear of relapsing. I had a nice nest egg and if I couldn't make it off that plus the advantages of being white, middle class, and bright, then I was a pretty sorry case. I had come to think of smuggling as almost like cheating and knew I would never be happy unless I was able to make a living in a straight, legal way. Not that I thought smuggling pot was immoral exactly. I thought of it as just as moral, say, as being a beer distributor and way more moral than distributing cigarettes. But I was cut out for something better.

One day Mary's brother Clint appeared at my door with a proposition. In the days when Abelardo was delivering grass to me in AAA storage spaces, Clint and Jenner, who didn't know each other, happened to meet at the space despite my efforts to stagger their visits. On chatting, they discovered that they could do a brisk business together in the acid trade, but code required that they obtain my permission first. This was Clint's reason for visiting me. He said if I gave them the OK to deal together, he would give me $10,000 up front right now in cash he had in his pocket. This was $10,000 that entailed no risk and didn't require that I do a lick of work—as close to free money as you could get. I turned it down knowing they would deal together anyway.

Then came the most difficult phone call of my life—a call from Abelardo. "*Tengo muy buenas noticias para ti, Tom* — I have really great news for you." He said his people had just delivered six tons of high-quality sinsemilla to the AAA storage facility south of San Francisco, adding that this was just the beginning. His method of crossing was now foolproof and his fields were on the point of yielding many tons more.

This was more than I had ever dreamed of. This was the ultra-Big Time and represented the culmination of years of work during which I had established a reputation so solid that a major Mexican supplier was willing to lay six tons of sinsemilla at my doorstep without even discussing terms or asking for an advance. If smuggling could be compared to science, this was the Nobel Prize.

Turning Abelardo down was one of the hardest things I ever had to do. I couldn't tell him the reason either. To tell him I no longer felt pot was that great for people would have made no sense to him, and to tell him I felt I was cut out for something better would have risked offending him. Instead, I told him that all my contacts had been busted and that I myself was in danger of getting indicted and was living in hiding. I had no one left to sell to, I told him. His disappointment was heartbreaking.

A new life lay before me. What had felt so right for so long was now gone. I sometimes thought of myself as like an ace fighter pilot once the war has ended. Or a bootlegger with the repeal of Prohibition. The times had changed and I had changed somewhat too, but I had to change a lot more. Changing who you are is a hard thing to do. I liked the psychiatrist I had seen and decided to see if he could help me.

*

The year is 1992 and I'm in Mazatlan—place where it all began. I've rented a cottage on the beach and have taken a week off to study for the internal medicine boards. I finally got myself into medical school, graduated AOA, and have just finished an internal medicine residency. Back home my wife is pregnant with our first child.

Poor Mazatlan is a shadow of the paradise it used to be—more of a hellhole really. I tried to find the stretch of beach where we camped that very first run, but the entire beachfront is now lined with hotels. The romantic thatched-roofed restaurants that hung out over the water have been replaced by cinder block structures thanks to a decree by a demented mayor who considered thatch unsightly. The red cross painted on the seawall where Manuel Salas was gunned down has faded into oblivion, and the neighborhood kids who could tell you the story behind it have grown up and gone. Even the Tropic of Cancer monument is gone, replaced by a lesser monument in a different location after scientists discovered that the original location was off. The Hotel Olas Altas, where we stayed so often, is boarded over.

Meche is still selling hats along the beach. I have no idea if he is still selling grass. He and I had a wonderful visit in which the subject didn't come up. He knows there will be no next run for me.

I visited Jesus in Tierra Blanca and he and Alicia are doing well. Abelardo is dead. He died several years ago in a hail of gunfire right here in Mazatlan along the malecón. The malecón . . . place where young lovers neck, old men sell *paletas* out of rusting ice chests, and drug dealers die dramatic deaths. I learned this from Miguel shortly after it happened and couldn't help but cry. "Some deal gone bad," Miguel surmised. I asked if he was gunned down by police or other *contrabandistas* and Miguel had to remind me how little point there was in trying to distinguish the two.

On my last day here, I took a walk along the malecón just to reminisce. An old woman was selling peanuts and I bought a small bagful from her. She had trouble picking out my change and I noticed that the joints of her fingers were enlarged in a squared-off way I had learned to recognize as osteoarthritis. I wondered if her fingers hurt her.

I took a seat on the beach wall and ate peanuts as I stared out over the ocean. It was mid-afternoon and there was a light haze over the water, robbing the three islands offshore of some of their color. I thought how I had once stared out over these same waters and felt just like a Marseilles gangster. That notion seemed strange to me now. During my training, enough patients had called me Doc that I now felt more like a real doctor and less like the imposter I imagined myself to be when I first started medical school. Gradually, I am losing the feeling that I have something to hide.

Going through medical school and residency has changed me. I feel I am getting to know people in a way I never knew them before. I have seen enough suffering to make me wish never to cause any more for anyone. I look back at the things I used to do and most of them are things I would not do now. This is a gratifying metamorphosis I am going through, and in the coming years I look forward to medicine changing me even more.

I stared out over the calm, blue water and a deep sense of satisfaction welled up in me. Medicine is a good field. It offers the opportunity to help others and be recognized and respected for it. I chose to become a doctor.

Even though I was born to be a smuggler.

EPILOGUE

A SLEW OF MINOR CHARACTERS APPEAR IN this story: the two secretaries, Marie, the pipe-smoking lieutenant, Dutch, the family from Oregon, the creator of the fat Mexican judge, whoever it was who shone a light at the Rio Grande that night—too many to mention. If you recognize yourself in these pages, I would love to hear from you. You can reach me via the email address on my copyright page. Who knows? If enough people respond, maybe we could throw a party!

GLOSSARY

ADF Automatic Direction Finding, a navigational aid

AOA Alpha Omega Alpha, a medical honor society

attitude (*aero*) a plane's relationship to level, includes pitch (fuselage relative to horizontal) and roll (wings relative to horizontal)

beaner (*vulg*) Mexican person

benny Benzedrine pill

BFD Big Fucking Deal

blotter acid blotter paper impregnated with LSD

boss (*adjective*) cool, neat

bougie member of the bourgeoisie

bread money

BSA brand of British motorcycle

chip, to to shoot heroin recreationally on occasion

cherried out (*said of a car*) made to look nice by removing dents, repainting, etc.

come on, to (*said of a drug*) to take effect

cook up, to to heat heroin in water to dissolve it so it can be injected

cop, to (*a drug*) to acquire, usually by purchase

crash, to to go to sleep

cut up fish, to to cheat suckers in a card game

dead reckon, to to navigate by compass

dime bag a packet of heroin (usually costing ten dollars)

do up, to to self-inject a drug

dualie a pickup truck having dual rear tires

ETA Estimated Time of Arrival

factory rod hot rod straight from the factory (as opposed to customized)

Family Dog, The a rock-promoting commune in Denver

fix a self-injection of heroin

flash, to (*on LSD*) to see flashes of color induced by the drug

front, to to advance without prepayment

get off, to to get high

hip hip person, hippie

hip, to to clue (*someone*) in

holding possessing drugs

IFR Instrument Flight Rules (apply in bad weather), loosely means "flying blind"

joint marijuana cigarette

junk heroin

key kilogram of pot

kilo kilogram of pot

kit drug injection paraphernalia

Loran LOng-RAnge Navigation, a navigational aid

Man, the the law, a law enforcement officer

MCAT Medical College Admission Test

Michoacan type of grass from the Mexican state of Michoacan

munchies, the the hunger that follows getting high on marijuana

narc narcotics agent

off, to (*drugs*) to sell

Pan Am Pan American World Airway

PSA Pacific Southwest Airlines

raise, to (*someone on a radio*) to establish contact

red (*drug*) secobarbital tablet

reefer marijuana

reg weed mediocre quality marijuana

roach butt of a marijuana cigarette

R&R Rest and Relaxation

rush feeling of suddenly getting high from a drug

shake portions of the marijuana plant that have low THC content, such as leaves and stems

soul-kiss, to to French kiss

stepped on cut, adulterated

stiff, to to fail to pay money owed

straight (*adjective*) not hip, not tuned into drugs or alternative thinking; (*noun*) a person who is not hip, not tuned into drugs or alternative thinking

strung out addicted

tie someone off, to to apply a tourniquet for injecting a drug intravenously

toke a hit off a joint

Vic Tanny one of the first modern health clubs

VOR VHF Omnidirectional Range, a navigational aid

Zig-Zag brand of cigarette paper commonly used to roll joints

Dr. Jenkins has used the fluent Spanish he acquired smuggling to provide healthcare to Spanish-speaking patients in various safety net settings, both rural and inner city. He has taught clinic-based and hospital-based medicine at a major medical center and has volunteered at clinics in Sinaloa, Mexico.